EXPLORING RELIGION AND THE
SACRED IN A MEDIA AGE

In recent years, there has been growing awareness across a range of academic disciplines of the value of exploring issues of religion and the sacred in relation to cultures of everyday life. *Exploring Religion and the Sacred in a Media Age* offers inter-disciplinary perspectives drawing from theology, religious studies, media studies, cultural studies, film studies, sociology and anthropology. Combining theoretical frameworks for the analysis of religion, media and popular culture, with focused international case studies of particular texts, practices, communities and audiences, the authors examine topics such as media rituals, marketing strategies, empirical investigations of audience testimony, and the influence of religion on music, reality television and the internet.

Both academically rigorous and of interest to a wider readership, this book offers a wide range of fascinating explorations at the cutting edge of many contemporary debates in sociology, religion and media, including chapters on the way evangelical groups in America have made use of *The Da Vinci Code* and on the influences of religion on British club culture and electronic dance music.

THEOLOGY AND RELIGION IN INTERDISCIPLINARY PERSPECTIVE
SERIES IN ASSOCIATION WITH THE
BSA SOCIOLOGY OF RELIGION STUDY GROUP

BSA Sociology of Religion Study Group Series editor:
Pink Dandelion and the publications committee

Theology and Religion in Interdisciplinary Perspective Series editors:
Douglas Davies and Richard Fenn

The British Sociological Association Sociology of Religion Study Group began in 1975 and provides the primary forum in Britain for scholarship in the sociology of religion. The nature of religion remains of key academic interest and this series draws on the latest worldwide scholarship in compelling and coherent collections on critical themes. Secularisation and the future of religion; gender; the negotiation and presentation of religious identities, beliefs and values; and the interplay between group and individual in religious settings are some of the areas addressed. Ultimately, these books reflect not just on religious life but on how wider society is affected by the enduring religious framing of human relationships, morality and the nature of society itself.

This series is part of the broader *Theology and Religion in Interdisciplinary Perspective Series* edited by Douglas Davies and Richard Fenn.

Other titles published in the BSA Sociology of Religion Study Group Series

Religion and the Individual
Belief, Practice, Identity
Edited by Abby Day
ISBN 978-0-7546-6122-1 (HBK)

Women and Religion in the West
Challenging Secularization
Edited by Kristin Aune, Sonya Sharma and Giselle Vincett
ISBN 978-0-7546-5870-2 (HBK)

A Sociology of Spirituality
Edited by Kieran Flanagan and Peter C. Jupp
ISBN 978-0-7546-5458-2 (HBK)

Materializing Religion
Expression, Performance and Ritual
Edited by Elisabeth Arweck and William Keenan
ISBN 978-0-7546-5094-2 (HBK)

Exploring Religion and the Sacred in a Media Age

Edited by

CHRISTOPHER DEACY
University of Kent, UK

ELISABETH ARWECK
University of Warwick, UK

Formission
Rowheath Pavilion
Heath Road
Bournville
Birmingham B30 1HH

ASHGATE

Published by
Ashgate Publishing Limited
Wey Court East
Union Road
Farnham
Surrey, GU9 7PT
England

Ashgate Publishing Company
110 Cherry Street
Suite 3-1
Burlington
VT 05401-3818
USA

www.ashgate.com

British Library Cataloguing in Publication Data
Exploring religion and the sacred in a media age. –
    (Theology and religion in interdisciplinary perspectives series)
    1. Religion and sociology
    I. Deacy, Christopher II. Arweck, Elisabeth III. British Sociological Association.
    Sociology of Religion Study Group
    306.6

Library of Congress Cataloging-in-Publication Data
Exploring religion and the sacred in a media age / [edited by] Christopher Deacy and Elisabeth Arweck.
        p. cm.—(Theology and religion in interdisciplinary perspective series)
    Includes bibliographical references and index.
    ISBN 978-0-7546-6527-4 (hardback : alk. paper)
    1. Religion and culture. 2. Mass media—Religious aspects. I. Deacy, Christopher. II. Arweck, Elisabeth.

    BL65.C8E93 2009
    201'.7—dc22

2008036050

ISBN 978-0-7546-6527-4

Transferred to Digital Printing in 2014

Printed and bound in Great Britain
by Printondemand-worldwide.com

Contents

List of Figures

Notes on the Contributors

Elisabeth Arweck is Senior Research Fellow at the University of Warwick (Instutute of Education). She is a Council member of the International Society for the Sociology of Religion and an editor of the *Journal of Contemporary Religion*. She has co-edited a number of volumes, including *Reading Religion in Text and Context* (2006), *Materialising Religion* (2006) and *Theorising Faith* (2002). She is author of *Researching New Religious Movements in the West: Responses & Redefinitions* (2007) and co-author of *New Religious Movements in Western Europe: An Annotated Bibliography* (1997).

Tom Beaudoin is associate professor of practical theology in the Graduate School of Religion and Religious Education at Fordham University. He is the author of *Virtual Faith* (1998), *Consuming Faith* (2003) and *Witness to Dispossession: The Vocation of a Postmodern Theologian* (2008). His current research takes place at the intersection of theology, Foucault studies and psychoanalysis.

Nicholas Buxton is a minor canon of Ripon Cathedral. He was one of the participants in BBC2's *The Monastery* and has a PhD in religious studies from the University of Cambridge. Research interests include religion and culture, and contemporary spirituality. He has lectured, published and broadcast widely in these areas.

Nick Couldry is Professor of Media and Communications at Goldsmiths, University of London. He is a participant in the Goldsmiths Media Research Programme and the author or editor of seven books including *The Place of Media Power: Pilgrims and Witnesses of the Media Age* (2000), *Inside Culture* (2000), *Media Rituals: A Critical Approach* (2003), *Contesting Media Power: Alternative Media in a Networked World* (co-edited with James Curran, 2003) and most recently *Media Consumption and Public Engagement: Beyond the Presumption of Attention* (2007).

Christopher Deacy is Lecturer in Applied Theology at the University of Kent and a member of the UK Theology, Religion & Popular Culture Network Group. He has published widely in the field of theology and film. His publications include *Screen Christologies: Redemption and the Medium of Film* (2001), *Faith in Film: Religious Themes in Contemporary Cinema* (2005) and *Theology and Film: Challenging the Sacred/Secular Divide* (co-authored with Gaye Ortiz, 2008). He is currently working on a monograph which critically examines theological perspectives on cinematic representations of death and the afterlife.

Michael W. DeLashmutt is Lecturer in the Study of the Christian Church at the University of Exeter. He has published widely on issues related to theology and popular culture, including articles and chapters in books dealing with science fiction, technology, speculative science, animated television, pornography and sexuality. An eclectic practical theologian, Dr DeLashmutt is interested in how the beliefs and practices of the Christian Church interact with the often marginalized aspects of the quotidian life.

Carlton Johnstone is a PhD candidate in Sociology at the University of Auckland, New Zealand. His thesis is an exploration of Christian faith journeys of Generation X and Y and their experiences of church in New Zealand.

Danielle Kirby is a PhD Candidate at the University of Queensland, researching fiction and media as conjunct locales for new forms of metaphysical questing and spiritual understanding. She has published and lectured in the areas of online religion, new religious movements and popular culture and co-organized the 2006 conference *Alternative Expressions of the Numinous*. A founding member of the Queensland Society for the Study of Religion, Danielle was also co-editor and co-creator of the peer-reviewed journal *Khthónios*. Her research interests include mythology, popular culture, New Religious Movements and contemporary cultural trends.

Sarah Lawther is currently working for Nottingham Trent University researching Learning Development in Higher Education. Her previous position was as a lecturer in the School of Social Sciences also at Nottingham Trent University. Her research interests include religious representation on the Internet and Internet research methods.

Jolyon Mitchell is a Senior Lecturer at New College, Edinburgh University. A former BBC World Service producer and director of the *Peacemaking in the World of Film* conference (Edinburgh, 2007) his publications include: *The Religion and Film Reader*, co-edited with S. Brent Plate (2007), *Media Violence and Christian Ethics* (2007), *Mediating Religion: Conversations in Media, Religion and Culture*, co-edited with Sophia Marriage (2003), and *Visually Speaking: Radio and the Renaissance of Preaching* (1999).

Katharine Sarah Moody is a PhD candidate in the Department of Religious Studies at Lancaster University, exploring how truth is conceptualized within the UK emerging church milieu. Her primary research interests are the interrelationships between Christianity and culture, working from within multiple disciplines, including continental philosophy, deconstructive theology and the sociology of religion and spirituality. She has published on the relationship between technology and theology and on the nature of text in the blogosphere. Her research blog can be found at http://opensourceresearch.blogspot.com/. She would like to thank the

Arts and Humanities Research Council for the grant that enabled her to undertake her doctoral studies.

Ellen E. Moore is a lecturer and PhD candidate at the Institute for Communication Research at the University of Illinois, Urbana Champaign. Her research focuses on the relationship between the mass media, evangelicalism, and politics in the USA. Specifically, she examines how the commodification of contemporary religion, with its reliance on secular, commercial media, impacts American evangelicals' political actions and beliefs. Other publications include 'Raising the Bar: the Complicated Consumption of Chocolate' (2008), on the ethical implications of chocolate consumption and production, and 'American Evangelicals and Environmental Politics: the Impact of Media and Religion on Environmental Politics in the United States' (in review).

Stephen Pattison is Professor of Religion, Ethics and Practice in the University of Birmingham. His recent publications include *The Challenge of Practical Theology* (2007) and *Seeing Things: Deepening Relations with Visual Artefacts* (2007).

Milja Radovic is a PhD candidate at the University of Edinburgh. Her research is in the field of Film and Religion and she is completing her dissertation on how films depict society in her native Serbia during the Milosevic era. She has participated in several festivals as a member of the Ecumenical Jury and is a member of the World Association for Christian Communication.

Rupert Till is Senior Lecturer in Music Technology at the University of Huddersfield. His publications include 'Popular Music as Religion: from trance dancing to worshipping popular music icons' in *Faith Is, Es Glaubt in German* (2008), and 'The Nine O'Clock Service: mixing club culture and postmodern Christianity' in *Culture and Religion* (2006). He has also written about the appropriation of African American dance music forms in *Cross the Water Blues* (2007). He is a composer and performer and his latest research ranges from investigating the acoustics of Stonehenge to studying electronic dance music culture as a form of contemporary Western possession trance cult.

Yam Chi-Keung is currently an Honorary Research Associate at the Divinity School of Chung Chi College, the Chinese University of Hong Kong, where he also teaches courses in theology, media, and popular culture. His research includes the theological and religious study of Chinese language popular culture (especially film). He worked for twenty years as a media producer and director, with experience across television, film and the new digital media. He did his PhD at the University of Edinburgh, after pursuing theological study in Boston and communication study in Hong Kong.

Acknowledgements

The editors would like to express their thanks to a number of people who have been instrumental in bringing *Exploring Religion and the Sacred in a Media Age* to fruition. The present collection of essays arose from the joint conference, organized by Prof. Gordon Lynch, of the British Sociological Association Sociology of Religion Study Group conference and the UK Research Network Group in Theology, Religion and Popular Culture, which took place at St Catherine's College, Oxford, 2-4 April 2007. The conference gathered a range of international participants and thus offered a broad base from which to choose the contributions to this volume. The members of the BSA Sociology of Religion Study Group have been interested and supportive of this project and its officers, chair Prof. Linda Woodhead, Convenor Dr Peter Gee and Publications Officer Dr Ben Pink Dandelion, have facilitated various aspects of the project. Finally, the editors greatly appreciate the support and assistance of Sarah Lloyd at Ashgate who accompanied the assembly of this volume through its various stages.

Introduction

Why Study Religion and Popular Culture?

Christopher Deacy

In recent years, there has been a growing awareness across a range of academic disciplines of the value of exploring issues of religion and the sacred in relation to cultures of everyday life. This is evident in the growth of interest in the study of religion and 'popular culture', including the intersections between religion and consumer culture, leisure cultures and lifestyles, changing forms of household space, technology and emerging forms of social network. There has also been growing attention paid to the relationships between religion and the media, such as the use of new media and communication technologies by religious groups, the representation and exploration of religion and spirituality in the media, the religious significance and content of media texts and rituals, and the popular consumption of religious and spiritual media.

But, why study 'religion' at all? After all, religion is often perceived by cultural theorists as an inescapably negative, indeed corrosive, phenomenon, which must be jettisoned if we as a society are to mature. As the success of Richard Dawkins's *The God Delusion* and other writings on the New Atheism have demonstrated, there is still a widespread suspicion, certainly at a popular level, that discourse involving religion has nothing constructive to offer in the twenty-first century. Identifying an unbreachable dichotomy between 'science' and 'religion', the image of 'warfare' or 'conflict' is a common one, in a manner which corresponds to the language adduced by two instrumental late-nineteenth century publications—John William Draper's *History of the Conflict Between Religion and Science* (1874) and Andrew D. White's *A History of the Warfare of Science with Theology in Christendom* (1896). For many people today, science is believed to provide the only reliable path to knowledge—it is seen as objective, universal, rational and based on solid observational evidence, whereas religion is perceived as belonging to the realm of the emotional, irrational and the subjective (see Barbour 1998: 77). As Robert Pirsig attests, 'When one person suffers from a delusion, it is called insanity. When many people suffer from a delusion it is called Religion' (qtd in Dawkins 2006: 28), and Dawkins himself writes that if *The God Delusion* 'works as I intend, religious readers who open it will be atheists when they put it down' (ibid.).

Influential though such perspectives are, however, McGrath is right that '*The God Delusion*, more by its failings than its achievements, reinforces the need for high-quality religious education in the public arena' (McGrath 2007: 4). No one—whether theist, agnostic or atheist—exists in a cultural vacuum and Dawkins is no less immune from the social, economic and political matrix within which his work is promulgated than the most conservative of Christian theologians. As I have suggested elsewhere, for instance, the distrust of human judgement that permeates Karl Barth's *The Humanity of God*—with the underlying understanding that God is Wholly Other and that we can only know God through God's own revelation, to the point that theology should thus be self-validating—cannot be dissociated from what Barth witnessed at first hand as the folly of the First World War and the sincerely held belief that humanity was utterly lost before God (see Deacy & Ortiz 2008: 3). Similarly, Dawkins, although coming from an antithetical ideological starting point—one which posits that 'Natural selection not only explains the whole of life; it also raises our consciousness to the power of science to explain how organized complexity can emerge from simple beginnings without any deliberate guidance' (Dawkins 2006: 141)—concedes that he would have written a very different book, had the contemporary cultural climate been different. Dawkins bemoans the prevalence in the world today of what he calls 'the genie of religious fanaticism' (ibid.: 61), which, whether in the form of Islamic extremism or the naïve and educationally backward teachings of Creationism and Intelligent Design, have relegated the existence of 'subtle, nuanced religion' (ibid.: 15) to the margins. Such is Dawkins's disdain for anything that impedes the advance of rational, empirically proven scientific discourse that even the academic study of theology is deemed worthless. Whereas, as he attests, 'Science has eradicated smallpox, can immunize against most previously deadly viruses' and 'can kill most previously deadly bacteria', theology 'has done nothing but talk of pestilence as the wages of sin' (Dawkins 1998: 6). Accordingly, 'If all the achievements of scientists were wiped out tomorrow, there would be no doctors but witch doctors, no transport faster than horses, no computers, no printed books' and 'no agriculture beyond subsistence peasant farming' (ibid.). On the other hand, 'If all the achievements of theologians were wiped out tomorrow, would anyone notice the smallest difference? ... The achievements of theologians don't do anything, don't affect anything, don't mean anything', prompting Dawkins to ask: 'What makes anyone think that "theology" is a subject at all?' (ibid.).

It is largely in response to these sorts of questions that this volume has been conceived. Dawkins may well see science and religion as engaged in a battle to the death from which only the former can emerge triumphant, but, as McGrath construes it, 'The Dawkinsian view of reality is a mirror image of that found in some of the more exotic sections of American fundamentalism' (McGrath 2007: 23). No matter how persuasively Dawkins argues, as he did in an article for *The Guardian* newspaper just four days after 9/11, that 'To fill a world with religion ... is like littering the streets with loaded guns. Do not be surprised if they are used' (Dawkins 2001), it is questionable that this warfare model, by which 'Religion is persistently and consistently portrayed in the worst possible way', to the point of 'mimicking the worst features of religious fundamentalism's portrayal of atheism' (McGrath 2007: xii), ought to comprise the final, definitive word on the subject. As Barbour put it a whole decade before the publication of *The God Delusion*,

'The image of warfare is common today, partly because conflict between extreme views lends itself to dramatic media coverage, while more subtle and complex intermediate positions tend to be neglected' (Barbour 1998: 77). Compelling though his rhetoric may be, the way forward is to move from binary oppositions— whether construed in terms of the 'sacred' vs. the 'secular', the 'Church' vs. the 'world', or, indeed, the 'virus' of religion vs. the sophistication of science—towards according critical attention to the manner and the extent to which the boundaries are deemed to be much more fluid and malleable. Without denying that Dawkins's concern about the way in which Creationism has entered the school curriculum is legitimate—in his words, 'Any science teacher who denies that the world is billions (or even millions!) of years old is teaching a preposterous, mind-shrinking falsehood' (Dawkins 2002)—we ought to find ways of bringing the 'religious' and the 'secular' spheres into serious dialogue in an effort to do justice to the complex dynamics at work in the contemporary world.

As Gaye Ortiz and I have argued elsewhere, 'Whether we are speaking of religious fanaticism and fundamentalism or the media's trivialization of cultural values and moral standards, there is much work to be done in continuing mutual conversation instead of resorting to authoritarian edict, censorship, or even hostilities as remedies for the cultural crisis of the new millennium' (Deacy & Ortiz 2008: ix). In the world of both religious fanaticism and Richard Dawkins (and to this end, it is worth commenting that the differences between them are not all that pronounced, inasmuch as Dawkins sees himself as on an evangelical crusade to rescue science from the evils of religion), there is a clear and ontological distinction between 'right' and 'wrong'. For Dawkins, religion is 'bad' and science is 'good', and there can only be peace and progress in the world if and when religion in all its manifestations is exposed as a dangerous illusion and supplanted by science, while for adherents to more evangelical and fundamentalist forms of religion, it is religion that is a force—the force, indeed—for good and it is atheistic thinking that must be rejected. In actuality, however, there are considerably more sophisticated forms of theological and cultural enquiry 'out there', as this volume will attest. In my own field of Religion & Film, for example, Melanie Wright is correct that 'the past ten years or so have witnessed a remarkable growth in scholarship predicated on the religion–film interface' (Wright 2007: 11), for example, along the lines of my own thesis that the 'secular' medium of film is one of many cultural agencies that has challenged traditional religious institutions and even taken on their functions (see Deacy 2007: 253). As Clive Marsh argues in *Cinema and Sentiment*, for many people the act of going to the movies may be no less part of their 'life structure' than working, eating, sleeping and socializing, to the point that 'As a major component (binding commitment) in a person's life … cinema-going is functioning as a religious practice for some' (Marsh 2004: 1). Might it even be the case, Marsh suggests, that those who work in film 'may be functioning more authoritatively or at least more influentially than bishops' (ibid.: 3)? After all, as Christine Hoff Kraemer has recently argued, 'In some cases, the communal viewing of a film in a darkened theater and the lively discussion it inspires have become a more vital site of spiritual exploration and reflection than the mainline church service' (Kraemer 2004: 243), and I have previously written that there is something theologically significant about the way in which 'groups of people file into a theatre at a specified time, choose a seat, and prepare with others for what could be said to amount to a religious experience' (Deacy 2001: 4; cf. Ostwalt 1995: 154–5). Whereas for Dawkins, religion and the secular sphere can (and should) be clearly distinguished, Marsh correctly affirms that the 'secular' medium of film often works by getting people to do something that is identifiably theological in nature, since it is 'not possible to be moved to the core of one's being, or to ask questions about ultimate meaning and value without raising theological questions' (Marsh 2004: 10). He continues that this is not a strategy for trying to surreptitiously bring theology in through the back door—a charge one can imagine issuing from Dawkins and other detractors of religion—but 'a response to the fact that this is where theological discussion … is happening already' (ibid.).

Despite all the talk, therefore, of secularization—in terms of statistical evidence, we learn that 'only 7.5% of the population in England attended church on a regular basis' (Lynch 2005: 166) at the end of the twentieth century and according to some estimates 'around 1,500 people leave the church each week in Britain alone' (Pope 2007: 9)—Robert Pope is correct in his affirmation that 'religion, or at least the religious questions of origins, meaning and destiny in life, have maintained their potency in contemporary culture even when the popularity of institutional religion has declined' (ibid.: 1). Many theologians are already taking on board, for instance, the empirical reality that the reason students are interested in studying theology at university is not because they are necessarily interested in learning about ecclesiastical history or theological doctrines, such as those pertaining to sin, salvation and redemption, *per se*, but because they have encountered the use of theological vocabulary in popular culture and want to see what theology has to say about this. In my own case, I have increasingly found that one of the most popular undergraduate theology modules is in the area of religion/theology and film; Marsh is spot on in his attestation that the theology students of today 'are those who sit in lecture- and seminar-rooms across the world and may not have begun to examine the differences between salvation, liberation and atonement, but *are* interested in tackling them and have seen *The Shawshank Redemption*' (Marsh 2007a: 4). Moreover, Marsh maintains that 'There is no escaping this and it is not a situation to be regretted. It is simply the way things are' (ibid.: 2). In a very real sense, there is no reason why this should come as a surprise, although in Dawkinsian terms it might seem remarkable that such a debate is actually taking place at all. If the line of demarcation between religion and culture is permeable, John Lyden is correct when he affirms that 'there is no way to completely separate religion from culture' and that, conversely, 'if those aspects of culture that are usually viewed as nonreligious or opposed to religion meet many of the same functions of what we call religions, then we also cannot really separate culture from religion' (Lyden 2007: 205). Stewart Hoover takes a similar line, in his contention that the realms of religion and the media 'occupy the same spaces, serve many of the same purposes, and invigorate the same practices in late modernity', such that 'it is probably better to think of them as related than to think of them as separate' (Hoover 2006: 9).

Irrespective of whether one takes the line that religious practices are being displaced and dispersed by secular agencies such as film, or whether one could go even further and affirm that the entertainment industry has superseded and replaced religious institutions in the quest for meaning-making (cf. Deacy 2001: 4), this is a far cry from the black-and-white, 'religion' vs. 'secular' dichotomy adduced by proponents of the New Atheism. Even if it is held that we have entered some kind of post-Christian era, where non-institutionalized forms of spirituality and religion have taken the place of churches (and the popularity of yoga, devotion to fitness regimes and preponderance of 'Mind, Body, Spirit' sections in mainstream bookstores all testify to the fact that alternative agencies may be taking on religious functions in the modern world [see Marsh 2004: 11]), there is no reason why theologians should not be involved in the ensuing discussion, rather than, as Dawkins would have it, be relegated to the periphery. In Dawkins's eyes, theology is not 'of the smallest use to anybody ... When has theology ever said anything that is demonstrably true and is not obvious? I have listened to theologians, read them, debated against them. I have never heard any of them ever say anything of the smallest use, anything that was not either platitudinously obvious or downright false' (Dawkins 1998: 6). As Marsh suggests, however, 'theological discussion is necessary, for those who do it, and for the society of which they are a part' (Marsh 2007a: 176). After all, are not religious traditions 'carrying vital resources for people to work with in their quest to understand how to live' (ibid.)? Instead of drowning out the theologian, a more measured response would to be to take the line, as Marsh does, that 'societies will be all the poorer without theological traditions to inform them' (ibid.).

The fact that Marsh observes that 'Indifference or hostility to religion may be mixed up with very religion-like practices and a very human desire to find or construct meaning' and that even those people 'who regard themselves as religious do their meaning making in relation to a range of resources and practices that is wider than they realize' (Marsh 2007b: 150) serves to show that the contours of the debate are more fluid than the Dawkinsian mindset allows. Over the last decade, for example, there has been a growing range of literature on religion, media and popular culture, including Bruce David Forbes & Jeffrey H. Mahan's *Religion and Culture in America*, which has moved away from a traditional focus on the beliefs and practices of established groups and cultural élites in order to concentrate more on the lives of everyday people (see e.g. Mahan 2000: 292). Sporting rituals, for example, 'shift our attention from the "official" performance of the work of art to the performance activity of the audience' (ibid.: 293), while Michael Jindra, writing in the same volume in relation to the concept of TV science fiction fandom, establishes that, when fans of a programme such as *Star Trek* 'fill out a mythological universe and keep it consistent through the formation of a canon of acceptable and unacceptable ... events', together with the 'schisms and oppositions' (Jindra 2000: 167) that such movements regularly generate, this is territory that the scholar can ill afford to overlook. Similarly, writing in 1982, M. Darroll Bryant claimed that 'as a popular form of the religious life, movies do what we have always asked of popular religion, namely, that they provide us with archetypal forms of humanity—heroic figures—and instruct us in the basic values and myths of our society' (Bryant 1982: 106). This also links with Lyden's more recent thesis, as expounded in *Film as Religion*, that 'If the religious dimensions of film were better understood, we might see both how film's views may parallel those of various religions and how film functions religiously in its own right' (Lyden 2003: 34). Accordingly, as I have written elsewhere, 'if our definitional net is woven in too conventional a mode, then a great deal of fascinating contemporary religiosity will just pass through it' (Deacy 2005: 18).

It is not therefore wide of the mark to propose that a 'secular' practice such as cinema-going 'does not simply fill in the time left by the absence of religion, but actually enables film-watchers to participate in the business of religion' (Marsh 2004: 6). The fact that those participants do not bring religious commitment in the conventional sense thus militates against Dawkins's assessment that religion is dangerous, because so many of its adherents subscribe to archaic, superstitious and irrational pre-scientific teachings on the question of the origins of the universe. In a nutshell, Dawkins's understanding of religion is too limited. He equates religion unequivocally with 'belief in God', such that the bottom line is that 'God's existence is a scientific fact about the universe, discoverable in principle if not in practice' and that 'If he existed and chose to reveal it, God himself could clinch the argument' (Dawkins 2006: 73). There is, however, rather more to the definition of religion than Dawkins's rather simplistic position permits. In sociological terms, for instance, there are important questions relating to ritual practices, and social and behavioural dispositions, which do not necessitate a concomitant belief in a Creator God. Writing in relation to Durkheim's theory of religion, Paden argues that

> Like a creator god, society fashions the world and its sacred institutions, even affixing hallowed times and places. Like a lawgiver and moral guardian, society ordains the behavioral order of things and punishes violations ... Like a god, society gives to us and expects to receive back from us. Religious behavior really *is* social behavior. (Paden 1992: 32)

On this reading, even though religion may be a fundamental human endeavour, the existence of a supernatural God is not the be all and end all of religion. For Durkheim, indeed, group solidarity gives the believer 'more strength in himself, either to cope with the difficulties of existence or to defeat them. He is raised above human miseries because he is raised above his condition as man' (Durkheim 2001 [1912]: 311).

It may be Dawkins's position that 'one of the truly bad effects of religion is that it teaches us that it is a virtue to be satisfied with not understanding' (Dawkins

2006: 152), but, as the case of Durkheim has highlighted, religion is considerably more nuanced than such a picture suggests. Indeed, if, as a Durkheimian model indicates, religion comprises 'a unified system of beliefs and practices relative to sacred things, that is to say, things set apart and surrounded by prohibitions ... that unite its adherents in a single moral community ...' (qtd in Durkheim 2001 [1912]: 44), it is hard to defend Dawkins's categorical affirmation that, if religion is abolished, the divisions and tensions within humanity will also thenceforth disappear. As Dawkins puts it, 'If children were taught to question and think through their beliefs, instead of being taught the superior virtue of faith without question, it is a good bet that there would be no suicide bombers' (Dawkins 2006: 348). Yet, as Milja Radovic's chapter in this volume reveals, there is a very fine line between religion, ethnicity and nationalism—and one could add to this mix such factors as language, gender, age, sexual orientation, class, wealth, political views and tribal allegiance (see McGrath 2007: 52)—such that the 'simplistic belief' as espoused by Dawkins that, *per se*, 'the elimination of religion would lead to the end of violence, social tension or discrimination' (ibid.) is very wide of the mark.

   To sum up, the treatment of religion by authors such as Dawkins tends to miss the point of where religious belief, expression and commitment tend to be located and can be encountered in contemporary society. Dawkins may see religion as a wholly negative phenomenon—a virus, no less—but there are less fundamentalist (and for that matter less monotheistic) types of religiosity present in society and, if there is any scepticism advanced even among academics regarding the viability of work undertaken at the intersection between religion and popular culture (see Deacy 2001: 16–17), this is because there is still too often a tendency to understand religion as having very strict, and clearly demarcated, boundaries. Religion is alive and well in the twenty-first century, but since it is not bound up with God, the Bible and the Church in quite the way Dawkins has in mind, the debate is too often incomplete and impoverished. Reading Dawkins, one would think that the study of religion and theology were only for 'religious' people. Yet it certainly does not follow that the study of religion entails an uncritical and naïve religious adherence and commitment on the part of the investigator. As the case of John Hinnells demonstrates, one can be an atheist while at the same time being sympathetic to the religious beliefs and practices of others (as evinced by Hinnells's pioneering work on Zoroastrianism). In his words, 'Of course one does not have to agree with something in order to study it' (Hinnells 2005: 5)—rather, it is vital to study religion because of the massive power throughout history that religious traditions and institutions have wielded.

   Moreover, has anyone even come up with a satisfactory string of words to describe what 'religion' actually is? As Peter Connolly succinctly puts it, 'Like many territories, religion has a number of disputed borders' (Connolly 1999: 4), and Hinnells rightly notes that all labels have limitations, making 'religion' a useful, but nevertheless potentially misleading term. In the words of John Hick, 'Religion is one thing to the anthropologist, another to the sociologist, another to the psychologist (and again another to the next psychologist!), another to the Marxist, another to the mystic, another to the Zen Buddhist and yet another to the Jew or Christian' (qtd in Crawford 2002: 3). Accordingly, for Hick, there is 'no universally accepted definition of religion, and quite possibly there never will be' (ibid.). Hinnells asks, indeed, whether there is even such a thing as 'Christianity', as opposed to a variety of different types of Christianit*ies*—'Are Primitive Welsh Methodists a part of the same religion as the Russian Orthodox?' (Hinnells 2005: 10). The US Presidential election campaign in 2008 of former Massachusetts Governor Mitt Romney ensured that the question of religious affiliation became a pivotal component of the race to succeed George W. Bush in view of Romney's affiliation to the Mormon Church. As the BBC's North American Editor, Justin Webb, wrote in December 2006: 'Is the Republican party too bigoted to select a Mormon as its presidential candidate?' (Webb 2006) At the root of the controversy is the uncertainty among many Americans as to how to categorize the Church of Jesus Christ of Latter-day Saints vis-à-vis 'mainstream' Christianity. To cite Webb again, from November 2007:

> At a party here in Washington recently, I conducted a scientific survey of my own. I asked all those I met what they thought of Mormonism. The respondents (including a very senior member of a mainstream Christian denomination) all thought it was weird, weird, weird. Several sniggered about multiple marriages, despite the fact that official Mormons have not been polygamous for a century (Webb 2007).

There may not be any ready-made answers to hand, but it is clear that, instead of seeking to ask whether religion is 'good' or 'bad' or whether a particular tradition such as Mormonism is 'mainstream' or 'deviant', a more fruitful starting point would consist of the attempt—indeterminate and ambivalent though the results may be—to *define* what religion is (or might be) in the first place, rather than to impose one's own prejudices and/or ignorance on to the agenda.

To this end, *Exploring Religion and the Sacred in a Media Age*, which addresses the very question of the diversity of religious experience and encounter with respect to contemporary culture, is a fitting counterpart to the work I have been involved in over the last decade in the emerging field of Religion & Film, where I have made the case for bringing two discrete, but potentially complementary, disciplines into critical dialogue. We live in societies where the media plays an increasingly integral role—film, for example, has arguably become 'Western culture's major storytelling and myth-producing medium' (Johnston 2007: 16)— yet theologians and religious studies scholars have only started to address this phenomenon in recent years. It is thus anticipated that this volume will make a significant contribution to the growing interest in this area of study by bringing together a selection of the best papers from the joint conference of the British Sociological Association Sociology of Religion Study Group conference and the UK Research Network Group in Theology, Religion and Popular Culture, which took place at St Catherine's College, Oxford, in April 2007. This was one of the first conferences in the UK to explore this area in depth, and it attracted interest from a range of international participants contributing to this area of research. Of the 57 papers accepted for the conference, 14 have been selected for inclusion in this book. These range from chapters by key-note speakers at the conference, who are international leaders in this field, to contributions from other scholars with established or emerging expertise.

A key strength of this book is also its interdisciplinary range, offering perspectives on the study of religion, media and popular culture from a range of disciplines, including theology, religious studies, media studies, cultural studies, film studies, sociology and anthropology. With contributions from the United Kingdom, New Zealand, North America, Hong Kong, Australia and Serbia, the collection reflects the international dimension of this field. Each of the chapters consists of focused case studies of particular texts, practices, communities and audiences and is at the cutting edge of contemporary debates in sociology, religion and the media. Topics include the examination of media rituals, marketing strategies, empirical investigations of audience testimony and the influence of religion on music, reality television and the Internet.

The collection begins with Tom Beaudoin's insightful call for scholars who conduct research in religion and culture to pay closer attention to their underlying motivations, attachments and methodologies. What exactly is their relationship to the academic disciplines and practices that they use? He queries whether such studies are the pure and objective scholarly productions that they deem them to be or whether they say rather more than they might be prepared to allow about their own idiosyncrasies, fantasies, daydreams and fictions—indeed, their 'fandoms'. He is especially concerned about the problematic theological assumptions that guide the generation, classification and reportage of sociological data pertaining to, for example, the religious and spiritual lives of modern American teenagers. Beaudoin's concern is that such studies, one of which he examines here in depth, misread the nature of everyday faith. As he observes, the definition of what constitutes real or authentic faith is provided in such studies by institutions and their representatives and it is against these that the testimony of, say, teenagers themselves are measured. Priority in such surveys is given to 'pure official teaching', with anything that falls short of this standard a deviation. In reality, however, Beaudoin attests that the particular beliefs that are sanctioned by religious leaders are implicated in non-theological, cultural, political, social and economic factors, yet such surveys continue to hold fast to an unproblematic and self-evident ahistorical and idealized view of Christianity. Beaudoin therefore calls for a proper analysis of the practices that comprise the study (and those who do the studying) of popular culture to be conducted in order that, for example, researchers may consider, instead, how sociological data may actually have something spiritually constructive and new to teach the larger church. Academics may see themselves as detached, rational and able to decode the discourses of others, but, he proposes, they have more in common than they care to acknowledge with the category of 'fandom' as developed in popular culture studies. Academics, like fans, are inclined to venerate—no less irrationally—particular passions, attachments and subjectivities. Intrinsic to both academia and fandom is an obstinacy concerning the superiority of one's chosen object of engagement and Beaudoin highlights the need for academics to undergo a self- and communal examination of their motivations and fandoms before they even attempt to speak on behalf of other people's faith. A richer academic conversation is thus needed about the cost of the stability of the scholar in the studies and research that they carry out.

In chapter 2, Nick Couldry asks whether contemporary mediated societies are inclined to become increasingly ritualized, with the reality TV programme *Celebrity Big Brother* cited as a prime example of a media ritual. He is not writing as a religious studies specialist, but Couldry's argument has a clear affinity with the argument adduced by Emile Durkheim in his *Elementary Forms of Religious Life*. Couldry stresses that his concept of 'media rituals' does not involve arguing that some aspects of contemporary media are rituals because they carry some of the feelings that we may associate with religious ritual. Rather, he chooses to look at purely structural and formal analogies that may be constructed between media rituals and Durkheim's thinking. According to Couldry, Durkheim's understanding of ritual can refer to practices that are secular as well as religious and ritual practice reinforces the distinction between the sacred and the profane. Couldry attests that the rhetorics of order that underlie media rituals are increasingly prevalent in contemporary societies and that through media rituals we acquire a direct and immediate connection to certain central social realities. Just as Durkheim saw religious rituals as organized around the mutually exclusive categories of sacred/ profane, so media rituals are organized around the categories of 'media' vs. 'ordinary' (as shown by the perceived distinction between 'celebrities' and 'ordinary persons'). Couldry argues that media rituals enact and reproduce the categories which underlie beliefs in the social institution of the media, just as religious rituals reproduce the categories which underlie religious beliefs, and he examines the extent to which the 'media world' in some sense 'stands in for', and gives us special access to, our collective 'reality'. In Durkheimian terms, Couldry asks whether religious authority is based in the same type of social source as the media's authority, that is, the claim to stand in for the social, and then proceeds to examine the ethical ramifications of this. Can we obtain a framework for thinking about media ethics that can take on the challenges that an intensely mediated and ritualized public sphere will generate for our chances of living peaceably together?

In the third chapter, Stephen Pattison makes the bold and provocative case for engaging more deeply from the perspective of Christian practical theology with artefacts. He argues that while artefacts—works of human creation—of a sacred or aesthetic significance may be objects of academic analysis, they are mostly ignored by commentators and critics who tend to assume that there is a disjuncture between the material/inanimate and the human. The material world of artefacts thus lacks fundamental interests and rights and exists solely for human use and manipulation. Yet, Pattison contends, there is a need to redress the balance, not least because artefacts make claims upon the human world—our bodies, persons, beliefs, societies and practices—and a relationship of mutual recognition and respect for all things is preferable to one of domination and exploitation. The fact that artefacts are among the highest forms of human self-realization exacerbates the need to see them more as we presently relate to persons and agents and to cultivate person-like relations with them. After all, artefacts shape us and make us who and what we are—because of the bicycle, for example, a whole generation of pedestrians have been transformed into tourists. In theological terms, Pattison suggests that artefacts may even be seen to constitute the products of and witnesses to embodied human logos—they are the products of and witnesses to embodied human logos. Not to engage with, or to admire, artefacts thus comprises a lost opportunity. Artefacts need our appreciation, care and respect if they are to survive and flourish, and many artefacts, from the most lofty (cathedrals) to the most prosaic (doors), outlive and outlast their progenitors—to the point, even, of acting as memorials to the humans that created them. Sometimes, he argues, they have a value over and above that of human beings themselves—valuable paintings, for instance, may be evacuated in times of war ahead of the exigencies of living people. The fact that artefacts do not have free will is no reason, according to Pattison, for consigning them to the (literal and metaphorical) rubbish heap. Some humans and animals lack the ability to undertake reciprocal responsibilities, but that does not mean we accord them no moral significance—whether we are talking about an embryo, a person who is comatose or the environment. Pattison argues strongly that if we invest in relationships with artefacts, we can be more properly engaged in the experience of living, thereby challenging attitudes of unthinking acquisition and consumption. In response to the charge that a relationship with artefacts might lead us away from relationships with fellow humans, he concludes that the opposite may be the case and that there is no reason why we cannot be concerned with both. If human life is shaped by artefacts, to care about humans is to care about our relations with material things.

Jolyon Mitchell's chapter (chapter 4) examines how various media are used to promote, celebrate and offer a critique of purported martyrdoms, with particular reference to how mediated representations of recent martyrdoms within Islam reverberate across various cultural and religious settings. This is a pioneering study as very little work to date has accorded adequate consideration to why the concept of 'martyrdom' has become a point of contest. Mitchell begins with the recent assassination in Pakistan of Benazir Bhutto, and, by paying attention to testimony on the Internet, where the story of her murder has already been amplified and elaborated, he appraises whether the manner and form of Bhutto's death determines her 'martyr' status and what kind of martyr she will become—will she be a martyr for freedom, social justice and democracy, or a martyr for Islam? Moving on to discuss memorials to those who were killed during the Iran–Iraq war of the 1980s, Mitchell questions whether any links can be forged between contemporary Iranian martyrdoms and the death 1,300 years ago of Hussein, the grandson of the Prophet Muhammad, and as to whether there is a distinction between describing, on the one hand, volunteer soldiers who lost their lives, and, on the other, suicide bombers, as martyrs. Mitchell also looks at the work of scholars who have gone beyond purely religious and theological explanations for what motivates suicide bombers—to what extent, for example, do political goals play a role, especially in the light of claims that suicide bombing is primarily a response to foreign occupation and a strategy for political liberation? Significantly, Mitchell notes that despite the often vociferous support that suicide attacks receive within Islam, more nuanced pictures emerge on the Internet, where the appropriateness and legitimacy of suicide bombings are often condemned on religious grounds. Many sites, for example, advocate that 'true' Islam is peaceful and life-bringing, such that there is a clear distinction between Islam and Talibanism. Mitchell then concludes by examining how the apparent democratization of Internet communication has helped to ensure the further fragmentation of the contested term 'martyrdom', to the point that modern media is a pivotal site for Muslims and Christians alike to express their strongly held beliefs in the face of violence, terrorism and war.

In chapter 5, Michael W. DeLashmutt raises vital questions about the extent to which technology has become a central facet in the construction of self-identity and personal values. His focus is on the religious self-identity of IT workers in Seattle, a city where religious identity is disproportionately lower than in other regions of the US and where the rate of employment within the IT industry is high. DeLashmutt is particularly well qualified to undertake research in this area, having worked for a number of years within the information economy in Seattle. Using Paul Tillich's understanding of technology as a starting point, DeLashmutt asks whether technology contributes to the radical construction of identity, community, ethics and even religious faith. He says that as a Christian practical theologian he is interested in exploring how cultures produce forms of expressing something akin to what Tillich meant by Ultimate Concern. To what extent can technology convey the Ultimate (so that the language of techno-theology becomes apt)? If technology offers a plausible functional alternative to religious devotion, does this account for the low religious adherence of those who work in the IT sector in the Seattle metropolitan area? According to statistics, DeLashmutt notes that more people living in the Pacific North West choose 'none' as their religious identity than anywhere else in the United States. But, looking at the evidence, he indicates that no definite correlation can be made between this particular region's employment data and its rate of religious affiliation, which was low even before the likes of Amazon, Microsoft, Real Media and hundreds of small Internet corporations took root there in the last couple of decades. He draws on three case studies and reaches the conclusion that religious views have little to do with his respondents' choice of vocation and, vice versa, that their choice of vocation has little to do with their religious views. Rather, DeLashmutt points out, issues of religious affiliation have more to do with family, community and life situations and his research subjects' reasons for working in this sector are entirely pragmatic, such as wishing to make money or pursue a challenging career. This is one occasion, DeLashmutt acknowledges, in which his research has produced results contrary to his original expectations and which causes him to reflect on his research in new and challenging ways. He concludes that we need to pursue new ways of conceiving of spirituality apart from functionalist accounts of religion and that the onus is on the academic to appreciate that the way in which a research subject may understand religion is not necessarily identical or equivalent to the manner in which it is used in academic discourse. The same words may have different definitions. Rather than see religion as being on the defensive when it comes to the challenges posed by technology, DeLashmutt makes the instructive point that the Church might actually be better served by placing technology in the background, not the foreground, especially in an age when contemporary users of technology are favouring the ability of technology to facilitate collaboration and community (as evinced by the popularity of social networking sites such as *Facebook*)—'two things for which the Christian church could find an immediate resonance' (p. 99). Technology may thus be complementing, rather than competing with, organized religion.

Carlton Johnstone's chapter (chapter 6) also draws on the unexpected and unconventional ways in which religious language and knowledge have the capacity to be drawn upon and appropriated in more 'secular' contexts. His focus is on the study of billboard advertisements in Auckland, New Zealand, which challenge claims that Christianity and the Church are anachronistic and redundant in the modern world. With particular reference to two recent marketing campaigns which heavily exploited religious vocabulary, Johnstone's chapter raises important questions about the disparity between people's positive response to Jesus and their negative response to organized religion as well as significant broader questions concerning the representation of God in popular culture. Is God an old man with a long white beard, as conveyed in the depiction by Michelangelo in the Sistene Chapel, or could he be black, as in the case of the film *Bruce Almighty* (Tom Shadyac, 2003)? To what extent are perceptions of Jesus culturally assimilated and historically located rather than normative? Are we passive consumers or is it the case that there is no such thing as a natural or correct reading of an image or text? To what extent does social position play a role in the interpretation of media texts? The billboards that Johnstone refers to enable people—as his study of empirical testimony has shown—who are reluctant to engage in conversation about God and Christianity to build a bridge and have a dialogue about religion and theology. The main focus of his study is the 'Hell Pizza' advertising campaign which reappropriates the biblical idea of Hell as a place of eternal torment and punishment to refer to a gourmet pizza outlet. Ironically the net result of this, as Johnstone identifies, is to bring back to the discussion table a concept that 'has virtually been eliminated from the vocabulary and doctrinal repository of most churches' (p. 112). He refers to the way religious ideas are being emptied and refilled with branded meaning and indicates that the adverts do not transmit messages by themselves—without the viewer as decoder they are meaningless. Similar to the above chapter, which questions whether technology might be taking on religious functions, Johnstone raises a broader question: whether advertising comprises a form of religion. Is advertising, in a consumer society, one of the institutions creating meaning and thus replacing the Church? Or is it the case that, rather than a new form of religion, religiousness is being exploited for the purposes of advertising? Johnstone then examines Michel de Certeau's concepts of strategies, tactics and textual poaching to explore the marketing of God and Hell in two rival marketing campaigns. Johnstone's conclusion is that, if the biblical rivalry between God and Satan is being successfully played out in the streets of modern-day Auckland, there has been a sea-change in people's religious and cultural values in the last 20 years and we are now witnessing 'a semiotic landscape that is fluid and polysemic' (p. 118).

In chapter 7, Ellen E. Moore also examines the manner in which secular media can help—or even hinder—personal faith. Her focus is the nature of contemporary American evangelism as it is shaped by the media and the questions it poses to churchgoers concerning the importance of truth and objectivity. She pays specific reference in this regard to the various ways in which evangelical Christian congregations engaged with *The Da Vinci Code* (Ron Howard, 2006) upon its theatrical release in May 2006. Moore observes that whereas many Roman Catholic leaders advocated a boycott of the film, a number of evangelical churches appropriated its style in their worship and literature: not only did they screen the film to churchgoers, they also made their websites resemble scenes from the movie and created 'code breaking' games to play on church grounds. Although at first glance there would appear to be a conflict between a secular, mainstream media culture and evangelical Christianity, Moore raises the possibility that the values they espouse are not all that different. Looking at the concept of a 'spiritual marketplace', she examines how church leaders are increasingly adopting a consumerist strategy and ideology, to the point that there is an ongoing redefinition of churches as businesses and the faithful as 'clients' in which the individual is privileged over and above the institution. Accordingly, individual churchgoers can even reject the Church's teachings, if they impede, or stand in the way of, the individual's search for meaning and happiness in life. Finding that the media are an important evangelizing tool for reaching out to 'unchurched' individuals, who may be either unfamiliar or disillusioned with traditional religious institutions, Moore suggests that it can prove difficult for pastors to call for an outright rejection of popular culture when the media play such an integral role in attracting new members and 'bringing them to God'. She even cites one Presbyterian pastor who invoked *The Da Vinci Code*'s lead actor, Tom Hanks, as a source of religious authority, since the minister concerned had read or heard somewhere that Hanks was a Christian. Drawing on her observations of several evangelical church services in Illinois, which she supplemented by focus group discussions, Moore also argues that church leaders are being forced to confront their congregations' acquaintance with, and dependence on, rationalism and scientific reasoning, in which ordinary churchgoers are predilected to frame their religious beliefs in the language of science, evidence and knowledge, rather than faith alone. To this end, Moore cites the testimony of churchgoers whose relationship to the Bible and Church teachings was changed by *The Da Vinci Code*, in that following the disclosure in the film that one of the characters is the last living descendant of Jesus Christ, they wanted to know whether the Church could use DNA testing in order to establish whether or not Jesus' bloodline was continued. Moore's chapter thus raises fascinating questions about how the 'sacred' is being redefined in the light of scientific and media discourse and points to broader issues about how changing religious practices influence contemporary culture and politics beyond the specific context of American evangelicals.

In chapter 8, Danielle Kirby continues the search for the sacred within the context of secular culture. Her focus is the way in which the popularization of the Internet has facilitated the establishment and growth of 'virtual', albeit loosely affiliated, communities, whose adherents believe in the existence of a non-human world, populated by mythological souls and selves. This raises key questions about the ways in which works of fiction—in the form of books, films, television and comics, to name some of the more obvious ones—can be drawn upon to carry and convey sacred and spiritual meaning. Irrespective of whether such groups believe literally in the worlds portrayed in narrative fiction or whether such texts 'merely' provide support and inspiration for religious, metaphysical and spiritual beliefs, Kirby's exercise is important, if we are to avoid misrepresenting what 'alternative', syncretic religious groups stand for. While such groups tend to acknowledge the explicitly fictional basis of the texts to which they relate, they nevertheless believe, as in the case of adherents to Jediism, in a 'personal acceptance of the moral and spiritual code' (p. 143) that is attributed to their fictional counterparts—in this instance, the Jedi of the *Star Wars* films. Rather than literally believe in the existence of the Death Star, for instance, a Jedi might find that the ideals espoused by fictional characters are worth emulating in his or her own life. The central focus of Kirby's study is the Otherkin, who exemplify a far more literal interpretation of narrative fiction than Jedis, to the point of believing that they are themselves more-than-human. They are a community aimed at personal metaphysical enquiry and mutual support. Kirby raises fascinating questions concerning the nature of how they may be said to comprise a 'community'. She notes, for example, that despite being dispersed geographically and comprising a 'virtual' phenomenon, there are off-line group activities and meetings, too. The conclusion she draws is not that the Otherkin are religion-like or implicitly religious, in the way that football may be deemed to encompass religion-like traits and tendencies, but that they are actively religious—their concerns are of a spiritual and super-empirical nature. Kirby's chapter also encompasses a discussion of the nature of fan cultures more generally and whether the alternative worlds that such groups adhere to is pre-existent, thus existing prior to their composition by an author, with the author 'merely' channelling the worlds concerned, or whether the 'fictional' worlds concerned have been constructed by the readers or viewers themselves, through their various interests, predilections, hopes, aspirations and needs.

Nicholas Buxton's chapter (chapter 9) draws on first-hand experience of taking part in a British TV documentary series, when he lived in a Benedictine monastery (Worth Abbey) for six weeks. One of the other participants, a self-confessed atheist, underwent a religious experience during his time at the monastery, prompting Buxton to ask whether a Reality TV series can really be the right medium for fostering such a personal journey. Besides the legitimate question whether it can ever be possible to have a religious experience without also having a religious faith in which to situate it and a religious language with which to describe it, Buxton's chapter raises significant questions about how the monastic principles drawn upon in the programme, such as silence and simplicity, correlate with the world of Reality TV. Is a medium of entertainment and escape from reality capable of communicating something real and authentic? Can a line of demarcation be drawn between reality and Reality TV? How porous is the distinction between fact and fiction in television? Can a TV documentary be anything other than a constructed narrative as opposed to an unmediated, neutral record of reality? Is there a disjuncture between the 'transformation' or 'self-improvement' of the 'contestants' (and/or their houses and gardens) that has now become a staple of Reality TV and the spiritual transformation one might expect to happen in a monastery? Buxton discusses the paradox of effectively having two monasteries to contend with—the 'real-life' experience of living in Worth Abbey and the media event of a Reality TV programme that is set in a monastery. Would his, and that of his fellow contestants', experience of spending six weeks in this environment have been any different had the event not been televised? Did the process of being observed by a television audience have any effect on the experience of being there? Buxton suggests that, although physically absent, the viewer was nonetheless ever-present, which raises questions whether viewers are seeing the 'real' self or the 'performed' self. He notes that even the attempt to avoid acting and performing in front of the camera itself became an act and that there was a perceptible difference in the group's behaviour when the camera crew were not present. Buxton raises important questions about the media 'packaging' of religion, like Johnstone's chapter, and, in particular, the way filmmakers subsumed the 'radical otherness' of the transformative experience of the atheist-turned-believer into the nature of religion as a form of therapy. What is the media's role in the construction of selfhood in the modern world? Instead of, as in traditional religious terms, having one's attention directed away from oneself on to something higher and transcendent, Buxton concludes that Reality TV is interested only in exploring the move towards the self and one's inner life—thus creating a distinction between the 'virtual' and the 'real' monastery.

In chapter 10, Rupert Till examines the relationship between religion and Electronic Dance Music Culture (EDMC). He asks whether there is such a thing as EDMC spirituality. As in the case of DeLashmutt's first-hand experience of working in the Seattle Metropolitan area and Buxton's time spent in a monastery, Till has insider knowledge of club culture: he has worked in it since 1991 and has thus been in a prime position to undertake participant observation over a long-term period. In functionalist terms, Till examines whether the design of clubs might be found to resemble churches, with, for example, the DJ booth taking on the characteristics of an organ loft or pulpit—an analogy that extends to the club names which often have overt religious connotations, while clubbers can be seen raising their hands upward towards the light in the manner of a Pentecostal Church service. The clubs themselves also denote separation from mainstream culture, being places of escape, release and transgression, although Till notes the irony that it is often Christianity that is the target of transgression, rather than, say, Hinduism or Islam, while at the same time clubs borrow from Christian culture. Till argues that the most obvious evidence of religion and spirituality within EDMC is the many instances of transcendent experiences, described by clubbers, which he recounts at length. He observes, however, that most clubbers do not regard themselves as 'religious' or see EDMC as having a religious or spiritual dimension. Like DeLashmutt, who found that workers in the IT sector had a different understanding of the term 'religion' to those in the academy, Till suggests that there is a dichotomy at work, in which it is the language, traditions and history of religion that are being rejected, rather than its philosophical essentials. Dismissive of religion though his respondents may be, Till nevertheless finds that, in Weberian terms, clubs are providing a focus of community for the homeless self, created by the individualization of society in the modern industrialized world—a role that traditional religions fulfilled in the past. That there is a social and community dimension to EDMC is evident from Till's fieldwork, with individuals seeking closeness, attachment and empathy—even ecstatic merger—with the group, in what amounts to 'sacred space', both separate from the everyday world and a key focus of community and identity. Accordingly, Till concludes that EDMC enables us to understand the importance within our cultures of tradition, ritual, community and transcendence and the importance of dancing together to music.

Milja Radovic's chapter (chapter 11) looks at the interplay between Serbian films from the 1990s and the socio-political regime of Slobodan Milosevic, with particular reference to the representation of nationalism and its connection with institutional religion (the Orthodox Church of Serbia) in *Pretty Village, Pretty Flame* (Srdjan Dragojevic, 1995). Radovic interrogates what the film says about the cultural context of the time and whether there is a link between ecclesiastical mission and political activities. She suggests that the film comprises an important barometer of the particular mindset of Serbian people during this period and of the way Milosevic's regime affected people from various backgrounds. Although the film bears witness to a number of competing symbolisms, Radovic attests that ultimately there is a strong, although indirect, message which opposes the regime. She refutes the charge that the film is pro-Milosevic by virtue of the way it deconstructs the very stereotypes and myths upon which Milosevic's populism was based. Dealing with questions of implicit versus explicit religion, Radovic notes that Orthodox Christianity is not specifically analysed in the film, nor were the filmmakers interested in dealing with religion *per se*. But, she argues, *Pretty Village, Pretty Flame* discloses much about the Serbian Orthodox Church and its impact on the people of Serbia, with its religious elements inseparable from the representation of nationalism, and religious intolerance is presented as an integral part of the conflict. Her conclusion is that the film provides a critical depiction of religious-mythological concepts of nationhood as well as pointers to the way nationalism and religious intolerance are equated and connected, in particular, how Milosevic's regime presented the conflict as a continuation of the historical battle for Serbdom, of which Serbian Orthodoxy was an integral part.

The focus on world cinema continues in chapter 12, in which Yam Chi-Keung focuses on two films by Hong Kong actor and filmmaker Stephen Chow. Yam recognizes that East Asian cinema has not been accorded much attention in the emerging Religion & Film field. His chapter is an important attempt to redress this imbalance. Using textual and contextual analysis, he examines the manner in which *Shaolin Soccer* (2001) and *Kung Fu Hustle* (2004) may be found to comprise parabolic representations that express important aspects of the mass psychology of the people of Hong Kong in the years following political reunion with China in 1997. Although Chow's work has been neglected in major scholarly works on Asian cinema, Yam argues that despite the films' appearance as non-sensical and irreverent entertainment, aimed at a mass audience and devoid of serious substance, they manifest, in their depiction of marginalized underdogs struggling for survival in a changing world that is hostile towards them, some of the deepest collective concerns of contemporary Hong Kong and proffer a vision of hope. In *Kung Fu Hustle*, for example, the characters may well be displaced from mainstream society, but they are portrayed as heroes who exhibit both extraordinary physical strength and moral courage. Placing the marginal at the centre subverts the conventional relationship between the centre and the margin and redefines what it means to be socially excluded and powerless. In particular, the impetus to transform the destiny of the marginal community comes from within this very socio-economic class itself, rather than from an outside élite who, in the manner of, say, the American Monomyth, would break into the world from above in the form of a saviour-figure. Yam suggests that hope for the future comes from the ability to reconnect with the collective memory of hardship that has been common in Hong Kong's recent past. While not explicitly religious films, Yam argues that there is a religious undertone at work in Chow's movies—they preach a 'secular gospel' devoid of explicitly sacred, eschatological and transcendental content, while nevertheless addressing fundamental issues that the contemporary local audience deem to be 'sacred'. The absence of a dichotomy between sacred and secular is a useful corrective, Yam concludes, to the tendency in Western academia to set up just such a dichotomized paradigm, in the form, for instance, of the secularization thesis.

In Chapter 13, Sarah Lawther examines the impact that the Internet has had on the way in which religions are depicted and understood. In a way that mirrors Kirby's discussion of the relationship between the Internet and the rise of alternative religions, Lawther examines the inter-connection between religious involvement in the online world and the extent to which this has the capacity to change what happens offline (although the focus here is specifically on mainstream religious traditions). Looking primarily at the homepage—the initial point of contact—of religious websites from the Buddhist, Christian, Hindu,

Muslim and Jewish traditions, Lawther examines how religions choose to present themselves and asks a number of pertinent questions: what are the differences between religion *in* cyberspace (religion online) and religion *on* cyberspace (online religion)? Is there a difference between the way religion is presented and the extent to which the Internet offers a new form of religious experience? Can the boundaries between the two categories be tightly drawn? Does the Internet enable or encourage religious experimentation? If so, how challenging might this be to traditional forms of religion? To what extent does the medium shape the message? While anyone can access the sites concerned in her study, Lawther notes that this may not have been the intention of the authors, who may, for instance, have a local, select audience in mind and certainly did not create these Internet sites for the purposes of social scientific research. Lawther's chapter investigates a number of ethical and methodological questions that thus arise. As there is no central source of control or authority on the web, does this tend to favour non-hierarchical traditions? Is the medium swallowing the message to this end? How objective can sampling be, if some religious organizations are using 'pay-for-placement' advertising where they appear as the sponsored link for any searches that are conducted on search engines for religions? Does this skew the results? Does the updating of sites reflect the fact that religions are evolving—or is this simply down to skilful marketing strategies? Finding in the course of her research that a significant number of images on the home pages of religious sites are of the social and communal dimension of religion, Lawther asks whether this reflects the fact that the motivation for, say, Christians who join online communities is not information, but a need for relationships? Or is it the case that 'community' images are easy to show and can be uploaded easily and economically from a digital camera? Lawther concludes by examining the effect that online images of sacred figures are having on offline religious experience and the extent to which offline communities are being sustained by their online presence.

In the final chapter (chapter 14), Katharine Sarah Moody also looks to the Internet. The focus here is on the way the Internet is a site where people are working out their self-identity, with particular reference to blogging and open source software. Similar to Kirby's study of virtual communities, Moody is also interested in the websites of emerging groups, although her focus is mainly on Christian communities. Recognizing that much research to date has tended to ignore the online aspects of emerging Christian communities, Moody offers an invaluable corrective to scholarship in this area by facilitating the inclusion of seldom heard voices, using the methodology of Radical Orthodoxy's post-secular understanding of theology. Her research finds that the Christian web bloggers concerned tend to reflect in a Christian fashion upon all manner of phenomena and events, including music, film, football, beer, food, fashion and politics, as well as specifically theological concerns. She identifies in particular a website which has been created by an online community of users who are engaged in the reconstruction of theology following an open source methodology (similar in form to Wikipedia, which allows users to update entries, edit pages and alter page content and layout). She examines how the source code of the Christian tradition—whether the Apostles' Creed or anything to do with such topics as eschatology or ethics—is being questioned, reinterpreted and modified by web users. The effect is that 'the conventional understanding of theology as a bounded discipline reserved for "the experts"' (p. 234) is being exploded. The ramifications are, she observes, being experienced off-line, too, with what is happening online providing a model or template for what is going on in the 'real' world. Moody's conclusion is that the blogosphere presents researchers with an opportunity for conducting research that would be constrained by more conventional research methods. In interview situations, for example, there is not the same sort of flexibility or scope for allowing discussion topics to develop. The advantage with blogs as data is that the participants' own personal theorizing can be expanded through their engagement with other voices. There is therefore something far more collective and up-to-the-minute happening with web-based research than conventional, library-destined academic research permits, although Moody acknowledges that a number of ethical and practical questions still need to be addressed. How far ought one go, for example, to enable potential respondents to access and contribute to, or participate in, a web blog? The dangers that Moody spells out of 'link slutting' and 'link whoring', and of other inappropriate 'netiquette', makes for a very topical chapter which explores innovative and pioneering directions for future empirical research.

Exploring Religion and the Sacred in a Media Age is thus a very creative and academically rich counterpoint to some of the more dismissive treatments of religion that have been so much in vogue of late, not least through the advances of Richard Dawkins, Christopher Hitchens and other advocates of the New Atheism. In the place of what McGrath discerns in *The God Delusion* as the 'atheist equivalent of slick hellfire preaching' and the substitution of 'turbocharged rhetoric and highly selective manipulation of facts for careful, evidence-based thinking' (McGrath 2007: x), this volume has sought to ensure that a more multi-faceted and creative engagement with religion is on offer. It has been written with an international audience in mind, and is recommended reading for the growing number of undergraduate and postgraduate courses in religion, media and popular culture—of which there is a particular concentration in North America, Britain and Scandinavia, but also a growing number in other parts of Europe, Latin America and Asia—that are at the cutting-edge of contemporary academic discourse.

References

Barbour, Ian, *Religion and Science: Historical and Contemporary Issues* (London: SCM Press, 1998).
Bryant, M. Darroll, 'Cinema, Religion and Popular Culture', in John R. May & Michael Bird (eds), *Religion in Film* (Knoxville: University of Tennessee Press, 1982): 101–14.

Connolly, Peter (ed.), *Approaches to the Study of Religion* (London: Cassell, 1999).

Crawford, Robert, *What is Religion?: Introducing the Study of Religion* (London: Routledge, 2002).

Dawkins, Richard, 'The Emptiness of Theology', *Free Inquiry*, 18/2 (Spring 1998): 6.

Dawkins, Richard, 'Religion's Misguided Missiles', *The Guardian* (15 September 2001), www.guardian.co.uk/Archive/Article/0,4273,4257777,00.html [access date 27 May 2008].

Dawkins, Richard, 'A Scientist's View', *The Guardian* (9 March 2002), www.guardian.co.uk/uk/2002/mar/09/religion.schools1 [access date 27 May 2008].

Dawkins, Richard, *The God Delusion* (London: Transworld, 2006).

Deacy, Christopher, *Screen Christologies: Redemption and the Medium of Film* (Cardiff: University of Wales Press, 2001).

Deacy, Christopher, *Faith in Film: Religious Themes in Contemporary Cinema* (Aldershot: Ashgate, 2005).

Deacy, Christopher, 'From Bultmann to Burton, Demythologizing the Big Fish: The contribution of modern Christian theologians to the theology–film conversation', in Robert K. Johnston (ed.), *Re-Viewing Theology and Film: Moving the Discipline Forward* (Grand Rapids: Baker Academic, 2007): 238–58.

Deacy, Christopher & Ortiz, Gaye, *Theology and Film: Challenging the Sacred/ Secular Divide* (Oxford: Blackwell, 2008).

Draper, John William, *History of the Conflict Between Religion and Science* (New York: Appleton, 1874).

Durkheim, Emile, *The Elementary Forms of Religious Life* (Oxford: Oxford University Press, 2001 [1912]).

Hinnells, John, 'Why Study Religions?', in John Hinnells (ed.), *The Routledge Companion to the Study of Religion* (Abingdon: Routledge, 2005): 5–20.

Hoover, Stewart, *Religion in the Media Age* (London: Routledge, 2006).

Jindra, Michael, 'It's About Faith in Our Future: Star Trek Fandom as Cultural Religion', in Bruce David Forbes & Jeffrey H. Mahan (eds), *Religion and Popular Culture in America* (London: University of California Press, 2000): 165–79.

Johnston, Robert K., 'Introduction: Reframing the Discussion', in Robert K. Johnston (ed.), *Re-Viewing Theology and Film: Moving the Discipline Forward* (Grand Rapids: Baker Academic, 2007): 15–26.

Kraemer, Christine Hoff, 'From Theological to Cinematic Criticism: Extricating the Study of Religion and Film from Theology', *Religious Studies Review*, 30/4 (October 2004): 243–50.

Lyden, John C., *Film as Religion: Myths, Morals and Rituals* (New York: New York University Press, 2003).

Lyden, John, 'Theology and Film: Interreligious Dialogue and Theology', in Robert K. Johnston (ed.), *Re-Viewing Theology and Film: Moving the Discipline Forward* (Grand Rapids: Baker Academic, 2007): 205–18.

Lynch, Gordon, *Understanding Theology and Popular Culture* (Oxford: Blackwell, 2005).

McGrath, Alister, with Joanna Collicutt McGrath, *The Dawkins Delusion?: Atheist Fundamentalism and the Denial of the Divine* (London: SPCK, 2007).

Mahan, Jeffrey H., 'Conclusion: Establishing a Dialogue about Religion and Popular Culture', in Bruce David Forbes & Jeffrey H. Mahan (eds), *Religion and Popular Culture in America* (London: University of California Press, 2000): 292–99.

Marsh, Clive, *Cinema and Sentiment: Film's Challenge to Theology* (Carlisle: Paternoster Press, 2004).

Marsh, Clive, *Theology Goes to the Movies: An Introduction to Critical Christian Thinking* (London: Routledge, 2007a).

Marsh, Clive, 'On Dealing with What Films Actually Do to People: The Practice and Theory of Film Watching in Theology/Religion and Film Discussion', in Robert K. Johnston (ed.), *Re-Viewing Theology and Film: Moving the Discipline Forward* (Grand Rapids: Baker Academic, 2007b): 145–61.

Ostwalt Jr, Conrad E., 'Conclusion: Religion, Film, and Cultural Analysis', in Joel W. Martin & Conrad E. Ostwalt (eds), *Screening the Sacred: Religion, Myth and Ideology in Popular American Film* (Boulder: Westview Press, 1995): 152–9.

Paden, William E., *Interpreting the Sacred: Ways of Viewing Religion* (Boston: Beacon Press, 1992).

Pope, Robert, *Salvation in Celluloid* (London: T&T Clark, 2007).

White, Andrew D., *A History of the Warfare of Science with Theology in Christendom* (New York: Appleton, 1896).

Webb, Justin, 'Is America ripe for a Mormon president?', BBC News (23 December 2006), http://news.bbc.co.uk/1/hi/programmes/from_our_own_correspondent/6203179.stm [access date 27 May 2008].

Webb, Justin, 'Defending One's Faith', BBC News (19 November 2007), www.bbc.co.uk/blogs/thereporters/justinwebb/2007/11/defending_ones_faith_1.html [access date 27 May 2008].

Wright, Melanie J., *Religion and Film: An Introduction* (London: I.B. Taurus, 2007).

Chapter 1

The Ethics of Research in Faith and Culture: Scholarship as Fandom?

Tom Beaudoin

Introduction

The serious attention given to 'popular culture' in the study of religion and theology in the last two decades has generated a rich range of research—from studies of the lived faith of non-élites, to erudite theological exegeses of media productions, to sophisticated sociological deconstructions of religious practices. It also represents, at its best, diverse examples of the worthiest that an academic life concerned with religion can be: an intellectually serious engagement with everyday life, a deep curiosity and respect for the strangeness of sacrality as lived, an awareness of the necessarily political position of the scholar or the creativity to test religious claims in the domains of the quotidian, the lay, the invisible or—in the case of media—the often too simplistically visible.

However, as I have argued elsewhere, scholars who research faith and culture and those whose lives feel the impact of our scholarship could benefit from paying more attention to learning what is going on when scholars write about popular culture and religion (Beaudoin 2007).[1] Do we read our readings of the works of others in this field as having to do with our own subjectivity? How indeed have we learned to read our scholarly productions? Why do we so often only read them as scholarly interventions vis-à-vis a particular school, debate or person, instead of also reading them as they relate to our own weirdness, the strangeness that we are made to be by our cultural and personal unconsciousnesses and the different strangeness that we might be by attempting to let through and re-place our histories, socially and individually? What politics of scholarly production prevent us from reading our writings as fictions, fantasies, daydreams, reports of desire and conflict or *rapports à l'ésprit* yet unimagined?

Such questions turn us to the problem of the 'government' of the ethical placement of the scholar as cultural interpreter. Can we answer to what is 'really going on' when scholars make religious or theological sense of the cultural practice of faith?

---

[1] For a more indulgent presentation of the ideas contained in this chapter, see Beaudoin (2008).

When Scholars Study Others' Faith: *Soul Searching*

A case will serve to develop why a turn to the ethics of studies of faith and culture might be important. The recent volume *Soul Searching: The Religious and Spiritual Lives of American Teenagers* is a major sociological report about the faith lives of American adolescents (Smith & Denton 2005). In this book, the authors, Christian Smith and Melinda Lundquist Denton, present the results of the most comprehensive study of teenage faith ever attempted. Over 3,300 teens were surveyed by phone and 267 were subjects of personal follow-up interviews.

Through summary charts, brief biographical narratives and rich quotations, the authors argue that a clear picture of contemporary teenage faith emerges. Far from being 'spiritual but not religious' seekers, teens are surprisingly conventional in their faith. Indeed, they frequently profess to enjoy being religious or at least lacking suspicion about it. Mostly they end up believing what their parents believe. They affirm spiritual 'seeking' in theory, but almost never do it in practice, and they do not bother to talk to each other in depth about faith. Nor are they generally concerned about what their professed traditions actually teach about faith and practice. Often treading cautiously among peers, they do not want to publicly offend anyone else's faith (or lack thereof). Rather, they seek to believe what 'works' for them. And teens, the researchers discovered, want religion to provide them, above all, with individual health and wealth: an American-styled happiness.

Smith & Denton coin a phrase for this everyday teen faith: 'Moralistic Therapeutic Deism' (2005: 118–71). By this they mean that teens like to make value judgements, but are highly inarticulate at defending them. They use their faith to further their own sense of individual entitlement and they imagine God as indifferent to, or unable to be involved in, worldly affairs in general or their own moral decisions in particular. The teen credo that cuts across denominations is: believe what you need to believe in order to fulfil yourself. This is the contemporary teenage faith in the United States. Far from inventing this new religion, however, teenagers learned it from their culture, particularly through their moralistic, therapy-positive, functionally deist parents.

This book will have concrete effects in religious and academic environments. Those involved in the National Study of Youth and Religion (NSYR) have made numerous academic presentations of the findings and multiple academic productions are planned: another 6 books, 17 articles or chapters, and 8 Master's or doctoral theses presenting and interpreting the data.[2] Smith & Denton's authoritative interpretation has already been cause for hand-wringing in popular Christian periodicals and their conclusions, along with presentations of the larger NSYR data, have been the stuff of dozens, perhaps now hundreds, of presentations

---

[2] I am grateful to Terri Clark of the NSYR for providing access to these compilations.

to ministry professionals and church leaders.[3] Such use of this research also matters because of the resources being invested in 'effective' youth and young adult ministries in the United States. The first new Catholic Catechism for the United States in over a century has recently been produced (United States Conference of Catholic Bishops 2006); it was ostensibly written with reference to sociological data on young adult Catholic faith in America, signalling an interest in official Catholicism about studies of everyday faith.[4] Such a mobilization of scholars and presenters in academic and religious life reinforces and reflects the presumption, in most theological and ecclesial circles, that, when sociologists present data on faith and culture, they are telling the more or less objective truth. Some questions and objections can be raised, however, about this research that will set us within the theme for this chapter.

Soul Searching should be credited with many serious achievements in the study of American youth and religion.[5] My purpose here, however, is to underscore the problematic theological assumptions that seem to implicitly and explicitly guide the generation, classification and reportage of these sociological data. Such assumptions prevent this study from comprehending everyday faith in its specificity, that is, the ways in which everyday faith is amalgamated from multiple ways of operating in everyday life (see Bender 2003); is practised as 'fragments',

---

[3]   I wish to express gratitude to Kenda Creasy, Dean of Princeton Theological Seminary, for a helpful conversation about the conclusions of *Soul Searching* for church life today. Even in my own Roman Catholic Church, so often averse to creative and serious attention to the faith lives of young people, the NSYR data have received considerable attention. As of April 2007, there have been presentations to a group of Catholic bishops, to diocesan youth ministry leaders and in 30 dioceses to pastoral ministry leaders. The National Federation for Catholic Youth Ministry (NFCYM) has been instrumental in arranging these presentations. See McCorquodale *et al.* (2004); McCarty (2005). I am grateful to NFCYM Executive Director Robert McCarty for his overview of these activities.

[4]   Denton & Smith acknowledge the link between sociological research in religion and the formulation of social policies and practices that affect those studied. When encouraging parents of teenagers to cooperate in such studies, they counsel, 'It may be helpful to stress that participation is important because the research will be used to help generate better policies or resources for teens and parents' (Denton & Smith 2001: 13).

[5]   From my perspective, the achievements of *Soul Searching* include a remarkably comprehensive presentation of teenage faith, surpassing the scope of all previous studies; the quotation of a great diversity of adolescent voices; exhaustive cross-analyses of data; productive categories for analysis, such as grouping teen beliefs according to 'traditionally Christian', 'non-Christian' and 'paranormal' (Smith & Denton 2005: 43); productive internal comparisons, such as the description of similarities between young Catholics and Jews in religious practices and identities (ibid.: e.g. 46); considerations of wider factors of influence on teenagers, such as the authors' argument that the moral rules that teenagers rehearse are strongly informed by lessons learned about drugs and sexuality (ibid.: 155) or the evidence for how overrun explicitly religious practice is by popular electronic media (ibid.: e.g. 179). These are just a few examples.

'side plots' and 'tangents', more than theorized (Ammerman 2007: 226);[6] is irreducible to a 'logical syllogism' (Davidman 2007: 65) and is speakable only after something like 'therapy'[7]—none of these dimensions of faith as practised are allowed in *Soul Searching*, except as deformations of a supposed ideal form of faith.

This misreading of everyday faith stems from *Soul Searching*'s conception of personal religious identity as derivative of official conceptions of identity. Institutions and their representatives get to define what counts as authentic faith and it is these contemporary declarations against which teens' own declarations (narrowly understood, as will become evident) are measured. This misreading operates through four strategies in the analysis, which I shall delimit.

Firstly, *teen faith is framed as a problem for the power of religious leaders*. Smith & Denton define institutional representatives as the 'agents of religious socialization' and describe their ineffectiveness in contemporary American culture (2005: 27). The authors presume, but do not defend, any theological ground for evangelical exhortations such as 'there may be more than a few Catholic and Mormon leaders who may be justifiably concerned that roughly one in every seven of their teenagers are not even convinced that God exists' (ibid.: 42).[8] They write elsewhere that 'all religious groups seem at risk of losing teens to *nonreligious identities* ...' (ibid.: 88), betokening a suspect theological assumption—that of an easy distinction between a religious and non-religious identity. Such 'top-down' analysis also lacks psychological–sociological curiosity regarding the ways in

---

[6] As Ammerman writes, a 'person may recognize moral imperatives that have a transcendent grounding without ever having a "religious experience" or being able to articulate a set of doctrines about God' (Ammerman 2007: 226).

[7] See, for example, the work of theologian Riet Bons-Storm, who found in her interviews of Dutch women that it took at least a full hour of conversation before she could even begin to have access to the 'survivor theology' of those she interviewed—by which she meant the personal beliefs that do not necessarily square with the perception of the received tradition on the part of the interviewees. These 'survivor theologies' are the hard-won fruit of having gone through difficult life experiences and reworking personal belief systems as a result. These were typically buried below more official sounding reports of their beliefs during the first hour (Bons-Storm 2007; see also Bons-Storm 1996). From a different perspective, this claim has also been developed for nearly three decades in the work of psychoanalyst Ana-Maria Rizzuto, who has argued that personal images of God and individual religious beliefs cannot be read off people's conscious speech: 'Believing has complex unconscious components and the resulting belief content may remain completely unconscious for the believer ... Most beliefs require psychic work to become consciously verbalized descriptions ...' (Rizzuto 2002: 443, 436.) For a fascinating and bewildering compilation of attempts by social scientists to measure faith, from a psychology-of-religion perspective broadly construed, see Hill & Hood (1999).

[8] Note the double qualification, which is a clue to the moral burden of the book. Such judgements are anchored in these sorts of rhetorical formulations.

which 'religious' identities may be necessarily related to 'non-religious' identities in a life or a social circle.

The authors imagine religious beliefs as starting from pure official teaching, stewarded by contemporary religious leaders, well or poorly, through official channels, such as programmes of religious education. Beliefs that begin as given at the 'top' are corrupted by American culture, sometimes with the assistance of weak delivery systems for education in faith. Thus, on one page, the study states three different times that teen faith has suffered significant 'slippage' from the official doctrines of religious tradition and religious education (Smith & Denton 2005: 44). The authors report with evident surprise that 'a number of religious teenagers propounded theological views that are, according to the standards of their own religious traditions, simply not orthodox' (ibid.: 136).

The preoccupation with what 'slippage' might actually reveal seems, as transpires over the course of the book, to be an anxiety regarding the maintenance of religious power. Typical evidence can be found in the survey question presented to teenagers whether it is legitimate to pick and choose beliefs without having to accept the teachings of the faith as a whole (ibid.: 74). Such a strange question boxes teenagers in unnecessarily, adopting a 'with us or against us' tone that lacks sophistication. No one, of course, can possibly know all the teachings or even all the 'important' or 'foundational' teachings of a religious tradition. Moreover, as theology itself is discovering with ever greater complexity, the particular beliefs that are 'sanctioned' by religious leadership, at any particular time and place, are deeply implicated in 'non-theological' or 'non-religious' political, social, cultural and economic factors. The very opposition between 'picking and choosing' and 'accepting the whole' is itself a recent way of imagining, often for the sake of an intended control, what the 'options' for belief are today—much like the opposition between fundamentalism and enlightenment or relativism and moral foundationalism. (Or, for the authors of *Soul Searching*, the dualism between inhabiting 'morally significant' and 'morally insignificant' worldviews [Smith & Denton 2005: 156–8].)

Part of the anxious defence of institutional religious authority happens through another dualism that runs through the study: between individualistic and communal faith. Individualism is cast as that which threatens the communal maintenance of traditional religious identity and convictions. But this bifurcation leaves important theological points in the study lacking nuance. For example, after discussing several examples of teenagers who say that they want to glorify God, live for God, have Christ in their heart or give up old behaviours by being saved, the authors write that these teenagers 'illustrate something of a departure from the individualistic instrumentalism that dominates U.S. teen religion by making God and not individuals the center of religious faith' (ibid.: 150).[9] Or consider the contention that conservative Protestant and Mormon teenagers 'tend to hold

---

[9]   Note again the qualifier 'something of' that both allows the subtle moral claim and renders difficult or impossible any assessment of it.

the most particularistic and exclusive views of religion and tend to be the least individualistic about faith and belief' (ibid.: 76). To the contrary, it is not evident that those who say such things have transcended 'individualism' in their faith or whether the category of individualism allows a sufficiently rich screen through which to hear such statements. Such theological claims might well be heard in other ways: as self-serving affirmations, as testaments to surviving hardships, as ways of showing love or honour to the authorities from whom one learned such statements or as phrases that cover a theological terrain very different from that intended by an 'official' 'theocentric' understanding. It could indeed be argued that a 'conservative' theology can effectively be an individualist theology. The point is that an individualist/communal dichotomy fails to capture the richness and complexity of such statements to register the 'rough ground' (see Pilario 2005) of everyday life that makes American Christian faiths such interesting foci for study.

Secondly, *the authors accept religious—effectively, Christian—leaders 'placing of the boundaries between religious traditions.* The study therefore employs the discourse of 'eclecticism' or 'syncretism' and of course comes out strongly critical of it, even as the alleged phenomenon rarely shows up in their study.

Smith & Denton claim that the 'absolute historical centrality of the Protestant conviction about salvation by God's grace alone ...' is 'discarded' by many teens (2005: 136). Such hyperbolic language as 'absolute historical centrality' is already a clue that an ahistorical theological claim is being advanced. No such historical– ahistorical 'conviction'—held by all (authoritative?) clergy, all (authoritative?) theologians or even all 'the faithful'—exists, as the turn to 'historicism' in theology would expect and as histories of Christianity, especially from 'below', increasingly show.[10]

Further, no attempt is made to distinguish 'eclecticism' from other attempts at plural faith inhabitations, including practices such as what theologians are presently naming 'multiple religious belonging' (see Cornille 2002). As it is, 'eclecticism' is labelled as the domain of 'religiously promiscuous faith mixers' (Smith & Denton 2005: 32)—a rhetorical dismissal of any potential case for a pluralistic holding by invocation of a sexually dangerized ('promiscuous') religious identification. According to the study, however, not many practise it anyway, since 'almost all stick with one religious faith, if any' (ibid.). The phrase 'one religious faith' is another problematic designation that the authors leave as a natural category. This seems especially worth questioning when the authors themselves find that 14–20 per cent of five of their religious sub-groups (black Protestant, Jewish, mainline Protestant, conservative Protestant and Roman Catholic) attend services at more than one congregation.

---

[10] For a recent attempt to read Christian history through the 'popular culture' of material Christian practices, see McDannell (1995). On recent historicisms, see Davaney (2006).

Moreover, they set an unrealistically high academic bar for someone to be considered a spiritual seeker: those who truly qualify must satisfy at least a half-dozen conditions. They must be 'self-directing and self-authenticating individuals pursuing an experimental and eclectic quest for personal spiritual meaning outside of historical religious traditions' (ibid.: 79). Not surprisingly, only 2–3 per cent of teens do this, they report. However, this description sounds like a critique of a romanticized view of the Baby Boomer searching of a generation ago. How many adults would even qualify as 'seekers' under that description? While it seems unhelpful as a way of gauging spiritual *bricolage* today, it is consistent with the book's frequent segregation of 'new age' from 'biblical' views of God—without argument or rationale (Smith & Denton 2005: e.g. 42)—and the book's striking continual recourse to theistic terminology without a discussion of the limits of God-references for theistic traditions themselves or for teenagers in our culture. For example, references are made to survey questions designed to elicit views on 'belief in God', 'views of God' or of 'God's judgement' (ibid.: 41).

Thirdly, *Soul Searching accepts as unproblematic and self-evident many theological concepts, allowing them neither cultural context nor sociological-theological critique.* For example, the authors state that 'two out of three teens profess to believe in something like the Bible's personal, historically active God' (ibid.). This simplistic theological statement is made to sound common-sense regarding the Bible. On the contrary, it is far from evident that 'the Bible' manifests an unproblematically 'personal' and 'historically active' God. The key phrase here is 'something like', which allows the authors a zone of ambiguity regarding both the sociological and theological aspects of the claim: as if to say that a lot of teenagers operate in a zone of belief that bears some affinity to a theological claim that may or may not be quite right, but it does not need to be justified, anyway, because the correlation is not being too tightly claimed. The very provisionality of the association between teens and the true meaning of the Bible is the rhetorical key, paradoxically, to the illusion of tight association/dissociation between the Bible and teens.

Smith & Denton also report that half of Roman Catholic youth believe in communicating with the dead and proceed to group this belief with significant levels of Catholic teen belief in reincarnation, astrology, psychics and fortune tellers (2005: 44). These are portrayed as evidence of deficient religious education and as a consequence youth are going over to magical or paranormal beliefs. The authors report this, despite praying to the dead and the communion of saints being not only quite commonplace in Catholic teaching, but part of the symbolic order of many churches and of home altars, especially for Hispanic/Latino Catholics. Further, the authors do not give any indication that what they call reincarnation, astrology or divination has ever been seriously considered in, conceptually congenial toward, or an historical influence upon, the Christian tradition.

Indeed, an ahistorical and idealized view of Christianity is evident throughout the analysis, such as in the statement that 'the religion to which most [teens] appear to be referring seems significantly different in character from versions of the same faith in centuries past' (ibid.: 154). They then make theological judgements that rely on stock theological formulae: teen religion as practised today is not orthodox, nor is it 'revealed in truth by [a] holy and almighty God who calls all to a turning from self and a serving of God in gratitude, humility, and righteousness'; nor does it fashion teens 'into a community of people embodying a historically rooted tradition of identity, practices, and ethics that define[s] their selfhood, loyalties, and commitments' (ibid.). It does not witness to a 'life-transformative, transcendent truth ...' (ibid.). As a theologian, I wonder where, apart from experiences of the religious 'ghetto'—if even there—such descriptions of [Christian?] religion's purpose really hold true. These idealizations structure the study throughout, perhaps most tellingly displayed in the important claim that 'a significant part of Christianity in the United States is actually only tenuously Christian in any sense that is seriously connected to the *actual historical Christian tradition*' (Smith & Denton 2005: 171, emphasis added). As in 'absolute historical centrality' earlier, the hyperbole is a clue to the anxiety of the power of religious authority underpinning the study. Readers then learn in a footnote the revealing claim that this 'actual historical' tradition is given in Christianity by 'creeds and confessions', a motley and contradictory Protestant and Catholic mix of which is listed, presumably for the reader to sort out (ibid.: 322, n. 21).

Fourthly, *the authors make their own a critique of teenage articulacy and inconsistency that becomes a characteristic form of moralizing.* The authors note their discovery of the 'apparent logical inconsistency of some teens in relating to God' and when teen 'deists' report that they, too, feel close to God—the authors name this a 'conceptual confusion'— they mockingly add, 'go figure' (ibid.: 42). These criticisms indicate the lack of a creative sociological–theological research frame for the vicissitudes of everyday faith. Such criticisms make me wonder which religious, or even non-religious, persons the authors would point to as models of logical consistency. (They seem surprised to report that it is 'not easy to find someone who is clear and articulate about what [spiritual seeking] means' [Smith & Denton 2005: 83] and they moralize about a 17-year-old who lacks 'solid grounding' for his 'moral reasoning' [ibid.: 95; cf. 131, 132]—something that has eluded even the best of our contemporary moral philosophers.)[11]

It seems at least unfair, as well as theologically problematic, to overvalue what comes to teenagers' minds to say to an interviewer as a key to their deep moral commitments. That is why it is particularly striking to note the piling-on that the researchers do, salting their book with various moralizing comments whenever the topic of teen articulacy surfaces. It is characteristic of the way in which sociology can rhetorically produce theological truths that the claim that 'some' teenagers are

---

[11]   Of course, a mature moral philosophy that turns out to lack 'solid grounding' is quite different from what many 17-year-olds might articulate. The point is that a discussion of theological literacy would be better served by a different kind of attention to what teenagers say and how they live, including attention to the analogies between complexities in their own praxis and that of their elders.

'Machiavellian moral relativists' (never mind that Machiavelli was a sophisticated political philosopher who articulated his views as an adult) comes with disavowal of any interpretive action on the part of the scholar: after all, these teens 'openly profess' it (ibid.: 156). It is as if, to quote the old saying, their words go 'from their lips to God's ears', with the sociological researcher having the divine clairaudience, the ear of the Other. It must be so: teens 'profess' it, and 'openly'. The rhetoric of confession is precisely what a theological account of this study must protest. After Foucault, we know too well the reasons for regarding confession as an unproblematic route to theological truth.

There are some acknowledgements of teen articulacy, but these tend to be swallowed by the study's moralizing approach. The authors claim that most teens are more articulate about sex or the media than about their faith. However, they do not see these other kinds of literacy as bearing on teen faith or as a way of articulating faith as such. This seems to be part of a larger problem in the book of a lack of letting sociology be informed by scholarship on theological understandings of spirituality, such as research in spiritual direction and pastoral care and counselling. Such a lack is evident throughout the book, for example, when the authors report that 'One 17-year old black conservative Protestant boy from New York … readily slid from discussing how religious faith influences him into how having faith *in himself* has been helpful: "How is religious faith important? Well, like school. If I didn't have faith in myself, I wouldn't be going to school right now, wouldn't have the motivation"' (Smith & Denton 2005: 140).[12] The authors do not ask about the potential links between the two types of faith in self and God.

Despite all this, the simplest evidence for this moralizing is that *Soul Searching* never considers that contemporary teen belief may have something substantially spiritually constructive and new, not just alarming, to teach the larger Church.

What *Soul Searching* offers, then, is an example of academic study that generates, while seeming to reflect, a stabilized discourse about faith. This discourse is a result of the indulgence of the power of the disciplines of sociology and theology to tell the truth about younger generations, that is to say, to be able to assign a truth to younger generations and their faith, to include populations of young adults in social-scientific and religio-theological discourses of truth. The dream of a stabilized discourse concerning young people's faith is the fevered dream of marketing religion in America (Moore 1994). Young people's faith must be stabilized in order to be put in motion in the economy of American morality and religion, to safeguard the proprietors of the tradition, including those theologians who think that faith identity moves from a pure 'above' to a messy 'below'.

Although this study does not show evidence that the authors are fans of the teen culture that they study—perhaps just the opposite—the authors of *Soul*

---

[12] See all of chapter 4, 'God, Religion, Whatever' (118–71), for dozens of examples of teen faith testimonies that could benefit from a more generous, patient and theologically informed ear.

Searching nonetheless seem to be fans of a different sort: of a certain academic approach to studying faith and culture. It is the fandoms that enable and govern academic identity that run deeper than the study results themselves, to which I shall return below. If the case of *Soul Searching* is not an isolated example, if this book and its reception are not the only exhibits of an argument in analysis of faith and culture needing an ethical-theological critique, there may be larger points for those who are concerned about how academic work on such topics is a part of our lives and the lives of others, how thinking and writing these concerns functions as interventions in our own lives and in the lives of our readers and all those influenced by our living.

Reflexivity as Ethical Task: Religious Research and Academic Fandom

Scholars committed to investigating ethics of scholarship can look to popular culture studies for assistance in talking about the cultural dynamics of formation for advocacy and attendant developments of forms of governing methods of interpretation, texts and membership: the sub-discipline of fan studies.

Making fan studies into a reflexive discourse for the work of scholars in faith and culture—that is, raising the question of the ways in which 'we academics' are fans of our own disciplines—gives a 'non-religious' language for the investigation at hand. I suggest a popular cultural analysis of the practices that constitute the study, and studiers, of popular culture. This is to ask not only whether and how academics are fans of the cultures and the things they hold as sacred, about which we write, but how we are fans of the academic disciplines and practices through which we are subjectified. Such a focus may allow us to read our research not only as a valorization of the freedom of the everyday or as the effect of social forces exposed by the scholar or some combination of these ('habitus', 'reflexivity', etc.), but to read our work and its constitutive practices as exercises of what could be called 'academic fandom'.

Cultural studies theorist Matt Hills has come to a similar conclusion in his recent synoptic account of fan studies, *Fan Cultures* (2002). Hills makes two points which are relevant for present purposes. Firstly, he specifies how fans of media culture, and academics, are often the 'others' of each other's discourses. Both communities operate within 'imagined subjectivities' over against the other: the academic is rational, committed to argument, adopts a broad-minded view and has the authority to decode the discourses of others. The fan, by contrast, is intense and passionate, an expert in the minutiae of the frivolous, a fantasizer whose primary associations with like-minded individuals fosters an irrational way of relating, grounded in fetishistic returns to venerated superficial objects. The fan has an immediate relation to pop culture; the academic a discerning and learned distance. This binary is even kept in place, Hills observes, by well-meaning fan studies in 'reception' or 'audience' theory that privilege fan creativity and resistance, in so far as the fan becomes theorized as something of an academic-without-portfolio, decoding media culture with pleasure and political savvy, just as academics imagine themselves doing.

As Hills pays attention to the influential binarity in media and cultural studies, he shows how, within fan cultures, fans do their own kind of theorizing that borrows from, but reworks, academic theorizing, by the way that they practise their relation to each other and to their cultural objects. Fan knowledge is situated within and across binaries: it is consumption as well as resistance, both communal and hierarchical, concerned both with displaying knowledge as well as justifying it, inhabiting worlds of both fantasy and reality, existing as both cult and culture, being both 'textual' and 'extra-textual'. By looking at material practices with an awareness of the seductions of binary, moralizing or valorizing thinking, fan cultures can be appreciated on their own complex and ambiguous terms. They are spaces of contradictory values whose very contradictions are essential to their workings.

Included in Hills's account is a development of the idea of fandom as the personal tending of 'secondary transitional objects'. Hills works this idea out from his reading of ambiguities in D.W. Winnicott's psychoanalytic account of primary transitional objects. Hills argues that Winnicott allows that primary objects can and must dissipate over time, return to the cultural milieu from which they came (and, Hills points out with reference to research on consumer culture, may more likely happen when those objects come from a plastic culture of disposability, as does so much of Western youth culture). But 'faded' objects do not lose all affective importance in the project of developing a self, Hills observes. Secondary objects are objects that retain significance less intensely after serving as primary objects, are less affectively operative and available in the inner life of subjectivity, but not altogether absent. In American society, childhood toys and television characters, along with pop stars from pubescence, may continue to bear emotional resonance for us and help us constellate our identities. They are more susceptible to being conditioned by culture and its governing powers than primary objects are. Hills's research goes a long way towards dispelling the idea of the fan as needing to be split along a binary: either passive or active, creative or consumptive, childish or mature, and the like. His account shows how these dualities do not need to be valorized on one side or the other, but rather that their interplay constitutes the creativity of fan life.

Hills's philosophy of fandom leads him to recommend that fan studies take up investigations that 'look beyond cultural groups which self-identify ... or which have ... been described as 'fans'; groups, for example, such as academic subcultures' (2002: 183), the sub-cultures of the very academics who study fan culture, who focus their scholarly work on the passions of others. I take Hills and myself to be saying something similar: that we join the emerging discourses about 'reflexivity' as scholars and this is an ethical next step for our fields.[13]

---

[13]   See Nick Couldry's excellent discussion of some approaches to reflexivity in chapter 6, 'Accounting for the Self' (Couldry 2000: 114–33).

I agree with Hills that an 'approach to fandom *within* the academy [will] continue to tease out the many ways in which fan attachments, affects, and passions permeate "academic" work, institutions and the *embodied*, rather than imagined, subjectivities of academia' (2002: 183).[14]

While there is scarce work on academics as fans of their own academic cultures or disciplines, this is where my present investigation of the dynamics of research into 'other people's faith' has led me. It has made me consider that there may be an unacknowledged, or more strongly, disavowed fandom that the scholar has towards his or her own discipline or, more likely, of an 'object' within it, such as a specific method, field, problem, community of inquiry or a person who can represent any of these. It has been argued that academics can be usefully understood as defenders of 'tribes' and 'territories' (Becher & Trowler 2001) and that we may be playing out an unacknowledged narcissism, when we think we are initiating students into our disciplines (Ellsworth 1997).[15] Such clues to disavowed fandoms in academic life gain greater traction when we appreciate the contingent and contradictory, even 'dangerous', character of a very specific scholarly telling of other people's faith, like *Soul Searching*.

This approach contrasts with the principle of conscious identification that guides much research in fan studies: that intrinsic to the value of studying fan

---

[14]   It is difficult to imagine such a thing as 'reflexivity' as such, despite the way it is commonly and perhaps increasingly used in research discourses. Reflexivity seems a rather mobile concept that can be marshalled for all sorts of different cultural work, identity straitening, or enforcements of knowledge. One can imagine, or reference, many kinds of reflexivity, although often having a similar function: failing to interrupt the scholarly understanding and practice of work. This can be the case particularly if reflexivity means the invocation of popular culture pleasures without analysis or merely a report about that increasingly unhelpful category called one's 'social location'. I here advocate a specific meaning of reflexivity, that of making fan studies into studies of academics as fans, in their academic and non-academic fandoms, because of the ethical questions posed to our common work, questions that come to us first in a general acknowledgement of an unacknowledged placement of our subjectivity in our scholarship, leaving our understanding of our work incomplete, if we cannot begin to think through its askesis on us; and secondly, because of what we can see happening concretely with the way knowledge of popular religious practice can be constructed, through a work like *Soul Searching*, which may leave us desirous of a way to pay attention to the power we indulge in such thinking. Such intellectual work needs this reflexivity, this self-examination as fans of our academic and non-academic disciplines, because cultural studies, sociology and theology, in their own ways, claim for themselves the right and responsibility to tell other people the truth about themselves. Couldry's underscoring of the importance of the work of Kamala Visweswaran (1994: esp. 101–6) for theorizing reflexivity is germane to my present argument. He notes that Visweswaran wants anthropologists to involve themselves in (in her phrase) 'anthropology in reverse', by (in Couldry's telling) 'questioning the process by which she came to be in a position to write about culture' (Couldry 2000: 124).

[15]   For the danger of being tempted to recover personal losses through teaching, see also Grumet (1988).

cultures is that fans own their fandom, that is that there are people who delight, at various levels of self-awareness, in being 'fanatic' about a music group, celebrity or comic book series, who take pride in their partisanship in what the rest of society considers quaint, ephemeral, juvenile or even repulsive. Fan studies and the turn to 'low culture' have typically gone together, with the former being one extension of the latter. But what of academics who are, almost by definition, not given to 'fanaticism'? It is just here that I believe inquiry opens on to a space of a disavowed fandom. This fandom will be an attenuated form of the more self-conscious fandoms of popular culture in which the contestation of fan identity is often a part of the constitution of fan identity. Hence it will not necessarily bear the relative creative richness present in some accounts of fan culture. It must be a fandom by disavowal, because passionate attachments, dwellings in the artificial and mass-produced, pleasure in mere assertions of value and arguments that primarily justify emotional investments are not phenomena that can typically be tolerated in academic spaces. This disavowal will most typically be unconscious and as repressed will likely manifest itself in conceptual contradiction, claims that exceed evidence and minute enactments of the relationships between knowledge and power that pertain to the discipline in question. There is no need here to choose superficially between, say, 'Freud' and 'Foucault'. The space of disavowal is a convergence of a personal and cultural unconscious: personal because confabulated out of the affections of the scholar's mind in having invested oneself emotionally in a scholarly identity in part out of individual psychic conflicts, and cultural because the meaningful forms of intellectual experience in the scholar's history and in their scholarly productions will be historically constellated in relations of truth, subjectivity and power. Such disavowed fandoms in the scholarly life seem inordinately resistant to disentanglement, which is why I prefer to focus on a specific text, in the hope that the specificity of analysis can link up to other such studies of the ethical emplacement of researchers in religion, in aid of ethical theories of academic 'motivation' and production—and academic life together.

The Difference a Fandom Consciousness Introduces

We can think of fandom as a kind of caughtness in objects, in the multiple sense of 'catching' and 'being caught'. It is a way of catching cultural objects, in the negative sense of something that has worked its way into oneself: catching a cold, catching a disease; the positive sense of catching a thrown object, like a ball: aligning oneself with an incoming object, an active kind of receptivity in the face of something given. It is also a way of being caught by cultural objects. This has the positive sense of having one's attention arrested, a summons from a surprising entry into our awareness. It also has the negative sense of being dragged along unwillingly and abrasively, in the way a branch is caught in the undercarriage of a car.

Hills's Winnicottian object-relations perspective suggests that objects of fandom are both taken by persons in some measure of freedom to balance their interior and exterior realities and also afforded or denominated by the culture in which the person attaches to objects. One could thus see fandom as a way of catching and being caught, in the complexity of registers of 'caughtness' noted above, by objects that promise the working-through of consent to lived reality. These objects are 'owned' in the 'passion' of the fan as striated by the passions available discursively in a cultural setting. We become fans of objects that help us 'come to terms', but only with the palette of objects available. This caughtness of our caughtness should lead us into a genealogy of ourselves, which is why theologies of everyday life and sociological inquiries into everyday faith demand both radical critique in and of their claims about, and productions regarding the truth of, 'external' reality: society, history, culture; and 'internal' reality: psyche, mind, soul, conscience. A theology of this sort needs, in other words, both a critical genealogical consciousness as well as a critical psychoanalytic consciousness. These seem essential for comprehending both the fandoms at work in everyday life and faith and the (everyday academic) fandoms that inform academic study of these (everyday non-academic) fandoms.

Soul Searching indicates a fandom whose subjective provenance is difficult to identify, given that the work was written by a primary author (Smith) as well as secondary author (Denton) and is the product of consultation with dozens of scholars over several years.[16] In the absence of material that would provide more personal access to the authors, such an approach must be tentative. But given what I have argued, it seems reasonable to suggest that their study exhibits a fannish caughtness in the adequacy of sociology of religion to everyday faith. The method of the study, the truth value of the objective comprehension of young people's faith, so often discussed, defended and rearticulated in the book's pages, is a strong candidate for an object of fandom. Such 'over'-investment in method may, according to sociologist Nancy Ammerman's recent review of research in lived religion, be common: 'The concerns of sociologists [of religion] have been shaped both by our theoretical preoccupation with secularization and by the survey methodology that has been our dominant epistemological technology'[17] (Ammerman 2007: 224).

---

[16]   See Smith & Denton (2005: vii–viii) and Denton & Smith (2001: 29–30) for the lists of individuals consulted on the project. On my (fallible) reading, the list of those consulted includes many Protestants, including many Protestant theologians, and few academically or ministerially identified Catholics and no self-identified Catholic theologians.

[17]   In line with the critique developed in the present chapter, Ammerman argues that the prevailing methods 'privilege religious adherence and institutional affiliation as measures of religion's strength'. Likewise, '[d]efining strong religion in terms of "strict" [read "orthodox"] beliefs and practices leaves much of everyday religion unanalyzed' (Ammerman 2007: 224).

Whether Smith & Denton were drawn to methods that stabilize young people as the conduits for a new civil religion and as objects for a possible institutional management or whether the methods employed taught them to understand faith as susceptible to their study, the social-scientific methods employed can be understood as both created and found—a key quality of primary and secondary objects—by them. The basic and even passionate trust in the method, the obligatory rhetorical gestures stating its limits, the shoring up of colleagues who do similar work, the marshalling of a scholarly community to tell and re-tell the NSYR story from various angles—all of this suggests a fandom at work. We can speculate, and no more than that, that the method both allows and closes off a possible balancing of 'interior' and 'exterior' for that problematic category of academic production: 'the authors'.

Intrinsic to fandom in our culture is an obstinacy about the superiority of one's chosen objects (Frith 1996). Because the authors cannot imagine themselves, in the writing, as fans, they cannot appreciate fandom as a practice that they have in common with the teens they study. Thus they cannot see 'inarticulacy' as having any positive meaning. But seeing teens themselves as fans of belief systems would enrich their analysis. As Hills reminds us, 'the ethnographic process of "asking the audience", although useful in many cases, constitutes a potentially reductive approach. It assumes that cultural activities can be adequately accounted for in terms of language and "discourse"' (2002: 66). Indeed, thinking through what we know of fans could illuminate what happened in the *Soul Searching* study: 'Addressing the question "why are you a fan of this particular text?", it seems that fans typically register some confusion or difficulty in responding, before then falling back immediately on their particular fandom's discursive mantra'[18] (ibid.: 67). We can learn then that, when researchers ask teens to explain and justify their beliefs, they are constructing an image of a 'teen believer' (or 'teen unbeliever') that from the outset cannot comprehend the affective complexities of faith, the positive significance for teen life and faith of what looks to scholars like 'inarticulacy' and the ways in which teen faith may be registered indirectly through other 'non-theological' interests, questions, even fandoms. In other words, if scholars who research faith and culture could think through their own fandoms, this would invite a rethinking of the moralizing categorization of teenage inarticulacy.

Academic fandom does not make Smith & Denton's *Soul Searching* unique; such fandom stands only as a symbol for a process as typical in academic life as it is underappreciated and undertheorized. In Hills's formulation:

> We are, perhaps, *all* 'stuck' on something, whether that thing is the dogma of Lacanian lack, sociological anti-subjectivism, Deleuzian philosophy, or the dogma of a specific fandom. I would suggest that it is whether or not our

---

[18] Compare the many quotations in *Soul Searching* wherein teens express bewilderment and then appear to fall back on certain formulas as a way of explaining their faith.

'stuckness' can act as a personal and good enough 'third space' for affective play that is significant. (2002: 112, emphasis added)

Acknowledging academic fandom is a move against disavowal—of the 'other' of academic reasonability as described by Hills and of the governance of affective investments that induce us into uses of academic power in the interpretation of others. The 'disavowal' I mean here is not a narrowly personal, much less intentional, kind of denial. It is a historical and social phenomenon, a way of having been fashioned by the constellation of cultural forces that shape perception in the study of religion in particular and Western academic life in general. It is a living absence in the scholar, 'a practice forgotten in its origins and its meaning, but always used and always present' (Foucault 1988: 276), the mark of precluding forms of attention in the history that produced our present academic truths for religious and theological studies. At the same time, it is also a personal kind of denial, in two senses. Firstly, in so far as our academic subjectivities, so bound up with our individual hopes and plans, are given in prespecified histories and cultures, as the academic study of academic life increasingly shows.[19] Secondly, because many of us in academic life already know better at some level—that we are in more or less active disavowal about our disavowed fandoms, aware that there are unexamined scenes backstage of all our smartest writing and most rigorous thinking, backstage scenes of misrecognized and unfulfilled desire, unrequited and unworthy love, uncompensated losses, malevolence. In this sense, the fandoms of the scholars are made of personal objects, once known and now mostly disowned, in Matt Hills's Winnicottian sense—objects that may run the gamut from a compelling 'Protestantism in sociology of religion' *per se*[20] to a relation and an advisor, *Doktorvater*, book or other person or object who was 'transitional' for

---

[19]   I have in mind here works like Becher & Trowler (2001); Slaughter & Leslie (1997); Slaughter & Rhoades (2004); Washburn (2005); Johnson, Kavanagh & Mattson (2003). Such studies have hardly begun to deeply influence the everyday consciousness of those who toil in academic fields.

[20]   Although it lies beyond the scope of the present writing to settle, could what Hills discusses as the religiousness of fandom, in this case for method in sociology of religion, be sustained in part by the religious quality, by which I mean religious genealogy, of sociology of religion, in its investment in Christian assumptions about religious practice? Among others, sociologist Lynn Davidman has suggested that 'Most sociological studies of religion, and the methods used to study religion, have been based on assumptions derived from Protestant theology and praxis. As the dominant religion in the United States, Protestantism has shaped sociological study, often presuming to stand for religion in general' (Davidman 2007: 64–5). Substantiating Davidman's claim is social theorist Philip Mellor, who argues that various 'constructive conceptions' of the relationship between faith or religion and culture that are used by otherwise non-confessional social theorists have a 'recognizably Protestant character, even if this is generally concealed by a representational system that is, ostensibly, religiously neutral' (Mellor 2004: 149).

the scholar. It is the domain specified by overlaying, say, a 'Freudian' creative individual repression and a 'Foucauldian' historical unconscious.

Theology's Contribution to the Ethical Question

Limning the ethical placement of the scholar of faith and culture is one way to bring Christian theology, and its tradition of spiritual exercises, to bear on a multidisciplinary conversation. One way in which Christian theology is relevant for cultural analysis is found in the fact that Christianity is already so deeply embedded in much of Western culture and its popular culture, on the one hand, and the potentially 'humanizing' contributions that theology can make to multi-disciplinary considerations of culture, on the other hand. Giving theology a place at the scholarly table can thus be a recognition of Christian power in all its ambiguities and an opportunity for theology to test what can be said about reality in the face of other people of good will, including sociological colleagues who have understood something of reality that is far from theologians' minds. Theological engagements of culture show not only how complicated it is to talk about lived faith in contemporary culture, but these engagements also make themselves visitors in practices, disciplines and debates that theology may not recognize, thereby risking their claims to truth in a contemplative kind of travelling-through, learning and shedding along the way. Theologians in cultural studies are thus themselves residents of their own popular culture and sociologists, religionists and other scholars make 'us' take up many strategies that we find in those we study: resistance, assimilation, refiguring, *bricolage*, experimentation. And beyond.

I agree with Matt Hills, and have tried to indicate here, that self- and communal examination of our ignored 'power relationships', our 'others', our 'moral dualisms' is an ethical task for scholars who want to speak on behalf of other people's faith. This is not to simplistically try to prize ourselves apart from the ways in which we are fans of our studies, methods, disciplines, networks or institutions and the cultural practices that place us in these fandoms, but it is to ask us to let through a richer ethical conversation about the cost of the stability of the scholar in our studies, in favour of 'academic commitment which is modelled on fan commitment', for 'impassioned thought rather than the parroting of academic ... mantras [and] for an "affective reflexivity"' which can contemplate our 'own fandoms' and the ways we give ourselves as fans to our academic studies (Hills 2002: 183–4). Is it possible that, on this point, theologians may be able to have a dialogue with other scholars of religion, to not only continue the slow revolution in the turn to the religious everyday, but to make ourselves more worthy of it?[21]

---

[21] I am paraphrasing Friedmann (1970), as quoted in Hadot (1995: 70).

References

Ammerman, Nancy T., 'Studying Everyday Religion: Challenges for the Future', in Nancy T. Ammerman (ed.), *Everyday Religion: Observing Modern Religious Lives* (New York: Oxford University Press, 2007): 219–44.

Beaudoin, Tom, 'Popular Culture Scholarship as a Spiritual Exercise: Thinking Ethically With(out) Christianity', in Gordon Lynch (ed.), *Between Sacred and Profane: Researching Religion and Popular Culture* (London: I.B. Tauris, 2007): 94–110.

Beaudoin, Tom, 'The Ethics of Characterizing Popular Faith: Scholarship and Fandom', in Tom Beaudoin, *Witness to Dispossession: The Vocation of a Postmodern Theologian* (Maryknoll, NY: Orbis, 2008).

Becher, Tony & Trowler, Paul R., *Academic Tribes and Territories: Intellectual Enquiry and the Culture of Disciplines*, 2nd edn (Philadelphia: Open University Press, 2001).

Bender, Courtney, *Heaven's Kitchen: Living Religion at God's Love We Deliver* (Chicago: University of Chicago Press, 2003).

Bons-Storm, Riet, *The Incredible Woman: Listening to Women's Silences in Pastoral Care and Counseling* (Nashville, TN: Abingdon Press, 1996).

Bons-Storm, Riet, 'Practical Theology in a Secularized World: Beyond the Obsession with Guilt and Atonement', paper presented at the International Academy of Practical Theology, Berlin, Germany, 30 March 2007.

Cornille, Catherine (ed.), *Many Mansions? Multiple Religious Belonging and Christian Identity* (Maryknoll, NY: Orbis, 2002).

Couldry, Nick, *Inside Culture: Re-imagining the Method of Cultural Studies* (Thousand Oaks, CA: Sage, 2000).

Davaney, Sheila Greeve, *Historicism: The Once and Future Challenge for Theology* (Minneapolis: Fortress Press, 2006).

Davidman, Lynn, 'The New Voluntarism and the Case of Unsynagogued Jews', in Nancy T. Ammerman (ed.), *Everyday Religion: Observing Modern Religious Lives* (New York: Oxford University Press, 2007): 51–67.

Denton, Melinda Lundquist & Smith, Christian, 'Methodological Issues and Challenges in the Study of American Youth and Religion' (University of North Carolina—Chapel Hill: National Study of Youth and Religion, 2001), www.youthandreligion.org/docs/methods.pdf [access date 5 December 2007].

Ellsworth, Elizabeth Ann, *Teaching Positions: Difference, Pedagogy, and the Power of Address* (New York: Teachers College Press, 1997).

Foucault, Michel, *Madness and Civilization*, trans. Richard Howard (New York: Vintage, 1988 [1961].

Friedmann, Georges, *La Puissance et la sagesse* (Paris: Gallimard, 1970).

Frith, Simon, *Performing Rites: On the Value of Popular Music* (Cambridge, MA: Harvard University Press, 1996).

Grumet, Madeleine, *Bitter Milk: Women and Teaching* (Amherst: University of Massachusetts Press, 1988).

Hadot, *Philosophy as a Way of Life: Spiritual Exercises from Socrates to Foucault*, ed. Arnold Davidson, trans. Michael Chase (New York: Blackwell, 1995).

Hill, Peter C. & Hood, Jr, Ralph W. (eds), *Measures of Religiosity* (Birmingham, AL: Religious Education Press, 1999).

Hills, Matt, *Fan Cultures* (New York: Routledge, 2002).

Johnson, Benjamin, Kavanagh, Patrick & Mattson, Kevin (eds), *Steal This University: The Rise of the Corporate University and the Academic Labor Movement* (New York: Routledge, 2003).

McCarty, Robert, *The National Study of Youth and Religion: Analysis of the Population of Catholic Teenagers and Their Parents: A Brief Summary* (Washington, DC: National Federation for Catholic Youth Ministry, 2005).

McCorquodale, Charlotte, Shepp, Victoria & Sterten, Leigh, *National Study of Youth and Religion: Analysis of the Population of Catholic Teenagers and Their Parents* (Washington, DC: National Federation for Catholic Youth Ministry, 2004).

McDannell, Colleen, *Material Christianity: Religion and Popular Culture in America* (New Haven: Yale University Press, 1995).

Mellor, Philip, *Religion, Realism, and Social Theory: Making Sense of Society* (Thousand Oaks, CA: Sage, 2004).

Moore, R. Laurence, *Selling God: American Religion in the Marketplace of Culture* (New York: Oxford University Press, 1994).

Pilario, D.F., *Back to the Rough Grounds of Praxis: Exploring Theological Method with Pierre Bourdieu* (Leuven: Leuven University Press, 2005).

Rizzuto, Ana-Maria, 'Believing and Personal and Religious Beliefs: Psychoanalytic Considerations', *Psychoanalysis and Contemporary Thought*, 25/4 (Fall 2002): 433–63.

Slaughter, Sheila & Leslie, Larry L., *Academic Capitalism: Politics, Policies, and the Entrepreneurial University* (Baltimore: Johns Hopkins University Press, 1997).

Slaughter, Sheila & Rhoades, Gary, *Academic Capitalism and the New Economy: Markets, State, and Higher Education* (Baltimore: Johns Hopkins University Press, 2004).

Smith, Christian & Denton, Melinda Lundquist, *Soul Searching: The Religious and Spiritual Lives of American Teenagers* (New York: Oxford University Press, 2005).

United States Conference of Catholic Bishops, *United States Catholic Catechism for Adults* (Washington, DC: USCCB, 2006).

Visweswaran, Kamala, *Fictions of Feminist Ethnography* (Minneapolis: University of Minnesota Press, 1994).

Washburn, Jennifer, *University, Inc.* (New York: Basic Books, 2005).

Chapter 2

Media Rituals: From Durkheim on Religion to Jade Goody on Religious Toleration

Nick Couldry

Introduction

Ernesto Laclau wrote almost two decades ago that contemporary societies 'are required by their very dynamics to become increasingly mythical' (1990: 67) —a positive sociological claim that on the face of it is surprising from a philosopher who is highly influenced by Derridean deconstruction. The paradox is only intensified by the title of Laclau's essay which is 'The Impossibility of Society'. Yet I think Laclau identified something very important about the possibilities and requirements of 'social order' today, even if, as I note elsewhere, the foundations of Laclau's argument lie too much in the abstractions of philosophy of language to provide a secure basis for social enquiry (Couldry 2008). Nonetheless, it is in a broadly similar spirit to Laclau that I have argued in my work that contemporary mediated societies are at least inclined, if not required, to become increasingly 'ritualized'—ritualized in a particular sense appropriate to mediated societies.

My chapter is not the work of a religion specialist; indeed I claim no specific expertise on religion at all. I am a media cultural and social theorist who is interested in the consequences of what media institutions do for the organization of social space and everyday life.[1] In researching these issues, I make no claims, as some have done, that contemporary media is somehow 'like' religion, let alone performing a similar 'function' to that once played by religion: indeed I will do all I can to avoid such functionalist language which is quite unhelpful in understanding complex societies and the media's role in that complexity (Lukes 1975; Couldry 2005). *All* I will claim is that one feature of media institutions' current representations of the social world—the feature I refer to as 'media rituals' (Couldry 2003a)—is worth understanding as a facet of contemporary relations between religion and culture, since it may be crucial in *distorting* the terms of exchange between members of a largely secular, religiously plural society such as Britain. That potential distortion provides the starting point for the reflections on media ethics with which I end the chapter.

---

[1]   See, for example, Couldry (2000; 2003a; 2003b; 2006).

However, while my argument will not depend at any point on substantive claims about the nature of contemporary religion—and therefore, as a non-specialist, I will operate within a 'common sense' definition of religion as a set of practices, values and beliefs grounded in a transcendental reference point that is regarded as explaining the order of life and the material world—my argument will share a lineage with a still influential perspective in the sociology of religion: Emile Durkheim's *Elementary Forms of Religious Life* (Durkheim 1995). I will explain how my notion of 'media rituals' emerged and its particular relationship to Durkheim's account of the social origins of religion. While, as I hinted, I will sharply distinguish my approach from any idea that contemporary media might in some sense equate to, or reoccupy the position of, religion, I want to take one example of a media ritual, *Celebrity Big Brother*, which recently generated some fierce debates about racism, and ask what would be the consequences of such a reality TV show becoming the site of equally fierce debates *about religious difference*. If that happened, how exactly would it help us to think of such a programme as a ritualized format and how could we build a framework for thinking about the ethics of such a programme's hypothetical presentations of religious difference?

The Idea of 'Media Rituals'

What do I mean by 'media rituals'? Rather than rush straight into a definition, I first want to explain the wider argument within which I developed this concept and its particular relationship to Durkheim's classic account of the social origins of religion. This is essential to understanding the ways in which I, as a media sociologist, perhaps can, and the ways in which I certainly *cannot*, even if invited to, contribute to the understanding of contemporary religion.

My proposed concept of 'media rituals' does not involve arguing, for example, that some aspects of contemporary media are rituals because they carry some of the feelings that we associate with religious ritual, although arguments of that sort have been made (Martin-Barbero 1997). My argument develops instead via a purely *structural or formal analogy* with a particular reading of Durkheim's sociological deconstruction of the basis of religion.

Let me very schematically run through what I see as the shape of Durkheim's argument in the *Elementary Forms*, because this will enable me to make clear which parts of it are salient to the concept of media rituals and which are not. Durkheim argues

(1) that religious practice is based on the category distinction between sacred and profane.

Clearly Durkheim's position has been disputed, with many arguing that it misses out a great deal of what is important and distinctive about religion; since

I am not a sociologist of religion, I will not take a position on this one way or the other. Durkheim then offers

(2) a sociological account of the emergence of the sacred/profane distinction from experiences of the social bond and how ritual practice reinforces that distinction.

Two alternative interpretations of the purpose of Durkheim's argument result from this, which depend on whether you give weight to step (1) or emphasize step (2) without step (1).

Taking the first route, you would see Durkheim's overall argument as an attempt at a sociological explanation of religious experience; taking the second route, you would see it as an attempt at a much broader sociological explanation of all major categories of social thought and an analysis of how they are reinforced through formalized practice (what Durkheim, in his re-reading of religious experience in particular, calls 'ritual'). Note that, if we look at Durkheim's argument from the second and broader perspective, our discussion of ritual, or formalized practice, need not, and should not, be limited to religious ritual, that is, ritual directed at a transcendental reference point that explains the whole of life and the world. 'Ritual' in this context can be secular and aimed at a different type of 'transcendental', the social transcendental in which Durkheim was undeniably interested. The argument relied upon here—that the concept of 'ritual' can refer to practices that are either secular or religious—was settled 30 years ago in anthropology (Moore & Myerhoff 1977).

Therefore, if my account of media rituals does draw on Durkheim's argument in some way, what routes does it take? As you will already have guessed, my account brackets out step (1) (claims about the particular origins of religion) and thus leaves aside the first reading of Durkheim's purpose and emphasizes step (2), offering a version of the second reading of Durkheim's purpose. My approach tries to apply Durkheim's explanation of social categories to specifically *media-related* categories of social thought and their reinforcement through specifically *media-related* rituals. However, my argument does so—and here is the extent of the parallel between my argument and what Durkheim says about religion—*via an analogy* with Durkheim's account of the emergence of the sacred/profane distinction and how ritual practice reinforces that distinction.

This makes clear once more that my notion of media rituals is *not* a claim that media outputs, or media practices, are in some way religious. Instead, my definition of media rituals (to which I am now ready to come) tries to abstract from the definitions of Roy Rappoport (1999) and other ritual theorists and to generate a term whose specific reference is quite distinctive to the media. 'Media rituals', as I define them, 'are formalized actions organized around key media-related categories and boundaries, whose performance frames, or suggests a connection with, wider media-related values' (Couldry 2003a: 29).

I will mention some examples of media rituals in a moment, but let me first emphasize another point: in adapting parts of Durkheim's classic arguments about religion in this way, I also want to read that earlier argument *against the grain*. I fully recognize the many critiques of structural functionalist versions of Durkheim (in Talcott Parsons, Edward Shils and others—see, for example, Shils 1975). In so far as my argument is based on an analogy with Durkheim, I want to apply this analogy to anti-functionalist ends that, as I suggested earlier, owe rather more to sociological critics of functionalism (Lukes 1975; Wrong 1994) and to post-structuralist writers (Laclau 1990) than to Shils and Parsons. I am not claiming that media rituals somehow make social order possible, but only that the *rhetorics* of order that underlie media rituals are increasingly prevalent in contemporary societies and that it is the prevalence of particular claims to 'order' and their condensation in particular formalized practices or rituals that requires us to go back to Durkheim's *Elementary Forms* and see its new, perhaps surprising, implications for intensely mediated societies.

What rhetorics do I mean and what specifically do I mean by media-related categories and values? I mean media institutions' claims to speak for, or to be our privileged access to, 'the social'. These claims are very often not explicit, but they are embedded not only in the practice of media professionals and the discourse of countless media texts (see Couldry 2000 for a detailed argument), but also in the various categories of thought that underlie what I call media rituals (Couldry 2003a). I call the overall package of those categories, and the orientation to the media they sustain, 'the myth of the mediated centre' (Couldry 2003a: ch. 3; 2006: ch. 2).

Here are some examples of the categories that encode that myth and specifically the idea of a social 'order' in which media institutions have a central explanatory and evaluative role. There is the category of 'liveness' which suggests that through media we acquire a direct and immediate connection to certain central social realities, so important we must be connected to them 'now'; there is the category of the 'media personality' or 'celebrity' somehow imagined to be different from its opposite, the 'ordinary' or non-media person; there is the category of a 'media world' imagined to be different from, more glamorous than, somehow higher than, the 'ordinary world' in which the rest of us live. Just as in Durkheim's account religious rituals are organized around the absolute and mutually exclusive categories of sacred/profane (behind which lies the mythical value of the social bond with which they are associated), I would argue that media rituals are organized around the categories of media (things, people, world) versus ordinary (things, people, world), a category distinction that naturalizes a sense of media as socially central, what I call 'the myth of the mediated centre'.

Media rituals are practices that enact and reproduce the categories which underlie beliefs in the social institution of the media, just as religious rituals reproduce the categories which underlie religious beliefs. Examples of media rituals that I have argued for elsewhere in detail (Couldry 2003a) include: *talk shows*, places where people confess often very private things to audiences of millions, where what I would call the 'ritual frame' of the talk show is crucial to making sense of the transformative effect of these confessions; *media events*—first, and classically, theorized by Dayan & Katz (1992); the scope of these events goes well beyond single rituals, but they often contain media rituals, such as the coordinated broadcasting and watching of a state funeral;[2] and *Reality TV* about which I must say a little more, since it will help introduce the later discussion.

'Reality' programming is a large and, it seems, continually expanding dimension of contemporary media, whose expansion, for sure, is closely linked to economic factors—not so much a *genre* any more as a 'meta-*genre*', with the claim of being 'reality-based' now attaching to an increasing diversity of documentaries, quasi-dramas, game shows and so on. Seeing Reality TV as a media ritual foregrounds the ambiguity of its claims to present 'reality' while also being 'mere entertainment' (Couldry 2002), a structuring ambiguity that it shares with all ritual (Bloch 1989). This approach is no doubt contentious and this is not the place to defend my argument in detail. Rather, I want to explore those features of reality programming that the concept of media ritual helps us hold in focus, assuming in what follows that, as reader, you grant the 'media rituals' perspective some value. The importance of all this for understanding the challenges of media presentations of contemporary religious difference will become clear later. For now, I ask you to suspend your disbelief!

Firstly, seeing Reality TV formats as media rituals foregrounds the banal, but fundamental, claim of all such programming to present some aspect of social 'reality' and thus to exemplify the claim underlying all media rituals that the 'media world' somehow stands in for, and gives us special access to, our collective 'reality'. *Secondly*, it foregrounds the ambiguity of this claim: what distinguishes ritual is its ability to be both a *mere* 'game' or presentation and something *more* 'real' than 'ordinary life'. Recall the *Celebrity Big Brother* racism furore in January 2007 when spokespersons for the programme and format owners, Endemol, alternated between downplaying the incident's seriousness (implicitly relying on its status within a mere game) and on other occasions insisting that the programme was important precisely because it showed the 'reality' of racism in Britain today. (For an example of the latter, see Bazalgette 2007.) I shall build on this example later. *Thirdly*, the concept of media rituals also helps us understand Reality TV better by identifying what is at stake in performing in the game of Reality TV: taking part in a media ritual inserts you into an apparently separate and 'higher' space (of media), even as you act out an aspect of perfectly 'ordinary' everyday reality (another ambiguity). *Fourthly*, the concept of ritual highlights the framing power of such programmes in the sense of the late Mary Douglas (1984: 64): their ability *to focus attention on common objects*—a particularly important point when we come to think about the presentation of religion and religious difference. *Fifthly*, the Durkheimian analogy developed earlier helps explain the 'contagion' of the categories involved in media ritual: for example, the continual expansion of

---

[2]   For my own anti-functionalist reading of Dayan & Katz's well-known theory, see Couldry (2003a: ch. 4).

the notion of mediated 'reality' from one example to another, which is at the basis of the meta-*genre* of Reality TV. *Finally*, the concept of media rituals provides one way of explaining how Reality TV relates to wider issues of power: because, if Reality TV formats are best seen as 'media rituals', their enactment must further legitimate and naturalize the very categories on which their performance is based. In this case, the categories are associated with the underlying claim that the media (what we construct as 'the media') somehow stand in for, and gain their special authority from, the social (what we construct as the supposed totality of 'the social'). Therefore, the process of media rituals[3] in turn helps further naturalize the power of media institutions and the very intense concentration of symbolic resources and symbolic power from which they benefit.

To sum up, the point of this chapter is not to argue that Reality TV programmes are media rituals in some sense—that is more a matter for media research itself— but to bring out how, if there were something valuable in this idea, it might prove useful when we assess the contribution (positive or negative) of media rituals, for example Reality TV programmes, to how we live with religious difference. To develop this, I need a hypothetical example whose invention I believe is justified by recent events.

Reality TV and the Presentation of Religious Difference: A Hypothetical Case

Let me use as my starting point the UK version of *Celebrity Big Brother* which in January 2007 caused major controversy because of the racist bullying by Reality TV 'celebrity' Jade Goody[4] and others of the Bollywood film star Shilpa Shetty: the controversy spread far beyond Britain, to India and North America as headline news. Let us leave to one side the specific issue of racism and consider the *only slightly* hypothetical situation where the abusive comments in question had covered issues of religious as well as, or even instead of, ethnic difference. Incidentally, one interesting reason why they did not, perhaps, was that Jade Goody's white English mother, as *The Guardian* (20 January 2007: 2) noted, is, it seems, a practising Muslim: a factor clearly known to the production team when choosing the programme's cast, but not one, we must presume, that the producers wanted to have highlighted in this particular version of the show. It is not difficult,

---

[3]   If I had more space, I would go further here and explain how the relatively exceptional cases of 'media rituals' emerge out of a wider everyday field of media 'ritualization', by drawing on the work in the anthropology of religion by Catherine Bell (1992).

[4]   Jade Goody was a contestant in an earlier series of UK *Big Brother* who, although voted out, subsequently acquired high popularity (for discussions, see Holmes 2004). The hostile reaction to Goody's racist comments led the paperback version of her autobiography *Jade, My Autobiography* to be pulped and caused Goody to undertake a trip of 'atonement' to India in Spring 2007.

however, to imagine a case where religious differences were not downplayed, but highlighted from the outset by the editorial decisions of the producers and by the actions of participants. How does the concept of media ritual help us gain a critical distance from the controversies that might develop in this hypothetical case?

We can readily imagine the claims that might be made that such a programme showed us the 'real' state of religious discrimination in Britain and thus 'revealed' to the wider world something 'representative' about inter-faith relations in Britain. We can also easily imagine the claims of others that, despite the artificial context of the mediated reality-game, its events offered us an 'index' of what is now 'at stake' around religion in 'our' society (the ambiguity I noted earlier). Thinking of such programmes as media rituals would also help explain why they have the framing power that can generate an interpretational vortex such as developed around Jade Goody's racist remarks. This perspective would therefore licence us precisely to be more cautious, more sceptical, about what that vortex might tell us about wider social attitudes or tendencies.

We can also imagine cases where, as such a dispute over religious insults in a Reality TV game intensified, religious authorities felt impelled to get involved. There are cases, from Brazil for example, of politicians becoming involved as actors in television fictions that re-presented current political disputes (Hamburger 2000), so that we cannot ignore the possibility that, under certain circumstances, religious authorities might feel pressure to intervene in disputes in the supposedly representative 'space' of a Reality TV show. Such a hypothetical situation not only brings out the importance of holding on to the concept of media rituals, because of the scepticism towards the supposed representativeness of mediated 'realities' that it supports, but also points to some interesting cases where media institutions' underlying claim to social authority—their claim to be our best access points to social 'reality'—*cuts across* the quite separate and traditional claim to the social authority of religious institutions.

There is indeed a theoretical issue at the intersection of media theory and sociology of religion. For, at least in Durkheim's classic account of the origins of religion, religious authority is based in the *same type* of social source as we have just argued media's authority is based—the claim to stand in for 'the social'—even if within religion that claim is differently inflected and has been developed over a very different historical trajectory. For a rare discussion of this interesting sociological possibility, see Knut Lundby's recent analysis of the media-intensive election campaign for the Bishop of Oslo (Lundby 2006). It may well be that we can go even further and argue that in contemporary mediated societies, media institutions place general pressures on religious professionals and religious believers that have transformed what we might call, after Bourdieu, the 'field' of religious practice, altering what counts as prestige or 'symbolic capital' in the religious field and thus affecting the operations of the religious field and their entanglement with the journalistic field (applying Couldry 2003b). Developing that argument would take me too far afield here.

We need also for the purposes of this chapter to keep in mind how the media rituals concept (if *wrongly understood*) might obscure our understanding of how religious difference is played out in the media age. I emphasized earlier that the idea of media rituals involves no claim that contemporary media literally are functioning like religion. Indeed my argument has relied only on the minimal claim that there is a sufficient descriptive difference between media and religious forms (institutions, practices, experience) to licence us to treat them, at least initially, as broadly separate domains.

However, things would be very different, if we claimed a wider *fusion* between media and religion. General claims of that sort have been made by various scholars (for example, Goethals 1997) and are in play more recently in Eric Rothenbuhler's brilliant argument (Rothenbuhler 2005) that media institutions are now literally *the* churches of a new cult of the individual (focused on celebrities) similar to what Durkheim anticipated in some writings. The problem with this line of argument, for all its rhetorical force, is that we lose sight of the distinctive and independent force of media forms and therefore blur the media's ability to *influence* religious practice in a variety of ways. Indeed we blur exactly the sorts of tensions that my hypothetical extension of the *Celebrity Big Brother* case has raised. The reason why throughout I have emphasized that media rituals are distinctive rituals based around the authority of media institutions (rather than being an extended or ersatz religion) is exactly to clarify the workings of the potential interactions between media and religious spheres in the media age.

To summarize my argument so far about my hypothetical *Celebrity Big Brother* episode, I have claimed that it is a form of media ritual that relies on certain claims to present 'social reality' which must be deconstructed; this ritual focuses commentary and claims about 'the social', leading often to intense debates on multiple scales about aspects of 'the social', including, potentially, debates about religious and ethnic differences. As such, this ritual form may have significant consequences for how we can live together. The question of how we can live together *well* is, of course, the question that motivates the long tradition of ethics in philosophy that began with Socrates and Aristotle; in the next section I want to use this to frame the broader consequences of my argument.

Towards a Framework of Media Ethics in Multi-faith Societies

How might we develop a framework for considering the ethical consequences of Reality TV or indeed other media forms that re-present religious differences in multi-faith, partly secularized societies? The first step in this direction is the one I have been preparing all along: to regard such 'reality-based' media forms as precisely that—as generic forms that rely on certain condensed claims about the media's authoritative access to reality. By deconstructing in this way these media forms as rituals, we can distance ourselves from claims that these media forms somehow display 'our reality'. Such distance is essential, if we are to think calmly about the ethicality, or otherwise, of such media forms and the representations made by, and about, them.

The second step is to recognize that any attempt at ethical reflection about the 'debates' within such programmes will get us nowhere, unless we distinguish between the various levels, or scales, of dialogue and commentary that a programme such as *Celebrity Big Brother* elicits. This is partly because, as I mentioned earlier, media rituals provide an intense 'frame' in which participants can act and viewers can place their comments. The result, however, is to make the space of ethical judgement very complex in relation to 'reality' media. In our hypothetical *Celebrity Big Brother* case, there are of course first the original interactions in the house (before any editing). Then there is the commentary on those interactions embedded in the editing choices made by the producers: we can easily imagine editing down raw footage in such a way as to enhance an impression of disagreement over religious difference. (Did something parallel go on in the Jade Goody case? We cannot know.) The broadcast version provides a further level of presentation which is in turn commented on in the press, in magazines, television news bulletins and so on, but not just there; increasingly we need to take account of a further level of recorded *audience* commentary on sites such as YouTube. A still further level, again only possible because of sites such as YouTube, is the circulation of 'mash-ups' of televised material, which offer a more complex form of commentary in the margins of the original media text: we can imagine exceptional cases where an individual's reworking of a programme clip has a significant audience, to rival that of the original broadcast. Finally, we have to take account of how versions of the original behaviour in the Reality TV setting—particular representations of religious difference—are replayed, in stereotyped or normalized form, in everyday culture.

All of these levels are relevant to considering the ethics of how religious difference is represented in Reality TV formats. An obvious difficulty arises when originally improvised behaviour (admittedly improvised in a highly artificial and constraining setting) becomes 'text' within a programme and then, in extracted form, becomes '*the* text', as it were, for an open-ended chain of commentary stretching far beyond the original context. Of course, the ethical complexities of disseminating texts and images have been inherent to modern media from the outset, as John Durham Peters (1999) has argued, but Reality TV raises two distinct problems: firstly, what is disseminated (for commentary) started its life as (at least partly) *spontaneous* interaction, not text; secondly, the *representative* claims inherent to Reality TV always have a potentially provocative relationship to the highly stratified societies those programmes supposedly represent. Claims about differences of religious denomination also involve differences in the very broadest narratives of belief, history and practice by which people identify themselves. The representative playing out of 'differences' between atheists, Muslims and Christians in a Reality TV setting before a national audience is not trivial, even if it emerges from an entertainment format and is driven overwhelmingly by economic motives which are only thinly masked as 'democratization'. If you doubt whether Reality

TV is a sufficiently serious topic for ethical analysis, consider the implications of saying that Reality TV—and the claims about contemporary societies that are made within its frame—is *beyond* ethical evaluation.

Let me clarify where I am heading. Two factors—the ritual status of Reality TV and the complexity of levels on which such programmes operate as texts and textual commentary—require us to hesitate before drawing any simple ethical conclusions about behaviour represented in programmes like *Celebrity Big Brother*. There is inevitably a gulf between the original pretext and the interpretative chains that develop out of such programmes. The ethical implications of an original gesture may be very different from those of the token version of that gesture commented upon in the interpretative vortex provoked by the programme. However, far from this gulf blocking off ethical enquiry, it entitles us to require very careful thought on the part of Reality TV producers concerning the long-term ethical implications of what they do. We should not be afraid to ask whether Reality TV as a media form—with its generic claim to represent a slice of everyday unedited 'reality'— itself raises ethical questions. Suppose it becomes true that we increasingly see religious discourse and inter-religious differences caught up in the interpretative vortices encouraged by Reality TV. Would this represent an important opening up and broadening out of the debate about religion's role in societies such as Britain, until recently assumed by many to be unproblematically secular? Or would it be the start of something more disturbing and unstable—the end of any possibility for non-prejudicial public discussion of religious difference? Perhaps neither, and it is the tendency to draw drastic conclusions from such programmes which itself must be undermined through careful formal/ritual analysis.

If Reality TV formats provide us with ready-made incentives to generate dispute and to enjoy the dramatization of difference (we cannot always assume that such dramatization will meet a strong negative reaction as it did in the Jade Goody case), how might other media formats provide a positive vortex of interpretation—a stimulus to listen better, to reflect more calmly, to acknowledge the importance of accommodating difference? Perhaps we find that alternative difficult to imagine: until then, we cannot rely on Reality TV formats to de-dramatize religious difference, because this goes exactly against the commercial imperatives on which they are based.

Conclusion

All of this suggests that we need a framework for thinking about media ethics that can take on the challenges that an intensely mediated and ritualized public sphere will generate for our chances of living peaceably together. There are, of course, many dimensions to media ethics and the representation of religious difference is just one of them. However, there is, I believe, a long-term issue about the representation of religious difference through 'reality' media that has appeared on the horizon and that will not go away. In some recent writing (Couldry 2006:

ch. 7), I have speculated on whether some version of an Aristotelian approach to ethics might help us in building the foundations of a global media ethics— an approach that comes from outside any of today's major religious traditions, yet is not exclusively secular either. The appropriate representation of religious difference would be a central issue for any such global media ethics, since on any view religious differences are salient to our prospects of global peace. An approach that starts not from moral principles with which particular groups most strongly identify—for those we know others may well not share—is likely to be less productive than one which starts instead from our overriding need: for all of us to live together safely and peaceably and make effective use of our shared resources, whether environmental or economic, social or cultural.

Developing such a framework of media ethics would, of course, be a topic for another chapter, indeed another book. My aim in this chapter has been more modest: to explore one approach to media analysis, which coincidentally draws on some of the same insights of Durkheim that still flow through sociology of religion, but which, more importantly, allows us to see clearly not the sacred's imagined merger with media culture—a crude and improbable outcome—but rather how particular media forms—and the mythical rhetoric of 'the social' associated with them—represents and is quite possibly liable to distort the space of religion and religious difference. For all our differences of priority, this is perhaps a problem towards which both media researchers and researchers of religion should orientate themselves for the longer term in order to see what common frameworks of understanding we can develop.

References

Bazalgette, Peter, 'Why We're Right about Celeb BB', *Observer*, 25 February 2007: 26.

Bell, Catherine, *Ritual Theory, Ritual Practice* (New York: Oxford University Press, 1992).

Bloch, Maurice, *Ritual History and Power* (London: Athlone Press, 1989).

Couldry, Nick, *The Place of Media Power: Pilgrims and Witnesses of the Media Age* (London: Routledge, 2000).

Couldry, Nick, 'Playing for Celebrity: *Big Brother* as Ritual Event', *Television and New Media*, 3/3 (2002): 283–94.

Couldry, Nick, *Media Rituals: A Critical Approach* (London: Routledge, 2003a).

Couldry, Nick, 'Media Meta-Capital: Extending the Range of Bourdieu's Field Theory', *Theory and Society* 32, 5/6 (2003b): 653–77.

Couldry, Nick, 'Media Rituals: Beyond Functionalism', in Eric Rothenbuhler & Mihai Coman (eds), *Media Anthropology* (Thousand Oaks: Sage, 2005): 59–69.

Couldry, Nick, *Listening Beyond the Echoes: Media, Ethics, and Agency in an Uncertain World* (Boulder, CO: Paradigm Press, 2006).

Couldry, Nick, 'Form and Power in an Age of Continuous Spectacle', in David Hesmondhalgh & Jason Toynbee (eds), *The Media and Social Theory* (London: Routledge, 2008): 161–76.

Dayan, Daniel & Katz, Elihu, *Media Events: The Live Broadcasting of History* (Cambridge, MA: Harvard University Press, 1992).

Douglas, Mary, *Purity and Danger* (London: Routledge, 1984 [1966]).

Durkheim, Emile, *The Elementary Forms of Religious Life*, trans. K. Fields (Glencoe: Free Press, 1995 [1912]).

Goethals, Gregor, 'Escape from Time: Ritual Dimensions of Popular Culture', in Stewart Hoover & Knut Lundby (eds), *Rethinking Media Religion and Culture* (Thousand Oaks: Sage, 1997).

Goody, Jade, *Jade, My Autobiography* (London: HarperCollins, 2006).

Hamburger, Esther, 'Politics and Intimacy: The Agrarian Reform in a Brazilian Telenovela', *Television and New Media* 1/2 (2000): 159–79.

Holmes, Su, '"All You've got to Worry About is the Task, Having a Cup of Tea and Doing a Bit of Sunbathing": Approaching Celebrity in *Big Brother*', in Su Holmes & Deborah Jermyn (eds), *Understanding Reality Television* (London: Routledge, 2004).

Laclau, Ernesto, *New Reflections on the Revolution of Our Time* (London: Verso, 1990).

Lukes, Steven, 'Political Ritual and Social Integration', *Sociology*, 29 (1975): 289–305.

Lundby, Knut, 'Contested Communication. Mediating the Sacred', in Johanna Sumiala-Seppänen, Knut Lundby & Raimo Salokangas (eds), *Implications of the Sacred in (Post)Modern Media* (Göteberg: Nordicom, 2006): 43–62.

Martin-Barbero, Jesus, 'Mass Media as a Site of Resacralisation of Contemporary Cultures', in Stewart Hoover & Knut Lundby (eds), *Rethinking Media Religion and Culture* (Thousand Oaks: Sage, 1997).

Moore, Sally & Myerhoff, Barbara (eds), *Secular Ritual* (Assen/Amsterdam: Van Gorcum, 1977).

Peters, John Durham, *Speaking into the Air* (Chicago: Chicago University Press, 1999).

Rappaport, Roy, *Ritual and Religion in the Making of Humanity* (Cambridge: Cambridge University Press, 1999).

Rothenbuhler, Eric, 'The Church of the Cult of the Individual', in Eric Rothenbuhler & Mihai Coman (eds), *Media Anthropology* (Thousand Oaks: Sage, 2005): 91–100.

Shils, Edward, *Center and Periphery* (Chicago: University of Chicago Press, 1975).

Wrong, Dennis, *The Problem of Order* (New York: The Free Press, 1994).

Chapter 3
Deepening Relationships with Material Artefacts

Stephen Pattison

Introduction

The world is full of the works of human hands—artefacts. While being without other living humans is not too difficult for individuals to accomplish, it is almost impossible to conceive of a situation in which one might be unaccompanied by at least one artefact—clothing, a ring, a watch, a chair, shoes. Dant puts this graphically: 'If you think that interacting with things is not important, just try to remember the last time that you were not engaged in some sort of "material interaction"' (2005: xi).

Artefacts, many of them humble and unnoticed, vastly outnumber their human progenitors. They accompany us from cradle to grave. Some of them pre-exist and survive us by centuries. While they are made by humans, they also help to make humans what they are, transmitting culture and shaping bodies and minds. Somehow, however, they mostly manage to remain beneath our active notice and attention. The undifferentiated realm of 'things' or 'stuff' seldom attracts much active interest or comment.

While a few sacred or aesthetically significant artefacts may be the objects of considerable analysis and discussion, the vast majority of them, especially mass produced artefacts, are ignored by contemporary critics and commentators, even by most of those interested in cultural analysis. It is as if the more artefacts that are produced, the less overtly interesting they are to their users and consumers.

In this chapter, I want to suggest that we need to develop much more positive attitudes, and engage in deeper, more conscious relationships, with at least some of the humble, inconspicuous artefacts that surround us, at least some of the time. Indeed, we need to develop more person-like and loving relationships with them, not least because they shape human persons and the human world. The kinds of artefacts I have in mind are radiators, pens, toasters and chairs as well as more prized, overtly meaningful, and special artefacts like paintings, sculptures and buildings, the traditional objects of cultured and academic attention. I approach this topic from the perspective of practical theology rather than social science or cultural criticism. Hence a few words about practical theology.

The Practical Theological Approach[1]

Practical theology (PT) critically considers the implications of belief and thought for practice and the implications of practice for belief and thought. Practical theologians are students of action-influencing worldviews—undergirding beliefs and assumptions—that structure life and practice. They work from the perspective of being critical, but committed, inhabitants of a particular worldview (in my case, Christianity). Practical theology is concerned with what people do, why they do it and the implications of this for their faith, thought and practice. This is then related in a critical way to faith traditions which are taken to contain insight, truth and validity. The most important question in PT is, 'So what?' Thinking, analysis, understanding and faith must be correlated with concrete ways of acting or this kind of theology is clearly not actually practical.

PT proceeds from description—what is the case—to prescription—what might be done and considered differently—and then to action. It thus encompasses an element of ethical and value normativity which would be alien to many academic disciplines (see Lynch 2005). It focuses on the contemporary world and on the experience and practices of people in that world. It attempts to start where people are and to remain near to everyday experience.

To understand the contemporary world critically, PT draws upon the methods and findings of many different disciplines, such as sociology, psychology and anthropology. Thus it is interdisciplinary in its methods and overall approach.

PT focuses on relationships within and between humans and between humans and God or 'ultimate reality' (see Hick 1989). Here, however, I turn to human relations with artefacts. I have come to think that these powerfully shape bodies, persons, societies, beliefs and practices.

It is appropriate to use a PT approach to suggest more understanding of, and deeper relationships with, artefacts. In the first place, all people, whether conventionally religious or not, inhabit action-guiding worldviews which structure their thinking and actions. Furthermore we all have the potential to become more critical actors and thinkers in relation to our assumptions and practices. In a sense we can all become more critical 'theologians' of practice—in this case, the practice of relating to the artefactual world.[2] Secondly, in Western culture, Christian theology and attitudes have helped to shape general cultural views and practices. Therefore, for example, Christian attitudes to the material and to idolatry have influenced, and been influenced by, wider social attitudes.

---

[1] See, for example, Woodward & Pattison (2000) for an introduction to practical theology, its concerns and methods.

[2] In Pattison (1997), I argue that modern managers, while not theists, make certain faith assumptions and entertain action-guiding myths about the world, for example, that the future can be controlled and that it will be better than the past. I suggest that managers would be helped, if they saw themselves as believing inhabitants of a worldview who could become more critical of their own beliefs and practices.

Here I argue that we make assumptions about artefacts which contribute to certain kinds of practices. If we become more critical inhabitants of our artifactual world and the myths and assumptions that support it, it may be possible for us to be more sophisticated, responsive and responsible agents within it.

In the remainder of this chapter, I will make some comments on why Western culture has become so dualistic and indifferent to everyday artefacts that it mostly ignores them. Then I will set out some factors which might lead us to want to take them more seriously. Finally, I will consider some of the inhibitions that might prevent our developing more positive, nuanced relationships with them.

The 'Dead' World of Artefacts

One aspect that modern Westerners consciously take to be incontrovertibly true and ultimately 'real' is that there is a great gap between the realm of material, inanimate things and that of humans. For us, the world is divided into the living, animate and sensible, while on the other side of an invisible chasm stands the realm of the inanimate, material, insensible and dead. Our hierarchical world order of significance and attention is something like this:

1. Living animate beings
—Humans
—Higher animals
2. Living inanimate beings
—Plants, trees, single celled animals, etc.
3. Dead inanimate beings
—Natural phenomena (rivers, mountains stars, etc.)
—Unnatural phenomena (humanly made artefacts)

In this schema, artefacts, the works of human hands, are positioned as far away from humans as they can be. They occupy a place of total 'otherness', even beyond natural phenomena like rivers, mountains and stars, for which humans have no direct responsibility and over which they can have little or no influence. This way of thinking about the world, which completely separates the animated, enspirited, personal and living from the inanimate, material and dead is not universal.[3] Even in the West, it is relatively recent (see Latour 1993).

Space precludes a full account of the evolution of this dualistic worldview. Suffice it to say that it seems to have coincided with the rise of experimental science

---

[3]   Appadurai states that 'the powerful contemporary tendency is to regard the world of things as inert and mute, set in motion and animated, indeed, knowable only by persons and their words. Yet, in many historical societies, things have not been so divorced from the capacity of persons to act and the power of words to communicate' (1986: 4). See also Abram (1997) and Harvey (2005).

with its objectifying view of the world, which tends to separate human mind from matter, observer from observed. Accompanying rationalism and disenchantment of the material world seems to have been exacerbated by the rise of capitalism and consumerism, with its emphasis upon making and selling things to people in such a way that the artefacts created are not in themselves regarded as having much intrinsic value or significance as material objects (see, for example, Campbell 1987 and Ritzer 1999). Now, ironically, we find ourselves living in a so-called materialist society where humanly created objects are 'seen through' and regarded as valuable mainly for their symbolic significance.[4] This allows us continuously to manufacture and purchase new things because there can be no satisfying our symbolic and imaginative lust for things. We can create and exploit the material world, including the world of artefacts, without let or hindrance, because they are dead and inert. As far as we are concerned, they lack fundamental interests or rights and exist solely for the benefit of contemporary humans (see Latour 1993).

Re-valuing the Realm of Artefacts

If we think of artefacts in terms of a dead, more or less undifferentiated world of 'stuff' or 'things' separate from the world of people—human persons being the entities which we treat as morally significant—we are unlikely to give them much attention or to recognize that they may have interests or claims upon the human race. Therefore, if we are to take artefacts of all kinds seriously, we need to change our fundamental assumptions about the world and what is significant in it. To include them more directly within our moral purview and considerations, we need to change our ways of perceiving and relating to them. Effectively we need to regard and treat at least some of them more as subjects, agents or persons.

But why do artefacts of all kinds in principle deserve our attention? Why should we even begin to think of treating at least some of them as more like persons than mere 'things' that can be used and disposed of at our unthinking pleasure? I will

---

[4]   Artefacts are implicated in human life and society in both symbolic and non-symbolic, or material, ways. See, for example, Dant (2005). The symbolic/non-symbolic interaction is simultaneous and integral in relationships with artefacts—the two aspects are coiled around each other like the double helix of the DNA. When I get into my Jaguar XJ6, this 'says' something about me symbolically in terms of identity, status, etc. But the car also extends my physical range of travel and, as I sink down into its seat, my body is contorted in a particular way. When I become a bike rider, I not only become something different from the pedestrian I used to be in now understanding myself to be a cyclist; I can also physically get to places much faster. Unfortunately, it is the symbolic and figurative side of relations with objects that has mostly been studied and articulated, not the non-symbolic, material aspect (cf. Dant, 1999; 2005). Even materialist cultural critics have been more interested in the economic aspects of artifactual production and consumption, for example, their exchange, than in their ongoing non-symbolic lives with their users and owners. See further, for example, Miller (1987; 1998).

now outline some reasons as to why artefacts might deserve to be regarded and treated in more person-like or morally significant ways.

Why do Artefacts Deserve Human Attention?

The first reason for attempting to foster person-like relationships with artefacts is because *subject–subject relations are a more appropriate paradigm for dealing with the world than subject–object relations* (see Code 1991 and McFague 1997). In arguing that we should recognize and cultivate more person-like relationships with at least some artefacts, I am appealing implicitly to a subject–subject, rather than a subject–object, model of relating to things and people generally.

The roots of a respectful, subject–subject model for relating to inanimate as well as animate things lie in the post-Heisenbergian notion that all things are related to, and affect, each other (see Code 1991: 164–5; see also Levin 1988). Rocks and cells and the scientists who observe these things are all involved in mutual relationships, however slight, and there is no position of objectivity, or detachment, from this kind of relationship. Indeed, it is relationship itself that co-constitutes the beings involved in it. Perception is thus a capacity for relationship between perceiver and perceived, not the exercise by perceivers of a particular instrumental capacity upon an object (see Levin 1988).

The implication that some thinkers, especially phenomenologists and feminists, draw from this is that it is better to work on a paradigm of mutual recognition and respect for all things rather than to adhere to the dualistic paradigm of scientific objectivity and distance, which often seems to lead to relations of domination and exploitation (McFague 1997: 97). In some sense, all things, including artefacts, are subjects within interdependent relationships. The knower and the known are not entirely different in all ways, as objectifying Western understandings of the dead, inanimate world maintain.

If all things are acknowledged as subjects, perhaps on a continuum of subjectivity, we are more likely to treat them in ways that respect their integrity and differences rather than as objects. This may be more positive and less risky than objectifying things. Code argues that

> It is surely no more preposterous to argue that people should try to know physical objects in the nuanced way that they know their friends than it is to argue that they should try to know people in the unsubtle way that they claim to know physical objects. (Code 1991: 165)[5]

---

[5] McFague (1997: 47) notes that it is better 'to elevate trees and mushrooms, the sun and moon, ticks and tigers, to subjects' rather than to reduce everyone and everything to objects. Strangely, neither she nor any of the other feminists I have read think it fit to include artefacts in this re-subjectification of the world.

The next factor that might lead us to want to cultivate person-like relations with some artefacts is that *artefacts are among the highest forms of human creation and self-realization.*

The world is full of humanly created things—artefacts. Because they are ubiquitous and common, it is easy to forget what artefacts represent in terms of human endeavour, imagination, thought and craft. They are some of the main vehicles whereby humans create and pass on their culture and they have decisive effects upon both the animate and inanimate parts of the world. Arguably artefacts are the cultural equivalent of DNA and genetic inheritance (see Dant 2005; Ingold 2000). They shape people and make them what they are.[6] Furthermore artefacts vastly extend the scope of human survival, identity and flourishing. The bicycle, for example, turned a whole generation of pedestrians into tourists.

Many of the artefacts around us are 'fearfully and wonderfully made' (Psalm 139.14). Often they are amazingly complex and ingenious solutions to problems, both practically and aesthetically. They have evolved over centuries, if not millennia. And they materially embody human purpose, agency, emotion and communication.[7] In other words they have many person-like qualities, even though they are not themselves living members of the species *homo sapiens*.

In theological terms it could be argued that artefacts are to humans what humans are to God. Just as humans embody divine characteristics and *logos* or reason, artefacts are the products and witnesses to embodied human *logos*. It can even be suggested that the divine creation is not just significant because of the human beings it supports. If God has implanted certain potentialities and properties in the material world, thus for the whole creation to reach its potential, both people and the material environment in all its aspects, including the artifactual aspect, need to work closely together (Staniloae 2000). What I am suggesting is that we should not let utility and familiarity dull us to the importance of having a 'high' doctrine of artefacts. One way of expressing this appreciative way of thinking about them

---

[6] A personal example here. Since the age of four, I have been reading and writing almost every day. The artefacts with which I have been engaged in these activities—chairs, desks, books, paper, pens, computers, reading glasses—require me habitually to crane my head forward. The consequence is that I am now round shouldered and somewhat stooped. I have a tendency to look down rather than up, so I often do not look people in the eye. All of which means that I have actually become to outward appearances an academic, physically as well as by interest and profession. The artefacts I have used have changed me physically and this has probably contributed to how people interact with me and how I interact with myself. My curved spine is a permanent physical change, not just a symbolic reminder of my vocation.

[7] Gell (1998) argues that artefacts of all kinds index their creators and embody purpose, intention, emotion and other human qualities that allow humans to relate to them in person-like ways—particularly if they are very ingenious and complex. Gell believes that some artefacts are effectively indistinguishable from human persons, being the vehicle for person-like qualities.

is to acknowledge them as having the potential for person-like relationships with humans.

Another reason for developing person-like relationships with artefacts is that they (artefacts) *actually need our appreciation and care.*

Material artefacts often seem to be more robust and durable than their creators. Some of them, cathedrals, pictures, even doorsteps, seem destined to last for ever. They have a kind of immortality that mortal humans can envy. However, they can be easily destroyed. The Arena Chapel in Padua, with its epochal fresco cycle by Giotto, came within an ace of being destroyed by bombs in the Second World War. Coventry Cathedral was not so lucky. It takes but a moment to stick a knife through a picture and reduce it to shreds At a mundane level I am probably not the only person to have ruined a wood chisel by trying to use it as a screw driver or a wedge. Artefacts are vulnerable and need human interest and respect, if they are to survive and flourish. If neglected or abused, they can deteriorate or even disintegrate. Thus they need our care and attention.

It is easy to forget that *artefacts are admirable and delightful.* The Western world is full of complex, sophisticated, mass produced artefacts, many of which we cannot fully understand, much less attempt to make, or repair, ourselves. They are not just the quiescent, passive servants of humans. In their own right, even mass produced objects can be quite wonderful, enchanting and delightful. I still marvel at the beauty of aeroplanes in the sky, even at the many features that my mobile phone possesses in such a neat, compact form.

Perhaps there is a certain prejudice against acknowledging the delights of ordinary visible artefacts because they are associated with the evils of technology, consumerism or mass production (see Ellul 1964). But this failure to engage with, admire, and smile at the real delights that everyday artefacts provide represents a diminishment, or lost opportunity, in relationships between artefacts and humans.

Childish wonder and pleasure at the things we encounter in the world is not necessarily something we should seek quickly to outgrow. It adds value to everyday life as well as to the objects we possess and use. I agree with Jane Bennett when she asks, 'Why must nature be the exclusive form of enchantment? Can't—don't—numerous human artefacts also fascinate and inspire?' (2001: 171).

A further reason for developing more person-like relationships with artefacts is that *humans have a responsibility for what they create, obtain and use.* Like children, artefacts would not exist without the intentions, desires and actions of humans. They index their creators and can help to shape the material and social world, in some cases for years after their creators have died. Sir Christopher Wren's tomb in St Paul's Cathedral, London, bears witness to this in proclaiming that 'if you would see his memorial, look around you'. Clearly the individual historical creator or possessor of a particular object—a picture, a church, a gun or a fan—cannot be held responsible for everything that that artefact is used for, once it has become detached from its original context and purpose. In the same way parents cannot be held directly responsible for the actions of their children.

However, it seems to me that individuals may have some particular responsibility for the objects they have brought into the world—Mikhail Kalashnikov is responsible for the rifle that bears his name, although not for all the uses and causes in which it is now used. But more than this, the human race has a general responsibility towards the world of artefacts. They would not exist but for our intervention and exploitation. I would not dream of consigning my children to a rubbish heap. Perhaps we should regard old artefacts more like persons or children than as 'stuff' and do something to ensure that they exist and flourish for as long as possible. Thus we would honour the effort, resource and ingenuity that went into the creation of an artefact, together with its powers and ends. This would also do something to justify my part in exploiting the natural order to possess and use these things.

Artefacts form part of, and help to shape, the human and moral communities. Some artefacts, famous pictures and sculptures like the 'Mona Lisa' are accorded honorary person status and may have their interests and needs prioritized over those of living people. Thus in wartime, pictures and other significant objects may be evacuated before populations. But even less prominent artefacts have value to the human community. By virtue of the intentions and agency vested in them by humans, they affect what people can do and they shape them individually and socially (see Dant 2005). If the only artefacts in a culture are weapons, this affects what people can do physically and morally. Thus whether we like it or not, to a greater or lesser extent, artefacts have interests in, and help to shape, the human social and moral community. They do not have some of the qualities associated with human persons, such as free will and independent motivation. Nor can they take direct, reciprocal responsibility for their progenitors and users. This means that it is difficult to talk of artefacts and non-sentient beings having rights—which are usually only accorded to humans who can voluntarily undertake responsibilities in exchange for those rights. However, some animals and humans cannot necessarily undertake reciprocal responsibilities, yet they are still accorded moral significance and interest.

The language of rights applied to forests, wildernesses, mountains and other non-human things demonstrates the limits of thinking about all ethical responsibility in a reciprocal, rights and responsibilities-based, way (see Tamen 2001). If we move beyond this limited understanding to think about a morality based more on subject–subject relationships within an overarching ethical approach of solidarity and care, it is possible to admit artefacts to some place in the moral world (see McFague 1997: 40, 155–7; cf. Noddings 1986). This extends the boundaries of ethics and morality beyond the sphere of human persons and human–human relationships. But this is probably necessary, if we are to encompass all the aspects of the surrounding ecology that need active attention. Just because artefacts do not have rights and correlative responsibilities, narrowly understood, this does not mean that they are completely unentitled to appreciation and respect.

Not every artefact is as important to the human moral community as every human being. Nor does every artefact need the same degree of respect or attention.

However, if we do not recognize their potential moral significance and effects, we may fail to take proper responsibility for the realm of artefacts and indeed for the human realm, which is shaped with and by it.

Next it can be argued that *a basic stance of objectification will not serve artefacts or humans well in the long term*. Western subject–object, non–person-like views of relations applied to artefacts have allowed humans freely to exploit and manipulate the lifeless, inanimate material world for their own advantage. This attitude has permitted the growth of consumer capitalism, with all the real benefits that this has brought to the human race. However, seeing past or through objects is likely to produce 'hyper-consumption' and exhaustion of the world's resources in the long run. This will not be beneficial to artefacts, to humans or to the global ecology as a whole. Humans can actually live with very little materially (see Walter 1985). We have the potential to invest a few material objects with much affectivity and meaning (see Csikszentmihalyi & Rochberg Halton 1981). Appreciative subject–subject, person-like relationships in which fewer objects were invested with more care and meaning might then be much better for all the parties concerned.

If we were intensively engaged in friendly, person-like relations with some artefacts, we might not want so many of them. Humans cannot be attached to everything and everyone with equal amounts of love and attention. If we learned to have more intimate, attentive relations with artefacts, we might gain more satisfaction and therefore need fewer of them.

The owner of an intricate gold brooch in medieval times would probably have spent much time looking at this object and showing it to others. He or she would have regarded it as an intriguing marvel and been properly absorbed in an affective, person-like relationship with it, characterized by appreciation and respect. It is this kind of relationship that we need to develop more in the contemporary world.

There is an agenda here for designers, makers and users of artefacts (see Walker 2006). Modernist sensibility inclines towards making objects instantly appealing to customers so that they fall in love with them immediately (see Norman 2004). But then it is hoped that users' affections and wonder will fade and they will soon want to acquire new things. Creating 'sticky' artefacts that will continue to intrigue and delight their users in deepening relations of care and affection over the years is a task that now needs to be undertaken more vigorously.[8] Long-term relationships of fellowship and friendship with artefacts will require a difference in orientation on the part of all those who produce and use them.

Finally, I suggest that *humans need to become more affectively attached to the material world*. Attachment is fundamental to human beings, if they are to engage in, and enjoy, life (see Bennett 2001; Fonagy 2001). Consumer capitalism depends for its continuing existence upon creating a sense of detachment and non-engagement with things (see Berger 1972; Campbell 1987*)*. People move from one artefact to the next, buying one, throwing another out, with little thought. Against this I am advocating the cultivation of long-term attachment and

---

[8]   See Taussig (1993) for the 'stickiness' of objects.

intimacy with artefacts of all kinds. This is in the belief that people who invest in relationships with things as well as other people can be more appropriately engaged in the experience of living. If we can find meaning and delight in person-like relationships with artefacts, even humble artefacts in everyday life, this can be one means of attaching us to life (see Bennett 2001). Appreciating the depths and wonders of artefacts could enrich ordinary human living, challenging attitudes of unthinking acquisition, consumption and disposal and engaging humans more firmly in a subject–subject relationship with the material world.

Inhibitors and Obstacles to Deepening Person-like Relationships with Artefacts

There are, however, a number of possible inhibitors or obstacles to being open to deepening person-like relationships with material artefacts.

1. We do not believe that we are animists or 'primitives', nor do we wish to become such

Animism is the attribution of some kind of life or spirit to inanimate things. The term was coined by nineteenth-century Western anthropologists to describe the beliefs and behaviours of non-Western, non-industrialized peoples. They appeared to Western observers to mis-attribute characteristics of spirit, life and personhood to inanimate things such as trees, rivers, 'stocks and stones'. Along with cognate terms like 'fetishism', the term 'animist' is of course deeply pejorative and stigmatizing (Harvey 2005: xiii). It designates simple-mindedness, underdevelopment, infantilism and confusion. Animism is what Westerners are supposed to have developed from to live in the grown-up world of dead objects. To engage in person-like relations with artefacts is thus wilfully to regress.

Now, in post-colonial, pluralistic times, we are perhaps more appreciative of other peoples' relations with their environments and more willing to learn from them. In this context and in the light of the reality of our own ill-concealed, if unacknowledged, person-like relations with inanimate things, it is possible to re-define animism in more positive terms.[9] Harvey suggests that

---

[9]   There are a surprising number of intimate, person-like relationships with artefacts in the contemporary Western world which are mostly unremarked. Musical instruments, for example, are often treated as honorary persons, even as part of the person who uses them. They are admitted into intimate physical relationship with thighs, lips, etc. and may be given names. Some car and motorcycle owners similarly seem to enter freely into person-like relationships with their machines, naming them and even speaking to them as they interact with them. All of which seems to be regarded as fairly normal. Some art works and statues also enjoy person-like status and relations and many people have a limited number of 'biographical objects' which share their lives intimately, but may seem unexceptional

> Animists are people who recognize that the world is full of persons, only some
> of whom are human, and that life is always lived in relationships with others.
> Persons are beings, rather than objects, who are animated and social towards
> others ... Animism is [therefore] concerned with learning how to be a good
> person in relationships with other persons. (2005: xi)

Animism thus understood is probably something that Westerners need to grow into
rather than out of. There need be no necessary implication that we are recognizing
supernatural forces or spirits in acknowledging the person-like elements in
artefacts. Rather we may simply be being honest about the sedimented human
personhood that can be found, and related to, within them (see Gell 1998).

2. We are not, and do not wish to behave as, romantics, sacralizers or re-enchanters of the world

The inanimate, material world, in the eyes of a certain kind of rational science,
is officially dead (see Latour 1993). Its mysteries, complexities and effects are
potentially explicable. And as human knowledge and understanding grows, it is
becoming progressively disenchanted with no room for awe or wonder evoked by
divinities or spirits (see Bennett 2001; Moore 1996; Ritzer 1999). Unfortunately,
some people cannot live with the impersonal, desacralized world that reason and
investigation are exposing. Thus to make the world more habitable and hospitable
for themselves, these folks try to find inherent meaning and wonder within things
so that they seem more personally significant. Perhaps those who advocate more
person-like relationships with artefacts might be among these would-be escapees
from modernity? They are childlike, wilfully romantic re-enchanters and sacralizers
of the material world, deceiving themselves to make harsh reality more palatable.

There are certainly Western people who do maintain the magic quality and
sacrality of the world and all that it contains. Some of them see this as faithful
response to reality—and maybe they are right to do so. But it is not necessary
to be religious, a re-enchanter, or a romantic, to experience awe and wonder in
relations with artefacts. It is enough to acknowledge that they are complex human
creations which may have much personhood within them. Persons and personal
relationships are complex and mysterious. There is no reason why some objects
might not excite the same sense of depth, delight, awe and wonder that people
do. Awe and wonder are not the exclusive province of magic and religion. Plato
himself believed that philosophy begins in awe and wonder (Plato 1977: 155d).
Rational science, too, in investigating the universe, is not inured to these qualities
(Midgley 1999: 180–2). Indeed it could be argued that it is coldly rational to
acknowledge that some artefacts have wonderful, person-like qualities to which
humans can quite naturally closely relate.

---

to others, for example, pens, ornaments and photographs. See Hoskins (1998) and Daston
(2004).

3. We are not materialists or servants of objects (idolaters)

It may be felt by some in Western society, perhaps particularly middle-class logocentric intellectuals, that engaging in person-like relations with artefacts is a kind of materialist perversion. Religious people may have in the back of their minds the tradition of avoiding idolatry: that is, putting enticing things in the place of God. Materialist philosophers may be wary of the dangers of alienation and fetishism, whereby material objects abduct human interests and qualities and become inappropriately fascinating to people, possessing and controlling them (see Mulvey 1996; Marks 2000). Meanwhile, those of an ascetic turn of mind may think we are too concerned with producing fascinating objects that exhaust the planet while filling it up with unnecessary things.

Just as idolaters would never label themselves thus, probably none of us would like to be known as thoroughgoing materialists, enthralled to material objects and possessions. Cultivating person-like relationships with artefacts may then seem the last thing that we should do, even shamefully irresponsible.

It is easy to think of material 'goods' as 'bads' in the West, and to blame them for human failings (see Molotch 2003). However, the inappropriate enthralment of humans to artefacts is not an inevitable part of relating to them, nor is it the fault of the objects themselves.

Perhaps instead of trying to avoid person-like relations with artefacts— treating them as inevitably dangerous and corrupting—actually acknowledging and cultivating such relationships might help to get artefacts in proportion and minimize the repressed temptation to become inappropriately obsessed with them. Open relationships may be less exciting than covert ones, but they can be more honest and may be more fulfilling. In our unwillingness to engage personally with artefacts, we produce more and more of them and they mean less and less. This truly is an ecological and behavioural perversion that is likely to have serious consequences for people, artefacts and planet.

4. We are humanists

Closely related to the last inhibitor is the suspicion that cultivating closer relationships with artefacts might lead us away from more important concerns with fellow living humans. If the proper study and concern of humans are other humans, attending to artefacts might seem an unhelpful fetishistic diversion. And of course there are plenty of living humans who need our active interest and concern.

I would certainly not argue that a concern for relations with artefacts should be prosecuted at the expense of humans. Rather I would advocate that we should be concerned with both humans *and* artefacts. If artefacts are not only the creations of humans, but also help to create them in all their dimensions, individual and social, material and symbolic, then arguably we cannot care for humans and their world properly, if we do not also attend to artefacts. Human life is shared with and shaped by artefacts. To understand and care for human relationships is thus also to care about their relations with things.

Furthermore there is no necessary correlation between caring for artefacts and not caring for the humans who made them. On the contrary, some empirical research on relations with domestic objects revealed that subjects who 'were most vocal about prizing friendship over material concerns seemed to be the most lonely and isolated' (Csikszentmihalyi & Rochberg Halton 1981: 164). It seems that attachment to objects might even be an indicator of ability to attach to human beings and is not necessarily a sign of anti-humanism.

5. There are too many artefacts in the world for us to love them properly

This is a more practical, concrete obstacle than the others. There are indeed a great many artefacts in the world, probably many more than there are people. In the UK, the current Argos shopping catalogue alone boasts over 16,000 of them, available for instant purchase.[10] It is therefore physically impossible to relate to all artefacts attentively and in depth. So where should person-like relationships with particular artefacts begin and end? Do we have to engage with all of them equally and at the same level?

This kind of difficulty also applies to relations with humans. In practice, as moral philosophers recognize, we cannot relate to all people with equal seriousness and attention.[11] We ignore quite a lot of people, treating them essentially as background 'things' quite a lot of the time. This is not necessarily morally heinous. But it does not justify always treating all people as background objects. It is perfectly reasonable that our attention to artefacts should be selective. This does not justify avoiding some attentive relationships, with some significant artefacts, at least some of the time.

Conclusion

Gaston Bachelard observes that

> Whenever we live close to familiar, everyday things, we begin once again to live slowly, thanks to their fellowship, and so yield to dreams which have a past, yet

---

[10] Argos is a big UK retail store with branches on most high streets. It does not display goods, but instead makes available a huge catalogue from which people order on-line or in one of the shops.

[11] St Augustine, in *On Christian Teaching*, noted in the fourth century that 'you cannot do good to all people equally, so you should take particular thought for those who ... happen to be particularly close to you in terms of place, time, or any other circumstance' (1997: 21).

in which there is always something fresh and new. (cited in McAllester Jones 1991: 155)

Adopting a respectful attitude to the artefacts that share our lives should be enriching. It will allow artefacts to have more interest and a fuller place in the world, beyond mere usefulness. It will also permit humans to broaden their understandings of themselves and of the world in general. By cultivating deeper, closer, more person-like relations with things, human lives may well be richer, more nuanced and less cluttered. At the same time, the boundaries of the human and moral communities might be expanded, dissolving traditional boundaries between subjects and objects, things and people, to create more gracious and fruitful relationships with, and attachments to, the material world. A number of famous buildings, wildernesses and other inanimate phenomena have, over the last century, acquired official groups of friends who claim to care for and look after their interests (see Tamen 2001).[12] Perhaps the time has now come for us to widen the boundaries of friendship to include more of the material artefacts which share our lives.[13]

References

Abram, David, *The Spell of the Sensuous: Perception and Language in a More-than-Human World* (New York: Vintage Books, 1997).

Appadurai, Arjun, *The Social Life of Things* (Cambridge: Cambridge University Press, 1986).

Augustine, St, *On Christian Teaching* (Oxford: Oxford University Press, 1997).

Bennett, Jane, *The Enchantment of Modern Life: Attachments, Crossings, and Ethics* (Princeton, NJ: Princeton University Press, 2001).

Berger, John, *Ways of Seeing* (Harmondsworth: Penguin, 1972).

Campbell, Colin, *The Romantic Ethic and the Spirit of Capitalism* (Oxford: Blackwell, 1987).

Code, Lorraine, *What Can She Know? Feminist Theory and the Construction of Knowledge* (Ithaca, NY: Cornell University Press, 1991).

Csikszentmihalyi, Mihaly & Rochberg Halton, Eugene, *The Meaning of Things: Domestic Symbols and the Self* (Cambridge: Cambridge University Press, 1981).

Dant, Tim, *Material Culture in the Social World* (Buckingham: Open University Press, 1999).

Dant, Tim, *Materiality and Society* (Maidenhead: Open University Press, 2005).

---

[12]   Interestingly Canterbury Cathedral was the first inanimate object in the world to acquire human friends in 1927. The founder of the Friends of Canterbury Cathedral was the great Christian humanist, Bishop George Bell.

[13]   Many of the issues raised here are explored in greater depth in Pattison (2007).

Daston, Lorraine (ed.), *Things that Talk: Object Lessons from Art and Science* (New York: Zone Books, 2004).

Ellul, Jacques, *The Technological Society* (New York: Alfred Knopf, 1964).

Fonagy, Peter, *Attachment Theory and Psychoanalysis* (New York: Other Press, 2001).

Gell, Alfred, *Art and Agency* (Oxford: Oxford University Press, 1998).

Harvey, Graham, *Animism: Respecting the Living World* (London: Hurst and Company, 2005).

Hick, John, *An Interpretation of Religion* (Basingstoke: Macmillan, 1989).

Hoskins, Janet, *Biographical Objects: How Things Tell the Stories of People's Lives* (London: Routledge, 1998).

Ingold, Tim, *The Perception of the Environment: Essays in Livelihood, Dwelling and Skill* (Abingdon: Routledge, 2000).

Latour, Bruno, *We Have Never Been Modern* (Cambridge, MA: Harvard University Press, 1993).

Levin, David, *The Opening of Vision: Nihilism and the Postmodern Situation* (London: Routledge, 1988).

Lynch, Gordon, *Understanding Theology and Popular Culture* (Oxford: Blackwell, 2005).

Marks, Laura, *The Skin of the Film* (Durham, NC: Duke University Press, 2000).

McAllester Jones, Mary, *Gaston Bachelard Subversive Humanist* (Madison: University of Wisconsin Press, 1991).

McFague, Sallie, *Super, Natural Christians* (London: SCM Press, 1997).

Midgley, Mary, *Wisdom, Information and Wonder: What is Knowledge For?* (London: Routledge, 1999).

Miller, Daniel, *Material Culture and Mass Consumption* (Oxford: Blackwell, 1987).

Miller, Daniel (ed.), *Material Cultures: Why Some Things Matter* (Chicago: Chicago University Press, 1998).

Molotch, Harvey, *Where Stuff Comes From: How Toasters, Toilets, Cars, Computers, and Many Other Things Came to Be as They Are* (New York: Routledge, 2003).

Moore, Thomas, *The Re-enchantment of Everyday Life* (New York: HarperCollins, 1996).

Mulvey, Laura, *Fetishism and Curiosity* (London: British Film Institute, 1996).

Noddings, Nel, *Caring: A Feminine Approach to Ethics and Moral Education* (Los Angeles, CA: University of California Press, 1986).

Norman, Donald, *Emotional Design: Why We Love (or Hate) Everyday Things* (New York: Basic Books, 2004).

Pattison, Stephen, *The Faith of the Managers: When Management Becomes Religion* (London: Cassell, 1997).

Pattison, Stephen, *Seeing things: Deepening Relations with Visual Artefacts* (London: SCM Press, 2007).

Plato, *Timaeus and Critias* (Harmondsworth: Penguin, 1977).

Ritzer, George, *Enchanting a Disenchanted World: Revolutionizing the Means of Consumption* (Thousand Oaks, CA: Pine Forge Press, 1999).

Staniloae, Dumitru, *The Experience of God: Orthodox Dogmatic Theology, Volume II: The World: Creation and Deification* (Brookline, MA: Holy Cross Orthodox Press, 2000).

Tamen, Miguel, *Friends of Interpretable Objects* (Cambridge, MA: Harvard University Press, 2001).

Taussig, Michael, *Mimesis and Alterity: A Particular History of the Senses* (London: Routledge, 1993).

Walker, Stuart, *Sustainable by Design: Explorations in Theory and Practice* (London: Earthscan, 2006).

Walter, Tony, *All You Love is Need* (London: SPCK, 1985).

Woodward, James & Pattison, Stephen (eds), *The Blackwell Reader in Pastoral and Practical Theology* (Oxford: Blackwell, 2000).

Chapter 4

Contesting Martyrdom

Jolyon Mitchell

Introduction

In this chapter I investigate the ways in which martyrdom can become a point of contest. More specifically I will concentrate upon some of the debates which have surrounded three different kinds of killing: the assassination of a politician in Pakistan, the death of soldiers during the Iran–Iraq war and the attacks of suicide bombers in both the West and the Middle East. In the context of these discussions I analyse how various media are used to promote, celebrate and even offer a critique of the claim that these deaths are acts of martyrdom. Elsewhere I have considered the way in which martyrs are made or constructed, investigating the processes of amplification, reiteration, elaboration and reverberation (see Mitchell 2008). In order to understand these processes I concentrated in that discussion primarily upon the way in which different media were used following the execution of a well-known Filipino author, Jose Rizal, in 1896. In the current discussion I will primarily focus upon more recent deaths in predominantly Islamic contexts, considering various kinds of controversies which have emerged around these martyrdoms. In the last few years a number of books and essays have appeared analysing the history and evolution of martyrdom in Islam (see, for example, Pape 2005 and Bloom 2005). While both scholars and journalists have emphasized how certain kinds of martyrdom can be seen as forms of communication (see, for example, Snow 2006), few have considered where, how and why martyrdom has become a point of contest.

Contests over Definitions: A Martyr for Democracy?

Within a few hours of Benazir Bhutto's assassination on 27 December 2007 she was described as a *shaheed* (martyr). Several newspapers in Pakistan used the word 'martyr' in their headlines. For example, *The Post* ran a simple one-word headline: 'Martyred'. Similarly, the Urdu newspaper *Jang* called Bhutto a *shaheed*, while *The Tribune*, which is published from Islamabad and Rawalpindi, provided the following headline: 'Bhutto martyred, God save Pakistan'. National newspapers were reflecting a widespread belief expressed by many of her followers. Supporters of the Pakistan People's Party (PPP), clutching candles, congregated outside the Rawalpindi General Hospital, demanding that it should be renamed the 'Benazir

Bhutto Shaheed Hospital'. Her nephew, Zulfiqar Ali Bhutto, was widely cited as stating: 'She is a shaheed. It is incredibly tragic. She is the first Bhutto *shaheed.*' Others see Benazir Bhutto not as the first Bhutto martyr, but as standing in the tradition of her late father who was executed in 1979, under General Zia's rule. Even Benazir described her father Zulfiqar as a *shaheed.* Only a few months before her death Benazir changed her mind about her own burial site, requesting to be buried alongside her father in his domed mausoleum. For many followers it has become a martyr's shrine. Both in and outside Pakistan other, more makeshift, shrines have been set up (see Phillips 2007).

The claim by a PPP official, Rehman Malik, that 'She has been martyred' was widely cited in news reports around the world.[1] Many Western journalists reiterated such statements in their headlines or reports, describing how Pakistan was mourning Benazir Bhutto 'the martyr' (Wilkinson 2007). Even vociferous critics of her life asserted that she would be of 'greater use' to Pakistan 'as a martyr' (Peters 2007). In the midst of such claims, the news story itself evolved rapidly. Some discussions went beyond descriptions of her martyrdom and debated how she was actually assassinated or sought to understand why the way in which she was killed mattered. Many suggested that, if she was shot, at best it underlined the lack of effective government protection or at worst indicated government complicity in her assassination. Several commentators went further, suggesting that it was highly significant whether she was killed by a person or by an accident, as this would determine whether she could become a martyr. One contributor to a web discussion suggested that 'if she was killed by banging her head against the frame of the sunroof it would be considered an accident and she would not be considered a martyr. Although this seems trivial to Westerners, it makes a huge difference to Muslims.'[2]

Other writers seemed unperturbed by these discussions, claiming she was a 'martyr of freedom'[3] or a 'martyr for democracy'.[4] Another commentator developed this claim further: he saw Benazir as a 'reluctant martyr', who by 'Dying a violent, untimely and unexpected death', had 'joined the ranks of those political figures whose legacy in death is very different from the role they actually

---

[1]   Of dozens of reports which drew upon the Associated Press's report, see for example: http://abcnews.go.com/International/story?id=4055506 [access date 26 May 2008].

[2]   This was one of twelve answers provided to the question: 'Why does it matter exactly what killed Bhutto?' The answer provided by (ecvkennethmassie) claimed: 'That is why the government of Pakistan is saying this. They know that the people will revolt and possibly overthrow the government if She [*sic*] is considered a Martyr', http://answers.yahoo.com/question/index?qid=20071229062443AAUSAfb&show=7 [access date 26 May 2008].

[3]   See Bahraini blogger *Hayat* (Ar): http://hayatblog.blogspot.com/2007/12/blog-post_1312.html [access date 26 May 2008].

[4]   See www.cynicsunlimited.com/2007/12/27/benazir-bhutto-martyr-for-democracy/ [access date 26 May 2008].

played in life'.[5] While in life she 'was an inconsistent democrat', in death she 'has become the martyr of democracy and social justice'.[6] These claims raise the question of what *kind* of martyr Benazir is becoming. Describing her as a *shaheed*, a term with a long religious history, especially within Shi'ite Islam (see, for example, Cook 2007), is very different from describing her as a 'martyr for democracy'. Benazir herself appeared to be not as reluctant a martyr as sometimes suggested. In an interview with *Time* magazine in November 2007 she claimed: 'I am ready to die for my country' (Baker 2007).

It is clear from this brief discussion of accounts following Bhutto's assassination that she will be widely remembered as a martyr. One striking image appeared soon after her death: in a black and white portrait, she is wearing a white scarf and stares out of the frame. The monochrome colours are interrupted by her dark red lipstick and six letters above: 'Martyr'. The final 'r' is blood red, brighter even than the colour of the lipstick. The point of contest remains what kind of martyr she will become: a martyr for freedom and democracy or a martyr for God and the country of her birth? This dichotomy is, of course, a false one. For some the story of her death will not only be amplified and regularly reiterated, it will also be elaborated and, given the confusing circumstances, endlessly debated. These reverberations are already to be found in countless sites on the World Wide Web.

Contests over Necessity: Soldiers as Martyrs?

Virtual spaces are by no means the only place where memorials to martyrs are to be found. Driving through Iran it is hard to avoid encountering memorials to those killed during the eight-year Iran–Iraq war (1980–88), which claimed as many as one million Iranian lives (Rajaee 1993: 206). There are wall portraits, posters, shrines, cemeteries in every province of Iran. Our taxi driver in the city of Shiraz, for example, himself a war veteran, drew our attention to several large posters of Iranian pilots, including pictures of their planes and their names in Persian (Farsi). These represent a drop in the ocean of countless reminders of those killed in action during the Iran–Iraq war. The ubiquity of these memorials can be discerned by studying a set of 45 CD-ROMS, produced by the Iranian government, which preserve photographs, posters, printed documents, films, documentaries, poems and songs.[7] They provide a rich resource for understanding the extensive propaganda which emerged supporting the Islamic Republic of Iran's stand against Iraq. What is particularly striking is how the war is regularly depicted as a 'holy defence' or promoted in religious terms. Soldiers killed in action are repeatedly referred to

---

[5]   www.theaustralian.news.com.au/story/0,25197,22987921-7583,00.html [access date 26 May 2008].

[6]   Ibid.

[7]   This is available at the International Institute of Social History, Amsterdam, with more details at www.iisg.nl/archives/en/files/w/10930603full.php [access date 26 May 2008].

as martyrs or depicted as martyrs. There are also countless pictures of martyrs' graveyards, memorials and museums, now located all over Iran.

In Iran, Western journalists and writers tend to focus on accessible memorials, such as the martyrs' cemetery, which is about half an hour south-west of the centre of Tehran. The *Behesht-eZahra* cemetery, of which the martyrs' cemetery is only a part, consists of thousands of gravestones, for those who were killed not only during the Iran–Iraq war, but also in the 1979 revolution. While some of the gravestones have only the picture of a dove and 'unknown' engraved in Persian, many have more elaborate collections preserved in glass cabinets. These consist of fading photographs, plastic flowers or other tattered mementoes. In a vivid account entitled 'Iranian Lessons' for *The New York Times Magazine*, Michael Ignatieff describes this space as a 'vast city of the dead', with 'little shrines' that 'seem to go on forever, each one a family's attempt to confer immortality on some young man who died in the trenches at a place like Khorramshahr, the pinnacle of Iranian resistance to the Iraqi invaders' (17 July 2005: I).[8] Many of the cabinets also include a copy of the martyr's Qur'an, prayer beads and an Iranian flag. Through these simple symbols, as so often in Iran, the Islamic faith and the nation are brought closely together.

A number of Western journalists have visited and used the graveyard in Tehran as the setting for their reports. For example, in one of a series of reports from Iran, the web journalist Kevin Sites both describes and shows this cemetery through a photo essay (2006). He introduces his readers to two mothers who both lost sons in the Iran–Iraq war. On the one hand there is Iran Allahkarami, who states that 'It was for God's satisfaction ...' as 'our enemies were attacking our country. I say this on behalf of all martyrs' mothers. I'm not angered by the death of my sons'. Sites contrasts this description with Iran's friend Maryam Tavaghai, 'who has expressed misgivings about the war and the loss of her son, Hooshang'. He was a conscript, not a volunteer. In a couple of paragraphs Sites turns even the martyrs' cemetery into a site of contest. Admittedly, while these mothers may debate the rightness of the war, they are depicted as representative of a significant body of opinion in Iran who believes martyrdom to be a highly honoured status. Sites's report then quotes the spokesperson of a new organization, *The Commemoration of Martyrs*, which is said to recruit hundreds of volunteers to act as suicide bombers against Israel. The swift move from discussing soldiers who fell in war as martyrs to describing volunteers who will kill themselves as martyrs is noteworthy, as it reflects the common blurring between different kinds of martyrdom. I will return to this observation later when I consider debates about suicide bombing.

With the advent of web logs and other interactive websites, Western tourists and other visitors to the martyrs' cemeteries are able to record and make public their own personal responses. Some use their photographs to support their assertions and others use their descriptions to make a rhetorical point. For example, one travel

---

[8]   www.nytimes.com/2005/07/17/magazine/17IRAN.html?_r=2&oref=slogin&oref=s login [access date 26 May 2008].

review of this cemetery by a British woman had the following headline: 'War! What is it good for? Absolutely NOTHING—say it again!'[9] More experienced Western journalists also use their descriptions of the war cemeteries to contest the value or interpretation of such martyrdoms. Robert Fisk's article on 'Voices from the martyrs' cemetery' describes how he encountered a number of Iranian men at the cemetery, such as Mushtara Yussefi, who asserted that 'My dead father and brother fought for the *velayat e-faqih* (*sic*) ... for the Imam's Islamic republic'[10] (Fisk 2000) and for the maintenance of specific ways of life. Fisk explained that the '*velayat e-faqih* is the institution of the Supreme Guide—now Ayatollah Ali Khamenei' and then outlines his own personal response: 'I am stunned by all this. Did the dead of Behesht Zahra, did the men whose bones are still crated up here from the old battlefields, really sacrifice themselves to keep Iran's women in chadors, to ensure that no real democracy could flourish amid the autocratic clergy loyal to Khomeini? Was it for this they died?' Even as an outsider Fisk questions the way in which these deaths were and are being used in Iran.[11]

The martyrs' cemetery in Tehran is not the only memorial to become a site of contest. Christopher de Bellaigue's memoir draws its title from the martyrs' cemetery in Isfahan (Esfahan), which houses the remains of at least seven thousand men killed during the Iran–Iraq war: *The Rose Garden of Martyrs* (2005). This account of life in Iran draws together de Bellaigue's personal experiences as a Tehran-based British journalist and Iran's long and complex history. Reading his book it is hard not to reflect upon the origins, motivations and promoters of martyrdom in Iran. De Bellaigue starts the book by taking his readers to Karbala, the site where Muhammad's grandson, Hussein (or al-Husain), is believed by many Shi'ites to have been killed by the Sunni caliph Yazid in 680 AD. His father Ali may have been the Prophet's son-in-law and cousin, but he was assassinated in the mosque of Kufa (661). Like his father's murder, Hussein's death is commonly seen within Shi'ism as a founding martyrdom. The events surrounding the deaths are commonly re-enacted through colourful passion plays (*ta'ziya*). The stories of Hussein and Ali have become powerful narratives which are regularly amplified, repeated and elaborated upon. According to Malise Ruthven, 'the "massacre" of Karbala, a fight between rival clans that only lasts a day and results in the death of a few dozen dead, becomes the defining myth of Shi'ism, an emblem

---

[9] www.dooyoo.co.uk/destinations-international/martyrs-cemetery-tehran-iran/1044805/ [access date 26 May 2008]. This review appears at another travel review site, but with a different headline: 'A peaceful reminder of a turbulent past', a review by koshka on Martyrs' Cemetery, Tehran, 18 January 2007, http://travel.ciao.co.uk/Martyrs_Cemetery_Tehran__6610012 [access date 26 May 2008].

[10] Note that *velayat e-faqih* should be *velayat-e faqih*.

[11] Fisk may be underestimating the pull of the concept of *velayat-e faqih*, 'government of/by the Jurist', a term which some scholars claim Khomini made notorious through the way that he 'instituted' it and promoted a kind of 'reversal of the Shi'i tradition of staying politically underground' (Christian Lange, personal note January 2008).

of suffering and martyrdom' (1997: 55). While Ruthven may be downplaying the political significance of the killing at Karbala, it is useful to underline how in most Shi'ite villages on the anniversary of Hussein's death, many flagellants will process through the streets punishing themselves for 'the betraying of the Prophet's grandson' (ibid.). Hussein is widely referred to as 'Chief of Martyrs' and his picture is to be found in many of the graveyard cabinets. The significance of Hussein and Ali's lives and deaths over 1,300 years ago is of course contested beyond Shi'ite Islam, especially within the Sunni tradition. Nevertheless, in a country such as Iran, of which over 90 per cent of the population are Shi'a, their stories hold a significant grasp over many people's imagination.

The power of their stories can be seen in Fen Montaigne's extended *National Geographic* report on Iran (1999). This included an interview with Habib Eqbalpour, aged 70, and his wife, Zinat Parvaresh, aged 63. They lost two of their sons (one 17 and the other 21) in the Iran–Iraq war, but were clearly proud of the sacrifice their two children had made: 'We are proud we lost our children ... My sons are following in the path of Imam Husayn [Hussein], and when they are in the other world, they are helped by Imam Husayn [Hussein].' Like others who lost family members in the Iran–Iraq war, several 'government foundations, including *The Martyrs' Foundation*, provide them with a free apartment and pay them a stipend of 360,000 rials a month (about $120)'. While the financial support is valued, they are clearly proud that their sons were martyrs standing in the tradition of a founding martyr: Hussein.

Iran, however, does not have the monopoly of martyrs' cemeteries within Shi'ism. For example, following the American attack on insurgents in Fallujah, Iraq, in 2004, a football pitch was transformed into a burial ground, where as many as 500 local fighters were buried. This has been described as 'The Martyrs' Cemetery'; it has a sign outside which says: 'This cemetery is given by the people of Fallujah to the heroic martyrs of the battle against the Americans, and to the martyrs of the *Jihadi* liberations against the Americans, assigned and approved by the Mujahideen Shura council in Fallujah' (Fadhil 2005). Fallujah is a predominantly Sunni city, so most of those killed were Sunni Moslems. Even the road leading up to the cemetery has supposedly been renamed 'Martyrs' Cemetery Road'. It is not surprising that the claims that the fighters were martyrs are contested by other local Iraqis and by the Americans. Martyrs' cemeteries are also now to be found in Afghanistan and have become sites of devotion and controversy. Consider the burial site of over 70 Arab and foreign fighters and their families in the Southern Afghan city of Kandahar. For some locals this has become not only the resting place for these 70 'martyrs' who were killed by American bombing in 2001, but also a cemetery with miraculous healing properties. A member of the BBC's Pashto service subtly contested this belief in a recent account of how it has become a centre of pilgrimage. The report concludes: 'In a country with high unemployment and low literacy rates, it does not seem surprising that shrines are still the only hope for many sick and needy people' (Azami 2008).

In this section I have considered how soldiers are portrayed and remembered as martyrs. We have seen how different media are used to amplify and preserve the memories of such martyrs. I have also shown how the designation of 'martyr' is not always clear cut, nor without controversy. Such controversies are not new and they illustrate how the term can become a magnet for controversy. While I have primarily concentrated upon 'martyrs' from the Iran–Iraq war, claiming soldiers as martyrs is not a phenomenon found only in Islam. During the Middle Ages within the Christian tradition, it was not uncommon for the crusaders to be designated as 'martyrs' (Riley-Smith 1986: 152; see also Smith 1997). The executed leaders of the Irish Easter Rising in Dublin were also widely described in Ireland as 'martyrs' (see Fisk 2006). In particular, those arrested and then executed in the stone-breakers' yard in Kilmainham jail, Dublin, were soon venerated as martyrs. In the same year, one of the less well known English First World War poets, Robert Nichols, wrote 'The Last Salute' while serving at Ypres in 1916, claiming that even though he may die anonymous and alone, 'the soldier is the Martyr of a nation' (Osborne 1917).[12] It was not long after the end of the First World War that the value and necessity of such martyrdoms were being contested. Similarly for those commemorating the fallen of the Iran–Iraq war, such a description would not be full enough. As we have seen, such fighters are commonly described as far more than simply martyrs of a nation.[13]

Contests over Legitimacy: Suicide Bombers as Martyrs?

Sean Batty & Kevin Toulis's documentary account, *The Cult of the Suicide Bomber* (2005), makes a connection between soldiers as martyrs and the development of the popularity of using suicide bombers as a tool of war. The argument outlined in this documentary is more carefully developed than the connection hinted at by Kevin Sites and briefly discussed in an earlier section. For the presenter Robert Baer, a former CIA agent based in the Middle East and the man upon whom George Clooney's character was supposedly based in the feature film *Syriana* (Stephen Gagham 2005), the cult of the suicide bomber finds its origins in the Iran–Iraq war. More specifically, Baer claims that 'the world's first suicide bomber', was a 13-year-old Iranian, Hossein Fahmideh, who blew himself up under the treads of an enemy tank in 1980. Baer visits both the boy's highly adorned grave, also at *Behesht-e-Zahra* cemetery, and the boy's family, who like many in Iran see him as a hero. His image, like so many other Iranian martyrs, has been widely

---

[12]   This is one of nine poems from the 'In Memoriam' section and is also available at www.firstworldwar.com/poetsandprose/mia_lastsalute.htm [access date 26 May 2008].

[13]   There is not space in this essay to reflect on the question of devotion to the martyr, which appears less pronounced in many Sunni Islamic contexts than in some Christian settings, where the medieval custom of veneration of the martyrs' relics continues to this day.

disseminated. In Iran he may be portrayed as a brave soldier, but this documentary implies that he should be seen as a prototype suicide bomber.

In even more forceful terms than Kevin Sites, Baer argues against what he has discovered through researching this programme. In other words he is not afraid of stepping off the apparently objective fence of journalism to make a series of connected assertions. These merit quoting extensively:

> Like all cults, the cult of suicide bombing feeds upon itself. Log on to the internet or visit a militant Islamic bookshop and within a few minutes you will find enough inspiration in CDs, ranting sermons, DVDs, for a hundred suicide bombs. It swirls across the Islamic world as an expression of rage against the West for the invasion of Iraq, support for Israel, and for Western dominance of the world economy ... Amid the rage is the glorification of martyrdom. In a Gaza mosque I saw 'official certificates of martyrdom' being handed out like graduation diplomas to the families of suicide bombers. (Baer 2005)

Notice how Baer moves from describing a 'militant Islamic bookshop' to the whole 'Islamic world', creating the sense of an avalanche of rage expressed through glorifying suicide attacks. Notice also how he highlights the range of media that are employed to promote seeing suicide bombing as a form of martyrdom. This is a point reinforced by Anne Marie Oliver & Paul F. Steinberg's *The Road to Martyrs' Square: A Journey into the World of the Suicide Bomber*, which explores the 'cult of martyrdom in the underground media of the *intifada*', mostly in the Gaza Strip during the early 1990s (2004). They not only interviewed a failed suicide bomber, but they also gathered audiocassettes, videotapes, posters and other street media in over one hundred towns in Gaza and the West Bank. This book provides a valuable insight into a culture which encourages the embrace and celebration of death through martyrdoms which will kill the enemy.

More recently, scholars such as Robert Pape, in *Dying to Win: The Strategic Logic of Suicide Terrorism* (2005) and Mia Bloom, in *Dying to Kill: The Allure of Suicide Terror* (2005), have gone beyond purely religious or theological explanations for what motivates suicide bombers. While some groups clearly hope to increase news coverage of their cause, attract new followers, inspire fear among the wider public and even compete with other terrorist groups, there are other political goals. In the face of overwhelming force and power it may be perceived as one of the few remaining options available to comparatively weak organizations. Pape draws upon his extensive database of suicide bombing and a reading of the history of suicide attacks as well as the contemporary expressions of the current phenomenon to conclude that suicide terrorism 'is mainly a response to foreign occupation' (2005: 23; see also 45). For Pape a suicide attack is an 'extreme strategy for national liberation' (ibid.: 80).

Such a conclusion is contested, with some scholars emphasizing the religious roots and justifications of what are described not as 'suicide attacks', but 'martyrdom operations'. While suicide is explicitly prohibited in Islam (Qur'an

2:195, 4:429), some contemporary Muslim scholars see 'self-sacrificing' acts or 'martyrdom operations' as justifiable (see, for example, Cook 2005: esp. 128–61). Many different media, from books and pamphlets to television programmes and numerous web sites, are employed to promote these and other views. Attacks upon Iraqi Shi'ites by Iraqi Sunnis may be criticized in both Arabic and Western news reports, but on some web sites they are justified and celebrated. In such contexts, such acts are sometimes interpreted as going beyond purely 'a response to a foreign occupation'—as acts of religious obedience. It is noteworthy that following the American invasion of Iraq in 2003, Shi'a celebrations leading up to the Ashura festival, marking the anniversary of Hussein's death, have become occasions for suicide bomb attacks, presumed to be carried out by Sunni radicals intent on inciting further divisions.[14] Such attacks illustrate how certain Sunnis have also embraced martyrdom suicide operations, which—according to some scholars—is a comparatively recent phenomenon within Sunni Islam.[15]

Contesting 'Martyrdom' through the Web

While many suicide attacks regularly receive vociferous support as well as redefinition as 'martyrdom operations', on the web there are many examples of Muslims discussing the appropriateness and legitimacy of suicide attacks. These discussions take place beyond what Kevin Reinhart describes as the 'Muslim academy', in more informal digital settings. This is an example of what he describes as the 'Protestantization of Islam', where the 'laity' plays an active role in discussing the ethics of suicide bombings/martyrdom attacks (Reinhart 2008: 172–8). Following the attacks on Manhattan in September 2001, there were diverse reactions within 'Cyber Islamic Environments' where a few extremists celebrated, while many others unequivocally condemned them on religious grounds (Bunt 2003: 67–123).[16] As with every other diverse global religious tradition, rigorous discussions regularly take place on the web, with participants drawing upon a range of translated Muslim scriptures and authorities, including what Reinhart calls the 'Independent Magesterium'. For example, the Egyptian Sunni scholar Yusuf al-Qaradawi, who issued a *fatwa* (a religious edict to be followed voluntarily) about suicide bombing, is frequently cited on the web either as an authority for or an example of his support of suicide bombing in Palestine: 'Allah Almighty is just; through his infinite wisdom he has given the weak a weapon the strong do not have

---

[14]   See, for example, 'Shia worshippers killed in Iraq', at BBC News: http://news.bbc. co.uk/2/hi/middle_east/7194462.stm [access date 26 May 2008].

[15]   Cook (2005: 143–4). Cook also claims that in 'Sunni Islam examples of suicidal attacks are rare prior to the early 1990s'. For an example of martyrs from within the Sunni tradition in another setting, see Dale (1980).

[16]   For other research on Islamic use of the web see Bunt (2000; 2004)

and that is their ability to turn their bodies into bombs as Palestinians do.'[17] The way in which Qaradawi's pronouncements are used is significant, illustrating how not only members of the 'Islamic academy's' readings but also individual Islamic interpretations are becoming increasingly common on the web. For Reinhart, 'the popularization, Protestestantization, or even democratization of Islamic judgment is perhaps the single most significant change in contemporary Islamic intellectual life' (2008: 178).

These kinds of virtual debates draw not only on texts, but also on images. Elsewhere I have described the extraordinary success of the 'We are not afraid' site in the wake of the July 2005 London bombings (see Mitchell 2006).[18] Several other sites were created. One of the most interesting was the Islamic site 'Not in the name of peace' also set up only a few days after 7 July. The site's creator is a young British Muslim, Muhammad Ridha Payne. His opening statement to the site is passionate: 'We need to show these maniacs that none of us think what they are doing is right, justified or Islamically based.' Payne believes that 'Islam has very clear guidelines as to what is right and what is wrong.' He acknowledges that 'Of course we all feel aggrieved by actions in Afghanistan, Iraq and Palestine but this does not give anyone the right to kill further innocent people.'[19] The site attracted far fewer images than 'We are not afraid' and appears to have now been taken off the web, but nonetheless the several dozen pictures posted make powerful points. Some seek to reassure viewers. For instance, the words 'Don't Panic I'm Islamic' surround a man as he steps out of his British-looking house. He is wearing a simple black and white skull cap, pointing one finger and gently smiling. There is nothing threatening about his appearance. These images stand in sharp contrast to the more widely disseminated images taken from 'martyrdom videos', where bombers leave the equivalent of a video suicide note justifying their actions. There is nothing threatening in another image, a groomed young Asian-looking man, this time sitting on rocks with a harbour in the background: 'Don't EXPLODE, STRIKE a POSE! ... because terrorism is *never* pretty.' The comic twist here is found in several other postings such as one of a baby and the statement: 'I want to grow up not blow up.'

---

[17]   See, for example: Magdi Abdelhadi, 'Controversial Preacher with Star Status', BBC News, 7 July 2004, http://news.bbc.co.uk/1/hi/uk/3874893.stm [access date 26 May 2008]. See also Reinhart's translation of Qaradawi, 'On martyrdom Acts': 'The youth who defend their land—the land of Islam—and their religion and their honour and their religious community do not commit suicide: what they do is the farthest thing possible from a suicide. They are true martyrs, exerting their spirits willingly in the way of God. So long as their intention is towards God, and as long as they are compelled to this course by the terrorism of the enemies of God who persist in their enmity and who are deluded by their power and the support of the Great Power that they have' (Reinhardt 2008: 179).

[18]   Part of the following section is drawn upon and adapted from the final part of Mitchell (2006).

[19]   www.notinthenameofpeace.com/?p=55 is now no longer available on the web.

There are more serious religious depictions, from individuals reading sacred texts to crowds praying to God. A young girl in a white robe kneeling on a prayer mat with supplicatory hands and an open Qur'an in front of her is accompanied by a phrase that through repetition emphasizes the following phrase: 'Not in the name [new line] the name of Islam.' In a different picture, a young man is kneeling reading a Qur'an: 'Seek knowledge not war.' People in prayer are found in other pictures. For instance, above two men kneeling with heads touching the prayer carpet of a mosque are the words: 'the proverb says "slaughter your ego with the dagger of self-discipline"', below them three words are added: 'not slaughter people'. In another picture of rows of men at prayer, nearly fifty Muslims kneel; over the front row is the exhortation typed in white: 'stop the slaying and get down to some praying'. There is also a picture from Mecca with thousands of pilgrims at prayer with the words 'not in our names' superimposed in small white letters at the bottom of the photograph. Among a number of Shi'ite Muslim young people I spoke with in Tehran about these sites (Iran, November 2005), it was this image which proved most popular. They were more critical of the images described above which identified terrorism with Islam, suggesting that these images should be addressed against 'Talibanism', not Islam as a whole.

On the 'We are not afraid' site several contributors had digitally daubed words upon a photograph of the new dividing wall in Israel or at least a wall that looks strikingly similar to it. This image is recycled again on the 'Not in the name of peace' site, but is used for more explicitly religious reasons. The first line states 'Islam means peace'. The second, 'not in the name of Islam'. The same sentiments are expressed on a skilful adaptation of a London street sign found on the 'We are not afraid' site. The WNA team were so impressed they did something they very rarely do: comment on the image. 'We received this terrific photo along with a link to an online petition which condemns terrorist acts committed in the name of Islam, which can be found and signed here. We urge people to check it out!' On the connected site a similar image is to be found, along with a quote from *The Holy Quran* (5:32) which is in English: '... to kill one person is like killing the whole of mankind ... And to give life to one person is like giving life to the whole of mankind.' Many of these images assert that 'true' Islam is a peaceful and life-bringing faith. One overhead shot of a man apparently rapidly rotating and reading the Qur'an is overlaid with the claim: 'Islam "is a way of life" NOT "a way of death".' 'Life' is written in green and 'death' in red.

While it is no surprise that images connected with Islam dominate this site, it is not confined entirely to images of Muslims. One posting has a picture of Pope John Paul II respectfully kissing a large green Qur'an in the presence of a Muslim religious leader. The heading is 'united we can defeat terror'. Another posting is a photograph of U2 playing at the Arrowhead Pond arena in Anaheim, California, on 1 April 2005. In the original picture, projected in red lines above the band is the word 'Coexist'. This was created with a combination of normal letters and the major religious symbols of Islam (crescent in place of 'c'), Judaism (star in place of 'x') and Christianity (cross in place of 't'). The inspiration for this powerful linguistic image was drawn from graffiti that the lead singer Bono saw somewhere in the Midwest of the USA. Notice how the added copy which frames the image reinforces what the picture itself communicates: 'All GOD'S people MUST and U2 can … coexist!' Taken together, the use of the pictures of John Paul II kissing the Qur'an and U2 performing beneath this single word, partly created by religious symbols, are examples of how visual signs are recycled in new contexts to promote peace within and between religions.

Conclusion

In this chapter I have suggested that in certain contexts martyrdom is a highly contested term. There has not been space to consider how the deaths of children or innocents in war are sometimes described as martyrdoms.[20] Nor has there been the chance to analyse how a film such as *Paradise Now* (Hany Abu-Assad, 2005) depicts the contests surrounding the act of suicide bombing. I have also avoided entering into the discussions about the linguistic and theological evolution of the term in Islam. The actual word has clearly gone through many different phases, with its meaning expanding and contracting in different contexts. The contests that I have described stand in contrast to the supposedly classical view that *anyone* who died as a believer could be seen as a martyr (see, for example, Cook 2007). While these issues are beyond the scope of the current discussion, it is helpful to also be reminded of the importance of research which seeks to understand what *shaheed* actually means to different Muslims today. Further questions for research also include: What kinds of emotions, mythical associations or other images does the term evoke among Muslims? How might a genealogy of the term *shaheed* inform developing a clearer understanding of what 'martyrdom' currently means to different Muslims?

My intention has been to demonstrate how the term 'martyrdom' is currently used in a range of different ways, which reflect how descriptions of a shocking reality, whether the assassination of a political leader, the death of a soldier or the attack of a suicide bomber, are themselves highly contested. I have used a range of examples to highlight three different kinds of contest about martyrdom: firstly, contests over definition and description; secondly, contests over value and necessity; and thirdly, contests over legitimacy and practice. We have seen how web discussions have allowed such contests to become more global and free-floating, with a wide range of resources and authorities employed. The apparent democratization of communication through the internet has also helped to ensure the further fragmentation of these contests. The ability of the web to preserve and make easily accessible newspaper stories and amateur images related to martyrdom has facilitated even more lively global conversations. The memorable posting of images and opinions in the shadows of the London bombings is particularly

---

[20]   See for example the brief discussion of the children's deaths and their description as martyrs at Qana, Lebanon (Mitchell 2007: 1, 271–3).

noteworthy. Around the world, Muslims and Christians alike are expressing their strongly held beliefs in the face of violence through modern media in ways which would be hard to imagine one hundred years ago. Understanding these processes is important not simply for deepening understanding of the role of different media in these conversations, but also for creating spaces where different religious traditions can learn to co-exist.

References

Azami, Dawood, 'Kandhar's Cemetery of Miracles', 17 January 2008, http://news. bbc.co.uk/2/hi/south_asia/7193579.stm [access date 26 May 2008].

Baer, Robert, 'This Deadly Virus', *The Observer*, 7 August 2005, www.guardian. co.uk/attackonlondon/comment/story/0,1544259,00.html [access date 26 May 2008].

Baker, Aryn, 'Making a Martyr of Bhutto', *Time*, 27 December 2007, www.time. com/time/world/article/0,8599,1698472,00.html [access date 26 May 2008].

Bloom, Mia, *Dying to Kill: The Allure of Suicide Terror* (New York: Columbia University Press, 2005).

Bunt, Gary R., *Virtually Islamic: Computer-Mediated Communication and Cyber Islamic Environments* (Cardiff: University of Wales Press, 2000).

Bunt, Gary R., *Islam in the Digital Age: E-Jihad, Online Fatwas and Cyber Islamic Environments* (London: Pluto Press, 2003).

Bunt, Gary R., '"Rip. Burn. Pray": Islamic Expression Online', in Lorne L. Dawson & Douglas E. Cowan (eds), *Religion Online: Finding Faith on the Internet* (London: Routledge, 2004): 123–34.

Cook, David, *Understanding Jihad* (Berkeley: University of California Press, 2005).

Cook, David, *Martyrdom in Islam* (Cambridge: Cambridge University Press, 2007).

Dale, Stephen, *Islamic Society on the South Asian Frontier: The Mappilas of Malabar* (Oxford: Oxford University Press, 1980).

de Bellaigue, Christopher, *The Rose Garden of Martyrs* (New York: HarperCollins, 2005).

Fadhil, Ali, 'City of Ghosts', *The Guardian*, 11 January 2005, www.guardian. co.uk/Iraq/Story/0,1387460,00.html [access date 26 May 2008].

Fisk, Robert, 'Voices from the Martyrs' Cemetery', *The Independent*, 27 February 2000, http://findarticles.com/p/articles/mi_qn4158/is_20000227/ai_n1429285 [access date 26 May 2008].

Fisk, Robert, 'Traitors, Martyrs or Just Brave Men', *The Independent*, 15 April 2006, www.independent.co.uk/news/fisk/robert-fisk-traitors-martyrs-or-just-brave-men-474188.html [access date 26 May 2006].

Ignatieff, Michael, 'Iranian Lessons', *The New York Times Magazine*, 17 July 2005, www.nytimes.com/2005/07/17/magazine/17IRAN.html?_r=2&oref=sl ogin&oref=slogin [access date 26 May 2008].

Mitchell, Jolyon, 'Posting Images on the Web: The Creative Viewer and Non-Violent Resistance Against Terrorism', *Material Religion*, 2/2 (July 2006): 4–31.

Mitchell, Jolyon, *Media Violence and Christian Ethics* (Cambridge: Cambridge University Press, 2007).

Mitchell, Jolyon, 'Narrative', in David Morgan (ed.), *Key Words for Media, Religion and Culture* (London: Routledge, 2008): 123–35.

Montaigne, Fen, 'Iran: Testing the Waters of Reform', *National Geographic*, July 1999, www.nationalgeographic.com/ngm/9907/fngm/index.html [access date 26 May 2008].

Oliver, Anne Marie & Steinberg, Paul F., *The Road to Martyrs' Square: A Journey into the World of the Suicide Bomber* (Oxford: Oxford University Press, 2004).

Osborne, E.B. (ed.), *The Muse in Arms* (London: John Murray, 1917).

Pape, Robert, *Dying to Win: The Strategic Logic of Suicide Terrorism* (New York, Random House, 2005).

Peters, Ralph, 'Bhutto of Greater Use as a Martyr', *The Australian*, 31 December 2007, www.theaustralian.news.com.au/story/0,25197,22987921-7583,00.html [access date 26 May 2008].

Phillips, Adam, 'Bhutto Murder Hits Hard in New York City's "Little Pakistan"', *Voice of America*, 30 December 2007, www.voanews.com/english/2007-12-30-voa6.cfm [access date 26 May 2008].

Rajaee, Farhang, *The Iran–Iraq War: The Politics of Aggression* (Gainesville: University Press of Florida, 1993).

Reinhart, A. Kevin, 'Legitimacy and Authority in Islamic Discussions of Martyrdom Operations/Suicide Bombings', in David Linnan (ed.), *Enemy Combatants, Terrorism, and Armed Conflict Law: A Guide to the Issues* (Praeger: Westport, CT, forthcoming 2008): 167–83.

Riley-Smith, Jonathan, *The First Crusade and the Idea of Crusading* (Philadelphia: University of Pennsylvania Press, 1986).

Ruthven, Malise, *Islam: A Very Short Introduction* (Oxford: Oxford University Press, 1997).

Sites, Kevin, 'All My Fathers, All My Sons', 16 January 2006, Yahoo News Site, http://hotzone.yahoo.com/b/hotzone/blogs2234 [access date 26 May 2008].

Smith, Lacey Baldwin, *Fools, Martyrs, Traitors: The Story of Martyrdom in the Western World* (New York: Alfred Knopf, 1997).

Snow, Jonathan L., 'Hamas is Using its Media Properties to Back Terrorists and Incite Violence', *The Philadelphia Inquirer*, 17 November 2006.

Wilkinson, Isambard, 'Pakistan Mourns Benazir Bhutto "the martyr"', *Sunday Times*, 30 December 2007, www.telegraph.co.uk/news/worldnews/1573963/Pakistan-mourns-Benazir-Bhutto-'the-martyr'.html [access date 26 May 2008].

Chapter 5

Religionless in Seattle

Michael W. DeLashmutt

Introduction

> This is my computer. There are many like it, but this one is mine. My computer
> is my best friend. It is my life. I must master it, as I must master my life. Without
> me, my computer is useless. Without my computer, I am useless. (Coupland
> 1996: 104–5)

Douglas Coupland's *MicroSerfs* tells the story of a group of mid-1990s information
technology (IT) workers living in the eastern suburbs of Seattle in Washington
State. Based loosely around the real life experiences of Microsoft employees,
this paradigmatic novel frames the life of the dot-com era computer geek with
remarkable precision. Spending hours a day staring blindly into their computer
monitors, the computer science (CS) professionals gladly exchange their social
lives, their families, and at times their health, for writing code for their enigmatic
boss 'Bill'. There is an almost religious devotion to IT that is evinced by most of
Coupland's characters; for them personal identity has become utterly subsumed
under their all-encompassing concern for working in the IT industry. Hence the
quote, 'Without my computer, I am useless.'

For Coupland's characters, technology has become a central facet in the
construction of self-identity and personal values. Indeed, it is a commonly posited
thesis (see below) that technology—and in this case, IT—can pose significant
challenges to values, both social and religious. In this chapter, I wish to test this
thesis and determine the extent of IT's impact on the religious self-identity of IT
workers, who, like those in Coupland's *MicroSerfs*, seek to master their computers
as they master their lives. This chapter will endeavour to tap into the professional
computer geek sub-culture to determine if working within a computer profession
and living within a computer savvy culture necessarily results in the creation of a
pseudo-theological worldview which challenges or replaces traditional religious
beliefs and practices. I will explore these questions within the context of the
Pacific Northwest region of the United States, with particular focus on the Seattle
metropolitan area.[1]

---

[1]   My study makes use of data from the U.S. Census Bureau, the U.S. Department
of Labor, Bureau of Labor Statistics, the North American Religion Atlas (NARA), the
2001 American Religious Identification Survey (ARIS), and the 2000 National Surveys of

Given the confluence of a low self-selection for religious identity in Seattle and the region's high rate of employment within the IT industry (not to mention the technological ethos of the area, which is difficult to measure), it seems like an apt location to investigate if one's involvement within the IT and CS industry informs one's religious self-identity. I will begin by offering a brief survey of key literature, which outlines the potential relationship between theology and technology, in order to provide a basic framework for what I call 'techno-theology'. Following this, I hope to determine if techno-theologies are at play within the IT culture of the Pacific Northwest by providing an overview of the region's religious and vocational landscape. This will be done in three phases. Firstly, I will correlate national employment statistics with regional religious demographics in order to determine if regions with unusually high percentages of CS workers have a disproportionately low rate of religious affiliation. Secondly, I will provide a narrative profile of my own experiences as a participant observer working as an IT professional at a Seattle internet media company. Thirdly, I will explore the relationship between religion and technology described in three case studies of technology workers. I will then reflect on the way this kind of theological, historical, vocational and cultural analysis can contribute to the work of Christian ministry in the region.

Pursuing Techno-Theology

The role played by IT in contemporary life is undeniably significant. That most of us scarcely understand the machinations behind the vast global networks of information which we use in our daily lives (whether when flicking on the TV, checking e-mail, paying our bills or buying a sandwich with our credit cards at a local shop) says something about both the ubiquity of IT and its relative transparency to those who casually use it. Public and private corporations spend billions of dollars a year to update IT infrastructures in order to stay on the 'bleeding edge' of technology. In education, universities are under constant pressure to maintain the appearance of technological savvy to attract students who expect wireless internet around every corner, online course materials and technically competent lecturers. Because IT is both all around us and yet often invisible to the naked eye, we

---

Religion and Politics (NRSP). Most of my data on the growth and history of the Church in the Pacific Northwest is provided by the recent text *Religion & Public Life in the Pacific Northwest: The None-Zone*, which is an interpretation of the newly released NARA, ARIS and NRSP studies. Additionally, I rely on my ongoing conversations with individuals working within the IT economy in the wider Seattle area. I do not intend the findings from my own qualitative research as a participant observer to be construed as normative or even statistically relevant. I have pursued qualitative and indeed narrative examples of the religious life of technology in the Pacific Northwest for the purpose of uncovering specific stories of religiosity within the industry to illuminate the thesis of this project.

must endeavour to place our use of technology under the microscope, to better determine its impact upon the lived-life. What precisely is technology and how does theology engage with it?

For this chapter, space does not permit to engage in a dialogue with the likes of Dessauer (1972), Heidegger (1993), Ellul (1965), Ihde (1991) or Borgmann (2003)—to name only some key figures—in our effort to establish a 'proper' philosophy of technology. For the sake of brevity, I wish to only introduce the thought of Paul Tillich (1981); as a philosophical theologian with a keen interest in the cultural milieu, his reflections on technology and culture are informative for the work at hand.

Clearly, Tillich's notion of technology was rather different from our own. Writing in the early twentieth century, his work on the subject centred on industrial and military technologies rather than on communications and information technologies. Nonetheless, his analysis of creation and innovation within the technical *gestalt* is useful. Rather than focusing purely on the human agency in the use of technology, Tillich's latent philosophy of technology allows us to consider the material substrate as a viable object for theological reflection. His work opens our analysis to the cultural world created by technology, inclusive of its design, fabrication, use and dissemination.

For Tillich, the realm of technology is the realm of innovation. Technological manufacture is the introduction of something into the world which is an improvement upon a pre-existing condition and not, significantly for Tillich, pure creativity. For him, 'invention is in principle *subject to obsolescence,* while creation is inherently infinite and can become obsolete only on its technical side and never on its creative side' (1981: 106). Like Heidegger's later work, Tillich later makes a distinction between technology (as a conveyance of invention) and high art (as a conveyance of creativity). Heidegger (1993: 338–40) approached the problem by arguing that in the light of modern technology's use in the contemporary world, technologies can no longer function as a means of *poiesis* (a kind of in-breaking revelation). For both early-to-mid twentieth-century thinkers, high art appears to be the only poietic outlet in modern life. Yet, unlike Heidegger, Tillich (1981: 106) is willing to examine the liminal space 'where "art" or craftsmanship ends and science begins', at the nexus of poiesis and praxis, creativity and rationality, technology and the arts.

Although the ideal form of technology would seem to exist as the instantiation of scientific reflection upon a given goal, in reality this reflection is often superseded by a form of 'instinctive, acquired, and inherited praxis. And praxis retains its position even when science has been in effect for the longest time' (ibid.: 106). In this regard, technology reveals its latent ambiguity. It is neither pure theory nor pure action; all technologies reveal elements of both rationality and creativity. Within the technical act, '*science and craftsmanship* both cooperate and contend with each other' (ibid.: 107).

Thus, for Tillich, technology can be viewed both essentially and existentially. Essentially, technology is purely an extension of scientific rationality, designed to impose heterogonous goals upon materiality in an autogenous manner. Existentially, technology appeals beyond the sciences to a more spiritual dimension, whereby instinct transforms calculative praxis into an artistic form of craftsmanship. It is the aspect of the existential–spiritual nature of technology which informs my own analysis of IT culture below.

Within IT, the ambiguity or paradox between creativity and rationality is clearly evident. One is both able to employ technologies of information to extend the calculating reach of markets, militaries and economies, while simultaneously using the same technologies to openly distribute innovative research or artistic materials. Indeed, IT's ability to serve calculating and creative ends lends it the appearance of neutrality, whereby it seems to be able to facilitate both ethically appealing and ethically abhorrent activities.[2] Yet Tillich would encourage us instead to view technology's seemingly neutral characteristic as a paradox or ambiguity. The difference between ambiguity and neutrality is significant. When characterized as ambiguous, both the negative and the positive characteristics of an entity can be affirmed in tension; however, when an entity is characterized as neutral, neither the negative nor the positive can be affirmed. Ambiguous views of technology allow us to examine a technology by way of critical theological and ethical inquiry, whereas a neutral view of technology would limit our analyses to the agency of technology users alone. An ambiguous understanding of technology holds in tension technology's potential for both creative and destructive purposes, thus enabling us to assign ethical significance to the whole of a material culture, including, but not limited to, the agents within this culture.

The standing thesis is that technology—and, in this case, IT—contributes to the radical construction of identity, community, ethics and even religious faith. Given the ambiguities of a Tillichian technological *gestalt*, this would seem feasible. Within theology, philosophy and cultural studies, this ambiguity is often styled in destructive or even apocalyptic terms. Current commentators are quick to pick up on the latent ambiguity. In his *Techgnosis,* cultural commentator Eric Davis (1998) explores the subaltern cultures given voice and form by information technologies. He reflects on the capacity of any new technology to 'partially reconstruct the self and its world, creating new opportunities (and new traps) for thought, perception, and social experience' (ibid.: 3). Likewise, philosopher Albert Borgmann (1984) has voiced concern that contemporary technologies (inclusive of information technologies) disorient our proper concern for the good life, by entrapping us within a technological system which principally seeks to entertain and to perpetuate what he calls the 'device paradigm' (a shorthand for blind consumerism in a technological age). There is little time for religious devotion in Borgmann's dystopian vision of a highly technologized society (ibid.: 246). This theme is echoed in Christian theology by Graham Ward in his

---

[2]   Indeed, such a view of IT's neutrality was consistently articulated within my case studies, most of whom resisted assigning any kind of ethical value to technology, conferring the onus of ethical responsibility to the end user of technologies, themselves.

Cities of God (2000), where Ward seeks to find an ontological connection between IT and the human being, asserting that computer-mediated subjectivities, such as those of the 'cyborg/clone', speak to deeply theological notions of embodied identity (ibid.: 206). Yet Ward appears to be sceptical of communities and selves that are constituted through the mediation of IT, when mediation is a substitution for, or ancillary to, Christology or Eucharistic practices.

Beyond cultural studies, philosophy and theology, many technology practitioners and speculative scientists centre on the positive or even redemptive aspects of technology, couching their discussion of the ambiguous potential of IT in pseudo-religious terms. Physicist Frank Tipler (1994) holds to an eschatological vision of IT: in his *Physics of Immortality*, a future information processing device is ascribed the potential to facilitate a universal resurrection of the dead through cosmic computer simulations (ibid.: 138). Perhaps more in the realm of contemporary possibilities are the writings of technologists Ray Kurzweil (1999) and Hans Moravec (1988) where we read of a not too distant future when the human mind may be uploaded into a sufficiently robust computer substrate, facilitating a radical life extension for the lucky few who will be able to afford it. We could also look to the themes developed in artificial intelligence research which link computation with our understanding of consciousness or even with the construction of alternative forms of the soul or personhood (see Minsky 1986). It goes without saying that the spiritual dimension of information processing technologies has been a common theme in science-fiction literature and film.

The theological relevance of contemporary IT is a fascinating area of research. As a Christian practical theologian, I am keenly interested in the way cultures produce forms which express something akin to a Tillichian sense of Ultimate Concern. I have argued elsewhere that in the works of those listed above we find the appearance of a kind of techno-theology, where technology is invested with the potential to convey the Ultimate (DeLashmutt 2006). Wherever and whenever technology is reified and allowed to become the bearer of utopian or eschatological promise or dystopian projections, it carries within it a modicum of techno-theology.[3] In the extravagant examples of Kurzweil's *Spiritual Machines* or Moravec's *Mind Children* or in the more mundane references to new information technologies as a way of unravelling the mystery of consciousness or in the rhetoric that IT can bring about universal solidarity by breaking down communication barriers, I have argued, technology serves as a spring-board for a heretical eschatology and soteriology where transcendent possibilities are exchanged for the promises of immanently realizable solutions.

---

[3]   Techno-theology emerges when technologies are reified and divorced from their material and historical contexts. When concrete, materially and culturally instantiated technologies give way to flights of fancy, we lose sight of 'technologies' and begin to centre our hopeful musings upon wondrous Technology (the capital 'T' is intended). Technology removed from its social or economic context easily spirals into myth, transforming itself into a form of ultimate concern (see also DeLashmutt 2006: 268).

But the nagging question remains: does anyone outside the academy, apart from a handful of technologists, actually recognize that techno-theology is at play within everyday life? Does the literature about technology and society really represent the actual experiences of technology practitioners? If techno-theology is as pervasive as the thesis articulated above seems to maintain, surely technology practitioners would evince substantially different religious orientations in contrast to those in less IT-centred vocations or cultures. Indeed, it would seem that being involved with technology would radically diminish one's interest in organized religious practices, as technology would seem to offer a plausible functional alternative to religious devotion. In what follows, I attempt to test this thesis in three ways. Firstly, I wish to determine if there is a correlation between high levels of employment within the CS industry for a region and low rates of self-selection for religious adherence. Secondly, I want to offer my own qualitative data which I collected as a participant observer working within the dot-com sector as a CS professional in Seattle. Lastly, I wish to offer some representative case studies which explore the relationship between faith and technology among individuals of varying levels of religious affiliation within the IT industry.

Regional Religious Demographics

Coupland's depiction of the silicon forests of Seattle still resonate with many who work within the IT sector in the city today. Seattle, Washington, is a place renowned for its role in the internet economy. Within the greater metropolitan area lie the campuses of Microsoft, Amazon, Real Media and hundreds of small internet corporations. Living in Seattle one quickly gains the impression that the city's population is comprised of the young, the affluent, the well educated, and the technically savvy. According to the 2000 census, 31 per cent of Seattle's population are in the 20–34 year-old age bracket, compared to 21 per cent nationally (Seattle Department of Planning and Development). The state is also one of the most affluent in the country, with the thirteenth highest median income nationally and the second highest in the Western region. Further, 30.9 per cent of adult Washingtonians are in possession of a Bachelor's degree, making this population the most well-educated state in the West and the ninth in the nation.

Despite a decline in employment in the technology industry following the burst of the dot-com bubble in December 2001, there were, in May 2006, over 93,500 people employed within in the IT/CS fields in the State of Washington, a 10 per cent increase in the field since the height of the dot-com bubble in 2001 (U.S. Department of Labor, Bureau of Labor Statistics 2001; 2006). Today the city has one of the lowest unemployment rates in the nation, hovering around 3.9 per cent. As a leader in the IT sector, Seattle has the second highest percentage of computer technology workers (compared to the total percentage of workers) in the Western United States and the tenth highest overall. It is clear that once again IT is a leading source of the region's economic activity.

Like other West Coast cities, the core urban neighbourhoods have undergone continual gentrification throughout the past decade, driving up housing prices and driving out blue collar workers. Luxury cars are parked outside of 1920s bungalows, where 40-inch flat-screen televisions project the aura of middle class affluence on to the streets below. Among this upwardly mobile population, participation in organized religion is exceptionally low. The city is located in a distinctively non-religious region, as fewer people in the Pacific Northwest self-select for a religious affiliation than in any other region of the United States. In other words, there are more people who choose 'none' as their religious self-identity here than anywhere else in the USA.[4] Whereas 59.4 per cent of the nation admit to some kind of religious affiliation, the three constituent states in the region (Oregon, Washington and Alaska, combined) have an average adherence rate of 37.2 per cent (Killen & Shibley 2004: 26). The region is a spiritual and sociological anomaly compared to national data.

Employment Statistics and Religious Affiliation

Given the potency of techno-theology described above, I wonder if one of the reasons why the Seattle metropolitan area has such a low religious adherence rate has to do with the role played by IT workers and the information economy within the city's cultural ethos. To test if working in the computer technology industry somehow breeds scepticism or indifference regarding religious belief, I have examined other metropolitan areas which are marked by a high number of computer technology workers in order to determine if they also have a similarly higher percentage of unaffiliated persons. I correlated data from the U.S. Bureau of Labor Statistics with data from the North American Religion Atlas (NARA),[5] selecting the eleven metropolitan areas nationwide which have the highest percentage of CS workers in the total working population. Although in any one of the cities CS workers only make up a small percentage of the workers overall (and an even smaller percentage of the general population), the pull of the so-called information economy is strong enough for CS to be perceived, subjectively, as a major influence within the city's culture.

---

[4] Nationwide, 40.6 per cent of the population identify themselves as religiously unaffiliated, whereas 62.8 per cent of the Pacific Northwest do so. Nationally, 14 per cent claim no religious identity, whereas in the region 25 per cent describe themselves as non-religious. (see Shibley 2004: 141)

[5] NARA is the project of the Polis Center of Indiana University–Purdue University of Indianapolis. It was created as an interactive website based upon the 2000 census, the 2000 Religious Congregations and Membership Survey compiled by the Glenmary Research Center and supplemented by ARIS (American Religious Identification Survey) and other datasets.

The top 11 cities in the country for CS-related employment are San Jose, CA; Boulder, CO; the Washington-Arlington-Alexandria, DC-VA-MD-WV metropolitan area; Framingham, MA; Huntsville, AL; Durham, NC; Bethesda, MD; Seattle, WA; Colorado Springs, CO; San Francisco, CA; and Austin, TX. I have cross-referenced these metropolitan areas with the NARA data which contain statistics for religious affiliation by region. If computer technology produces some kind of rival theological world view, it would seem logical that within the regions that have the highest percentage of CS workers, a decline in religious affiliation would be indicated. However, as Table 5.1 (below) shows, the difference between the regional averages of un-affiliation rates and the rates of affiliation within the individual counties in which the cities are located indicate that (with regard to the CS sector) no definite correlation can be made between a region's employment data and its overarching rate of religious affiliation. Although the rate of unaffiliated persons within these metropolitan areas does vary from regional norms, the differences appear to fluctuate in both directions. It would seem that there is no strong correlation between the density of technology workers in a region and that region's general religious culture. In fact, in King County (the county in which Seattle is located), the affiliation rate goes up when it is compared to both the state and regional norms.

What is Significant about the Northwest Region?

If technology is not to account for Seattle's low rates of religious affiliation, what other factors could be considered? A combination of historical, environmental, social-psychological and economic reasons can prove insightful. As noted above, in contrast with other regions in the country, the Pacific Northwest is strikingly non-religious. According to the NARA data, the religiously unaffiliated make up 62.8 per cent of the population in the Pacific Northwest, compared to 34.1 per cent in the Mid-Atlantic Region, 41 per cent in the Midwest, 38.5 per cent in New England, 47.3 per cent in the Pacific, 48.3 per cent in the Rocky Mountain West, 40.3 per cent in the South and 32.5 per cent in the Southern Crossroads.

Historically, religions have failed to maintain a significant presence in the region. Throughout the Pacific Northwest's brief history, most people have tended not to affiliate with institutional religions and the plurality of religious institutions in the area has prevented any single religion from gaining a significant foothold (Killen 2004: 10). It is often said, with a measure of cheekiness, that the extreme westward journey for the region's first western settlers forced early frontiers people to unburden themselves from religious devotion before crossing the Cascades. Indeed, westward expansion required a remarkably independent spirit and for those who took up the journey, not having a religious community to leave behind 'back east' made the trek westward all the easier. This is not to say that early settlers were completely devoid of religion. Settlement of the Pacific Northwest included a diverse group which reflected any number of Christian religious traditions. However, the size of the region, the diffuse nature of early settlements and the absence of any single religious tradition or denomination emerging as a formidable social and cultural force all contributed to the area's historical lack of religious affiliation. Even today not having a religious confession is the norm rather than the exception in the Pacific Northwest. As the population has continued to grow, institutional religious adherence rates have continued to stay low (Killen & Shibley 2004: 31).

Although it may appear a trivial reason, the overwhelming presence of the area's grand natural environment could also play a role in the high rate of unaffiliated persons in the region. Surrounded by mountain ranges, rivers, inlets and vast supplies of natural resources, early settlers and residents today frequently reflect on nature as a place where they most acutely experience transcendence (Shibley 2004: 156). Finally, in more recent times the relative affluence of the urban centres of the Pacific Northwest (combined with the fact that the majority of the area's population live in urban centres) could be cited as a partially material cause for the region's current a-religious tendencies.

If lack of affiliation has always been the norm in the region, it would seem improbable that a demographic shift in employment (the rise of the so-called information economy in Seattle) would have any causal relationship to a pre-existing cultural disposition to religious 'un-affiliation'. Indeed, in the light of this, I argue that within the Pacific Northwest the historical lack of a concerted religious presence in the region and the characteristics of independent and hard-working people who live there could be a common cause for both the density of technology workers in the region and the general absence of religion in public life. The free-thinking entrepreneurialism of the region's computer technology industry has as much to do with the region's independent frontier spirit as it does with the region's lack of religious affiliation. Rather than religious 'un-affiliation' breeding CS workers or necessarily a-religious CS workers, it would seem that regional religious trends are influenced by factors outside individual employment statistics.

Spiritual Habits of Technology Workers

Hermeneutics and demography offer a high-level image of techno-theology and its role (or lack of role) in public life. For the remainder of this chapter I will examine the experiences of those who work within the technology industry, listening to their stories and determining the extent to which religion plays a part in their own lives. Although IT may not itself directly influence the spiritual habits of the region, perhaps by looking at a brief portrait of the religious dispositions of technology workers, we may determine if they reflect a distinct spiritual outlook. Perhaps then we could see if the aforementioned techno-theology is really at play within their culture.

The Portrait of a Company

My research into the particular spiritual practices of CS workers reflects nearly a decade of casual encounters as a participant observer within one particular internet company. Although I have worked at various points within the information economy in Seattle, what follows will reflect my time with a small internet media company (The Company) where I worked from 2000 to 2002 and again from 2006 to 2007. The Company swelled with millions of dollars of venture capital during the boom of the late 1990s and early 2000s and managed to survive the collapse of the dot-com economy in December 2001, despite a significant reduction of staff and available capital. The Company has turned into an internet success story, having recently been acquired by a larger multi-national media conglomerate. Typical of many early technology companies of that era, its initial technical staff included an eclectic mix of individuals from a variety of personal and professional backgrounds. In the light of the high demand and low supply of university trained computer scientists, The Company (before its acquisition) drew technologists from fields as far ranging as business management, English literature, anthropology and divinity. Many of its first computer software developers and IT specialists came into the CS field because of the promise of easy wealth, although most comment that they stayed in the CS field because they found the work to be creatively stimulating and intellectually challenging. The industry allowed a hobby-interest (in many cases) to blossom into a lucrative career with tremendous room for upward mobility. Not unlike the characters in Coupland's *MicroSerfs* or the tragically comical case studies in Lessard & Baldwin's *NetSlaves* (2000), employees were provided, in exchange for a work week of 80 hours and more, with free food and drink, a casual working environment and stock options. Today The Company's technology and software development groups include more properly trained technologists. In 2002 one in eight technologists was university trained, whereas in 2007 the ratio was one in two.

Interestingly, at the same time that The Company's technology staff was becoming increasingly professionalized, the ratio of staff who self-selected for religious affiliation also shifted. In 2002, of the eight technologists employed, only one self-selected for religious affiliation, whereas at the time of writing the ratio was one in four. Of those who self-selected for no religious affiliation, half were exposed to some kind of formal religious upbringing, but left their initial faith behind. The majority of these pronounced themselves to be agnostic and the most common reason for their agnosticism is the belief that religion is irrelevant to contemporary life. In casual conversation, several individuals on at least three occasions commented that the inconsistent attitudes of Christians on issues regarding sexuality and morality were reasons for their incredulity towards religion as a whole. Two objected to religious faith principally on intellectual grounds, citing the stories which organized religious told as interesting on an historical or pedantic level, but on the whole they viewed scientific narratives to be more convincing and more relevant for their personal lives. Among those with a religious affiliation, the sense that they were in the minority was readily felt. Even those with a proselytizing faith (evangelical Christians, for instance) rarely discussed religious matters unless prompted to do so. In conversations outside working hours or in social situations when religion was addressed, those with religious faith seldom contributed. A woman who described herself as an evangelical Christian said that it was her role to evangelize by her lifestyle and her love of her co-workers rather than by trying to discuss her beliefs in a public setting. Among both affiliated and unaffiliated, religion was perceived very much as a private subject.

Case Studies

To get to the heart of the religious practices and beliefs of The Company's staff, I interviewed a handful of technologists, asking them about their professional biographies, their exposure to religion (both in their formative years and at present) and if they recognized any overlap between religion (or religiously informed ethics) and technology. Three such studies follow.

The first is Phil, a software developer in his late 30s. He has been involved in CS for 14 years. He was attracted to a career in IT because of the potential for social networking online and he has never felt the stereotypical draw to gadgetry as a reason for his career choice. Phil sees the web as the great equalizer. It empowers individuals with disparate interests and levels of influence to be united through their use of a common technology. Although technology can be used for positive ends (like providing social networks or giving the disenfranchised a voice in society), technologies are generally 'benign'; Phil sees them as neither ethically positive nor negative. The ethics of technology emerge from technology use, not from technologies themselves.

Phil's spiritual life is varied. He grew up on an island in the middle of Puget Sound which was renowned for its New Age influences and openly practising neo-pagans. Though Phil was raised in a nominally Lutheran home, he was influenced by 'occult' spiritualities from a young age. When asked if he continues to practise either New Age spiritualities or Lutheran piety, he notes that no form of organized religion appeals to him. He considers himself to be non-religious, but spiritual, saying that 'God cares about you, not about you going to church.' However, he still feels some residual 'Lutheran guilt' for turning his back on his confirmation vows. When asked further about his idea of God, he says that God can be found in all things: 'God doesn't mind putting on drag, everyone comes to God [in some way] because God loves us [all].' Phil and his partner have a pre-teen daughter whom they have intentionally raised without any religious influences or education. They both feel that she should be allowed to find religion on her own rather than being forced into a religious mould by her parents.

Religion, Phil feels, may have some value to culture and society (by preserving concepts like honour or value), but on the whole it is simply an organized system which puts into practices and words what is intrinsic to all people. All people have a sense of the good, of honour and value; religion is merely a particular example of this. Whereas organized religion had little role to play in his day-to-day life, Phil claimed that spirituality was a powerful influence on him and his family. When asked what the practical components of their spirituality are, he commented that he believes in a kind of *open source* spirituality where they are free to draw on all traditions as they suit their present need. I found this to be an interesting metaphor, as it reflects the discourse surrounding the open-source programming movement in CS. Phil treats religion (or software, for that matter) as something which grows from the constant reworking of one's self and one's peers.[6]

Although technology may provide Phil and his family with a metaphor for talking about spirituality and ethics, it does not offer anything close to what we could see as a competing religious meta-narrative. Contrary to the concerns raised by Ward, the sociality which Phil experiences online empowers him to build a vibrant community of like-minded people. Unlike the hopes voiced by speculative scientists regarding technology's potential, technology for Phil and his family is firmly rooted in the practicalities of the lived life. They are not holding out hope for technology to usher in a utopian future.

The second case is Sam, who like Phil, has been involved in the CS industry for most of his professional life. Even as a child he was immersed in computing technology, as his father was a CS professional working with AT&T in Southern California. Growing up around computers, Sam took a shining to the problem-solving opportunities which CS provided. He was drawn into, and remains within, the field because of the creative aspect of CS and the thrill of problem solving which his career provides. He grew up in a strictly religious home, moving from the Adventist tradition of his youth to a non-denominational Evangelical church in his adulthood. Although he does not attend church every week, he and his family try to attend at least several Sundays a month. Outside public worship, he reads religious literature, particularly writings which deal with the relationship between religion and science. Unlike Phil and Peter (see below), Sam appears to be more attracted to the analytical rather than the creative element of CS. His relationship to religion and spirituality reflects this analytical perspective. Sam has persisted in his faith, because it is both a part of his core self-identity *and* because it provides a cohesive world view which he understands to be both rational and self-consistent. His interest in science and religion is an attempt to better understand this religious world view in conjunction with the scientific paradigm that informs his professional life.

Like the other interviewees, when asked about the relationship between technology and religion, he seemed to draw a blank. He understood technology

---

[6] A typical lay example of the open-source philosophy is the online encyclopaedia, Wikipedia. Anyone can add, remove or edit an entry, which makes all participants equals who have a common responsibility to maintain the encyclopaedia and make a common investment in the quality of the work. See Katharine Moody's chapter in this volume for more on this.

as a purely neutral entity which is assigned ethical significance by those who use it. Religion may influence our use of technology, but it has no other relevance to the field. For Sam, his religious world view is the principal locus for his sense of hope, identity and goodness. He sees technology and science as important, but in purely utilitarian terms.

The third case is Peter, a 27-year-old software developer who studied CS at university. He initially pursued software development because of the promise of easy wealth. In the late 1990s when Peter was trying to determine his college major, the promise of US$80,000 annual salaries in the industry was a powerful draw for a young man from a rural working class part of Washington State. Peter grew up in a nominally Christian home; during his early 20s while at university, he was a devout Presbyterian under the tutelage of a particularly dynamic minister in his university town. After he had left university, Peter's faith involvement lessened. Peter became disenchanted with the Church's anti-science stance, its position towards same-sex relations and evolution, arguing that those who work in technology and the sciences are rational people who look to science and reason to guide their ethics. He has no problem believing in an omnipotent creator God, the divinity of Christ or even miracles. His principal problem with Christianity is the Church, which he sees as both irrational and the source of a hypocritical and selective morality. In the light of his self-professed agnosticism and current lack of religious affiliation, I asked Peter how he arrived at notions of truth, beauty, goodness or meaning. He confessed that he seldom thought about such things. 'Religion isn't that complicated', he quipped, 'Religions are a source of guiding principles which are ultimately very personal.' When asked about the potential for technology to supplant religious beliefs or narratives, Peter wrinkled his forehead and appeared to be put off by what he characterized as a very 'science-fictiony' question.

In my conversations with technology workers in the Pacific Northwest, it emerged that their religious views had little to do with their choice of vocation and their choice of vocation had little to do with their religious views. When asked if they see any connection between religion and technology, no one was able to articulate any kind of sensible response which evinced anything like the techno-theologies posited by the cultural commentators, philosophers, theologians and technologists discussed above. It would seem that religious affiliation among computer technology workers are more influenced by family, community and life situations than by any conscious antinomy towards religion, as related to their sense of vocation.

When my respondents were plumbed further for indicators of techno-theology (reification of technology, utopian hopes invested in the future of technology or a sense of technologies' dystopian potential), none showed the least bit of interest in such speculations and most dismissed such talk as mere fictional musings. Rather than finding some kind of deeper meaning in technology, nearly all of those who were asked at this The Company why they originally pursued a career in CS either cited monetary reasons or a desire to solve problems and create interesting computer programs. CS has been a career that these individuals have pursued in order to facilitate particular lifestyle goals and to provide them with work that is enjoyable and challenging and that facilitates a solidly middle-class lifestyle. Their vocation does not correlate to an unusual love of, or hope in, technology. Their religious dispositions seem more related to regional norms than anything intrinsic to their choice of work.

Conclusion and Areas for Future Work

In late 2007 Thomas Goetz, an editor at *Wired* magazine, published a short piece outlining the importance of research which produces results contrary to the author's initial thesis. He stated:

> So what happens to all the research that doesn't yield a dramatic outcome—or, worse, the opposite of what researchers had hoped? It ends up stuffed in some lab drawer. The result is a vast body of squandered knowledge that represents a waste of resources and a drag on scientific progress. This information—call it dark data—must be set free. (Goetz 2007: 31)

When I started this project, I assumed that the connection between one's lack of religious affiliation and one's employment within the CS industry was a given. After all, nearly all of my reading suggested an antinomy between religion and 'technology cultures' and my casual encounters with those employed in the field gave me the impression that the logical and scientific mindsets of technologists were simply incompatible with religious faith. What I have found, however, is that one's religious self-selection reflects more variables than just one's vocational self-selection. This project has uncovered 'dark data' regarding the spiritual habits of technology workers. Even though this data may not conform to my original presuppositions, it does open up interesting avenues of reflection regarding the Church and its ongoing relationship with a technologically savvy culture.

Techno-theology may be implicit within certain strands of academic discourse, but as a concept it fails to fully account for attitudes towards technology advanced by those who work within the IT industry. Rather than replacing religious predilection with technological substitutes, the dot-com workers in Seattle come to, remain within, or reject religion for reasons unrelated to their involvement in the IT or CS field. As a practical theologian who works within the diverse interrelationships between Church and culture, I find this data supremely interesting. It suggests two points which could influence future work within the realm of Church and culture.

Firstly, with regard to practical theology's social-scientific interests in the study of religion in public life, new ways of conceiving spirituality apart from functionalist descriptions of religion need to be pursued. I came to this research assuming that a functionalist definition of religion or theology applied to the role played by technology in public life. I assumed that the hermeneutical study of technology and culture which repeatedly proffers such a position (in my own work as well as that of others) would somehow relate to the way individuals understood technology's role in their own lived life. In my study, I repeatedly found it difficult to identify (or correlate) a functionalist theory of religion which the idea of techno-theology relies upon. The problem with asking about the idea of 'techno-theology' is that it implies that the research subject would have some kind of reference for theology or religion in the first instance, apart from the way theology and religion are commonly understood. I would have had a similar problem using the term 'spirituality' with regard to technology, as all three terms (theology, religion, spirituality) have extant definitions within public life, which are different from the more rich and multivalent usage within academic discourse.[7] Simply put, I wonder how practical theologians who are attempting to think in a social-scientific way about theology and religion can have a meaningful dialogue with their research subjects, when they are in effect using different definitions of the same words.

Secondly, the ambivalent attitude towards technology as a cultural or religious force (e.g. techno-theology) evinced by my 20-something and 30-something respondents represents an important cultural disposition towards technology. Rather than the gadget-ridden or high-tech-loving stereotype that is often assigned to geeky CS and IT professionals, these individuals did not exhibit the kind of technological fetishism that one would expect. It would appear that the trend towards ubiquitous computing, social networking technologies and high-touch rather than exclusively high-tech uses of technology has become the dominant way of approaching technology in the life of the contemporary CS or IT worker. To this end, from the perspective of the ministry and mission of the Church in a technologically savvy culture, churches would be wise to rethink the importance of dazzlingly high-tech uses of technology in worship and proclamation. Is it truly necessary to seem cutting edge by employing the latest gadget or technique or would the mission of the Church be better served by placing technology in the background? As technologies of information continue to become increasingly ubiquitous and transparent, it would seem that less ostentatious uses of technology would be a prudent move. The gadget culture of the 1990s which was epitomized by the flamboyant spending among the newly minted dot-com rich seems to be in decline. In its stead, contemporary users of technology are favouring the ability of technology to facilitate collaboration and community, two things for which the Christian Church could find an immediate resonance.

In sum, this research has indicated to me that it is a false thesis to assume that technology is the idol of the masses. Rather than being viewed as objects of worship that are competing with organized religion, technologies are rather viewed as value-neutral functional tools which serve an end that is dictated by their use. Perhaps we have stepped out from the millennial techno-fetishistic frenzy of the 1990s and entered, in the twenty-first-century context, into an age

---

[7]   This is similar to problems found by Gordon Lynch in his study of the religious elements of rave culture in his *Understanding Theology and Popular Culture* (2005: 176).

where technology is rightly absorbed into the life world and becoming less a locus for hope or a portent of destruction and more a conveyance of pre-existing social goals. For theology, I would suggest that rather than treating technology as an evil to be overcome, we should begin to pursue critical reflection on technology which seeks to govern its use and implementation through the strong values of the Christian meta-narrative.

References

Borgmann, Albert, *Technology and the Character of Contemporary Life: a Philosophical Inquiry* (Chicago: University of Chicago Press, 1984).

Borgmann, Albert, *Power Failure: Christians in the Culture of Technology* (Grand Rapids: Brazos, 2003).

Coupland, Douglas, *MicroSerfs* (New York: Regan Books, 1996).

Davis, Erik, *Techgnosis: Myth, Magic and Mysticism in the Age of Information* (London: Serpent's Tail, 1998).

DeLashmutt, Michael W., 'A Better Life Through IT? The Techno-Theological Eschatology of Posthuman Speculative Science', *Zygon* 41, no. 2 (2006): 267–88.

Dessauer, Friedrich, 'Technology in Its Proper Sphere', in Carl Mitcham and Robert Mackey (eds), *Philosophy and Technology: Readings in the Philosophical Problems of Technology* (London: The Free Press, 1972): 317–35.

Ellul, Jacques, *The Technological Society*, trans. John Wilkinson (London: Jonathan Cape, 1965).

Goetz, Thomas, 'Freeing the Dark Data of Failed Scientific Experiments', *Wired* (2007): 31–2.

Heidegger, Martin, 'The Question Concerning Technology', in David Farrell Krell (ed.), *Martin Heidegger: Basic Writings* (San Francisco: HarperCollins, 1993): 308–41.

Ihde, Don, *Instrumental Realism: The Interface between Philosophy of Science and Philosophy of Technology* (Indianapolis: Indiana University Press, 1991).

Killen, Patricia O'Connell, 'Introduction: Patterns of the Past, Prospects for the Future: Religion in the None Zone', in Patricia O'Connell Killen and Mark Silk (eds), *Religion & Public Life in the Pacific Northwest: The None Zone* (New York: Rowman & Littlefield Publishers, 2004): 9–20.

Killen, Patricia O'Connell, & Shibley, Mark A., 'Surveying the Religious Landscape: Historical Trends and Current Patterns in Oregon, Washington, and Alaska', in Patricia O'Connell Killen and Mark Silk (eds), *Religion & Public Life in the Pacific Northwest: The None Zone* (New York: Rowman & Littlefield Publishers, 2004): 25–49.

Kurzweil, Ray, *The Age of Spiritual Machines* (London: Orion Business Books, 1999).

Lessard, Bill & Baldwin, Steve, *NetSlaves: True Tales of Working the Web* (New York: McGraw Hill, 2000).

Lynch, Gordon, *Understanding Theology and Popular Culture* (London: Blackwell, 2005).

Minsky, Marvin, *The Society of Mind* (New York: Simon and Schuster, 1986).

Moravec, Hans, *Mind Children: The Future of Robot and Human Intelligence* (London: Harvard University Press, 1988).

Seattle Department of Planning and Development, 'Seattle Population Demographics 1990 2000. Population & Housing Trends: Population Trends: Age', available at www.seattle.gov/dpd/Research/Population_Demographics/ Prior_Censuses/1900-2000_Population_Housing_Trends/DPDS_007032.asp [access date 1 September 2007].

Shibley, Mark A., 'Secular But Spiritual in the Pacific Northwest', in Patricia O'Connell Killen & Mark Silk (eds), *Religion and Public Life in the Pacific Northwest: The None Zone* (New York: Rowman & Littlefield Publishers, 2004): 139–67.

Tillich, Paul, *The System of the Sciences According to Objects and Methods*, trans. Paul Wiebe (Lewisburg: Bucknell University Press, 1981).

Tipler, Frank, *The Physics of Immortality: Modern Cosmology, God and the Resurrection of the Dead* (London: Doubleday, 1994).

U.S. Department of Labor, Bureau of Labor Statistics, Occupational Employment Statistics, '2001 State Occupational Employment and Wage Estimates Washington', available at http://stats.bls.gov/oes/2001/oes_wa.htm [access date 1 November 2007].

U.S. Department of Labor, Bureau of Labor Statistics, Occupational Employment Statistics, 'May 2006 State Occupational Employment and Wage Estimates Washington', available at http://stats.bls.gov/oes/current/oes_wa.htm#b15-0000 [access date 1 November 2007].

Ward, Graham, *Cities of God* (London: Routledge, 2000).

Empirical Data

The Polis Center, 'North American Religious Atlas', www.religionatlas.org/ [access date 1 March 2007].

U.S. Census Bureau, American FactFinder, 'Geographic Comparison Table', http:// factfinder.census.gov/servlet/GCTTable?_bm=y&-geo_id=01000US&-_box_ head_nbr=GCT-T1&-ds_name=PEP_2006_EST&-_lang=en&-format=US-9&-_sse=on [access date 1 March 2007].

U.S. Census Bureau, State & County QuickFacts, 'King County, Washington', http://quickfacts.census.gov/qfd/states/53/53033.html [access date 1 March 2007].

U.S. Census Bureau, Income, 'Two-Year-Average Median Household Income by State: 2003-2005', www.census.gov/hhes/www/income/income05/statemhi2. html [access date 1 March 2007].

U.S. Census Bureau, 'Educational Attainment in the United States: 2005', www. census.gov/population/socdemo/education/cps2005/tab13.xls [access date 1 March 2007].

U.S. Department of Labor, Bureau of Labor Statistics. Generated by Dr Michael W. DeLashmutt using 'Occupational Employment Statistics', http://data.bls. gov/oes/search.jsp?data_tool=OES [access date 1 March 2007].

Metropolitan Area	NARA Region (% Religiously Unaffiliated by Region)	% Religiously Unaffiliated Pop. (County)[1]	Working Pop.[2]	Pop. Working in CS	% Working Pop. In CS	Pop. Working in Dev.	% CS pros in Dev.	% all workers in Dev.
San Jose-Sunnyvale-Santa Clara, CA	Pacific (47.3)	51.3 (Santa Clara)	866300	67560	7.80%	22470	33.26%	2.59%
Boulder, CO	Rocky Mountain West (48.3)	44.2 (Boulder)	156250	11630	7.44%	2510	21.58%	1.61%
Washington-Arlington-Alexandria, DC-VA-MD-WV Metropolitan Division	South / Mid-Atlantic (40.3/ 34.1)	66 (Arlington)	2232510	163750	7.33%	24870	15.19%	1.11%
Framingham, MA NECTA Division	New England (38.5)	23 (Middlesex)[3]	154830	11120	7.18%	3060	27.52%	1.98%
Huntsville, AL	South (40.3)	32.1 (Madison)	190520	11250	5.90%	1630	14.49%	0.86%
Durham, NC	South (40.3)	40.8 (Durham)	252550	14770	5.85%	1810	12.25%	0.72%
Bethesda-Gaithersburg-Frederick, MD Metropolitan Division	Mid-Atlantic (34.1)	38 (Montgomery)	555860	31570	5.68%	4330	13.72%	0.78%
Seattle-Bellevue-Everett, WA Metropolitan Division	Coastal West (62.8)	55.2 (King)	1314870	69510	5.29%	16720	24.05%	1.27%
Colorado Springs, CO	Rocky Mountain West (48.3)	54.9 (El Paso)	243430	12040	4.95%	2400	19.93%	0.99%
San Francisco-San Mateo-Redwood City, CA Metropolitan Division	Pacific (47.3)	42.7 (San Francisco); 53.3 (San Mateo)	951240	45840	4.82%	10970	23.93%	1.15%
Austin-Round Rock, TX	Southern Cross-Roads	42.9 (Travis)[4]	686150	31670	4.62%	4080	12.88%	0.59%

1 Based on NARA data, Unaffiliated/Uncounted Adherents as % of total population, by county.
2 Labour Statistics Period: May 2005; NARA Statistics Period: 2000. Data extracted on March 3, 2007.
3 Massachusetts has an overwhelming Catholic population, state-wide of 71%.
4 Texas shares its religious population between Catholics (31.9%) and Baptists (27.2%).

Chapter 6
Marketing God and Hell:
Strategies, Tactics and Textual Poaching

Carlton Johnstone

Introduction

As I catch the bus into Auckland University from Takapuna, I enjoy the familiar and relaxing view of the Auckland harbour and the approaching city from the height of the harbour bridge. All that changes once the bus comes off the bridge into Fanshawe Street. The first available urban wall space is taken up by advertising, in the form of a colourful advertisement for coke. From here visual advertising is relentless, flowing down the sides of towering buildings, on billboards that dominate the urban landscape trying to persuade me to tune into Rock FM, wash my hair with Fructis shampoo and to wear Jockey underwear—after all, this is the underwear of choice by All Black Dan Carter. These advertisements function as narratives in the city that, as Michel de Certeau states, 'multiplies the myths of our desires and our memories by recounting them with the vocabulary of objects of consumption' (de Certeau *et al.* 1998: 142–3). Among all of this visual overload, or as some, such as Auckland City councillors, would say, 'visual pollution',[1] is a striking, simple black billboard with white writing that does not appear to be trying to sell me anything (see Figure 6.1).

The positioning of the sign is amusing and, indeed, clever, as it hangs on the outside of a multi-storey Auckland City Council car park building. Since 2005 these jet black billboards have been appearing in prominent locations around Auckland, with pithy thought-provoking and often humorous messages in white, signed by God. The messages aim to engage people in conversation about or with God. One of the unexpected conversationalists, however, ended up being 'The Guy from Hell' in a marketing campaign in 2005 for 'Hell Pizza', a franchise growing throughout New Zealand.

---

[1]   The Auckland City Council draft bylaw proposals (2007) aim to close around 200 billboard sites around Auckland. The Council claims that such a ban would bring Auckland up to standard as an international city by removing 'visual pollution' and draw more attention to its historic buildings.

Figure 6.1   Godmarks advertising billboard on the outside of a multi-storey
              Auckland City Council car park building. Photo courtesy of
              Godmarks.

It reads: '"Every day I get more prayer requests for car parks than anything
else. You people have to start thinking bigger"—God'.

In this chapter, I will draw upon Michel de Certeau's concepts of strategies,
tactics and textual poaching to explore two narratives of the city's marketing of
God and Hell. The two story tellers I will examine, 'Godmarks' and 'Hell Pizza',
draw on religious knowledge and language, but do so for very different purposes.
Reading the responses posted on the Godmarks website I will explore people's
tactics of reading the Godmarks billboards, particularly as a form of 'making do'. I
will then discuss two advertising campaigns run by Hell Pizza. Firstly, their 'Lust'
campaign and the public outrage that it generated. Secondly, I shall examine the
textual poaching of Godmarks involved in one of their billboard campaigns.

Godmarks as Tactic: Making Do in the Urban Landscape

In 2005 Auckland real estate agents Greg and Judi Gibson launched a billboard
campaign called Godmarks that has a striking resemblance to the successful 'God
Speaks' campaign which ran in America in 1998. This campaign began in America
when an anonymous donor had the idea for a local billboard campaign in South
Florida that would contribute to the spiritual climate and encourage people to
think about a loving and relevant God. The campaign went from nine billboards
in Southern Florida to 10,000 billboards in 200 cities across America, a donated
billboard space from the Outdoor Advertising Association of America worth
US$15 million (www.godspeaks.com/ATB/ATB03.asp, access date 5 November

2006). Those working in New Zealand advertising claim that they created the idea themselves and came across the American campaign afterwards. Whatever the case, Godmarks represents a localized version of a series of quotes from God written for Auckland drivers:

'Every day I get more prayer requests for car parks than anything else. You people have to start thinking bigger'—God

'I miss how you used to talk to me when you were a kid'—God

'I don't mind if you yell at me, at least we're talking'—God

Like the campaign in America, the Gibsons aimed Godmarks to be 'simple, entertaining and non-religious message[s] from the heart of God' (cited in Ngatoko 2005: 1). The messages also had to be non-judgmental. Such messages they hoped would challenge the findings of research recently carried out in Australia for the 'Jesus: All About Life Campaign' (Market Access Consulting and Research, 2003) funded by the Bible Society. The research found that Christianity and the Church are widely rejected by many non-Christians as anachronistic, boring and hypocritical. The findings highlighted the growing gap between people's response to Jesus, which was positive, and their response to the church as organized religion, which was perceived to be negative.[2] This might explain this humorous message: '"I love everyone, even Christians"—Jesus'. The Gibsons hoped to stimulate interest and conversation about God in a context where the number of people with no religious affiliation are a growing phenomenon in New Zealand. Those stating that they have no religion increased from 29.6 per cent (1,028,052) in 2001 to 34.7 per cent (1,297,104) in 2006.[3]

The Godmarks billboard campaign fits de Certeau's description of a tactic (1984). According to de Certeau, people deploy tactics to gain some control over the spaces of their everyday lives. Tactics take advantage of opportunities, playing on and with a terrain imposed on it. Tactics have no fixed place to call their own. They are about uses of consumption or what de Certeau refers to as 'making do' (ibid.: 36). Godmarks takes advantage of billboard space which is not rented and thus temporarily available and which various billboard companies offer them below market rates. The billboards are paid for by private donations. Although Godmarks has a website, it is not advertised on the billboards.

The way the Godmarks billboard messages are phrased also involves tactics. One of the ways that Godmarks hoped that people would 'make do' with the

---

[2] Harvey Cox (2000) found a similar disparity among his students at Harvard University among whom he had conducted a survey.

[3] www.stats.govt.nz/census/2001-national-summary/highlights.htm (access date 15 August 2007). The increase from 1996 to 2001 was even bigger, rising from 18.6 per cent to 29.6 per cent.

billboards is by challenging people's assumptions about God. A good example would be the message "'Isn't it weird how most people think I'm white?'—God'. Do most people think that God is white? What are the sources of people's image of God? Michelangelo's well known painting of creation adorning the ceiling of the Sistine Chapel portrays a popular image of God: he is a white man with a long flowing white beard. Such an image continues to be reinforced in *The Simpsons* (although technically he is yellow like the other characters). Popular culture is an increasingly influential source of God images, which has begun to challenge the traditional popular view of God as an old man with a long white beard. God in *Bruce Almighty* (Tom Shadyac, 2003) played by Morgan Freeman is certainly not white. New Zealand's *Bro Town*, an animation programme now in its third season, has given God a Pacific feel, with a lava-lava[4] and neat trimmed beard.

In popular culture and religious imagery, portrayals of Jesus are more prolific than portrayals of God. One can even buy Jesus as an action figure. Flicking through the pages of *On a Friday Noon* (Weber 1979), a book which depicts paintings and sculptures of Jesus' crucifixion from around the world, one is struck by the extent to which perceptions of Jesus are culturally assimilated and historically located.

People's image of God and Jesus, and their interpretation of the Godmarks messages, can be significantly shaped and influenced by what Stanley Fish (1980) has called 'interpretive communities'. Such communities provide a particular way of reading a text, interpretive strategies that are culturally constructed around similar values, worldviews and life experience. The Gay NZ website can be understood as an interpretive community: they ran an editorial entitled 'God billboards bring gay friendly message' in response to the Godmarks billboard "'Contrary to popular belief I don't hate anyone who's gay"—God' (www.gaynz.com/news/print. asp?artid=4139, access date 8 February 2007). Some billboard messages, such as "'Love thy neighbour is still the best bit of advice I ever gave you guys"—God', only make sense within the context of an interpretive community, such as a local church or synagogue, which place this propositional statement within the wider scriptural story. This is, after all, one of the functions of communities of memory.

Reading billboard messages is also an aspect of consumption. According to Fish, there 'is no single way of reading that is correct or natural, only "ways of reading" that are extensions of community perspectives' (1980: 16). De Certeau also challenges the image of passive consumers whose only freedom is 'that of grazing on the ration of simulacra the system distributes to each individual' (1984: 166). De Certeau views readers as travellers who are moving across a land belonging to someone else: 'Like nomads poaching their way across fields they did not write, despoiling the wealth of Egypt to enjoy it themselves' (1984: 174). Reading through the responses to the billboards[5] it becomes evident that people

---

4   Commonly called a sarong in English.

5   All the responses to the Godmarks billboards are taken from the Godmarks website, www.godmarks.co.nz/default.aspx (access date November 2006) under the 'impact' section.

are reading and 'making do' with the billboard messages in a number of ways. I shall discuss these in the following sections.

A Source of Encouragement

Messages, such as '"I was just thinking about you"—God', are interpreted as a word of encouragement, a reminder that God is interested in people's lives:

> Hi there, we got some of your fridge magnets at Parachute and stuck them on our fridge. One says 'I was just thinking about you'—God. I thought they would be great for visitors, but turns out they really help me to keep God on my mind during the day. Reminds me that God is always there. This is really helping me with my walk with God. (www.godmarks.co.nz, access date 15 November 2007)

This person has the billboard message as a fridge magnet which reminds him that God is always there. It has also assisted him in what Brother Lawrence (1977) has called 'practising the presence of God' as he turns his mind to God throughout the day. Of course, what kind of God is thinking about us depends upon our image of God. This could range from a retributive God waiting to punish us to a loving relational God or a very distant and removed God.

Making Do as a Personal Word

As C.S. Peirce has so concisely pointed out, 'A sign addresses someone' (1932: 135). The message, '"I don't mind if you yell at me, at least we're talking"—God', was read as addressing the following reader personally:

> I had just found out that the relationship with the woman I was looking to marry was coming to an end. I didn't understand why God would allow such a thing to happen so was very angry with Him. Driving along in my car while complaining to God and blaming Him for the course of events I got stuck in a traffic light on Fanshawe St. I then saw a sign that said 'I don't mind if you yell at me, at least we're talking'—God. It spoke straight to me, and helped me to remember His love and concern for my life. It turned me from shouting and frustration to thanking God for the way he speaks to us. Thanks. (www.godmarks.co.nz, access date 15 November 2007)

This quote demonstrates the important role which social position plays in the interpretation of media texts—the historical, cultural, social and technical context within which a text is 'read' (cf. Clarke 1997). This man read the billboard in relation to his lived reality of yelling at God and being angry with God for the break-up of a relationship. The message for him was a personal one: that it was acceptable to yell at God and that God understood. For him it had the effect of turning his anger into praise much like the Psalms of lament.

Conversation Starters

Godmarks provides tactical opportunities for people wishing to engage in religious conversations with other people, who do not always know how to start such a conversation, as the following quote demonstrates:

> Just wanted to say that you guys had a fantastic billboard on Victoria Park Market. I had lunch with some friends at the café across from it, and the conversation about God just started on its own. These guys usually shy away from the topic, so this was a real blessing. (www.godmarks.co.nz, access date 15 November 2007)

Another person travelling with non-Christian friends pointed out a Godmarks billboard which, he reported,

> led to a great conversation where we talked about ideas and issues raised by the different slogans then about God and Christianity in general. I found it incredibly exciting because these were people I only see in a specific context and the opportunity to share my faith would not usually come up … I think the billboards are a great resource, and I plan to use them to start similar conversations as often as I can! (www.godmarks.co.nz, access date 15 November 2007)

Both conversations started naturally in response to the billboards and the issues they raised. The responses suggest that there is a reluctance among many people to engage in religious conversation about God and Christianity. The Godmarks billboards have provided a bridge over the reluctance for some people in the form of a religious conversation starter.

Entertainment

For some people, 'making do' is about pleasure, enjoying the humour and providing a moment of relief from a bad day at the office, as the following comment illustrates:

> I am not a Christian, mainly due to those reasons you cited on the intro page— all the Christians I've known have put me off—but I was coming out of work the other day, driving up the ramp … I had had a really bad day and probably not laughed or smiled for at least eight hours. Right in front of me was the sign, 'Well, you asked for a sign.' I haven't laughed so much in ages. I think your strategy is fantastic and it affects the non-believers too. Congratulations! (www.godmarks.co.nz, access date 15 November 2007)

However, God is not the only spiritual entity trying to get our attention through the medium of advertising. Local 'Hell Holes', as Hell Pizza refer to their stores, have been popping up across the country. 'The Guy from Hell' has also been engaging in creative advertising inviting us for dinner. After all, God may listen, as the Godmarks billboards suggest, but 'The Guy from Hell' cheekily asks whether 'He can deliver'.

Hell Pizza: Renovating Hell

I walk into my local 'Hell Hole' up in Forrest Hill. I am greeted at the door by death himself. Inside are dolls representing the seven deadly sins in little coffin boxes attached to the walls. A male and female demon stare down at me from the wall. A text from Genesis 3 has been rewritten and framed. It is the biblical story of the Garden of Eden when God tells Adam and Eve they can eat anything in the garden except from the tree of life. Hell Pizza changes this to be anything except the pizza. Even when Eve saw that the pizza was good, she took a slice and gave another one to her husband. Hell 'rents' this biblical text and rewrites it or, in de Certeau's terms, 'renovates it' in favour of the Hell brand. My friends and I order Pandemonium, Lust and Mayhem pizzas which we eat while watching the DVD we have rented from the shop next door.

Hell Pizza is an example of what de Certeau calls 'strategies'. Unlike tactics, strategies require a place that can be delimited as its own. Hell Pizza as a strategy manifests itself physically through the sites in which it operates—the 'Hell Holes' that have been popping up across New Zealand—as well as in the products, which obviously include the pizzas, but also the advertising campaigns, website and the ongoing management of the brand identity. The 'Hell Holes' serve as the base from which relations with an exteriority, composed of targets or threats, in Hell Pizza's case, customers and competitors, not to mention complainers, can be managed. The PR management of Hell Pizza has recently found itself in overdrive, as it has attempted to deal with a torrent of complaints and calls to boycott the pizza.

From the humble beginnings of a small outlet in Wainuiomata[6] in 1996, Hell Pizza has now over 64 premises around New Zealand and has recently expanded to the UK. The company has won awards for its marketing savvy and creativity. It now proudly markets itself as 'The Underworld Icon of Aotearoa since 1996' (Aotearoa is the Maori name for New Zealand). Callum Davies, marketing director and founder of Hell Pizza, was named 'Marketer of the Year' at the 2005 *Marketing Magazine* Marketing awards. One can log on to find one's nearest Hell Hole (www.hell.co.nz) or call the 0800 number (which begins, appropriately, with the digits 666)—the 'Hell Emergency Number'. The company even offers deliverance. Hell Pizza's use of religious language raised, however, a complaint from a church in Tauranga[7] that the whole concept is anti-family and diminishes the seriousness of the Bible teaching on hell (Advertising Standards Authority (ASA) 06/396).[8]

---

[6]   Wellington, North Island of New Zealand.

[7]   Tauranga is in the Bay of Plenty, North Island, New Zealand.

[8]   The first number refers to the year (2006) followed by the complaint number (in this case 396).

Biblically speaking, hell may be the eternal place of torment and punishment. Gastronomically speaking, however, hell has come to represent a gourmet pizza outlet. While Jesus spoke about hell more than anyone else in the Bible[9] (ACUTE, 2000, xiiv), there has been considerable debate among biblical scholars about the proper interpretation of biblical teachings on hell. Should what the Bible teaches about hell be interpreted in a literal or metaphorical way? Will all be saved, as the Universalists believe? Is punishment forever or is eternal death of which the scriptures speak a state where unbelievers cease to exist, as those advocating 'conditional immortality' or 'annihilationism' maintain?[10] Despite the fact that Hollywood films keep the notion of hell alive in the popular imagination, Martin Marty (1985: 393) suggests, in an article entitled 'Hell Disappeared. No One Noticed: A Civic Argument', with a 'hyperbolic tinge' that 'Hell' has virtually been eliminated from the vocabulary and doctrinal repository of most churches. Hell Pizza has brought it back to the discussion table—around a culinary assortment of 'sinful' pizzas. A recent address by Pope Benedict XVI (2007) which reaffirmed the reality of hell as a place of eternal punishment is a case in point. Yet even this reaffirmation of the traditional Catholic understanding of hell is re-appropriated and renovated to serve the Hell Pizza's cause. The Pope has become an unwitting endorser of Hell Pizza, as the following billboard (Figure 6.2) illustrates.

Figure 6.2   Satirical appropriation of Papal address by Hell Pizza. Photo courtesy of Cinderella Marketing.

---

[9]   See Fudge 1982, chapter 11, 'Final Punishment in the teaching of Jesus'.

[10]   The various theological positions can be understood as interpretive communities that influence and inform how one interprets the biblical teaching on hell. For a concise overview of four main views on hell, see *Four Views on Hell* edited by William Crockett (1992). Chris Morgan (2004) presents an overview of prominent annihilationist theorists and evangelical responses to it.

Hell's marketing aims to build brand awareness, communicate the values of the Hell brand, being the 'slightly irreverent, cheeky kid on the block' (ASA 06/417), and to sell more product. Such marketing does not come without controversy, as the response to the Lust campaign demonstrates. From the outset, Hell Pizza has used guerrilla marketing tactics. The company has built a successful brand and business in an already existing and competitive environment. Limited by their marketing budget, Hell constantly seeks ways to grab attention by securing significant additional media coverage that it could never afford using paid-for advertising techniques.[11]

Redefining Lust

It is more obvious that the Hell Pizza brand can be interpreted as a means to diminish the seriousness of the biblical teaching on hell than it is to maintain that such language undermines the family. After all, Hell Pizza has also created a special kids' menu. (In keeping with their cheeky approach, it labels kids as 'little devils that need to be fed'.) What many families considered an offence was one of Hell Pizza's latest campaigns in early November 2006 which involved the delivery of 170,000 condoms in sealed foil and cardboard wallets to letterboxes surrounding Hell outlets as part of their 'Lust meat lovers pizza' campaign (see Figure 6.3). It quickly became the advertising campaign with the most complaints in New Zealand's history, totalling over 600 objections. Hell Pizza acknowledged that it knew the campaign would push the boundaries of marketing. It is proud to be the new custodian of this record. The complaints included a call by the *NZ Catholic* editorial (17–23 December 2006) to boycott Hell Pizza. However, such a boycott is expected to have very little impact on the company. Catholics are obviously not part of Hell Pizza's intended target market that needs to be managed. Kirk MacGibbon of Cinderella Marketing responded, saying that he is 'not sure how many Catholics buy from Hell, anyway' (Anon 2006). However, the gatekeepers of Catholicism do represent an influential interpretive community. Perhaps this explains why Hell Pizza poached the text of Pope Benedict's affirmation that hell is real and eternal.

However, the Chairman of the Advertising Standards Authority Complaints Board took quite a different view of the complaints relating to the extension of Hell Pizza's Lust campaign, ruling that there was no breach of the Advertising codes (ASA 06/433). The discrepancy between outcomes is based on the position of the Advertising Standards Complaints Board 'that each and every advertisement, whether part of a campaign or not, must be assessed in a "stand alone" capacity as

---

[11]   In August 2007, Cinderella Marketing pulled out of the advertising contract with Hell Pizza, as it had no confidence in its new, more conservative approach (Drinnan 2007: 7). Conservative that is by Cinderella's standards.

to whether it met the requirements of the Advertising Codes' (ibid.). The Chairman argued further that,

> there was no evidence in the advertisement before him to suggest that the packaging was in fact a condom packet, or that the advertisement referred to condoms. Furthermore, while some may consider that the name of the pizza 'Lust' and the wording '... for meat lovers' had sexual connotations, the Chairman was of the view that it was a reference to the product, and did not have overt sexual references. (ibid.)

The Chairman's ruling that there were no grounds to proceed overlooks that the consumption or reception of advertising messages is, as Stuart Hall (2001) argues, itself a 'moment' of the production process that follows on from the distinct moments of production, circulation, distribution and reproduction. Hall argues further that the consumption of messages predominates their production 'because it is the "point of departure for the realization" of the message' (ibid.: 168). Likewise, Judith Williamson (1978) states that adverts do not transmit messages by themselves. Without the viewer as the decoder of an advertisement, it remains meaningless: 'All signs depend for their signifying process on the existence of specific, concrete receivers, people for whom and in whose system of belief, they have a meaning' (Williamson 1978: 92). It is clear from the complaints that the silver packet from which the meat lovers' pizza protrudes signifies a condom packet. Further, the overall campaign is connected through the workings of intertextuality, where the same image of a pizza protruding from a condom packet (or 'silver packet' as the Advertising Standards Authority views it) is explicitly stated in other Hell Pizza Lust campaign advertisements.

Figure 6.3   The 'Lust' campaign extended to billboards and ads on the back of buses. Photo courtesy of Cinderella Marketing.

Connotations associated with hell and sin, such as lust, greed, sloth and envy, in a religious context are emptied and refilled with branded meaning and identity within the context of Hell Pizza. Lust, as their meat lovers' campaign demonstrates, is no longer about inappropriate sexual longing or a strong desire for sexual gratification, but, within the context of Hell Pizza, becomes Pepperoni, Salami, Ham, Bacon and Cabanossi, lashed with one's choice of sauce. It is a lust for pizza. 'Meaning', as de Certeau points out, 'is tied to the significance that comes from this new use' (1977: 49).

Sut Jhally (1989) argues that advertising is a form of religion. In a consumer society, advertising becomes one of the dominant institutions creating meaning, replacing traditional social institutions that were responsible for giving life and commodities meaning, such as family and religion. The flood of complaints in relation to the Lust campaign suggests that the family has not yet conceded such responsibility to the advertising masterminds of our world. Rather than seeing advertising as a form of religion, de Certeau observed the ease with which religiousness is exploited for the purposes of advertising. 'Marketing agencies', he states, 'avidly make use of the remains that were violently opposed as superstition. Advertising is becoming evangelical' (de Certeau 1984: 180).[12] Given the brand name 'Hell Pizza', it was obvious that any advertising would, and does, contain religious language, puns and references.

The Textual Poaching of Hell

In contrast to some of the more personal faith expressions of 'making do' with Godmarks messages, Hell Pizza had its own ideas for making do which involved what de Certeau calls 'textual poaching'. In response to the Godmarks billboard (see Figure 6.4), '"I've been thinking about you"—God', Hell Pizza put up a billboard (see Figure 6.5) with the words, '"I've been thinking about you too"—The Guy from Hell'.

The reader immediately asks, who is this 'Guy from Hell'? My mind automatically goes to Satan, the biblical enemy of God. Popular culture increasingly influences people's perceptions of the Devil, such as Al Pacino in *The Devil's Advocate* (Taylor Hackford, 1997), or the more seductive Liz Hurley playing the devil in *Bedazzled* (Harold Ramis, 2000). On further reflection, however, 'The Guy from Hell' could equally be the guy that served me pizza on Friday night or more plausibly Callum Davies, the owner and founder of Hell Pizza. I am sure he has been thinking about me as part of his target audience of people in their 20s and 30s and how he can sell me more pizza.

---

[12] The secularization of religion and the way consumption has become a vehicle for experiencing the sacred are explored in an article by Russell W. Belk *et al.* on 'The Sacred and the Profane in Consumer Behaviour: Theodicy on the Odessey' (1989).

Figure 6.4   Photo courtesy of Godmarks.

Figure 6.5   A prime example of 'textual poaching' by the Hell Pizza marketing
                    campaign from an original Godmarks advertising slogan. Image
                    courtesy of Cinderella Marketing.

Whoever the Guy from Hell is, the fact that he has been thinking about me 'too' involves what Julia Kristeva (1980) calls 'intertextuality', where one text is connected to another. This Hell Pizza billboard is dependent on the Godmarks billboard which says, '"I've been thinking about you"—God'. In order to make sense of some of Hell Pizza's billboards, or at least fully appreciate them, one needs to be familiar with the Godmarks billboards. Chandler called this 'a particularly self-conscious form of intertextuality: it credits its audience with the necessary experience to make sense of such allusions and offers them the pleasure of recognition' (Chandler 2002: 200). This particularly applies to understanding the 'too'. This billboard expects the readers' previous experience of having seen the Godmarks message, '"I've been thinking about you"—God'. Hell Pizza inhabits Godmarks with its own signature right underneath the message on the board.

De Certeau called the strategy of reconfiguring the meaning of a text, whether film, literature or billboard advertising, 'textual poaching'. According to him, it is analogous to inhabiting a text 'like a rented apartment. It transforms another person's property into a space borrowed for a moment by a transient' (Certeau 1984: xxi). Textual poaching is often the domain of viewers. It is a practice, however, that is becoming more common among the culture industries,[13] often as a form of counter-bricolage, as they re-appropriate the tactics of sub-cultures and include them in the mainstream. As we have seen above, Hell Pizza's billboard campaign is a form of textual poaching of the Godmarks campaign.

What we see is the nomadic grazing of Hell Pizza: it has settled temporarily on the lush plains of the Godmarks billboards which deal with the theme of prayer. Affirming and endorsing New Zealand's notorious binge-drinking culture, 'The Guy from Hell' encourages the inebriated babblings offered up (or down depending on one's geographical position of spiritual places) to him: '"I like the way you talk to me when you're drunk"—The Guy from Hell'.

Statistically, it is possible to work out whom the billboard addresses when it is placed within the context of New Zealand's binge-drinking culture. Twenty-four per cent of young people aged 14–17 who drink or drink to get drunk (Alcohol Advisory Council of New Zealand 2002) and nearly one in six adults have hazardous drinking habits (Ministry of Health 2001). (Binge drinking and risky drinking involve five or more glasses of alcohol during any one occasion.) The Guy from Hell, it would seem, has quite a few New Zealanders keeping him company. Hell Pizza claims that it wants to engage with social issues. Drinking is certainly one of them. I am not sure, however, how the billboard contributes to the debate about alcohol, apart from reinforcing binge drinking and the assumed links between drinking and having fun.

Continuing to play off the Godmarks billboards' theme of prayer, a cheeky Hell Pizza billboard asked, '"How do you know He is listening? At least I deliver"—The Guy from Hell'. The Advertising Standards Authority (ASA) received a fascinating complaint about this billboard. The complainant argued that the message suggested that 'He may not be listening (or may be deaf) to your prayers and this is contrary to the Bible.' The complainant went on to say:

> This advertisement in a Muslim country would lead to wholesale destruction and boycotts. It offends against the beliefs of all religions because of their faith in a god and the belief that he hears and answers prayers. Because Christians are

---

[13] 'Culture Industry' is a term coined by Theodor Adorno and Max Horkheimer of the Frankfurt school who argued that culture is commodified by capitalist corporations, particularly the mass media. See Adorno & Horkheimer (2001).

peace loving we do not react like that but we are very, very deeply offended by the suggestion contained in this advertisement. It is regarded as an insult against the Godhead and clearly directed at Him because of the use of a capital letter in 'He'. I am convinced that if it is brought to the attention of local Muslims it may release a reaction that will be damaging to this business and other innocents who may be caught in the crossfire. Perhaps it would be a good thing if it is brought to their attention. I await your decision before this is considered. I shall appreciate it if steps would be taken against them to force them to remove this insensitive and infuriating advertisement. (ASA Complaint 06/050)

This complaint demonstrates the way the media have influenced this person's image of Islam and Muslims. It is possible that the violent reaction to the caricature of Mohammed printed in a Danish newspaper is in this person's mind. The events of 9/11 and the war in Iraq have also distorted and shaped people's perception of Muslims and Muslim countries in a negative way. The person almost seems to threaten the advertisers to bring the billboard to the attention of local Muslims who 'may release a reaction that will be damaging to this business and other innocents who may be caught in the crossfire'. One cannot help notice the irony contained in this argument. There is the assumption that the Muslim reaction will be violent, unlike that of peace-loving Christians who merely bring Hell Pizza's deeply offensive advertising to the attention of Muslims, not to mention the ASA complaints board.

According to the 2006 New Zealand Census (www.stats.govt.nz/census/2006 access date 15 September 2007) there are 36,072 Muslims in New Zealand, the majority living in Auckland. People affiliated with Islam increased by 52.6 per cent between 2001 and 2006. Accordingly, it is unlikely that Muslims travelling around Auckland would not have seen the billboard or seen or passed by a Hell Pizza place. Maybe some of them have even bought pizza from Hell Pizza. Not only does this complainant misrepresent Muslims, but the 'we' claims general representation of all Christians. Maybe some of the complainant's Christian friends were equally offended. I know for a fact that a number of Christians, including myself and those at Godmarks, were not offended by this billboard and were therefore misrepresented by the 'we'.

Conclusion

The biblical rivalry between God and Satan is played out in contemporary times around the streets of Auckland on large jet black billboards. Both engage people as religious subjects in the narratives they tell, although some of Hell Pizza's billboard messages take the side of the cynical disbelieving in their irreverent and slightly cheeky mocking tone. The marketing of God and hell is played out in a semiotic landscape that is fluid and polysemic. Images of God, Satan and hell are historically, socially and culturally located. The billboard messages from both

Godmarks and Hell Pizza assume some religious knowledge or imagination, be that positive or negative.

It is hard to imagine that Hell Pizza as a creative brand would have been as successful 20 years ago. The fact that a pizza franchise can build a successful business branded on the imagery of hell suggests that there has been a change in people's belief in hell. Hell Pizza no doubt plays a part in shifting the public imagination of hell from a real place of eternal condemnation and fire to a place where you pick up pizza on a Friday night. Hell Pizza outlets visually represent the underworld and thus fictionalize hell. One could argue that such a belief makes it more tolerable for people to enter a Hell Pizza place and order pizza compared to those for whom hell is still very much a reality and not a place to buy pizza from. Some, however, continue to boycott Hell Pizza on religious grounds. The imagery is not inviting.

Godmarks constructs an image of a God that is personal, wants us to talk to Him, is interested in our lives and has a sense of humour. 'The Guy from Hell' constructed by Hell Pizza is not only cheeky, irreverent and 'delivers', but through the textual poaching of the Godmarks billboards, his messages call the Godmarks image of God into question. Hell Pizza billboards which ask questions such as 'How do you know He is listening?', do invite a response. Yet whoever 'He' is, along with images of God and 'The Guy from Hell' conjured up in people's minds, will depend not only on the cultural, social and historical context of the reader, but also on the tactics engaged in the art of 'making do'. Advertising critic Jean Kilbourne is correct when she writes that 'Advertising is our environment. We swim in it as fish swim in water. We cannot escape it' (1999: 57). However, even fish learn to play in their environment. Pizza anyone?

References

ACUTE, *The Nature of Hell* (Carlisle: Paternoster Press, 2000).

Advertising Standards Authority, www.asa.co.nz/decisions.php?year=2006 [access date throughout 2006].

Adorno, Theodor & Horkheimer, Max, 'The Culture Industry: Enlightenment as Mass Deception', in M.G. Durham & D.M. Kellner (eds), *Media and Cultural Studies: Keyworks* (Oxford: Blackwell Publishing, 2001): 71–101.

Alcohol Advisory Council of New Zealand, *Assessment of the Health Impacts of Lowering the Minimum Age for Purchasing Alcohol* (Alcohol Advisory Council, 2002). Available from www.alcohol.org.nz [access date 16 October 2002].

Anon, '"God" billboards bring gay-friendly message' (2006). Available from www.gaynz.com/news/print.asp?artid=4139 [access date 8 February 2007].

Anon, 'Boycott Hell Pizza, says Catholic Paper', *The New Zealand Herald*, 18 December 2006. Available from www.nzherald.co.nz/indexcfm?objectid= 10415923 [access date 31 January 2007].

Belk, Russell W, Wallendorf, Melanie & Sherry Jr, John F.,'The Sacred and the Profane in Consumer Behaviour: Theodicy on the Odessey', *Journal of Consumer Research*, 16/1 (June 1989): 1–38.

Brother Lawrence of the Resurrection, *The Practice of the Presence of God*, trans. John Delaney (New York: Doubleday, 1977).

Chandler, Daniel, *Semiotics: The Basics* (London: Routledge, 2002).

Clarke, Graham, *The Photograph* (Oxford: Oxford University Press, 1997).

Cox, Harvey, 'Jesus and Generation X', in Marcus Borg (ed.), *Jesus at 2000* (Colorado: Westview Press, 2000).

Crockett, William (ed.), *Four Views on Hell* (Grand Rapids: Zondervan, 1992).

De Certeau, Michel, *The Practice of Everyday Life* (Berkeley: University of California Press, 1984).

De Certeau, Michel & Giard, Luce, *Culture in the Plural* (Minneapolis: University of Minnesota Press, 1977).

De Certeau, Michel, Giard, Luce & Mayol, Pierre, *The Practice of Everyday Life, Volume 2: Living and Cooking* (Minneapolis: University of Minnesota Press, 1998).

Drinnan, John, 'Hell too Cold for Cinderella', *The Business Herald*, 7 September 2007: 7.

Fish, Stanley Eugene, *Is There a Text in This Class? The Authority of Interpretive Communities* (Cambridge, MA: Harvard University Press, 1980).

Fudge, Edward, *The Fire that Consumes: A Biblical and Historical Study of the Doctrine of Final Punishment* (Carlisle: Paternoster Press, 1982).

Godmarks website: www.godmarks.co.nz

Godspeaks website: www.godspeaks.com

Jesus All About Life Campaign website: www.jesusallaboutlife.com.au [access date 21 May 2007].

Jhally, Sut, 'Advertising as Religion: The Dialectic of Technology and Magic', in Lan Angus & Sut Jhally (eds), *Cultural Politics in Contemporary America* (New York: Routledge, 1989): 217–29.

Hall, Stuart, 'Encoding/Decoding', in M.G. Durham and D.M. Kellner (eds), *Media and Cultural Studies: Keyworks* (Oxford: Blackwell Publishing, 2001).

Hell Pizza website: www.hell.co.nz

Kilbourne, Jean, *Deadly Persuasion: Why Women and Girls Must Fight the Addictive Power of Advertising* (New York: The Free Press, 1999).

Kristeva, Julia, *Desire in Language: A Semiotic Approach to Literature and Art* (New York: Columbia University Press, 1980).

Market Access Consulting and Research, *Jesus, All About Life Campaign. Christian Media Project Qualitative Research* (NSW: Bible Society, 2003). Available from www.biblesocietynsw.com.au

Marty, Martin E., 'Hell Disappeared. No One Noticed. A Civic Argument', *Harvard Theological Review*, 78/3–4 (1985): 381–98.

Ministry of Health and Alcohol Advisory Council, *National Alcohol Strategy 2000–2003* (Wellington: Ministry of Health/Alcohol Advisory Council, 2001).

Morgan, Chris, *Jonathan Edwards & Hell* (Glasgow: Bell and Bain, 2004).

Ngatoko, Lavinia, 'Signs for the Times', *Challenge Weekly*, 63: 30 (8 August 2005): 1 & 3.

Peirce, Charles S., *Collected Papers of Charles Sanders Peirce, Volume II: Elements of Logic,* (Cambridge, MA: Harvard University Press, 1932).

Pope Benedict XVI, *Homily of His Holiness Benedict XVI,* 2007, www.vatican.va/holy_father/benedict_xvi/homilies/2007 [access date 24 May 2007].

Statistics New Zealand, *QuickStats About Culture and Identity 2006 Census.* Available from www.stats.govt.nz/census/2006-census-data/quickstats-about-culture-identity/quickstats-about-culture-and-identity.htm [access date 1 September 2007].

Weber, Hans-Ruedi, *On a Friday Noon: Meditations under the Cross* (Geneva: World Council of Churches, 1979).

Williamson, Judith, *Decoding Advertisements: Ideology and Meaning in Advertising* (London: Boyars, 1978).

Chapter 7

The Gospel of Tom (Hanks): American Churches and *The Da Vinci Code*

Ellen E. Moore

Introduction

On 19 May 2006, the blockbuster movie *The Da Vinci Code* opened in American movie theatres, holding the top box office spot and earned over US$77 million upon opening. The film—and the book of the same name on which it is based—purports to provide answers about the life of Jesus Christ, in the process calling into question some of the main tenets of Christianity, in particular whether or not Jesus was divine and whether or not he fathered children with Mary Magdalene. Catholic reactions to the movie were strong, with Vatican officials calling for boycotts (Wooden 2006), Catholic groups pressuring the Chinese government to ban the movie (Kahn 2006), religious hunger strikes in India and a ban in the Philippines (Goodstein 2006). In the US, however, it is fair to say that evangelical reactions to the movie were mixed at best. While one Presbyterian evangelical church rented an entire theatre for its members to see the movie and then take part in church-sponsored discussions, two other evangelical churches—an Assembly of God and a Vineyard church—provided alternative literature and held sermons refuting the principles of the movie. Meanwhile, religious leaders from a fourth church rejected the content of the film, but made their church grounds into a kind of *Da Vinci Code* movie set, hiding 'secret codes' for church members to find inside the sanctuary and outer areas and remaking their website and church map to look like an ancient scroll, taken directly from the movie itself.

These varied responses prompt some compelling questions, since at first glance the proper reactions of evangelical leaders and their churchgoers to a film with which they disagree might seem obvious. Why not simply boycott the movie, as many Catholic leaders advocated? Why refute the content of the movie while appropriating the style? The answer seems to rest partly in the fact that all of these churches have incorporated popular movies, commercials and television shows into the fabric of their religious messages and teachings, a strategy that increases churches' popularity and numbers (Roof 1999; Cimino & Lattin 1998). Examples of the adoption of secular media include: using contemporary game shows such as *Deal or No Deal* to discuss effective evangelizing methods, incorporating the communication company On-Star into a discussion about fostering strong

Christian values and showing a clip from the popular movie *Talladega Nights* (Adam McKay, 2006) to illustrate the power of prayer.

Although a clearly secular, mainstream media culture would seem on the surface to stand in conflict with religious beliefs and values to some degree, evangelicals themselves have typically not drawn such sharp distinctions (Hendershot 2004; Schultze 2001; Buddenbaum 2001; Marsden 1991). In fact, the values espoused by many evangelical churches do not seem that different from those in mainstream Hollywood films. According to Kellner (2000), American films typically define heterosexuality as the accepted social norm, reinforce the conception that certain conditions justify violence, focus on the importance of authority, and place clear emphasis on the value of consumption in society. Similarly, the films, commercials and television shows that many evangelical churches have incorporated into their sermons—including the film *The Guardian* (Andrew Davis, 2006) starring Ashton Kutcher, Mel Gibson's *Braveheart* (1995), *Nacho Libre* (Jared Hess, 2006) with Jack Black, and *Batman Begins* (Christopher Nolan, 2005)—consistently emphasize the importance of consumption, whiteness and heterosexuality as well as support a pro-military, pro-war stance.[1] While it seems as though reframing secular media to have a religious message has been successful for churches' success in terms of increasing numbers, it is evident that there is substantial tension underneath such reframing. It is this unease that becomes most apparent when popular culture goes too far in using religious symbols for a secularist message. In the case of *The Da Vinci Code*, what is directly attacked is the integrity of the most prominent and important symbol in Christianity: Christ himself.

A movie like *The Da Vinci Code* thus appears to pose two interrelated problems for evangelical churches. Firstly, it challenges the strategy of appropriating and reframing secular media symbols to create religious messages, and thus exposes the significant tension that arises when the boundaries between mainstream culture and religious faith are blurred. In addition, it recasts Christianity's own symbols by using a vehicle that resonates with evangelical individuals: popular culture itself. However, the research on which this chapter is based reveals a third issue: these churches are forced to confront their churchgoers' familiarity—and reliance on—Enlightenment concepts concerning rational thought, individualism, scientific reasoning and what constitutes 'fact'. In this case, the embrace of popular culture by both evangelical churches and their churchgoers complicates this issue, because what provides the 'truth' in some instances is popular culture itself.

---

[1] Other scholars have drawn similar conclusions regarding evangelicals' general support of war, with Bacevich (2005) noting the close ties between evangelical churches and the military during the Vietnam war, Martin (2005) describing Billy Graham's support of the military during the Korean War, and Marsden (1991) chronicling evangelicals' pro-war stance during World War I.

Methodology

Data for my research have been drawn from several sources, including multiple observations of church services before, during and after *The Da Vinci Code* was released in theatres. This included attending a screening of the film by one church (that had rented out an entire theatre so that churchgoers could see the movie together) and observing the pastor-led discussion group that followed. I also read the literature—including 'fact sheets' and books—that churches provided in response to the movie. Finally, church observations were supplemented by a series of interviews and focus groups with evangelicals—both churchgoers and church leaders—which explored the relationship between media and religion. The focus groups and interviews provided an in-depth exploration of the way in which evangelicals perceived the churches' use of secular media and how this shapes both private religious faith and perceptions about objectivity and truth.

This multi-method approach provides an understanding not only of churches' use of secular media and the messages being conveyed, but also of how individual churchgoers receive these messages and of the implications of this for faith and perceptions of science and objectivity. What becomes clear is that mainstream media, science and religion are connected in different ways: the portrayal of science in the secular media influences ideas about empirical reasoning and the scientific process and perceptions of science in turn challenge religious doctrine and private faith. *The Da Vinci Code* allows for an analysis of this intersection for various reasons, including its worldwide popularity, the close relationship that contemporary churchgoers have with American media culture and its appeal to scientific and historical evidence in the search for details about the human life of Jesus. My research thus provides a glimpse into the nature of contemporary American evangelicalism as it is shaped by mainstream media and into the beliefs held by modern churchgoers about the power of science and the importance of objectivity and 'truth'.

'A Diabolical Attack on Christianity': Evangelical Reactions to *The Da Vinci Code*

What emerges from the various methods is a surprising picture of the myriad, often conflicting, ways in which evangelical churches, with their heavy reliance on secular media, attempt to negotiate their churchgoers' immersion in, and love of, mainstream, consumerist culture—a connection that these churches have often encouraged (Hendershot 2004; Roof 1999; Cimino & Lattin 1998). What follows are examples of the various ways in which evangelical churches have responded to *The Da Vinci Code*. Of course, this list is not exhaustive and represents only the churches observed during the course of this research. However, all of these churches are part of much larger national and international organizations, allowing for the possibility that the results of this research may be indicative of larger trends within the US. In each reaction, the underlying tension becomes clear: the churches can neither completely embrace nor completely reject this instance of popular culture, partly because of their churchgoers' close relationship with secular media, and partly because of American individuals' perceptions of the nature of science and objectivity.

The leaders of one church—a Vineyard denomination 'megachurch'—reacted by rejecting the premise of the movie and many of the 'myths' it contained. However, the pastor stopped short of telling churchgoers not to see the movie, instead simply exhorting members to stay engaged and involved and implying that churchgoers could see the movie and read the book so as to be able to respond in conversations with 'non-believers' who were challenging the Christian faith. Encouraging members to be engaged did not mean that any part of the book was considered to be acceptable; in fact, the pastor called the book a 'diabolical attack' on the Christian faith and a 'grand deception' that had to be addressed. The fact that he perceived *The Da Vinci Code* to be a 'cultural phenomenon that is sweeping America' seemed to make it even more threatening. In addition, the pastor's statement about the role of popular culture in America revealed a great deal about the close relationship between evangelicalism and the secular media: 'We can't ignore that this is the water we swim in. It's here, it's part of our life, it's part of what we're living in.' To supplement the sermon, the pastor also provided online notes to refute the 'erroneous facts' in the movie.

Another church, an Assembly of God church, reacted by rejecting the movie outright, providing sermons and alternative literature to frame the discussion and help churchgoers refute the assertions made in *The Da Vinci Code*. Although they did not explicitly state that church members were not to see the movie or read the book, the message was clear: 'The Bible is the authority, not the book.' Oddly, however, in the strongest attempt to refute the statements made in the movie, the pastor relied not on the Bible, but on the words of a fictional character in the movie itself: 'As Langdon himself says, "All that matters is what you believe."' The pastor's reliance on popular culture to frame discussions about Christianity reveals the potential authority that is attributed to the secular media, especially when it comes to individual faith.

Similar to leaders of the Vineyard church, this pastor also expressed uneasiness about the potential influence of the secular media on evangelicals' faith, most notably in his statement that 'We live in a media-driven society, where images make impacts and imprints.' The pastor's main concern seemed to be that this popular movie would make church members vulnerable to doubts concerning some of the central tenets of the Christian faith. Ironically, however, this was the same church that had used the images of Victoria's Secret (an American lingerie company known for its provocative images of women) advertisements in its sermons a few months earlier in an attempt to frame a discussion about healthy family relationships (Moore & Press, 2007). Although church leaders consistently recast the symbols from secular popular culture to imbue them with religious undertones, they were extremely uncomfortable with religious symbols being employed for the decidedly secular, arguably anti-Christian message conveyed in *The Da Vinci Code*.

The third church, which identified itself as evangelical Presbyterian, rented out a local movie theatre for its churchgoers to view the movie and then held a lunch seminar immediately afterwards, when the pastor refuted the premise and some of the assertions made in the movie. To frame the discussion, the pastor provided a handout for churchgoers to read while he discussed the 'claims' and 'inaccuracies' of the book and movie. Churchgoers—whose questions are discussed in more detail below—were then invited to ask questions to be answered by church leaders.

Finally, an evangelical church based in Chicago strongly refuted the claims made by the movie and provided numerous works of literature for churchgoers to purchase that contradicted the film's premise. Quite clearly, this church viewed the movie as a direct threat to the Christian faith. At the same time, however, the church grounds were turned into a kind of *Da Vinci Code* set, so that members could go from the sanctuary to the outer buildings solving encoded puzzles and riddles, just as the characters in the book and movie do. In addition, the church's website contained a map of the church grounds that was re-drafted to resemble an ancient scroll, similar to the parchment shown in the film. Such incongruous reactions—rejecting the content of the movie, but appropriating its forms—reveal a great deal about the degree to which evangelical churches have adopted secular media. Interestingly, this Chicago church, which clearly exhibits the strong love/hate relationship with the media that characterizes many evangelical churches (Schultze 2001), was one of the first churches to make secular media—and consumer culture—the cornerstone of its marketing strategy (e.g. Cimino & Lattin 1998).

Doubt and Faith: The Effect of the 'Spiritual Marketplace'

What the four closely related reactions have in common is the perceived need to address the assertions made in *The Da Vinci Code* and the issues they raise in the minds of churchgoers. As set out above, the churches held discussions, provided 'fact sheets' and offered a plethora of alternative media (mostly books) that pointed out the factual errors in the movie and book. Yet, why did the churches feel the need to address the claims made in the movie and book for their churchgoers? First and foremost, this is because these churches have appealed to previously 'unchurched' individuals through secular media, to those who are either unfamiliar or disillusioned with more traditional religious traditions, a finding that was clearly supported in the interviews.

In an article in the *The New York Times* entitled 'It's Not Just a Movie, It's a Revelation (About the Audience)', Laurie Goodstein points out that the reactions to the film reveal a great deal about the changes in evangelical churches and American society that have occurred since the 1980s, when evangelical churches first began to appeal to 'seekers'—individuals who might be spiritual, but not necessarily strictly religious and who are immersed in the American media culture. According to Cimino & Lattin, declining church attendance in the 1970s and 1980s necessitated a new approach and evangelical churches responded by shifting to a 'market-based' strategy that resulted in a distinct change in the way contemporary evangelical churches in the US see their constituencies:

> Megachurch leaders unashamedly admit the influence of business and management theory … 'What is our business?' 'Who is our customer?' 'What does the customer consider value?' (Cimino & Lattin 1998: 57)

Einstein (2007) refers to this distinct shift as an adoption of the practices of religious marketing, in which religion is seen as a commodity in the marketplace that can be advertised and bought. Integral to this approach is a reliance on secular media and their concomitant emphasis on consumerism. The appeal to individual 'seekers' is largely conducted through a consumerist approach that employs various elements of popular culture, including rock music, television shows and coffee bars. According to Roof,

> 'Seeker churches' work at developing forms of worship … that convey a sense of authenticity and reality about contemporary life. Above all, they try not to be boring … Overhead projectors and large screens making possible visual connection with lyrics, cartoons, and Bible verses add to the overall experience. Drama and clips from film and television—mininarratives describing the joys and dilemmas of life—communicate effectively and relate to common, everyday experiences. (Roof 1999: 96)

What is created in the process is what Roof refers to as a 'spiritual marketplace', a marketplace where churches are seen to compete with one another for members. This relatively new 'marketplace', where churchgoers select churches to attend based upon individual needs and desires (akin to consumers), has been addressed by a number of scholars, including Schofield Clark (2007), Hoover (2006) and Cimino & Lattin (1998). According to Cimino & Lattin, 'The underlying concept of "seeker" congregations is that churches should meet the wider consumer culture on its own ground. Ideas and practices—however strongly they may be tied to one's denominational tradition—may be abandoned if they stand in the way of drawing new members' (Cimino & Lattin 1998: 68). The incorporation of secular media—including popular films and television shows—into church messages not only reflect evangelical churches' consumerist approach, but also continues to erode the distinction between the values of mainstream, consumerist culture and religious faith (Moore & Press 2007). In sum, the churches observed for this research fit the pattern recognized by many scholars of religion: evangelical churches are not based in older religious traditions, but embrace the individualistic search for meaning and self-fulfilment.

In the context of my research, treating churchgoers as customers—and consumers of popular films, television shows and contemporary music—creates the practice of privileging the individual over the institution, thereby creating the opportunity for churchgoers to reject or question the Church's messages, if they contradict the individual search for meaning or happiness. The perceived need by evangelical churches to address the doubts of churchgoers regarding *The Da Vinci Code* thus appears to be directly tied to the appeal through popular culture to 'seekers'—individuals who are 'unchurched' and who might be the most prone to doubt. When the Vineyard pastor expressed his anxiety that 'I've already had people come to me that are confused' after seeing the movie, it reveals the nature of the new evangelical churchgoers: they question the precepts of traditional religion, a tendency that is exacerbated by a movie such as *The Da Vinci Code*, which purports to be at least partly based on fact.[2] The blend of fact and fiction, of entertainment and supposed reality (in the form of scientific evidence regarding historical people and events) seems to pose the greatest difficulty for evangelical churches, although they have already crossed this line in the space of the Church by employing secular media for their purposes.

Fact, Fiction and Faith: American Evangelical Churches and Popular Culture

The redefinition of churchgoers as consumers and the use of secular media are not the only explanations why *The Da Vinci Code* elicited the controversial reactions among evangelical leaders. Another reason for the tension is revealed in the language used by the church leaders:

> *The Da Vinci Code* is filled with half-truths, distorted facts, and outright lies about the person of Jesus Christ and foundational Christian beliefs ... and these statements often appear deceptively as the truth. Christianity is not about simply believing what we want ... Truth does matter, truth is important, and truth must be fought for. (Vineyard sermon, 6 April 2006)

> ... the [*Da Vinci Code*] is filled with inaccuracies. It maintains that the Dead Sea Scrolls were discovered in the 1950s. They were actually discovered in 1947. The book reports that the pyramid at the entrance of the Louvre is composed of 666 panes of glass, thus evoking Satanic connections. Except that the pyramid is composed of 673 panes of glass. (Pastor at the Presbyterian church, 20 May 2006)

---

[2]   The author Dan Brown consistently blends fact with fiction, creating a story around imaginary characters, but including a section in *The Da Vinci Code* that lists historical and scientific evidence to support the claims made in the book.

What stands out in these statements is a sharp distinction being made between 'fact' and 'fiction', a point made previously by Press & Cole (1999) in their analysis of how the relationship between media, science, and religion influenced how women talk about abortion. Employing the language of scientific reasoning—including 'inaccuracy', 'truth' and 'proof'—reveals the churches' strategy in responding to *The Da Vinci Code*, which is to challenge the 'evidence': in this instance of popular culture. However, what constitutes 'truth' for evangelical church leaders and, perhaps more importantly, how do churchgoers themselves conceive of truth in their quest for faith? The first part of this question can be answered by data obtained in observations during church sermons and discussions, while the latter is addressed through interview and focus group material.

What my research reveals is that the churches used three main sources of information to contradict the assertions made in *The Da Vinci Code*: scientific and historical evidence, biblical sources and, surprisingly, popular culture itself. None of these categories is mutually exclusive: much of the biblical 'evidence' cited by the churches is based upon scientific analysis of historical texts, while contemporary secular media consistently blur the line between fiction and reality, thus shaping perceptions of science and the scientific process. What is surprising, however, is to note how infrequently church members were called upon to rely solely on faith—an omission that seems, at least on the surface, to privilege scientific knowledge and reasoning over personal religious conviction.

American Churches and Science

One of the primary ways in which churches attempted to refute the statements in *The Da Vinci Code* was by challenging the authenticity of the historical documents used by Dan Brown. The Presbyterian church pastor, in his lunch discussion, noted that 'the famous *Gospel of Philip* text 63:32 is actually broken', so that the specifics of Jesus' relationship with Mary Magdalene could not be known with certainty. In addition, the church leader stated that, regardless of its state of preservation, the gospel was not 'authentic', which was due to the late time frame in which it was written, calling it instead a 'misguided forgery'. The Assembly of God church took a similar approach, providing literature which indicates that 'bona fide' scholars have dated the *Gospel of Philip* and the *Gospel of Mary*, both of which featured in the film, hundreds of years after Jesus' time.[3] The Vineyard church relied on historical data to challenge statements in *The Da Vinci Code* about events that occurred at the Council of Nicaea. The churches also discussed historical figures, such as the Roman Emperor Constantine and his role in the creation of the gospels' idea of Christ's divinity.

---

[3]   The book provided by the Assembly of God church was Josh McDowell's *A Quest for Answers: The Da Vinci Code* (2006). Similar to *The Da Vinci Code*, this book contains 'Fact or Fiction' sections, provides timetables for the dates of certain gospels, and cites 'eminent' scholars to support biblical and historical claims.

In relying on historical and scientific evidence to assess the authenticity of the claims in *The Da Vinci Code*, it appears that the churches attempted to provide a body of knowledge that churchgoers can use to counter the assertions made in the book and movie. The reliance on evidence to verify truth claims reveals a great deal about the close relationship between American Christianity and science, most clearly in assumptions about the power of the scientific process to reach an absolute objective truth. As Christian Smith notes, science and Christianity were considered to be mutually supportive in the nineteenth century:

> The Bible would reveal God's moral law and certain natural truths; science, for its part, would confirm the teachings of the Bible and expand human understanding beyond what the Bible revealed. Together, the Bible and science were expected to render a rational validation of the veracity of Christianity and lay the foundation for a healthy national moral and social order. (Smith 1998: 3)

This line of thinking keeps science and religion particularly close, especially in the US. One well-known example comes from Dr Francis Collins, the head of the Human Genome Project, whose recent book *The Language of God: A Scientist Presents Evidence for Belief* presents the idea that scientific knowledge can be used to aid faith instead of contradicting it (Masci 2008). Press & Cole recognize this connection, noting that in their study the pro-life evangelical women often framed their discussions in scientific terms, emphasizing the need for documentation and scientific fact to understand abortion issues. In the course of the current research it was clear that evangelicals were quite comfortable about talking about science in relation to their religion. Far from the uneducated, backward stereotype of Christians portrayed by the media during the Scopes Trial in the 1920s (Marsden 1991), the evangelicals I interviewed had all completed high school (with the majority of the women in one group having college degrees), were fairly media literate and were, for the most part, immersed in mainstream culture: many watched popular television shows, used the internet and were familiar with the latest political and social events. In addition, one taught high school science and several others considered themselves to be amateur scientists. One man in particular had a set of fossils that he had collected in a nearby town. He emphasized that he did not doubt that the fossils were 43 million years old (a fact which a local scientist had provided through analysis), indicating that an older age for the earth did not pose a threat to his religious beliefs.

Interestingly, however, evangelicals' acceptance of both science and the media was tempered by certain issues, including a perceived 'liberal' bias in the media and the problems posed by certain components of science, such as evolution. These findings fit well with a recent study conducted by Keeter and colleagues at the Pew Research Center, who note the potential point of tension between scientific evidence and religious belief in the U.S. However, Keeter *et al.* (2007) see this tension as being extremely limited, stating that 'the theory of evolution as a means to explain the origins and development of life remain the only truly concrete example of such a conflict'.

What becomes clear is that, although the evangelicals in this study appeared to be immersed in mainstream American culture, discussions about the media and certain aspects of science highlighted significant points of tension. However, the general acceptance of science was made clear when the churches I observed framed their arguments in scientific language about evidence and authenticity in a way that was clearly understood by the churchgoers.

Biblical Authority

In responding to *The Da Vinci Code*, the churches I studied also relied upon the Bible, predominately by citing numerous biblical passages to refute the claims made in the movie. For instance, an Assembly of God pastor referred to 1 Timothy 3:16: 'Every Scripture is God-breathed and profitable'. This was followed with a list of 'heresies' in *The Da Vinci Code* which were systematically refuted through reference to scripture. For instance, in response to the assertion that the Council of Nicaea invented the divinity of Jesus, the pastor provided John 10:30: 'I and the Father are one.' The question whether Jesus was married to Mary Magdalene was answered by the pastor with reference to Revelation 21:9: 'And he spoke with me, saying, "Come here. I will show you the wife, the Lamb's bride."'[4] The pastor of the Presbyterian church used biblical verses in a similar fashion, stating that 'passages like John 4:6 and John 11:35 clearly show Christ's humanity'. Interestingly, however, the Bible was also subject to questions concerning truth and authenticity. In response to *The Da Vinci Code*'s claim that the Roman emperor Constantine himself created the Bible, one church listed the criteria that were used to select the gospels for the New Testament. In essence, the church leaders provided 'evidence' for the authenticity of the biblical canon.

The pastors' statements indicate reliance upon the Bible and it is clear that faith plays a significant role in the churches' discussions of Jesus' divinity. However, it is both striking and significant that the Bible itself—as the 'ultimate authority'—is subject to scrutiny; hence the need to provide evidence for the authenticity of some of the gospels. Thus, it appears that, for the churches in this study at least, faith in the Bible is insufficient: in order to be compelling (from both an intellectual and religious standpoint), the Bible must first be subjected to the rigours of scientific inquiry.

The Authority of Tom Hanks: Popular Culture and Evangelical Churches

The churches in this study did, however, not rely solely on scientific reasoning and the authority of the Bible. What provides striking insight into the relationship

---

[4]   The 'wife', or 'lamb's bride', thus appears to be the city of Jerusalem, and not Mary Magdalene.

between popular culture and religion was the frequency with which popular culture was invoked as a definitive way to distinguish fact from fiction. This included comments from the pastor of the Presbyterian church: he made an odd attempt to discredit the veracity of the movie by stating that '*The Da Vinci Code* is a work of fiction. Tom Hanks said so himself.' Later the pastor commented on the actor's private life, stating that 'I heard Tom Hanks might be a Christian. Perhaps the story in the well came from him.'[5] In this case, a popular actor is invoked as an authoritative source in a discussion about Christianity. As mentioned earlier, the Assembly of God pastor also resorted to popular culture by quoting Robert Langdon, the main character in *The Da Vinci Code*: 'The most important thing is what you believe.'

These comments indicate a significant blurring of the line between reality and fiction, as the purported real-life beliefs and behaviour of Tom Hanks the actor are integrated into his fictional character Robert Langdon. In addition, an appeal for faith that stems from a character in a fictional work is a powerful indicator of evangelical churches' perceptions of what might constitute 'truth' for individual churchgoers: popular culture itself. It is also a testament to the churches' beliefs regarding the power of popular culture to change perceptions and challenge beliefs through the presentation of what is true and what is not true. This was evident in both the Assembly of God pastor's comment about the potential 'impacts and imprints' that images can have on individuals and in the Vineyard pastor's concern about 'confused' members of the congregation who had seen the movie. Comments such as these indicate strong convictions about the power of the secular media to challenge religious beliefs about Christianity and the power of knowledge—not faith—to provide answers.

At this juncture it is important to ask what individual churchgoers themselves feel about the secular media—in the space of the church and in their own private lives—and how this affects evangelical perceptions of a movie like *The Da Vinci Code*. Many evangelicals I observed fit the profile of the description by Roof and Cimino & Lattin of 'seekers': those who are immersed in the American media culture, make no hard and fast distinctions between spirituality and traditional religion and have the potential to question the more traditional aspects of their religion. This aspect of American evangelicalism has the greatest potential to influence individuals' perceptions of a movie like *The Da Vinci Code*. While the church leaders' reactions were overwhelmingly negative, I observed that evangelical churchgoers voiced no explicit criticism of the movie; their reactions were surprising positive, revealing a great deal about the influence of secular media consumption on perceptions of science and personal faith.

---

[5]   In the movie, the main character Robert Langdon (played by Tom Hanks) recalls a childhood event when he was trapped in a well overnight. The character states that he felt as though he was not alone in the well, an experience that gave him faith as an adult in later life.

Testing Jesus' DNA: Churchgoers' Perceptions of Popular Culture, Science and *The Da Vinci* Code

The Da Vinci Code, which purports to tell the 'truth' about Christianity, has created an opportunity to discuss the relationship between the secular media and religion. During my interviews with evangelicals, I noted that they were careful to distinguish between what they considered 'good' and 'bad' science; they were able to accept the general principles of science—the process of scientific reasoning, testing, empirical evidence and so forth—while completely rejecting the concept of evolution. Therefore many felt comfortable about discussing biology as long as evolution was not included in the discussion. Thus, when an immensely popular movie, such as *The Da Vinci Code*, draws upon (or contends to draw upon) scientific principles in order to challenge central principles of the Christian religion, it is not surprising that this sparks fierce debate and controversy in evangelical churches. However, the somewhat positive reaction from churchgoers themselves stands in marked contrast to the negative responses by the church leaders and merits exploration.

The analysis of reactions to *The Da Vinci Code* indicates that evangelical churchgoers do not make hard and fast distinctions between science and faith: they are comfortable about blurring the boundaries. Part of this ease rests in the historically close relationship between religion and science. Another reason may be the consumption of American mainstream media, as entertainment television increasingly blurs the lines between fiction and reality, a point taken up in conjunction with evangelicals' statements below. In this sense, this study provides an interesting insight into American media culture and the effect it has on perceptions of science and questions of faith.

Churchgoers' Reception of The Da Vinci Code*: The Nature of 'Seekers'*

As described earlier, when *The Da Vinci Code* first opened in theatres in May 2006, I went to a private screening held by a local evangelical Presbyterian church that had rented an entire theatre complex so that its churchgoers could see the movie together. After the movie I attended a lunchtime discussion which was held by the pastor at the church. When he had finished speaking, the pastor invited questions. The questions and comments from the churchgoers provide significant insight into the way evangelicals themselves negotiate the intersection of science, popular culture and faith.

Many questions revealed the individualistic focus and 'seeker' character of contemporary evangelical churches. Countering the pastor's vehement assertion that there was no scientific or historical evidence that Jesus was married to Mary Magdalene, one woman in her 50s asked, 'If he hungered or thirsted, couldn't he have married? What would it matter if he had?' Although the churches stressed the importance of believing in the Bible's inerrancy and strict adherence to the scriptures (Roof 1999; Smith 1998; McDannell 1995; Marsden 1991), this woman questioned whether new evidence (in the form of new gospels that were not in the New Testament) could shed more light on the subject. She was thus open to the idea that the Bible—and perhaps her pastor—did not provide all the information required to understand her version of Christianity. In addition, she asked about the possibility that Jesus' bloodline may have continued, referring directly to claims made in the movie and the questions they raised for her.

Another evangelical, a man in his 60s, told the pastor he had difficulty seeing Jesus as divine, since it was so clear that he had lived a human life. Even more telling, perhaps, was a question posed by a third person who asked if it was possible to conduct DNA tests in the laboratory on the remains of potential members of the bloodline created by Jesus and Mary Magdalene. This sparked an unusual exchange between pastor and congregation: the pastor replied that it would be possible to test for DNA, but only if Jesus' remains could be found to provide a baseline with which to compare with the descendants from the bloodline. Many members of the congregation nodded in agreement, when this was said, apparently understanding this point.

Questions like this—and the ones asked before it—indicate that the claims in a popular movie had made individuals reconsider or question information in the Bible and church teachings. Such questions caused the pastor at the Vineyard church to lament that the movie was creating 'confused' Christians. The unusual conversation between the Presbyterian pastor and the churchgoers about the possibility of conducting scientific tests on Jesus' remains indicates several things, including compatibility between science and religion; thus, to find out if Jesus fathered children with Mary Magdalene, one simply tests the DNA. The most unusual part of this is, however, the clear association between popular culture, science and religion: not only were the questions about Jesus' life sparked by a popular movie, but the potential answer to these questions could be provided through reference to popular television crime dramas that include plot lines about DNA testing.

According to Delli Carpini & Williams (1994), the line between entertainment and reality has been blurred for some time; they cite the example of the way lawyers are now forced to approach real-life legal cases differently, because *LA Law* has had an impact on jurors' understanding of certain aspects relating to the legal system. In a similar vein, the churchgoers in this study discussed issues of faith in terms of contemporary crime dramas like *CSI*: 'Couldn't we get the DNA and test it?' Interestingly, the pastors appeared to recognize the importance of the secular media for the way their churchgoers understood their faith, which was revealed by their willingness to engage not only in conversations about scientific testing of Jesus' DNA, but also with references to Tom Hanks's private religious beliefs and the stated convictions of fictional characters in the movie. Quite clearly, *The Da Vinci Code* had created questions in their minds that the pastor was not able to address and church leaders were aware of the authority of the secular media to challenge churchgoers' faith.

Focus Groups: A Closer Look at Evangelical Churchgoers and Secular Media

Statements such as those made in the church discussions indicate evangelicals' ready familiarity with the mainstream media and underscore how easily the secular media are brought into the space of the church and into discussions of personal faith. The focus groups revealed that the use of secular media, far from detracting from personal religious experience, actually enhances the notion of the sacred and strengthens personal faith. All the focus groups were conducted in the months before *The Da Vinci Code* opened in theatres, thus precluding in-depth discussions of the movie. The focus groups can, however, shed light on the close relationship that evangelicals have with the media and how this intersects with their personal religious faith.

In the conversations with evangelicals I found that many had left more traditional churches, including Catholic, United Methodist and Synod Lutheran, because they felt they had very little connection with them. One participant, a high school teacher, explained it as follows:

> I grew up in a Missouri Synod Lutheran Church, you know, very traditional, the organ playing, and you sing out a hymnal and, you know, so everything is *very* different from here, and you know I think … I have much more of a connection to God when I'm at New Beginnings in a more modern setting, than I do when I go to my grandma's church.

A woman, a homemaker and mother of two, had a very positive view of media use in her church, stating that it ultimately helped her to develop a 'connection', or relationship, with God:

> So I think that it actually makes a point, to try to meet people where they're at, so that God can make a connection with them, and then they make a connection with other people as a result of that.

For many evangelicals interviewed for the study, the media were seen not only as an effective evangelizing tool to attract new members and 'bring them to God', but also as an instrument to strengthen their own personal connection to their faith. The emphasis on a personal relationship with God is a primary defining characteristic of contemporary evangelicalism (Marsden 1991) and, according to the evangelicals I interviewed, the secular media are seen as integral to fostering this relationship. Thus media use in a contemporary church setting seemed to make churchgoers feel more closely connected to their faith than they considered possible in more traditional churches (one participant referred to them as being 'dead') without any media. One evangelical woman, who discussed the use of the movies *National Treasure* (Jon Turteltaub, 2004) and *Batman Begins* (Christopher Nolan, 2005) in her church, provided an especially clear example of the way in which the connection between secular media and faith occurs:

But actually pay attention to what you're looking at, what issues this character is facing, you know, are those issues that you maybe face as well? And so, I think in that way, you know, here's somebody with a bunch of money [in *National Treasure*] and what's he going to do with it? Well, what do you do if you have a whole bunch of money, you know, what does God say about having a lot and how you spend your money? Or, you know, you have all this unresolved guilt [in *Batman Begins*], what does God say about how can you resolve that guilt and where can you look for comfort, and ways to take care of that?

Such statements provide strong support for the idea that secular, entertainment media can be used to strengthen personal faith. Although it seems that on the surface movies like *National Treasure* or *The 40 Year Old Virgin* (Judd Apatow, 2005) hardly contain anything that speaks to religious values, Roof notes that reframing is part of evangelicalism's strength: 'Reframing has potential in a media age, where words and symbols are manipulated in ways that often disassociate them from a historic and grounded tradition … Rather than approach a symbol as doctrinally formulated, allow the possibility that people may freely associate with it, drawing from their own experiences' (Roof 1999: 170). In sum, the focus groups provide strong support that the secular media, at least for the evangelicals I observed, play a powerful role in their personal faith. This in turn provides crucial insights into the reactions by evangelical churches—and their churchgoers—to *The Da Vinci Code*.

Conclusion

The research described in this chapter has explored the close, often uneasy relationship between American evangelical churches and the mainstream media at a specific moment when secular and religious values stand in direct contrast. The churches that I observed responded in different ways to the movie *The Da Vinci Code* in several respects, but had a number of features in common, including reliance on scientific reasoning, search for the 'facts' and demonstration of close connection with secular, entertainment media. Evangelical churches have been employing secular media as an evangelizing tool for some time, effectively reframing the symbols in secular culture into messages with religious undertones. The problem for evangelical churches is, however, that *The Da Vinci Code* did the reverse very well: it challenged the authenticity of Christianity's own symbols while using the conventions of popular culture and appealing to Americans' love of science.

Evangelical leaders appeared to find themselves in a bind: the very instrument that was so effective in evangelizing—the secular media—had become a competing source of information and 'truth'. The focus groups and church discussions revealed evangelicals' positive perceptions of the use of mainstream media in church sermons: many felt that they could make closer connections with God through the experience of the secular media during worship. However, an important question is what happens when the mainstream media—especially an incredibly popular movie about Christ—stands in direct conflict with evangelical Christian values? As this research has shown, *The Da Vinci Code* proved exceptionally effective in challenging contemporary evangelicals' faith, as indicated by church observations.

The 'spiritual marketplace' described by Roof has so far been largely successful in intertwining religion, the media and consumerism to attract churchgoers. The argument here is this: when evangelical churches begin to open the door to accepting secular culture—even embracing it through the use of secular media in the space of the church—this places limits on their ability to respond when an instance of popular culture contradicts the tenets of religious faith. Ultimately, a movie like *The Da Vinci Code* reveals the significant pitfalls of fostering a connection between private religious faith and the mainstream media, not only because of the individuality that the secular media encourage, but because the media, used by evangelical leaders so readily for evangelism, have the potential to become a competing source of information and truth.

Bibliography

Bacevich, Andrew, *The New American Militarism: How Americans are Seduced by War* (Oxford: Oxford University Press, 2005).

Buddenbaum, Judith, 'Christian Perspectives on Mass Media', in Daniel Stout & Judith Buddenbaum (eds), *Religion and Popular Culture: Studies on the Interaction of Worldviews* (Iowa City: Iowa State University Press, 2001): 81–94.

Cimino, Richard & Lattin, Don, *Shopping for Faith: American Religion in the New Millennium* (San Francisco: Jossey-Bass, 1998).

Clark, Lynn Schofield, 'Introduction: Identity, Belonging, and Religious Lifestyle Branding (Fashion Bibles, Bhangra Parties, and Muslim Pop)', in Lynn Schofield Clark (ed.), *Religion, Media, and the Marketplace* (New Brunswick: Rutgers University Press, 2007): 1–36.

Collins, Francis, *The Language of God: a Scientist Presents Evidence for Belief* (New York: Simon & Schuster, 2006).

Delli Carpini, Michael X & Williams, Bruce A. (1994), '"Fictional" and "Non-Fictional" Television Celebrates Earth Day: or, Politics is Comedy Plus Pretense', *Cultural Studies*, 8/1 (1994): 74–98.

Einstein, Mara, *Brands of Faith: Marketing Religion in a Commercial Age* (New York: Routledge, 2007).

Goodstein, Laurie, 'It's not just a Movie, it's a Revelation (about the Audience)', *New York Times*, 21 May 2006, www.nytimes.com/2006/05/21/weekinreview/21goodstein.htm [access date 26 May 2006].

Hendershot, Heather, *Shaking the World for Jesus* (Chicago: University of Chicago Press, 2004).

Hoover, Stewart, *Religion in the Media Age* (London: Routledge, 2006).

Kahn, Joseph, 'China Bans 'Code' After Warning from Catholics', *New York Times*, 6 June 2006, www.nytimes.com/2006/06/09/world/asia/09cnd-china. html?ex=1151121600&en=d8a80022b1cadb92&ei=5070 [access date 26 June 2006].

Keeter, Scott, Masci, David & Smith, Gregory, 'Science in America: Religious Belief and Public Attitudes', *The Pew Forum on Religion and Public Life*, 18 December 2007, http://pewforum.org/docs/?DocID=275 [access date 12 May 2008].

Kellner, Douglas, 'Hollywood Film and Society', in John Hill, Pamela Church Gibson, Richard Dyer, E. Ann Kaplan & Paul Willeman (eds), *American Cinema and Hollywood: Critical Approaches* (Oxford: Oxford University Press, 2000): 128–36.

Marsden, George, *Understanding Fundamentalism and Evangelicalism* (Grand Rapids: Eerdmans, 1991).

Martin, William, *With God on Our Side: The Rise of the Religious Right in America* (New York: Broadway Books, 2005).

Masci, David, 'The "Evidence for Belief": an Interview with Francis Collins', *The Pew Forum on Religion and Public Life*, 17 April 2008, http://pewforum. org/events/?EventID=178 [access date 12 May 2008].

McDannell, Colleen, *Material Christianity: Religion and Popular Culture in America* (New Haven: Yale University Press, 1995).

McDowell, Josh, *A Quest for Answers: The Da Vinci Code* (Holiday, FL: Green Key Books, 2006).

Moore, Ellen & Press, Andrea, *Where Would Jesus Shop?* (Unpublished manuscript, 2007).

Press, Andrea & Cole, Elizabeth, *Speaking of Abortion: Television and Authority in the Lives of Women* (Chicago: University of Chicago Press, 1999).

Roof, Wade Clark, *Spiritual Marketplace: Baby Boomers and the Remaking of American Religion* (Princeton: Princeton University Press, 1999).

Schultze, Quentin, 'Touched by Angels and Demons: Religions' Love–Hate Relationship with Popular Culture', in Daniel Stout & Judith Buddenbaum (eds), *Religion and Popular Culture: Studies on the Interaction of Worldviews* (Iowa City: Iowa State University Press, 2001): 39-48.

Smith, Christian, *American Evangelicalism: Embattled and Thriving* (Chicago: University of Chicago Press, 1998).

Wooden, Cindy, 'Vatican official suggests Catholics boycott *The Da Vinci Code* film', *Catholic News Service*, 1 May 2006, www.catholicnews.com/data/ stories/cns/0602483.htm [access date 21 June 2006].

Chapter 8

From Pulp Fiction to Revealed Text: A Study of the Role of the Text in the Otherkin Community

Danielle Kirby

The search for the sacred within the secular is not a new process in the modern world. Since the advent of theories of secularization, evidence of the opposing trend has been mounting (see Hanegraaff 2000: 301; Introvigne 2004: 981–2; Partridge 2005: 1–2). New Age beliefs (Heelas 1996), contemporary occultism (Hanegraaff 1998), Wicca and paganism (Harvey 2006; Hume 1997) are but some of the many movements that have taken an individually driven and eclectic approach to religion and spirituality that has at least a partial premise in the creations of popular culture. The popularization of the Internet has intensified this already existing trend, allowing for the establishment and growth of groups previously unknown, or at least those diffused to the point of non-existence within the public realm (Dawson & Hennebry 1999). The Otherkin, a loosely affiliated virtual community with an alternative metaphysical foundation, is one such group (www.otherkin.net). The unifying feature of the Otherkin community is a shared belief in non-human, often fantastic or mythological, souls and selves. Their beliefs are heavily constituted in relation to popular culture texts of all media (books, films, TV, comics, etc.) and the community holds a variety of approaches to the personal spiritual meaning of these narratives. This group, among others, demonstrates a range of beliefs that use fiction in a variety of ways: from the adoption of a code of behaviour, the evocative illustration of a worldview to the content of belief. While the actual integration of beliefs is extremely individual for participants, they all share a common factor: the conscious integration of explicitly fictional narrative into a sacred or spiritual context. This chapter seeks to explore the spectrum of approaches to the text by viewing four separate groups which are located in a broadly similar position within the cultic milieu (Campbell 1972: 122–4): Jediism, Paganism, the Church of All Worlds and the Otherkin. Particular attention will be paid to the latter, the Otherkin, as an example of the most deviant position with regard to a general understanding of spiritual relationships to texts. It is argued that the relationship of text to participant is not only of central importance in certain alternative spiritualities, but that it can in some ways provide a clearer view of the metaphysical assertions and related practices within a community that leaves practical manifestations of belief entirely up to the participant.

The centrality of the text has been well acknowledged, if perhaps undertheorized,[1] in relation to new and alternative religious movements (Partridge 2004: 53–8). Graham Harvey, for instance, in his numerous works on Paganism, has pointed to the importance of fantasy fiction[2] in support of pagan worldviews (Harvey 2006; 2000; 1997). Similarly, the Church of All Worlds is well known for its relationship with the fantasy novel *Stranger in a Strange Land* by Robert Heinlein (1961): the group explicitly attributes the religion described in the book with the founding principles of their church (Partridge 2004: 55). Also, the horror fiction of H.P. Lovecraft and the occultist psychedelia of Robert Anton Wilson all resonate deeply with certain elements of the contemporary occult world (see, for instance, the Church of the SubGenius and Discordianism). Indeed, the initial rise of contemporary occultism has been strongly linked with the development of gothic and fantasy literature in the nineteenth century (Hanegraaff 1998: 421). There are many other examples, of which the majority fall within the broad category of syncretistic personalized religion. By and large, however, within the worlds of alternative religion, analysis tends to assume that such texts function as support only or, at their strongest, as evocative representations of truths of the spirit, rather than holding literally sacred or spiritual meaning. Certainly, fictional texts do function as evocative support and representation for beliefs, but in some cases this relatively temperate position is superseded by something closer to a literal interpretation, or an outright belief, in the worlds or creatures portrayed within narrative fiction. I propose that the spectrum of analysis be expanded from simple acknowledgement of the text as support and inspiration, to encompassing an idea of literal adherence as well. Unless such approaches are included within academic discourse, we run the risk of fundamentally misconstruing both the beliefs and practices of alternative religious groups such as these.

Locating the types of groups that are being viewed in this chapter is a somewhat fraught task. Firstly, it is important to note that all four groups hold in common some type with fictional narrative. The point to focus upon here is the emic rather than the etic stance: a (rather tedious) argument can be made for all sacred texts to be works of fiction; this is not the point. Rather, the groups in this study all acknowledge the explicitly fictional basis of the texts to which they relate. The specific relationship certainly varies between participants as well as between groups. However, more broadly, it is central to note that this study is limited to groups that engage with fictional texts in full view of the authorial intention to create a narrative of fictional, not sacred, meaning.[3]

---

[1]   Sutcliffe (2004: 482) refers specifically to New Age texts, but the point holds true in the broader context of new religious movements.

[2]   Lacking the space to delve into the varying arguments surrounding the definition of fantasy literature, I here refer to that most common of categories: the bookstore *genre* definition.

[3]   A well-known example of an alternative religion that does not fit within the parameters of this study is Scientology.

Secondly, to situate these groups within the broader field of religious and spiritual activity is also challenging. At first sight it would seem promising to locate these groups within the stream of Western esotericism. Faivre, however, postulates four defining features of Western esotericism (Faivre 1994: 10–15) as well as two more that are often, but not always, present. These central four ideas are Correspondences, Living Nature, Imagination and Mediation, and the Experience of Transmutation. The two associated but unessential components are the Praxis of the Concordance and Transmission. While some forms of these themes are apparent, such as imagination in relation to the Otherkin and Paganism, they could not be said to be always present, nor are they central. Likewise, if one takes occultism as the frame of reference, there is both common ground and significant divergence. With the broad definition posited by Hanegraaff, that occultism 'comprises all attempts by esotericists to come to terms with a disenchanted world or, alternatively, by people in general to make sense of esotericism from the perspective of a disenchanted secular world' (1998: 422), the Otherkin, Paganism, the Church of All Worlds and Jediism all fall under this rubric. On the other hand, however, certain elements of such groups resonate strongly with Romanticism in its rejection of science and the disenchanted world, a movement that is distinct from occultism (ibid.: 423).

It can be seen, then, that while partaking somewhat in the body of knowledges and practices associated with Western esotericism and occultism, these groups do not fall easily within the parameters specified. In terms of situation, perhaps the most useful is the idea of the cultic milieu put forward by Campbell (1972) or Occulture proposed more recently by Partridge (2004: 62–86). The cultic milieu is conceived as a broad pool of underground knowledge, related to but distinct from the underground or counter-culture of the 1960s, and comprising deviant or disregarded sources of knowledge. Occulture as a category furthers this idea, drawing it away from the mystical associations put forward by Campbell, while highlighting its relationship to the popular mainstream as well as subcultures. While perhaps broad, the notion of an alternative culture that encompasses the counter-culture in all its forms highlights the eclectic mix of ideas that is so relevant to the groups in this study.

Jediism

One good example of fictional narrative used as evocative support for a developing belief system is Jediism. Jediism, simply put, appears to be the personal acceptance of the moral and spiritual code attributed to the Jedi, characters in George Lucas's classic film trilogy *Star Wars*. This community appears closely related to the fan culture surrounding *Star Wars*, as the following quote will attest, but still self-consciously separates itself from a more mundane reading of communities of appreciation:

> We've all seen the movies. We bought the DVDs and the toys. We imagined what it would be like to be a Jedi. We went online and met others who thought like we did. We met online, we grew online, and we began organizing online. We encouraged each other to take the life we talked about online, offline; at work, as neighbours, as friends. We were no longer 'role-playing', but Jedi Realists, making the Jedi way how we lived our lives. (The Jedi Resource Centre and Jedi Gatherings Group www.jediresourcecentre.org/index.php, access date 21 January 2008)

Primarily, this emergent belief appears to revolve around adherence to the idea of 'the force'. 'The force ... [is] an energy field created by all living things. It surrounds us and penetrates us. It binds the galaxy together' (Lucas, 1977). This power goes beyond simple energy and includes a concept of intentional use. 'A Jedi can feel the force flowing through him. You mean it controls your actions? Partially, but it also obeys your commands' (ibid.). It should be noted that most Jedi sites specifically disclaim anything more than an evocative reading of the films, while also explicitly denying any form of role playing. Belief in the force can be feasibly construed as a form of magic, although explicit techniques for accessing it seem limited to inferences of meditation in the films. Beyond this, the group states that peace is, both globally and personally, a central goal (www.geocities. com/xitongutaro/, access date 21 January 2008). Although Jediism seems to be considered somewhat dubious in some circles,[4] it has certainly made its presence felt both on- and off-line. While apparently simplistic, it appears that this text has genuinely inspired some form of spiritual engagement for participants. To the best of my knowledge, however, no Jedi is proposing that the death star truly exists or that Darth Vader—a central character in the *Star Wars* series—is literally walking among us. In this group we can see that it is an adherence to the ideals espoused rather than a fidelity to the created world that is appealing.

Paganism

Another example of the use of fiction as evocative support for a spiritual stance is Paganism. Although general statements about this movement are well-nigh impossible to make accurately, their tendency to find paradigmatic support in fictional texts has been well noted (Harvey 2000). Indeed, as a group they are unusual for relying far more upon creative texts than polemic literature (ibid.) and many pagans find the path to their faith through immersion in the fantastic worlds of speculative fiction (Hume 1997: 80; Ringel 1994: 66). Paganism draws upon a vast range of texts to support its worldviews, as a brief perusal of any Pagan booklist will attest. These texts are often seen as ideal type examples of the world

---

[4]   See, for instance, the 2001 Australian and UK census data on religion and the associated uproar. For more information on the group, see Possamai (2005).

as it should be, evoking the types of relationships between humanity, nature and divinity that are central to the Pagan paradigm. The works of Terry Pratchett and Robert Holdstock are central examples of the kinds of narrative fiction used in support of Pagan worldviews (Harvey 2000).

Another varying stance taken to fictional narrative is that of the Church of All Worlds (www.caw.org and www.geocities.com/Athens/9762/caw2.htm, access date 21 January 2008). In this case the relationship to the text can be seen as providing the inspiration for, as well as support of, the beliefs of its members. Founded in the 1970s, this group was the first Pagan collective to be granted legal status as a church in the United States. The Church of All Worlds pays homage to *A Stranger in a Strange Land* by Robert Heinlein (1961) as the source of its inspiration. A classic science fiction novel of the 1960s, the narrative follows the story of a Martian raised human who is returned to earth. This text portrays, for example, an ideal of human interaction: friends become 'waterkin' (an extremely intimate relationship within which everything is open and shared). This ideal, among others, resonated so strongly with the founding members of the Church that they adopted the associated terminology alongside the ideology into the practice of their faith. This case makes evident that the fictional text was central to both the origins and development of the group.

Otherkin

By and large, the approaches to the text demonstrated by Jediism, Paganism and the Church of All Worlds are representative of the relationships between religion or spiritual communities and narrative fiction. The Otherkin, while sharing many features with the previously mentioned groups, exemplify a far more literal interpretation of narrative fiction. The Otherkin appear to contain within the group the full gamut of approaches to the text, from the most playful stance of fan-based appreciation to an outright belief in the fantastic creatures of fictional narrative. Like the groups mentioned above, they often find evocative meaning in the creatures and worlds of fantastic narrative, but in practice some participants take this idea far further than is commonly the case in, say, Paganism. The Otherkin believe, primarily, that they are in some way other than human.[5] The non-human aspects appear to have been largely drawn from mythology and fantasy literature, such as dragons, elves and vampires, but also include more traditionally religious icons, such as angels, alongside cartoon characters. This relationship to the fantastic takes a variety of forms and can mean a non-human soul in a human body, multiple souls residing within the same person or inter-species reincarnation. This belief is the central factor of the Otherkin community and realistically presents the only definitive common ground between participants. Even starting from this primary assumption, there are any number of fascinating

---

[5] For a more detailed discussion of the Otherkin community, see Kirby (2006).

inferences in this type of approach. There is the tacit postulation that souls exist, that transmigration occurs, that these creatures exist beyond our literary traditions and that humans may somehow become intertwined with them. Further, that these creatures exist somewhere suggests the reality of alternative worlds, locales within which these creatures abide. These inferences are not necessarily concentrated on, or even explicitly acknowledged by participants, but give some broad idea of the body of knowledge upon which the group draws.

In order to summarize the Otherkin, it is important to attempt at least a brief overview of their philosophy, practice and concerns as well as more practical data, such as locale, population and so on.[6] Their shared philosophy is simply as stated above: the belief that members are something other than human. On one of the main otherkin websites, otherkin.net, a more detailed explanation is offered within an introductory article entitled *What are Otherkin?* written by Tirl Windtree (www.otherkin.net/articles/what.html, access date 21 January 2008). The article presents five alternative variants on the Otherkin position, stances based in either the biological, spiritual, psychological, escapist, or, finally, in some combination of these. A detailed discussion of these approaches is irrelevant here, but it should be noted that the spiritual position is by far the most common,[7] and may be summarized by the attitude that 'whilst their physical forms may be human, their essence, soul or equivalent term is not'(www.otherkin.net/articles/what.html, access date 21 January 2008).

The practices of the Otherkin are somewhat more difficult to specify. Practice is entirely individual. There are articles on magic and past life regression alongside discussions of role-playing in service to self-knowledge (www.otherkin.net/articles/bytitle.html, access date 21 January 2008). Realistically, it seems apparent that the Otherkin pick the practices rather than the other way around: the group seems strongly against any form of doctrine or limiting rules, beyond that of mutual respect.

Primarily, the group's concern seems to be self-knowledge. The participants give every indication that their interest is in exploring the nature of their 'Otherkinness' as well as sharing such thoughts and insights that they might have with other likeminded seekers. Little about the group seems aimed towards the broader public, although information is accessible to outsiders. Contrary to possible assumptions, participants give little indication that they are involved in order to appear sensational or in antagonistic opposition to the broader cultures of which they are a part.[8] There is no overtly stated political stance, nor does there

---

[6]   It should be noted that the sources used in this chapter are all drawn from the more static end of the web. I have not used discussion boards or mailing lists, simply as a necessary means of limiting the amount of material available online.

[7]   This is supported by both the article mentioned and my own research.

[8]   See the article 'Us vs Them' by Toscar for reflections on this undercurrent (see http://otherkin.net/articles//usThem.html, access date 21 January 2008).

seem to be an agenda of broad social change. To all appearances, this community is entirely aimed at personal metaphysical inquiry and mutual support.

Otherkin.net is one of many websites dedicated to the discussion of, and information about, the Otherkin. It particularly provides access to articles and mailing lists of Otherkin interests. Primarily, it appears to serve as a locus or gateway for other activity and, to some extent, as an archive.[9] Although in no way actually representative of the number of participants, the figures available on the site provide evidence that this type of belief is significant. Of the approximately 80 mailing lists on the site, the largest has some 782 members (see 'Haven of Kindred Spirits', www.otherkin.net/community/lists/index.html, access date 21 January 2008) and the Otherkin directory of participants had 1,535 entries at the time of writing.[10] To give a further sense of the scope of the community, it should be noted that, as sign-up is not required to access articles, it can be assumed that there are many more interested individuals who have chosen not to make their contact details public.

At this point it is worth digressing for a moment into some brief discussions of the Otherkin as a community. Thus far I have blithely referred to the holders of this particular position as 'a community', assuming both consensus on the use of the term and the fact that Otherkin interaction falls within this set of behaviours. This is, of course, problematic on both fronts. Although libraries could be filled with the research into the nature of virtual communities,[11] it can be difficult to pin down a specific definition. Certainly, in the case of the Otherkin, this is an extremely difficult undertaking. The participants are dispersed geographically and appear as a group to be primarily a virtual phenomenon. However, there are still group activities and meetings organized off-line. While the majority of participants are based in the USA, there are also small numbers scattered across the rest of the world. According to the Otherkin directory (www.otherkin.net/community/directory/geog.html, access date 6 November 2007), Australia has 28 listed participants, Romania 7 and Japan 4, whereas the USA has 1,085 Otherkin.

Before discussing the particular approaches to the text found within the Otherkin community, it is important to highlight their status as fans and audiences. With groups such as the Otherkin, their status as audiences and participants within popular culture should be seen alongside their position as spiritual seekers. The links between religion and the habits of fan cultures have been noted many times in the past. Studies such as those undertaken by Jindra (1994) and Frow (1998) both highlight the structural similarities between traditional religious behaviour and objects of popular culture (Star Trek and Elvis, respectively). The fervent belief that is so noticeable within fan cultures is equally evident within the religious

---

[9] For a particularly interesting take of the relationship between otherkin.net and the Otherkin community, see www.otherkin.net/articles//death.html.

[10] Both this and the previous figures were accurate as of 17 October 2007.

[11] For some particularly interesting research see, for instance, Dawson (2004); Dawson & Cowan (2004); Rheingold (2000).

world. However, it is important to maintain a separation between these two types of cultural engagement, even when focusing upon the same cultural product, as is the case with the Otherkin. It is entirely possible to adore and engage with cultural products without asserting any broader metaphysic inherently linked. This stance can thus be taken as the position of the fan. On the other hand, any claims pertaining to the super-empirical take beliefs into the realm of the metaphysical, into the worlds of religion and spirituality.

It would be most unlikely that anyone using narrative fiction in the creation of personal spiritualities could fall outside the classification of a fan, no matter what beliefs they may hold. Presumably, anyone so deeply involved in fiction as to make use of it in the creation of personal spiritualties has based such use on the premise of a wholehearted appreciation for the text(s). This factor does not detract from the sincerity or genuineness of participants' beliefs, but highlights another important element of this convergence of influences. Indeed, understandings of fan cultures have significantly developed in recent years. No longer is the fan relegated to the margins of the social world, nor are fans considered passive consumer dupes. Audiences are 'active, critically aware, and discriminating' (Jenkins 2006: 135). By focusing on both formal and informal societies of appreciation, theories of fan cultures offer an interestingly inverse approach to the issues central to this chapter as well as provide particular frameworks that help clarify passionate engagement with texts. Although, generally speaking, such theories treat groups as quasi-religions (Griel & Robbins 1994b), they are dealing with a similar convergence of devotion, media and cultural product, as can be seen in this study. Notably useful are some of the theoretical constructions of recent scholars who have attempted to clarify the particular location of cult discourses within fan cultures (Hills 2002: 117).

Of particular interest is Matthew Hills's location of cultic followings. Hills's approach highlights both the continuity and the disjunction between sacred and secular uses of the term 'cult', and he proposes the use of the term 'neoreligiosity' as a framework within which to understand fan approaches (Hills 2000). Hills emphatically denies religiosity as a formative aspect of fan cultures, but points to the shared language and characteristics to justify the use of this term (Hills 2002). Particularly relevant in this case is fans' self-conscious use of the term 'cult' in the face of its overwhelmingly negative popular connotations (ibid.: 121). Hills's thesis rests primarily upon fans' appropriation of the 'other' or 'outsider' status common to both religious and media cults, but also incorporates ideas of self-absence in fans' inability to fundamentally justify why they are fans (ibid.: 123). Hills's construction of 'neoreligiosity' is in some ways parallel to that of quasi-religion (Griel & Robbins 1994b), as he sees the discourses, but not the content of religion.

From the outset, Hills's claim that fan cultures 'cannot usefully be thought of as religions' (Hills 2002: 117) is important. Metaphysical endeavours like those of the Otherkin cannot be seen as fan cultures either. There is, however, common ground between these two that pertains to the structure and the content of both. The structural similarities are relatively clear: for instance, 'fan communities have long defined their memberships through affinities rather than localities' (Jenkins 2006: 137), a factor that is in line with the 'networked individualism' (Partridge 2005: 149) apparent within the Otherkin. The interests of the Otherkin, however, highlight the commonality between the narrative objects around which such communities are formed. This mutual interest in popular and, often, cult narrative bespeaks the importance of the particular nexus between passionate textual engagement and the specific appeal of speculative worlds.

It is imperative at this point to clarify the precise nature of the approach taken to the situation of the groups used in this study. I am not positing that these groups are *like* religions, as has been done in many cases, such as football events (Bailey 2004: 397), 'body beautiful' ideologies or twelve-step groups (Rice 1994). The use of the category of religion in this context is not intended as a metaphor to demonstrate similar modes of structure, practice or communication. These groups, I argue, are actively religious in so far as their concerns are of a spiritual and super-empirical nature (Griel & Robbins 1994a: 3) Although such groups deviate to a degree from the accepted or 'common sense' norms of what religion is (Barker 1994), they share the primary interest in the super-empirical that is arguably the only reliable linking factor in all that falls within the category of discourse. Given that this is the case, terms such as 'quasi-religion' (Griel & Robbins 1994b) or 'neoreligiosity' (Hills 2000; 2002) are perhaps inappropriate to describe the nature of the groups in question in this study, as such terms are intrinsically invested in maintaining tension and space between the conception of religion and the objects of study. While compelling the groups in this study into a pre-formed ideal of religion would do them a great disservice, it also appears that to exclude them from the field is fundamentally to misunderstand both their interests and their lived experience. While the concepts of quasi-religion and neoreligiosity have much to offer in aid of interpreting obscure and fringe groups and are indeed essential to understanding groups as obscure as those in this study, such theories point to the relationship with religion in order to eventually distance those studied from it.

Textual Engagement

The texts used by the Otherkin cover a range of territories, from fantasy fiction to non-fiction texts as well as mythology and classical literature. As Graham Harvey has noted, 'No Paganism has a dogmatic creed, few of its varieties are represented by allegedly authoritative texts, and certainly there is no single writer who is universally persuasive' (Harvey 2000: 1). This statement may be accurately applied to the Otherkin as well. Intriguingly, although fantasy and mythological narrative are clearly central to the community, if only as the sources for the creatures associated with it, the texts themselves do not generally loom large in the group's discussions. However, there are a large number of individual Otherkin book lists available on-line that give a clear indication of the general reading interests of the community.

The recommended reading section of otherkin.net provides a good example of the texts considered as worthy reading (www.otherkin.net/community/recommended/index.html, access date 6 November 2007). Although the list includes films and music as well, this chapter has not the scope to address them. Among others, the recommended texts include the works of Michael Ende, Christopher Paolini, Clive Barker, Neil Gaimon, Anne McCaffery, Terry Goodkind, J.R.R. Tolkien and Terry Brooks, all of which could be considered to comprise a fantasy canon. It should be noted that the use of the term 'canon' does not necessarily coincide with scholarly approaches to literature (Martin 2003: xx), but reflects a fan-type appreciation. While such texts may have somewhat dubious literary status, they are appreciated by readers for other reasons.

What I would particularly note is not any one specific text, although I am sure that, on the individual level, this may be highly relevant, but the conglomerate effects of a fantasy ideal-type world that is generally ascribed to by participants. In a similar vein to the idea of the cultic milieu, proposed as a method for discussing a body of associated practices and beliefs that are drawn upon freely by participants at their choice, I would posit what may be called a 'fantastic milieu'. The fantastic milieu could be viewed as a subsection of the cultic milieu, as the ideas are clearly entwined. The idea of hyperdiegesis, the 'creation of a vast and detailed narrative space' (Hills 2002: 137), is useful in this context. It has been noted that this type of world, in the light of its simultaneously immense, internally consistent and yet largely unexplored territories, may encourage 'creative speculation' (ibid.: 138). I would take this idea a step further and posit that, rather than a world bounded within a single narrative, such as *Star Trek* or the *Lord of the Rings*, the fantasy canon can be treated *en masse* as a case of hyperdiegesis. While not perfectly consistent, there are a number of features of the fantasy world that are regularly present, most particularly the use of magic and fantastic creatures, such as dragons and elves. Notably, these common elements are the particular focus of the Otherkin community, whereas specific textual engagement seems of less importance. The notion of a fantastic milieu could contribute to understanding the predominance of fantasy narratives being personally actualized while maintaining space for the apparent vast diversity of texts.

Another associated and fruitful area of inquiry is the role of the author in Otherkin conceptions of world creation. If, as is the case in the Otherkin community, the created worlds of fictional narrative are attributed with meaning beyond simple entertainment, it follows that the role of the author holds some interesting implications. There are two particular explanations offered on otherkin.net regarding this point (http://otakukin.otherkin.net, access date 6 November 2007). The first recasts the author as a channel or medium, expressing, perhaps unintentionally, another world or plane of existence. This process of pseudomimesis (Dolezel 1998: 9), although perhaps vacuous as a formal theory, nonetheless appears to be accepted as a valid argument by participants. The second possible explanation is that the readers themselves, through their attention and interest, actually create the worlds or creatures of the fantastic. This process seems to be based on the idea of energy transfer and implicitly assumes the validity of psychic powers and magic. The former proposal assumes the alternative world is already existent before the composition of the author, whereas the latter includes the audience in the process of world making, albeit as facilitators rather than creators. Subtly these two stances have quite different implications. The first, in assuming the alternative world as pre-existing, implies a cosmos, be it physical or otherwise, densely packed with discrete realities merely waiting to be discovered. Thus the participant taking this view is effectively an intrepid explorer through potentially limitless alternative worlds. The second proposition, on the other hand, implicitly limits these alternative worlds, rather asserting the existence of possible worlds: thought forms that can be made real by human engagement, but are not necessarily already so. This stance locates the participants in a far more active role in the world-making process.

It is worth noting that textual engagement within the community of Otherkin extends in turn to the creation of their own texts. This appears to run the full gamut from remix cultures, such as fan fiction extensions of narrative, to metaphysical reflection, as may be seen in the collections of letters made available by the Silver Elves. This type of behaviour extends the already evident participation with narrative.

Two important points must be raised at this juncture. Firstly, the implications that I find in the metaphysic of the Otherkin are not necessarily of particular concern to participants, nor are they engaged in any specific attempt to consolidate a singular or cohesive framework of belief. This group's premise is, first and foremost, an experientially-based metaphysic and as such it upholds the lived experience of the individual as the primary, and indeed only, arbiter of truth claims. Secondly, it is extremely important to note that any statements made about the community as a whole do not necessarily reflect the beliefs of specific individuals. The present overview is an attempt to highlight broad trends and point towards the underlying assumptions of the metaphysic rather than attempt an exhaustive case study.

What is found is a group that engages with and within narrative fiction to the point of positing reality of some type to the contents of the texts. The very process of ascribing reality to fictional creations, no matter how tentative, is one worthy of note. While by no means a simple process, the existence of groups such as the Otherkin denotes a particularly interesting shift in notions of fiction and the real. Although the step between fiction, on the one hand, as evocative support, and on the other hand, as the *source* for alternative realities is perhaps not large, the latter orientation merits recognition as an alternative and distinct stance.

Particularly interesting in the case of the Otherkin is the variety of sources used across the group. This variety ties in with the lack of a central narrative and the diversity is related to the priority of individual experience, but does not help to gain an understanding of the commonality demonstrably experienced between Otherkin. Of course, there is a kinship based in participants' shared experience of the non-human, but I propose that such commonality is, at least to a degree, established not just in the experience of textual appreciation, but also within a broadly shared vision of the conglomerate worlds of fantasy fiction. The recurring themes of fantastic creatures—dragons, elves, angels, demons, vampires and the like—the magical systems and the vividly realized territories dovetail enough to imply a mutually supportive set of alternative realities. While such a proposal is admittedly tentative at this stage, the idea of a fantastic milieu provides a framework within which positions such as those presented by the Otherkin may be understood.

References

Bailey, Edward, 'Implicit Religion', in Christopher H. Partridge (ed.), *Encyclopedia of New Religions* (Oxford: Lion Publishing, 2004): 397–9.
Barker, Eileen, 'But is it a Genuine Religion?', in A.L. Griel & T. Robbins (eds), *Between Sacred and Secular: Research and Theory on Quasi-Religion* (Religion and the Social Order, 4; Greenwich, CT: JAI Press, 1994): 97–110.
Campbell, Colin, 'Cult, the Cultic Milieu, and Secularisation', *A Sociological Yearbook of Religion in Britain* (London: SCM Press, 1972): 119–36.
Dawson, L., 'Religion and the Quest for Virtual Community', in L. Dawson & Douglas E. Cowan (eds), *Religion Online: Finding Faith on the Internet* (London: Routledge, 2004): 75–90.
Dawson, Lorne L. & Cowan, Douglas E. (eds), *Religion Online: Finding Faith on the Internet* (London: Routledge, 2004).
Dawson, L. & Hennebry, J., 'New Religions and the Internet: Recruiting in a New Public Space', *Journal of Contemporary Religion*, 14/1 (1999): 17–39.
Dolezel, Lubomir, *Heterocosmica: Fiction and Possible Worlds* (Baltimore and London: Johns Hopkins University Press, 1998).
Faivre, Antoine, *Access to Western Esotericism* (SUNY series in western esoteric traditions) (Albany: State University of New York Press, 1994).
Frow, John, 'Is Elvis a God? Cult, Culture, Questions of Method', *International Journal of Cultural Studies*, 1/2 (1998): 197–210.
Griell, A.L. & Robbins, T. (eds), *Between Sacred and Secular: Research and Theory on Quasi-Religion* (Greenwich, CT: JAI Press, 1994a).
Griell, A.L. & Robbins, T., 'Introduction: Exploring the Boundaries of the Sacred', in A.L. Griel & T. Robbins (eds), *Between Sacred and Secular: Research and Theory on Quasi-Religion* (Greenwich, CT: JAI Press, 1994b): 1–23.
Hanegraaff, Wouter, *New Age Religion and Western Culture: Esotericism in the Mirror of Secular Thought* (New York: State University of New York Press, 1998).
Hanegraaff, Wouter, 'New Age Religion and Secularisation', *Numen*, 47/3 (2000): 288–312.
Harvey, Graham, *Listening People, Speaking Earth: Contemporary Paganism* (Kent Town, S. Aust.: Wakefield Press, 1997).

Harvey, Graham, 'Fantasy in the Study of Religions: Paganism as Observed and Enhanced by Terry Pratchett', *Diskus*, 6 (2000).

Harvey, Graham, 'Discworld and Otherworld: The Imaginative Use of Fantasy Literature among Pagans', in Lynne Hume & Kathleen McPhillips (eds), *Popular Spiritualites: The Politics of Contemporary Enchantment* (Aldershot: Ashgate, 2006).

Heelas, Paul, *The New Age Movement: The Celebration of the Self and the Sacralization of Modernity* (Oxford: Blackwell, 1996).

Heinlein, Robert A., *Stranger in a Strange Land* (New York: Putnam, 1961).

Hills, Matthew, 'Media Fandom, Neoreligiosity, and Cult(ural) Studies', *The Velvet Light Trap: A Critical Journal of Film and Television*, 46 (2000): 73–84.

Hills, Matthew, *Fan Cultures* (London and New York: Routledge, 2002).

Hume, Lynne, *Witchcraft and Paganism in Australia* (Melbourne: Melbourne University Press, 1997).

Introvigne, Massimo, 'The Future of New Religions', *Futures*, 36/9 (2004): 979–90.

Jenkins, Henry, *Fans, Bloggers and Gamers: Exploring Participatory Culture* (New York: New York University Press, 2006).

Jindra, Michael, 'Star Trek Fandom as a Religious Phenomenon', *Sociology of Religion*, 55/1 (Spring 1994): 27–52.

Kirby, Danielle, 'Alternative Worlds: Metaphysical Questing and Virtual Community amongst the Otherkin', in Frances Di Lauro (ed.), *Through a Glass Darkly: Reflections on the Sacred* (Sydney: Sydney University Press, 2006).

Martin, Graham Dunstan, *An Inquiry into the Purposes of Speculative Fiction— Fantasy and Truth* (Studies in Comparative Literature; New York: Edwin Mellen Press, 2003).

Partridge, Christopher, *The Re-Enchantment of the West: Alternative Spiritualities, Sacralization, Popular Culture, and Occulture*, vol. 1 (London: T&T Clark International, 2004).

Partridge, Christopher, *The Re-Enchantment of the West: Alternative Spiritualities, Sacralization, Popular Culture, and Occulture*, vol. 2 (London and New York: T&T Clark International, 2005).

Possamai, Adam, *Religion and Popular Culture: A Hyper-real Testament (Gods, Humans & Religion)* (New York and Oxford: Peter Lang, 2005).

Rheingold, Howard, *The Virtual Community: Homesteading on the Electronic Frontier* (rev. edn; Cambridge, MA: MIT Press, 2000).

Rice, John S., 'The Theraputic God: Transcendence and Identity in two Twelve-step Quasi-Religions', in A.L. Griel & T. Robbins (eds), *Between Sacred and Secular: Research and Theory on Quasi-Religion* (Greenwich, CT: JAI Press, 1994): 151–64.

Ringel, Faye, 'New England Neo-Pagans: Medievalism, Fantasy, Religion', *The Journal of American Culture*, 17/3 (1994): 65–8.

The Silver Elves, *The Magical Elven Love Letters*, vols 1 & 2 (Silver Elves
    Publications, 2007).
Sutcliffe, S.J., 'The Dynamics of Alternative Spirituality', in James R. Lewis
    (ed.), *The Oxford Handbook of New Religious Movements* (New York: Oxford
    University Press, 2004): 466–90.

Chapter 9
Seeing the Self as Other: Televising Religious Experience

Nicholas Buxton

In May 2005, the BBC screened a television documentary series featuring a group of men who spend six weeks living alongside a community of monks in a Benedictine monastery.[1] The programme was billed as a 'unique experiment', whose stated aim was to discover if there was anything about an ancient monastic tradition that could be relevant to modern secular life. Towards the end of the series, one of the participants has what can best be described as a very profound and moving experience. Just as a piece of television, the scene is remarkable enough. For a full minute and a half, there is complete silence as Tony, sitting with his mentor Brother Francis, appears to be wrestling with thoughts and feelings that he is able neither to comprehend nor express. Eventually, Tony indicates that he wishes the meeting to end and it is brought to a close with a blessing.

Immediately afterwards, Tony speaks direct to camera and says that whatever it was, it was both the 'weirdest experience I've ever had in my life' and that it was without doubt a 'religious experience'. To describe it as a religious experience might, in the circumstances, seem like an obvious conclusion for Tony to draw, given that he had spent close to six weeks living in a monastery. Yet, Tony was a self-confessed non-believer: he had no faith. How then could he talk about having a religious experience, without having a religious faith in which to situate it and a religious language with which to describe it? Before going to bed that night he spoke to his video diary:

> Something happened, something touched me, something spoke to me very deeply, and very profoundly ... this isn't someone that wanted this to happen, or expected it to. When I woke up this morning, I didn't believe in this ... now, I do. Whatever 'it' is— and I still don't know what that is—I believe in it because I saw it, and I felt it, and it spoke to me, and that's something that will stay with me for the rest of my life. (*The Monastery*, BBC2, 2005)

I do not know what really happened, nor—I suspect—does Tony. Even with the event recorded on film, we are none the wiser; a sobering rejoinder to anyone

---

[1] *The Monastery*, © Tiger Aspect Productions, was a three-part series originally transmitted by BBC2, on 10, 17 and 24 May 2005.

who thinks that empirical data is unequivocal or self-evident. Whatever it was an experience of, however, we can say it was something categorically *other* than anything that Tony could comprehend or relate it to. In what follows we will be looking at the relationship between religious experience and the experience of selfhood, as reflected in the hall of mirrors that is Reality TV.

Reactions

Much to everybody's surprise—not least those who were personally involved— *The Monastery* turned out to be an unexpected success. In spite of being associated with a *genre* widely perceived as voyeuristic and exploitative, both critic and viewer deemed the programme to be sensitive and intelligent.[2] Worth Abbey, the monastery in question, received hundreds of letters and e-mails: moving testimony to the profound impact the series had on people from all walks of life and from diverse faith backgrounds or indeed of no faith at all. The following response, taken from a viewer's letter to her local newspaper, is typical:

> Original, thought-provoking and extremely interesting, *The Monastery* was both a pleasure to watch and a challenge to us all, for in the participants we see our own failings and weaknesses, and in the monks' unconditional love, we see Christianity at its best. (Miss D. Pfeiffer, *Gloucester Citizen*, 30 May 2005)

In this person's response we can identify two of the principal themes that attracted the most attention. First, it was good TV: 'a pleasure to watch'. This reflects a wider perception regarding the programme's status in relation to the *genre* of Reality TV, which is perhaps best indicated by the fact that industry professionals— including those from rival channels or production companies—continue to cite *The Monastery* as having set a new benchmark in religious broadcasting.[3] Second, that the content of the series was enlightening or inspirational. Many viewers were able to identify at a personal level with particular aspects of the programme ('we see our own failings and weaknesses') or found themselves reflecting on spiritual values ('in the monks' unconditional love, we see Christianity at its best'). Indeed, the good character of the monks, and the fact that they came

---

[2]   The label 'Reality TV' is applied to a wide range of popular factual programming, which typically features 'ordinary people' and unscripted dialogue. The *genre* includes lifestyle and makeover programmes, observational documentaries and game-show formats, with many more variations within these broad categories.

[3]   For this very reason, some within the industry try to make a distinction between 'serious' programmes, such as *The Monastery*, and the mass of 'infotainment' based on the increasingly ubiquitous game-show model, and consequently reject the label 'Reality' altogether. In spite of this, however, both the media and the viewing public unanimously perceived *The Monastery* as Reality TV, albeit of a higher quality.

across so well, were probably among the most frequently noted observations. For example, in the *Guardian* (25 May 2005: 22), Nancy Banks-Smith wrote: 'The intelligence, patience and gentle amusement of the monks were as soothing as the hypnotic swaying of their robes'. For many viewers, it was clearly something of an eye-opener to discover that monks could be so well adjusted, down-to-earth and human. Another journalist declared:

> Beginning as only a casual onlooker, I became intrigued, surprised and eventually moved by the sincerity and genuine kindness of the Benedictine brothers and, at times, humbled by their quiet wisdom in applying teachings of the 6th century to the muddled minds of their lay visitors ... I had to wonder how folk so detached from a contemporary way of life should be so aware of it and remain unfazed by the group's more sordid regrets and revelations. (David Prowse, *Western Morning News*, 31 May 2005)

Perhaps less surprisingly, many people also commented on the monastic principles—such as silence and simplicity—that were emphasized in the programme, recognizing these as desirable qualities that seem undervalued, if not completely non-existent, in today's world. Paul Vallely, writing in the *Church Times* (27 May 2005: 11), captured this sentiment well:

> Ours is a world of constant busyness, activity, noise, and stimulation. What these five men did was open themselves to finding something deeper in life, and gave themselves the time to do it. Openness and time: two things that our modern world is constantly short on.

The Monastery provoked extensive discussion in the public domain for several weeks after it was first shown: full-length features appeared in the broadsheets tackling issues as diverse as the 'crisis of masculinity' (Johnson & Sutch 2005) and what television comedy writer Armando Iannucci described in the *Daily Telegraph* as 'something very confusing about our current state of confusion' (28 May 2005: 17). Iannucci notes that rather than the so-called 'reality' of TV shows like *Celebrity Love Island* (ITV 2005), on at the same time as *The Monastery*, we clearly prefer the reality of people being made to think hard about life. *The Monastery*, he says, happens to have come at a time when

> We're ready for something to tell us that our grasp on reality has gone to pot. If we ever snap out of this brief pause of confusion, we'll take one ambiguity with us. It's this: were it not for some monks who let themselves become TV celebrities, we might never have realized how pointless television and celebrity actually are. (ibid.)

Comments such as this suggest that some people thought of *The Monastery* as more than just another Reality TV show: it was perceived as a serious documentary, which had something to say to and about us. It received extensive coverage in various broadcast and print media and was referred to in sermons and in classrooms.[4] Clearly there was something about *The Monastery* that resonated with a large number and a wide range of viewers, both as an example of quality television and as a programme that had spiritual and social significance. For at least some of the participants, too, the experience of spending six weeks in a monastery was genuinely transformative. At first glance, all of this would appear to contradict the view—articulated most pointedly by Neil Postman (1985)—that television, on account of being primarily a medium of entertainment, is intrinsically unsuited to the communication of serious issues. Yet, although *The Monastery* was credited with being an unusually thought-provoking series, which undeniably had a profound impact on many viewers, I would also maintain that it was at least partly conditioned by a discourse of religious commodification that sits in tension with its ostensible subject matter.

Ambiguity such as this permeates *The Monastery* at many levels. To begin with, a monastery, commonly perceived as an escape from reality, is made real for the viewer through Reality TV, a medium widely seen as being completely fake. Significant questions arise from this—concerning reality, experience, and the experiencing subject—often in interesting or unexpected ways. As one of the five participants, observing myself being observed, I have noticed when talking to people who saw the programme that the virtual monastery of the TV 'show' has become a reality for them; this is then projected back on to my own experience of the reality of my stay in the real monastery. This supports the view that one of the primary characteristics of factual television in general, and Reality programming in particular, is that it turns something seen second-hand into a first-hand experience for the viewer (Hill 2005: 82). Which, then, is the real monastic experience: the six weeks the participants spent at Worth Abbey or the media event of BBC2's *The Monastery*? In significant ways, these can be considered as two distinct phenomena; yet in other ways they are also, of course, one and the same. The question is, how do we understand the relationship between them? The answer may not be as obvious as might at first appear.

Reflections

Reality TV purports to be real, but as we all know, it is for the most part highly contrived. Richard Kilborn asserts that 'Factual programme makers are nowadays not so much concerned with the observational chronicling of events as the staging and shaping of events for viewer consumption' (2003: 73). This is often confirmed by

---

[4]   The impact of *The Monastery* continues to be felt in the media. In September 2007, the *Financial Times*—perhaps not the most obvious publication for such a subject—ran a five-page feature on monastic orders, focusing especially on Worth Abbey (*Financial Times Magazine*, 15/16 September 2007).

programme makers themselves. Gabe Solomon, series producer of *The Monastery*, is quoted in an interview as having said: 'I've now made a point of trying to watch so-called reality TV and my conclusion is, it's what I'd call artificiality TV because the directors are telling the participants what to do' (*Brighton Evening Argus*, 7 May 2005: 14–16). In much of what passes for factual programming, it seems that 'reality' has become something 'to be formatted according to television's designs and specifications' (Kilborn 2003: 74). *The Monastery*, by contrast, was widely perceived as marking a departure from the standard fare of over-contrived Reality programming. 'Could reality TV be about to get real?', asks Robert Shrimsley in the *Financial Times* (27 May 2005), comparing *The Monastery* with *Celebrity Love Island*, which he describes as 'as crude a piece of committee-crafted TV as has ever been laid before us'.[5] Indeed, similar comparisons were drawn by a number of other writers, for example in *Sunday Life* (15 May 2005):

> *Celebrity Love Island* has been described as a reality show. But what's real about it? When you come to think of it, what's real about most of those shows with the reality label? … It's a shame the reality label was attached to *The Monastery* … This was more than real. It was uplifting and inspiring, and I'm not the only one to find it so. Apparently the abbey website has been visited over 20,000 times since the first programme was broadcast.[6]

Yet what does it actually mean to describe *The Monastery* as 'more than real'? At the most obvious level it is to claim that this was an instance of Reality TV showing the viewer something genuine and authentic. The medium was for once, and almost in spite of itself, true to life.[7] In another sense, however, to suggest that a mediated representation of reality is real could have the effect of undermining the very reality that Reality TV purports to represent by blurring the distinction between them. The situation is further complicated when one considers that a monastery, often thought of as an escape from reality, is presented as something 'more than real'. This exposes the fault-line running between reality and Reality TV, neatly subverting the *genre* of a medium widely considered to be completely fake. Some reviewers seemed to instinctively grasp this irony, although they were perhaps unaware of all the connections. For example, in the *Sunday Telegraph* (15 May 2005), John Preston wrote:

> Here five men who didn't much like reality went off to spend forty days and forty nights in a Benedictine monastery in Sussex … Inevitably, the spectre of reality

---

[5]   http://search.ft.com/ftArticle?queryText=worth+abbey&y=0&aje=false&x=0&id=050527001109&ct=0

[6]   www.sundaylife.co.uk

[7]   Apparently 73 per cent of people think that what they see in Reality TV programmes is made up (Hill 2005: 64).

television hung over the whole venture, with the prospect of the contestants having to endure ever more grim privations.[8]

By describing the participants as 'contestants', Preston reveals that he views the programme as a Reality TV show (implying that it is not real, but contrived and manipulated) rather than a documentary about monastic life, which in any case is assumed to be an escape from the world, primarily intended for people unable to cope with 'reality'. The well-worn cliché that a monastery is somehow separate, or an escape from the world, was also evident in the way people talked about 'five men from the outside world' going 'into' the monastery (or worse, going 'on the show') and 'coming out' of it at the end of 40 days. Having said that, such perceptions are not entirely without foundation. The cloister is indeed supposed to be a place set apart—like a reserve perhaps—although at the same time it would also be understood by monks themselves as a place of deeper engagement with the truly real. In more ways than one, *The Monastery* was thus 'a world apart from other so-called reality TV programmes', as Martin Collins put it in the *Christian Herald* of 4 May 2005.

A question I am always asked (after 'How did you get on the programme?') is, 'Did it change you?' When people ask this, they usually expect me to answer in the affirmative. It is hard to know whether this expectation is due to an understanding of the monastery as a place where one might be likely to undergo some kind of personal transformation or whether it is engendered by the fact that Reality TV programmes are often explicitly concerned with the transformation of the participants (or their houses, gardens, lifestyles, etc.). It is possible the latter is the more dominant factor. As Jonathan Bignell asserts, 'the notion of the makeover and the ideology of self-improvement ... are crucial to contemporary Reality TV formats' (2005: 13). Bignell further notes (ibid.: 151) that contestants on the popular Reality TV show *Big Brother* themselves talk about the experience of being on the show in terms of an opportunity for self-improvement. However, it does seem reasonable to suppose that the monastic setting in this particular case would strengthen that expectation significantly. Indeed, the combination of these dual expectations—and their dramatic fulfilment—could help to explain the tremendous impact the series had on viewers. It is surely no accident that Tony's transformative experience features so prominently in many people's recollections: after all, the programme makers were intent upon telling a story about 'a challenging journey of self-discovery' from the outset.

Whether or not it changed me is an obvious question to ask, but not necessarily all that easy to answer, if only for the simple reason that there are effectively two monasteries to deal with here. On the one hand, there was the real-life experience of spending six weeks with a Benedictine community; on the other hand, there was the media event of a popular TV series. In short, I have been through it all twice: once in reality and once again on Reality TV. How much would my life

---

[8]   www.telegraph.co.uk

have been changed, had it not been on TV, I wonder? How would I feel about it now if the programme had been harmfully exploitative or negatively received? It is impossible to leave the effect of the observer out of the equation: the process of being observed undeniably contributed to the experience, even at the time, never mind afterwards.

By suggesting that our behaviour was to some extent conditioned by the viewer, I mean not only that we might have been tempted to perform for the camera, either overtly or by being more guarded, but also that we would not actually have been there at all, if it had not been for the camera. By extension therefore, the viewer, although physically absent, was nevertheless ever-present. There are thus two aspects of the observer effect to consider: participants showing off and the film-maker setting it up. Regarding the first, some scholars have noted an interesting tension between the 'performed self' and the 'true self' of participants in Reality TV programmes. Audiences expect participants to act up for the camera and have no trouble identifying such behaviour. Yet at the same time, they also feel they can get to 'really know' the characters, who often reveal something true about themselves in spite of their tendency to perform the self they wish to project (for further details, see Hill 2005: ch. 4). To some extent, acting—however subtle—would seem to be almost unavoidable in such circumstances. I can distinctly recall making a conscious effort not to, but this too was a consequence of being observed, which conditioned my behaviour and made me self-conscious or otherwise mindful of my actions. The attempt to avoid acting itself becomes an act. Regardless of how accustomed I became to the presence of the TV camera, I could never be entirely oblivious to it or completely unconcerned about how I might come across. Even if not consciously thinking about it all the time, I was nevertheless aware at some level that things said in private would one day be made public and could easily notice the difference in my behaviour and that of the rest of the group, when the crew was not around.[9]

As for the film-maker manipulating the subject, it is inevitable that a certain amount of what is seen in any documentary or factual programme has to be staged. Likely as not, the 'reality' in question will need to be manipulated simply in order to make filming possible. As it happens, in the case of *The Monastery*, intervention was fairly minimal, nor were there any games or special tasks to perform. Nevertheless, the distinction between fact and fiction in television is becoming increasingly porous. As a number of scholars have pointed out, Reality TV makes extensive use of narrative structures derived from fictional drama—especially soap opera—including the use of a single location, a central cast of characters, serial plot-lines, typical leave-taking devices between episodes and the segmented interweaving of parallel storylines (Kilborn 2003: 110). All of these feature in

---

[9] In an interesting counter-example, Anita Biressi & Heather Nunn (2005: 19) cite a situation in which the participants were being completely 'natural' (in fact they were drunk, therefore not so self-conscious about being observed). In this instance, the presence of a camera acted as a catalyst for a disclosure that would not otherwise have occurred.

The Monastery, together with other staples of the *genre*, such as the obligatory slanging match between argumentative participants—a narrative code derived from TV drama. We should not be surprised: no factual documentary could ever claim to be an unmediated or neutral record of reality as-it-is, but is always and necessarily a constructed narrative.

Whether deliberately or unconsciously, the film-maker necessarily selects or creates character storylines from the outset and does so according to their own predetermined notions concerning the story they intend to tell. This in turn affects not only editing decisions once filming has been completed, but also the filming process itself. In other words, the film-maker's agenda will not only govern casting choices, but also determine what they decide to film in the first place, the nature of their interaction with participants in terms of the questions they ask and so on. For example, by asking an apparently innocent and reasonable question such as 'what do you want to get out of being here?' the filmmaker forces the participant to 'buy into' their view of the monastic experience as reducible to transactions between consumers and spiritual commodities. Far from providing an objective record of events, simply pointing a camera at someone is already to become an author, to intervene in the natural flow of life and impose a particular interpretation on a reality that in itself could be read in a variety of different ways.[10] Thus, even if it is fair to say that what one sees in the programme is (almost) all true, it is certainly not the whole truth, but a story told about our experiences by someone else, from their point of view, not ours. This is reinforced by the role of the narrator whose reading of events is assumed to be normative. In all these ways, our experience of the real was 'framed and shaped by the production agency that made it possible' (Bignell 2005: 75).

Although this is not to say that a factual documentary is indistinguishable from a work of pure fiction, it does mean that in as much as a documentary conveys a structured narrative—which it must do, if it is to make any sense—it effectively tells a story that is not intrinsic to the ostensible subject, but supplied by the programme-maker, who in so doing processes the world into 'narrativized forms' with an 'established grammar' (Hill 2005: 61). Moreover, that narrative will, whether consciously or not, reflect and affirm a set of prevailing consensual discourses. This implicit coding was most clearly evident in the inevitable follow-up programme, in which the radical otherness of Tony's transformative experience appears to have been subsumed into the story of his recovery from alcoholism.[11]

---

[10]   Even news reportage, generally believed by both journalist and viewer alike to be a reasonably objective record of events that occur independently of their being observed, is highly constructed, with editors making subjective decisions about what counts as 'news'. If it seems far-fetched to suggest that 'the News' could become just another form of interactive infotainment, one ought to consider the fact that the BBC's news website features the following link: 'Help us *make* the news, with your pictures, views and stories' (emphasis added).

[11]   *The Monastery Revisited* © Tiger Aspect Productions, BBC2, 7 June 2006.

While I would not wish to diminish the significant part that being at Worth played in his recovery process, I cannot help thinking that something important is missing from this explanation of what 'really' happened. *The Monastery* began with a seemingly open question: is there anything that the monastic tradition—or for that matter, religion in general—can offer in the modern world? By the time they made the sequel, they had an answer: 'Yes—therapy.' Are we to infer therefore that religion is meant only for people with problems? Or is this just the media's way of packaging religion as an easily consumable product? Without wishing to denigrate the value of therapy in appropriate contexts or ignore the healing that is so central to Jesus' ministry—and thus Christian soteriology—there is nevertheless, and very broadly speaking, one important respect in which religion is not equivalent to therapy: the latter is primarily concerned with the self, while the former is all about the other. To reduce religion to therapy is to miss the point, which is that the function of religion is to point us towards that which is the point of everything— away from ourselves towards something beyond, something fundamentally *other* than self.

Revelations

Of the five participants, I was the only one who had ever stayed in a monastery before. This meant that, unlike the others, I had some idea of what I was letting myself in for—at least in terms of the monastic routine. I knew I would find it stimulating and fulfilling and expected to learn something about myself and about life in general. What I could not have anticipated, however, was the effect of sharing this experience with four strangers and a TV crew. Our five-man micro-community, consisting of people with very different attitudes to religion and reasons for being there, provided us with a first-hand experience of communal living that was deliberately intended to reflect that of the monastery itself. The lesson we were to learn was this: that genuine personal transformation only comes about through the rough and tumble of social interaction. It is hardly surprising then that tensions emerged. As one journalist astutely observed (*Sunday Tribune*, 15 May 2005), 'In a monastery the way of life brings you into direct confrontation with yourself and any inner problems that you may have been avoiding are thrown into stark relief.'[12] I soon realized that both the dynamic of the group and the presence of the TV crew greatly intensified an experience that would probably have been intense enough on its own. As well as grappling with the challenges of the monastic discipline, and dealing with each other, we were also constantly expected to articulate for public consumption much that would normally have remained private. Even at the time I noticed that having to reflect on and verbalize my inner experiences for the benefit of the camera forced me to think about everything much more deeply.

---

[12]   www.tribune.ie/home.tvt

While we were at the monastery, I kept a journal to note down thoughts and feelings, as I find I am able to work through ideas more thoroughly if I do so in writing.[13] Whether I had kept a journal or not, however, the TV programme itself provides a text on which to reflect. Because it is all 'on the record', the participants have been granted a rare and valuable opportunity to see how others might perceive them: as they present themselves rather than as they imagine themselves. In an interesting discussion of the narcissistic dimension of the consumerist therapy culture we currently inhabit, Biressi & Nunn point out that Reality TV highlights two interesting truths about us. First, that identity is performed rather than possessed, thus our so-called 'real' selves 'are only ever the performance of a role', and, second, that our sense of self is guaranteed by an imagined 'other' whose 'gaze confirms the solidity and worth of our existence' (2005: 101). Reality TV thus provides a means by which our existence is validated through being observed. That is reminiscent of Berkeley, who in *A Treatise Concerning the Principles of Human Knowledge* famously declared that to be is to be perceived (Fraser 1901: 259). Similarly, Biressi & Nunn claim that Reality TV highlights the ways in which our subjectivity is formed 'through a matrix of looks, of processes of seeing, being seen and of our self-conscious knowledge of being seen. It suggests that within media culture being publicly regarded can constitute an affirmation of the self' (2005: 102).

The role of the media in the construction of contemporary selfhood is plainly evident in the way in which people often define themselves—at least in part—by the media they consume: the TV programmes they watch, the music they listen to or the publications they read. Indeed, fans of different media, and of *genres* within particular media, sometimes base their identity very closely on the media product in question: one only has to think of 'Trekkies' or the fans of popular bands to see the connection between media and personal identities. A number of scholars have identified a correlation between the tendency to define selfhood in terms of media consumption and the rise of personal autonomy in matters of faith. Evidence for this is seen in the 'culture of therapy'—often shaped by the symbols and discourses of the mass media—that has emerged to service late modernity's 'project of the self'. As a consequence, new forms of religiosity, increasingly distinguished from traditional religion by the use of the term 'spirituality', have arisen which place the individual, free of institutional authority, at the centre of the meaning-making process. Summarizing this view, Stewart Hoover states that

> Whereas we once might have looked to a network of social relations in home, school, work, community, church, or family to provide the resources necessary

---

[13]   This tallies with the method of theological reflection on personal experience that Graham *et al.* (2005: 18) describe as turning 'life into text'. My own findings corroborate their conclusion that such a process 'presents the self as formed through intimate relations with God and others'.

to the making of our 'selves', today we think of this as being much more our *own* responsibility. (2006: 52)

These observations are supported by the work of others who have examined the 'turn to the subject' in late modern culture. In their attempt to map the terrain of contemporary religiosity, Paul Heelas & Linda Woodhead (2005) make a distinction between the 'congregational domain' of traditional forms of religious life and the 'holistic milieu' of new age and alternative spirituality. They sum up the difference as follows:

> To step into a worship service is to find one's attention being directed away from oneself towards something higher. By contrast ... to enter into the holistic milieu is to find attention directed towards oneself and one's inner life. (ibid.: 13–14)

The distinction in focus and orientation between the congregational domain and the holistic milieu captures the difference between the two monasteries—the virtual and the real—and also highlights the theological significance of the curious phenomenon that is the representation of a monastery on Reality TV. In fact the 'project of the self' is nothing new: the earliest Christian monks believed that if you wanted to know God then, you must first know yourself. But what does this actually mean? According to the Christian ascetic tradition, the life of prayer—even, or perhaps especially, in its most apparently introspective forms—is not so much about cultivating an intimate experience of one's self, but cultivating a relationship with something profoundly *other* than self, whether God or neighbour. Heelas & Woodhead noted a similar understanding in the congregations they observed: their members were

> united by the conviction that truth and goodness lie not in the cultivation of unique individuality so much as in curbing such individuality by way of conforming to a higher common, authoritative good. This good may be envisioned in different ways ... but it is always transcendent: it is higher than those who subserve it and, as such, it binds them into something more than they would be on their own. (ibid.: 14)

Towards the end of our stay at Worth Abbey, the monks encouraged us to think about vocation, which arguably implies a question about how an individual relates to the world and all that is other than them. Thus, when Tony sat down with Br Francis before that life-changing moment, he wondered what he would do when he left and he was concerned about losing what he had gained from being there. Vocation, said Br Francis in response, is all about 'discovering who we really are'. To my mind, this was the whole point of the exercise. During my stay at the monastery I came to understand that we only really come to know ourselves through other people: not as we imagine we are, but by becoming aware of ourselves as objects of someone else's perception. If self-knowledge was just about getting to know myself, it could not result in any significant change, for change only comes about as a result of engagement with something other and more than oneself, by mutual give and take, which in turn depends upon cultivating an attitude of receptivity and openness. As Graham *et al.* point out, 'self and identity are always formed through interaction with others' (2005: 20). To cultivate self-awareness, therefore, is to learn to see the self as other; to see others as yourself and yourself as others see you.

For the monk, the transcendent other through which the self is known initially presents itself in the form of the discipline and demands of the rule. Yet it is important to understand that according to St Benedict, monastic obedience is not primarily concerned with slavish adherence to regulations or being compelled to do things we do not want to do: true obedience is an act of will, freely chosen, not grudgingly given.[14] Moreover, St Benedict stresses the importance of the mutual obedience of monks to one another (RB 71.1), saying that: 'No one is to pursue what he judges better for himself, but instead, what he judges better for someone else' (RB 72.7). Obedience thus means listening attentively and responding appropriately, giving up all that comes between ourselves and others and ultimately between us and God. Community life is about putting the needs of others before one's own. But this is not a one-way sacrifice, for, if I am present for others, this means the other is (presumably) present for my sake as well. Obedience is about relationship, it is to show respect; ultimately it is the basis of love. This is why following a spiritual path is not just about withdrawing from the world, but a different and arguably more challenging mode of being *in* the world.

Conclusion

Far from asking an open question, *The Monastery* began with the answer. One cannot blame the individuals who made the programme because we are all complicit, products and producers of the culture we inhabit. For whatever reason, over the last two hundred years religion in Western society has been steadily relegated to the private sphere. Now it is being repackaged as a lifestyle accessory under the brand-label of 'spirituality'. Behind this lies an assumption that God, the putative object of religious experience, is a word in a language we no longer speak; therefore religion must be explained in terms of something else—such as therapy—in order that it may be the more easily digested. On this view, the success of *The Monastery* is a function of the media's success in commodifying religious experience and constructing the self in its own image. Regardless of its apparent claim to the contrary, it did not challenge our consensual norms of individualism and consumerism so much as affirm them.

Is this to say that we have all been duped? Surely one cannot simply disregard the testimony of the many people who were profoundly moved, or otherwise

---

[14]   Extracts from the *Rule of St Benedict* (RB), English translation in Fry (1982).

impressed, by *The Monastery*? Although the programme was undoubtedly conditioned by the discourses of Reality TV and the implicit dogma of spirituality-as-therapy, the story of five men spending forty days in a Benedictine monastery did nevertheless disclose something real for and about the participants, which communicated itself to the viewer. In spite of the ostensible focus on the self, it revealed something 'other'.

References

Bignell, Jonathan, *Big Brother: Reality TV in the Twenty-First Century* (Basingstoke: Palgrave Macmillan, 2005).

Biressi, Anita & Nunn, Heather, *Reality TV: Realism and Revelation* (London: Wallflower Press, 2005).

Fraser, Alexander (ed.), *The Works of George Berkeley, Vol. 1* (Oxford: Clarendon Press, 1901).

Fry, Timothy (ed.), *The Rule of St Benedict in English* (Collegeville, MN: Liturgical Press, 1982).

Graham, Elaine, Walton, Heather & Ward, Frances, *Theological Reflection: Methods* (London: SCM Press, 2005).

Heelas, Paul & Woodhead, Linda, *The Spirituality Revolution: Why Religion is Giving Way to Spirituality* (Oxford: Blackwell, 2005).

Hill, Annette, *Reality TV: Audiences and Popular Factual Television* (London: Routledge, 2005).

Hoover, Stewart, *Religion in the Media Age* (Abingdon: Routledge, 2006).

Johnson, Daniel & Sutch, Dom Antony, 'Why Male Spirituality Hasn't Got a Prayer', *The Times*, 16 May 2005.

Kilborn, Richard, *Staging the Real: Factual Programming in the Age of Big Brother* (Manchester: Manchester University Press, 2003).

Mitchell, Jolyon & Marriage, Sophia (eds), *Mediating Religion: Conversations in Media, Religion and Culture* (London: T&T Clark, 2003).

Postman, Neil, *Amusing Ourselves to Death: Public Discourse in the Age of Showbusiness* (London: Methuen, 1985).

Chapter 10

Possession Trance Ritual in Electronic Dance Music Culture: A Popular Ritual Technology for Reenchantment, Addressing the Crisis of the Homeless Self, and Reinserting the Individual into the Community

Rupert Till

Introduction

This chapter explores the relationships between Electronic Dance Music Culture (EDMC) and religion, meaning and spirituality. It briefly outlines some of the existing work in this area before presenting evidence of elements of religiosity found in EDMC during my research. A brief explanation of the historical roots of EDMC is followed by an investigation of transcendent experiences, of how these are perceived, the use of drugs to trigger them and how they relate to trance and possession. Evidence from the field of ethno-musicology is discussed in relation to EDMC, as is the way in which music and dance interact. The effect of individualization within postmodernity is addressed, as is EDMC as a ritual technology for social construction, creating community and openness with others. In conclusion, EDMC spirituality is defined and discussed.

Within Electronic Dance Music Culture (EDMC), there is no one author. The club is the text and both the experience of it and its substance are different for each clubber. EDMC is therefore very much part of postmodernity and demands a multi-level interdisciplinary approach to describe its many facets. An author-based approach is reflected here in the ethnographic field study and interviews. The ethnographic study involved long-term participant observation, which has resulted in a presentation one might describe as emic, as I have been a musician, clubber, disc jockey and event promoter working within EDMC since 1991. Insider knowledge of EDMC is important, as its illegal elements involve secretiveness and EDMC initiates have a greater access to all its activities. However, I have maintained an intellectual distance in this research where possible in order to ensure objectivity. A textual approach is also used to interpret cultural meanings and analyse content.

This work also addresses sociological analyses of EDMC and explores it through praxis, by involvement in composing, performing and creating club events. It has endeavoured to integrate concepts from fields such as the sociological study of religion, intrinsic religion, theology, philosophy, sociology and cultural studies where relevant.

I have used the term 'EDMC' as I consider it the best term available. It describes a coherent group of activities and cultural practices, including those in some nightclubs and at free parties and festivals, and it focuses on music *genres* such as trance, techno, house and drum and bass, while excluding mainstream chart music, rap and hip hop. I do not use the term 'club culture', as it includes too much mainstream or 'townie' culture and excludes festivals. I also avoid the word 'rave', as it is not used by those within EDMC and is considered inauthentic. My work is focused principally on England, although it resonates with and relates to EDMC worldwide.

Existing Theoretical Perspectives

Many publications have investigated the relationships between religion, spirituality, meaning and club culture. Gordon Lynch's interviews with clubbers made it clear that clubbing was meaningful for them: 'There is reasonable evidence that club culture did perform religious functions in some sense for the majority of participants' (Lynch 2005: 177). Graham St John's ethnographic research presents clubbers as parts of neo-tribes, with trance based ritual part of their culture, discussing EDMC as involving fearless leaps into uncertainty (St John 2004). Gauthier has commented that rave is 'a manifestation of the religious "fete", or celebration' (Gauthier 2004: 69) and investigated club culture in Canada as implicit religion referring to commitments, integrating foci and intensive concerns with extensive effects (Gauthier 2005). Olaveson suggests that 'rave' cultures 'do in fact exhibit many features of new religious movements and, while that phrase may lack precision here, the dance culture phenomenon of the past 15 years demonstrates sociocultural revitalisation on a massive scale' (Olaveson 2004: 86). He found 'raving' to be a 'highly meaningful and spiritual practice for many ravers' and that 'dance events are meaningful and transformative' (ibid.). Lynch & Badger (2006: 27–40) describe EDMC as a secondary institution. It has also been described in terms of cultural religion (Sylvan 2005), home (Rietveld 1998) or temporary autonomous zone (Bey 1985). It is clear that for those involved in EDMC it fulfils many of the traditional functions traditionally served by religions and that it bears many of the hallmarks and typical features of religion and spirituality.

Overtly and Covertly Religious Clubs

EDMC contains many references to religious or spiritual elements. Some events have an overtly spiritual agenda. One of these is the Boom Festival in Portugal. Boom's 'liminal village' includes meditation, yoga and Tai Chi sessions and explores spirituality through workshops, seminars, discussions of new age issues, exhibitions and art. Boom's website discusses its liminality as being

> characterized by ambiguity, openness and indeterminacy. One's sense of identity dissolves to some extent bringing about disorientation. Liminality is a period of transition, during which your normal limits to thought, self-understanding, and behavior are relaxed, opening the way to something new. According to the anthropologist Victor Turner the liminal stage of a ritual is a period during which one is 'Betwixt and between', 'Neither here nor there'.[1]

Other elements of EDMC contain references to religion that are less specific. Its lyrics rarely have the same youth culture themes as pop or rock music; the lyrics have different themes, they are often uplifting, encouraging or overtly sexual. The music makes little or no sense on the radio or purely for listening, but is specially designed for the ritual of clubbing, for groups of people to dance to together. The design of clubs often resembles that of churches. The DJ booth is placed high up in the air, much like an organ loft or pulpit, above the audience, and there is often a gallery. Indeed, there is a long history of using former churches as clubs. The Que Club in Birmingham, for example, was originally the city's Central Methodist building. One description of this club is 'The House of the Techno Gods, where the infectious grooves will make your booties move'.[2] Promoters Obsession who ran nights like 'Freedom at the Que Club' state on their website:

> there is something seductively religious about a club that is located in what used to be a place of worship. The DJs now occupy the altar, playing to a congregation of around 1,600, many of whom know what it truly means to have seen the light.[3]

Obsession and Freedom are typical of the names used for EDMC clubs and organizations. House of God, God's Kitchen, The Ark, The Monastery, Mass and Heaven (sacred space and a sense of community); Heresy, Sin, Seven Sins and Temptation (transgression); Passion, Release, Joy, Sublime, Blessed, Lost in Love,

[1]   Boom Festival, *Boom Festival 2006 Website*, available at www.boomfestival.org/afterboom06/index.html/ [access date 10 July 2007].
[2]   Stephen Williams, *dircon*, available at www.users.dircon.co.uk/~matrix/que/que_club.html/ [access date 9 August 2007].
[3]   Obsession, *Obsession Website*, available at www.obsession.org.uk/history/freedom.htm [access date 9 August 2007].

Ascension, Awakening, Rapture, Lifted and Bliss (transcendence); Source, Pure, Best, Revelation, Renaissance, Positiva, Empathy, Freedom, Liberty and Future Perfect (utopianism); Devotion, Praise, The Trinity, The Cross, Spirit of Soul, Labyrinth (Christian references); Cosmos, Voodoo, Destination Venus, Dionysus, Escape from Samsara, Return to the Source, The Gathering presents 'Highway to Hell', and Earthtribe (various religious and cosmological references)—these are all names of clubs that use terms related to religion.[4] Clearly the organizers want to signify that something like a religious experience will happen.

Clubbers can often be seen raising their hands up towards the light(s) in a fashion very reminiscent of a Pentecostal church service. For clubbers I spoke to, raising their hands was a sign of release, rapture, escape, ascension and ecstasy, as they reached upwards and outwards towards lights that came down from above, framing their heads with a nimbus or halo, a signifier in religious art of the sacred or divine, all set within heaven-like smoke machine generated clouds.

Figure 10.1   Decorative art from the Shamania festival 2007. Author's photo.

---

[4]   All these names are taken from a single edition of the club magazine *Mixmag*.

The imagery in clubs often refers to religious themes. Shamania is an annual EDMC music festival. The 2006 festival featured a number of hard trance music sound systems with workshops, stalls and other content derived from new religious movements, Paganism, Wicca and groups influenced by Shamanism. Figure 10.1 is a wall decoration from the festival featuring self-similarity, entopic imagery and magic geometry. I often found similar images at other club events. Other Shamania decoration included a painting of a bird spirit leaving a shaman holding a drum; this was accompanied by the words 'There is a fire burning in Bird Spirit land, My Bones smoulder I must journey there.' There were also circles and tunnels of dots and stars; Yin and Yang symbols; a complex mandala with an Om symbol at the centre; adverts for 'green witchcraft', 'sensory solutions' and 'herbal remedies'; an advert for 'the shaman's apothecary plant allies teachers and healers—rare psychotropic and visionary plants and herbs'; publicity for 'Murgen's Keep, the pagan festival stall', with 'witches parking only, all others will be toad', '666' and 'Give me that old time religion' all visible.

'Club décor' would in many circumstances have religious imagery, such as angels, demons, Hindu gods or magical geometry and entopic images, Turing or psychedelic patterns. Figure 10.2 shows an example which features the naked image of a female 'demon' surrounded by fire. She is smiling and sexual, placed on a psychedelic background pattern designed to play with perspective. Festival-goers told me how their perception of this image changed after they had taken liquid LSD, ecstasy or other drugs, from a flat painting to a realistic three-dimensional red and white room or tunnel, with the female image floating inside in the foreground. This typical EDMC imagery is transgressional and sexual, a demonic temptress from the Christian tradition, mixed with elements of Pan and other horned gods influenced by 1960s psychedelic imagery. Clubbers also use paints and colours that react to ultra-violet (or black) light to create other 3D effects.

Figure 10.2   Décor image from Boom Festival 2006. Author's photo.

Angels and Demons, often feminine and sexualized, regularly feature in EDMC. Plastic angel wings and devils' horns are often worn and demons, angels and wings are tattooed on backs and shoulders. A key element of club culture is its separation from mainstream culture. Clubs are a place of escape, of transgression, of release. They are also sites drenched in postmodernity, and as such witness the frequent clash of extremes, whether sacred and secular, old and new, or organic and technological. Christianity is usually the target of this transgression. Never does one see in EDMC a transgressional approach to Islamic, Hindu or Buddhist imagery or content, in fact these and other religions are presented in a positive light. Despite borrowing substantially from Christian culture, it is this mainstream religion of US and British culture that is opposed and contravened.

Club culture's oppositional and transgressive stance is expressed in its subcultural identity. Thornton has described how subcultural capital is gained: 'The social logic of subcultural capital reveals itself most clearly by what it dislikes and by what it emphatically isn't. The vast majority of clubbers and ravers distinguish themselves against the mainstream' (Thornton 1995: 105). As Hebdige (1979) has explained, subcultures are often created as cultural resistance to a hegemonic form. In this way it is an anti-religion (Demerath 2002) or a-religious approach, socio-political as much as religious in nature, but no less meaningful.

One of the reasons for the oppositional nature of club culture is its reaction against the idea of a single reading of what is healthy or constructive, the will to choose one's own path—an approach typical of postmodernity. In this case it involves the knowing transgression of what the mainstream regards as healthy and constructive, accompanied, authenticated and advertised by the moral panic of the tabloid press about the use of drugs. This is what gives EDMC much of its oppositional subcultural capital, an identity which is enhanced by the use of unofficial or unlicensed venues (the 'Free Party' scene); the use of uncleared samples and opposition to traditional ownership and copyright (Beadle 1993); the use of deregulated, unlicensed white label recordings; the focus on specialist, independent EDMC record shops and websites; and the use of micro-media for advertising, such as flyers, posters and websites.

It is clear that EDMC has elements of religion, spirituality and meaning. Its transgressional nature is partly a reaction to the history of Christianity, particularly Puritan and Lutheran Christianity, repressing traditions of ecstatic dancing. EDMC developed from Black and latino gay disco culture from which elements of Christianity (from black/gospel church culture), African trance culture (from African American secular music culture), and sixties psychedelia were transmitted into EDMC. Like its African American dance music form predecessors (blues, jazz, swing, rock'n'roll, rhythm'n'blues, soul, funk, hip hop and ska), EDMC has crossed over into mainstream British white culture (Till 2007).

EDMC's prehistory in African American culture explains its recurring Christian references including the use of gospel style vocals, pianos and organs. That gay disco is the primary route of transmission of this culture explains that these references are most often made transgressionally and oppositionally, following the persecution and demonization of homosexuality by traditionalist Christians. Pan, Bacchus and Dionysus, gods of revelry and pleasure, are celebrated by EDMC as positive figures. Reclaimed from their demonization by Christianity, the horned gods make ideal signifiers of transgression and hedonism.

Transcendent Experiences

The most conclusive evidence of spirituality and religion within EDMC are the innumerable accounts of transcendent experiences described by clubbers, some of which I collected. They are typical of the kinds of experiences I have heard clubbers describe over and over again and which are documented by other writers:

> I felt really amazed ... made me feel like I'd left my body briefly ... I thought I was in the matrix.

> I forget my everyday worries and remember how to just have fun. Often a great night out dancing puts things I'm worried or stressed about into perspective for me.

> I feel transported away to somewhere else, I lose myself in dancing. I feel like I'm connected to my body in a special way ... it gives me a chance to celebrate life.

> Unconcerned by the realities of everyday life ... nothing else matters except enjoying that moment ...

> It is the disappearance of the conscious self, my body moving instinctively in time with the beat of the music ... no sense of how long it goes on for ... just a sense that this is good, feels right and makes me happy.

> The most spiritual experience I have ever had was post-clubbing ... we went back to someone's house and I had my first ketamine experience ... I lost any sense that I had a body or ever had had one, and thought that I was a clicking noise that had existed for all time! Gradually I morphed into the entire universe, which was encapsulated in a single atom and as such ran the universe and I suppose was God by proxy ... gradually my vision returned as did a sense that I had arms and legs.

(Author's interviews, 2007).

These are mystical experiences of transcendence and rapture. Writer Simon Reynolds relates a similar experience:

Borne aloft in the cradling rush of sound, swirled up and away in a cloud of unknowing, for the first time I truly *grasped* what it was to be 'lost in music'. There's a whole hour for which I can't account. (Reynolds 1998: xxvii, emphasis in original)

Perception of Clubbers' Behaviour as Non-religious, Lack of Language or Context

Perhaps mainly due to inherited transgressional attitudes to Christianity, most clubbers made it very clear in interviews that they do not see themselves as religious or see EDMC as religious or indeed as spiritual, contradicting the clear references to elements of religiousity described above, and the elements of religion and spirituality that seem to be present. The following are comments made by clubbers when asked if they were religious or if clubbing was religious:

Absolutely not.

An altered state yes, but I associate spirituality with clarity and I'm not sure I've felt much of that when I've been clubbing.

I think a lot of the feelings stem from the drugs, but that's not to say it's insignificant ... I would feel naive to say clubbing is spiritual (it has a dirty side too), but the experiences I've had through my time of intensive clubbing and outdoor parties have certainly altered who I was.

They are good experiences for me, for my spirit/soul/id, but I don't get a sense that they are experiences directed by some higher force.

[I am] anti religious, I find the codification of spirituality into religion almost the antithesis of spirituality.

[Regarding religions and spiritual practices] Loathe the lot especially the ones that seek to foist their ideas onto you without being asked, these practices are evil.

I've always put it down to the drugs and consequently have reality issues about the whole thing.

I have never felt the presence of God or any one supernatural deity.

(Author's interviews, 2007).

Because EDMC is an escape from life and often involves the use of drugs, clubbers often do not recognize their activities as religious or spiritual. This does not necessarily mean that they are not. Bailey has explained how those within social institutions such as EDMC may not see their activities as religious, if this religion is implicit rather than explicit: 'It will not be seen, by the actor, as religious' (Bailey 2002: 9), with other terms being used instead of religion, such as 'philosophy', 'world-view', 'life-style', 'way-of-life', 'ideal' or 'identity'.

Bailey describes the need for a three-dimensional discussion of religiosity that includes the sacred, the profane and the everyday to make sense of experiences such as those in EDMC. The implicit religion he describes as arising from the everyday includes concepts that are also significant in EDMC, like commitment, identity and integrity. Despite the eloquence of many respondents, they lack 'a discourse that would enable them to describe their experiences' (Lynch 2005: 181), having no traditional religious context. The dimensions of the sacred experience and the human encounter are clearly present in EDMC, but the dimension of the holy, the encounter with God, seems to be missing and to be rejected. Encounter is with other people, although there is a sense of the infinite and the void, and it is perhaps the language, traditions and history of religion that are rejected rather than its philosophical essentials. Certainly if 'The sacred ... is that which is special and set apart' (Bailey 2001: 78), it would seem that EDMC is sacred.

Drug Taking in EDMC

The widespread use of illegal drugs in clubs is described in some detail by numerous writers, including Reynolds (1998), Shapiro (1999) and Deehan & Saville (2003). The rituals revolving around finding drugs, smuggling them into clubs, taking them, discussing them and recovering from them are an important part of EDMC's ritual practice. Ecstasy is the most prominent and common drug used. It floods the brain with serotonin, the chemical related to happiness and well-being, and dopamine, which stimulates motor activity, speeds up the metabolism, causing overheating, filling the person with energy, encourages them (in an EDMC context) to dance for hours on end and creates euphoria. Reynolds describes Ecstasy, its history and effects very clearly (1998: xxiv). The drug's initial effects can cause nervousness, discomfort, distraction, stomach aches and vomiting; this fits in well with Rouget's description of the crisis that occurs before a possession ritual (1985).

Clubbers who have taken Ecstasy described feeling their whole bodies glowing with pleasure, a physical and mental experience of being flooded with joy, ecstasy and love for those around them. Many clubbers told me that this is an experience that cannot be fully understood, unless one has tried it, that it is a key part of EDMC and that taking it for the first time was an initiatory experience that changed their perception of EDMC. They commented that Ecstasy had changed their perspectives on life, opened them up to other people and allowed and freed them to have closer friendships and greater levels of emotional intimacy.

Ecstasy users described how they felt an enormous empathy and connection with each other, a connection that was not the same with someone who had not taken the drug, and that they would feel a deep intimacy with a person within minutes of meeting them. This was something that bonds clubbers together, and has created an insider world within clubbing impenetrable to anyone who has never taken drugs.[5] Drug taking was clearly a powerful ritualized process for clubbers, and it is important to note the sense of transgression and excitement granted by illegality.

Trance and Possession

EDMC shares many similarities with possession trances in traditional cultures. As Sylvan puts it, 'connections between music, rhythm, dance, and trance induction are consciously recognized by ravers, and the induction of the trance state is a specific goal of the music' (2005: 68). One clubber told me that 'All concept of time disappears' (Author's interview, 2007) when clubbing after having taken ecstasy. Loss of memory is an important indicator of a trance experience. Malbon describes EDMC altered states as 'Oceanic experiences' (1998: 105–33). Saunders, Saunders & Pauli (2000) and Reynolds (1998) both discuss EDMC in terms of trance rituals and ecstatic states. Sylvan states that EDMC has taken its trance traditions from African Yoruba and Fon traditions, via African American music (2005: 90).

Rouget describes trance as involving movement, noise, being in company, crisis (or altered state), sensory over-stimulation, amnesia, no hallucinations,[6] as well as involving trembling, protruding eyes and thermal disturbances (1985: 11–14). These conditions are typical for a clubber in an Ecstasy-induced EDMC altered state. Rouget defines two kinds of trance: possession, when the entranced has little control over his experience, and shamanic, when the entranced journeys on a voluntary voyage to visit the world of the spirits (ibid.: 23). The latter seems to resemble most what happens in EDMC, but shamanic trance usually involves the shaman making his or her own music. More similar still to EDMC is the trance culture of the African Pygmies and Bushmen: the trance is shamanic, but unusually the music is made for the shaman, which is characteristic of possession. The Pygmies or Bushmen occupy a position between possession and shamanism (ibid.: 139–47), which is again similar to the state within EDMC.

---

[5]   Ecstasy is of course illegal. Clubbers understood, but played down the negative aspects of the drug, such as depression, mood swings, disruption of serotonin production or even death caused usually by mistreatment of the drug's symptoms.

[6]   Ecstasy is defined in comparison as being characterized by immobility, silence, solitude, no crisis, sensory deprivation, recollection and no hallucinations. This perhaps corresponds more closely to the experience of clubbers when 'chilling out' after clubbing. The two are opposite poles of the same continuum.

Rouget describes how hallucinatory drugs are sometimes used to trigger trance (1985: 25), as is continuous loud drumming (ibid.: 53), and how a person's character changes during a trance. He describes the crisis that precedes the trance state; the difficult transition from normal to trance state; how more recent initiates react more strongly and are more likely to achieve a trance state, while the more experienced have more control over whether they go into a trance; that music usually accompanies trance and is generally thought to induce it (ibid.: 44). Rouget states that music includes rhythmic breaks, complex rhythms, changes in stress and rhythmic irregularities, speeding up and getting louder and the collapse or breakdown. Trance dancing is described as frenetic and repetitive, as 'acting the music rather than simply undergoing it ... substituting a totally or partially passive relationship to music with an overtly active one' (1985: 91) while undergoing the effects of the music. 'The possessees are the ones who do the dancing ... the music is played for the purposes of dance' (ibid.: 114). Further, 'Dancing ... brings about modifications in the dancer's state, both at the physiological and psychological level' (ibid.: 117).

Rouget's descriptions of traditional trance elements reflect the altered states reached by clubbers within EDMC. Similarly, the trance dance movements mentioned by Rouget are what I have often seen in EDMC—familiar to any clubber, 'packed one against the other, the dancers bend their knees in time with one another, accompanying each beat with a kind of pounding of the ground and a back-and-forth swaying of the body' (1985: 312) and 'an alternating movement consisting of swaying the entire body from right to left and left to right while the head oscillates from one side to the other' (ibid.: 301).

Music interacts with dance in two ways: acting to trigger trance and then sustaining it. This is either done directly, in which case the trance makes people dance, or indirectly, in which case the music triggers dancing, which itself triggers trance. Dancing is a key element of EDMC. Barbara Ehrenreich makes it clear in her book *Dancing in the Streets* (2006) that there is a long tradition of vigorous dancing to music in England, a tradition that was systematically suppressed by the hegemonic institutions controlling society, as it was seen as containing elements of disorder in an Enlightenment world which was struggling to become a more controlled place. This indicates a further source of the oppositional and transgressive contextualisation of EDMC.

However, as Rouget states, the effect of integrated music and dance was too powerful to suppress:

> To dance is to inscribe music in space, and this inscription is realised by means of a constant modification of the relations between the various parts of the body. The dancer's awareness of his body is totally transformed by this process. Insofar as it is a spur to dancing, therefore, music does appear to be capable of profoundly modifying the relation of the self with itself, or, in other words, the structure of consciousness. Psychologically music also modifies the experience of being, in space and time simultaneously. (1985: 121)

Thus 'music and dance act in conjunction to produce an emotional state favourable to possession' (ibid.: 182). According to Rouget, 'The universality of trance indicates that it corresponds to a psychophysiological disposition innate in human nature' (ibid.: 3). He also points out that throughout the world trance is usually associated with religion and ritual as well as music and dance. Nettl addresses the universality of these associations, discussing

> The importance of music in ritual, and, as it were, in addressing the supernatural. This seems to me to be truly a universal, shared by all known societies, however different the sound. Another universal is the use of music to provide some kind of fundamental change in an individual's consciousness, or in the ambiance of a gathering ... And it is virtually universally associated with dance; not all music is danced, but there is hardly any dance that is not in some sense accompanied by music. (2000: 468)

In the same volume Freeman describes how these relationships may even be a part of human neurobiology (2000: 411–25). Ehrenreich describes the history of the loss of these traditions in some detail. She emphasizes that this kind of activity is a core part of traditional human activity:

> These ingredients of ecstatic rituals and festivities—music, dancing, eating, drinking or indulging in other mind-altering drugs, costuming and/or various forms of self-decoration, such as face and body painting—seem to be universal. (2006: 18)

The Crisis of Individualization

Chernoff states that the most fundamental musical aesthetic in Africa is that 'without participation there is no meaning' (1979: 23) so that 'we can clearly perceive African musical forms only if we understand how they achieve their effectiveness within African social situations' (ibid.: 30). He compares this with Western attitudes where 'we see art as in many ways something separate and distinct ... we isolate the work of art from the social situation in which it was produced in order to concentrate on our main aesthetic concern, those qualities which give it integrity as art' (ibid.: 31–2). Frith states that in Western culture 'the musical experience has been individualised. Music is no longer a necessarily social or collective affair' (1996: 237). In comparison, traditional 'African music is not set apart from its social and cultural context' (Chernoff 1999: 33), an issue discussed in further detail by Small (1987).

Trance is usually associated with a crisis. The crisis associated with EDMC seems to be related to the individualization of society, the loss of and discomfort with traditional forms of community, religion and ritual and the loss of communal celebration and regular connection to the essence of existence. This has created what Ehrenreich (discussing Weber) describes as 'the terrible sense of psychic isolation—"the unprecedented inner loneliness"—that a competitive sink or swim economy imposed' (Ehrenreich 2006: 143–4). D.H. Lawrence wrote in 1929 that

> We are unnaturally resisting our connection with the cosmos, with the world, with mankind, with the nation, with the family ... *We cannot bear connection.* That is our malady. We *must* break away, and be isolate. We call that being free, being individual. Beyond a certain point, which we have reached, it is suicide. Perhaps we have chosen suicide. (2002: 148)

Drawing on the Peter Berger, Brigitte Berger and Hansfried Kellner book *The Homeless Mind: Modernisation and Consciousness* (1974, orig. 1973), Heelas & Woodhead (2001: 43–72) have explored how clubs and other elements of counter-culture act as secondary institutions that provide a focus of community for the homeless self created by this individualization of society. EDMC organizations fit the concept of secondary institutions particularly well as, unlike for example Christianity, such entities provide no '*order of things* to be obeyed ... and therefore provide much greater freedom for people to exercise autonomy' (ibid.: 53). They adopt a role fulfilled in the past by primary institutions such as traditional religions, bridging and filling the gap between primary institutions and homeless selves caused by the inability of these large traditional institutions to remain culturally relevant due to both their inertia and the increasingly rapid speed of change of cultures, philosophies and ethics within postmodernity. Also quoting Weber they describe 'a world once charged with religious significance had been "disenchanted" by "the tremendous cosmos of the modern economic order"' (Weber 1985: 181, qtd in Heelas & Woodhead 2001: 44). EDMC is a process of re-enchantment, of addressing the problem of the homeless self.

Reinsertion into Society, Ritual as Social Construction

The sense of togetherness was important to the clubbers I met. In the words of one clubber: 'If you're dancing to the same beat as everyone else and equally loving it, then yeh there's a feeling of connection' (Author's interview, 2007). The use of drugs for pleasure in this context rather than for medical reasons employs medical technology for recreational purposes and it is an act of bricolage, the oppositional reuse of an object for other than its original purpose (Hebdige 1979: 104). As Rietveld puts it, 'by destroying a sense of self, the merging with technology becomes a cyborgian rite of passage which needs to be repeated for as long as the identity crisis prevails' (2004: 59), and the destruction of the self allows bonding with the group. The crisis of the self in an industrialized world brings machine and humans together musically, ritually and also pharmacologically. By taking Ecstasy, clubbers use chemical technology to short-circuit the lack of traditional ritual, use cultural and social technologies available to them in order to feel completely inserted into the dynamic of the group. Clubbers take an efficient short-cut, a direct route into trance, that bypasses the need for any artefacts of religiosity usually found in 'traditional' or 'ethnic' trance traditions. As Reynolds puts it, 'Ecstasy is self-medication for the societal illnesses caused by rampant consumerist individualisation in the 1980s' (1998: xxii).

Rietveld has discussed EDMC in terms of providing a sense of home: 'One may even go so far as to call a dance space, which involves the consumption of house music, a kind of night-time "church", where an experience can be achieved of a self-effacing identity which becomes part of a community' (1998: 195). As traditional community foci in Britain have become deconstructed, clubbers have sought out new places where they feel part of a community, in which 'the collective voice is given precedence over the individual voice of the artist or composer' (Hebdige 1979: 11), art leading the re-enchantment of culture and society (Gablik 1991: 167–83). Ehrenreich describes the rise of carnival traditions and other ecstatic dance/music traditions of blacks in the Americas in general (and the Caribbean in particular) as 'ecstatic, danced religions in which music and the muscular synchrony of dance are employed to induce a state of trance interpreted as possession by, or transcendent unity with, a god' (2006: 169). She explains that festivities and ecstatic rituals act to dissolve rank and other forms of social difference (ibid.: 44) and that this was one reason why they were repressed. She uses Turner's notion of 'communitas' (1969), 'the spontaneous love and solidarity that can arise within a community of equals' (Ehrenreich 2006: 10), and Durkheim's term 'collective effervescence' to describe 'that which leads individuals to seek ecstatic merger with the group' (ibid.: 14).

EDMC is both a reaction against and a result of postmodernity. It is an effort by postmodern culture to create its own forms of religion, spirituality and meaning. As Bauman states,

> postmodernity ... brings 're-enchantment' of the world after the protracted and earnest, though in the end inconclusive, modern struggle to dis-enchant it ... Dignity has been returned to emotions; legitimacy to the 'inexplicable', nay *irrational*, sympathies and loyalties which cannot 'explain themselves' in terms of their usefulness and purpose ... Fear of the void has been blunted and assuaged ... we learn to learn to live with events and acts that are ... inexplicable. Some of us would even say that it is such events and acts that constitute the hard, irremovable core of the human predicament. (Baumann 1993: 33, emphasis in original)

EDMC trance experiences are leaps into the void, into irrational enchantment, into the sacred, away from the everyday. It is religion 'without a strict and comprehensive ethical code... making a wager on human moral intuition and ability to negotiate the art and the usages of living together' (ibid.: 33).

Openness with Others

The importance of building community and of reinsertion within the group is clear from responses I had from clubbers:

> Usually the best nights are when I meet a great new person or have a really good time with friends ... One of the first times I went clubbing and ended up at an after party the next morning, I met a woman who gave me some acid. We had a great time and I'm still friendly with that woman now, years later ... It was a way of meeting new people (who weren't a part of 9–5 living), having an extended social circle and just having an interesting conversation with a person I've never met ... When I'm out and about in [name of town] I see a lot of people I know. I know there's another world out there which is very different from that of work and I feel my mind has been opened up to differences—I'm more open minded.

> It has made me more open to meeting different types of people ... the closeness and acceptance with/of other clubbers ... I really learned how important it is to let other people know how you feel.

> I enjoy the music & the openess of the friendships/interaction at clubs ... there was a community spirit that transcended the clubbing itself ... As well as accounting for the majority of my present social circle, clubbing has also resulted in a [positive] realignment of my base emotional state, given me a greater sense of empathy and has increased my ability to talk to people I don't know.

> Meeting certain people who will probably be friends for the rest of my life ... the place and my/their state of mind leading to a certain empathy that is difficult to replicate in any other social situation. That sense of empathy on a broader level ... ecstasy has rewired my brain and I now get emotional when I see something's on TV/at the cinema/theatre that would not have affected me before ... I don't dwell on it.

(Author's interviews, 2007)

These comments are typical and were reaffirmed by many others.

EDMC Spirituality

Lynch has identified three elements of EDMC spirituality: a deeper connection with oneself, finding this connection through an essential non-verbal form (dancing, ritual) and the enjoyment of freer and more intimate relationships with others (2002: 88–9). These elements combine and mix together. EDMC spirituality involves many elements, including the creation of sacred spaces; the emulation of images of heaven using clouds of smoke and moving lights; out of body, otherworldly experiences; opposition and transgression; subcultural authority and authenticity; ecstatic journeys; ritual possession trance practices triggered by dancing, drugs and music; no reference to an external deity that has an absolute right to obedience; the replacement of priests by DJs, drug dealers and promoters whose job is to facilitate and enhance the clubbers' mystical experiences. It is a democratized, postmodern, re-enchanting, reconstructive spirituality. It is autonomized, subjectivized, both individualized and rational/holistic, both individual and group/communal, emotionally intelligent and explorational, seeking sensation and ecstasy, mystical and it involves power and spiritual authority being owned, not passed or delegated. It relates to 'something-ism', connection to the earth, Gaia theory, the neo-pagan, direct connection with others and God, general (rather than special) revelation, the experiential, body positivism and liberal attitudes to sexuality. It is focused around community facilitation and celebration, *communitas* and collective effervescence. Ethical decisions within EDMC spirituality are the individual's responsibility, in line with Zygmunt Bauman's *Postmodern Ethics* (1993) rather than an 'absolute line of reference' (Lynch 2005: 94–5) or external power, sometimes guided by the concept of PLUR—Peace, Love, Unity and Respect.

EDMC is a significant cultural phenomenon. Ben Malbon quotes figures showing that 42 per cent of the UK's population visit clubs at least once per year, and that 43 per cent of 15–24-year-olds visit a club once a month or more often (Malbon 1999: 8). 1.8 per cent of 16–59-year-olds used Ecstasy in 2006–7, a figure that has stayed roughly the same (between 1.5 per cent and 2.2 per cent) since 1995 (Nicholas, Kershaw & Walker 2007). These statistics show that in any one year more people in the UK go to a nightclub than to a Christian church. The percentage of the UK population that take Ecstasy (1.8 per cent) is larger than the percentage of those that take part in Pentecostal (1 per cent) or charismatic evangelical (1.2 per cent) Christian churches (Ashworth & Farthing 2007).

It may be that, like other popular music forms, EDMC will be a short-lived cultural phenomenon. Perhaps history will look back on it as a millennial phenomenon, responding to the lyrics of the hit single by pop star Prince, 'tonight we're going to party like it's 1999'. EDMC has been criticized for maintaining participants in a liminal state of continual infancy and that its endemic drug use may cause brain damage to a generation of young clubbers. Lynch states, 'if club culture does serve religious functions for some people in Western society, this raises normative questions of whether it does so in ways that are healthy and constructive' (2005: 178). Healthy or not, EDMC reflects some of the needs of Western society and culture and the failure of traditional religions and contemporary society to meet them. It helps to understand the importance within our cultures of traditions, rituals, communities, transcendence and dancing together to music.

EDMC contains elements of spirituality, meaning and religion. As mainstream culture has become more individualized and less community orientated and as it has lost its celebratory traditions, rituals and religions, some aspects of the original role of organized religions have been replaced by EDMC, which acts much like a religion. It draws upon the traditions in a pick and mix, postmodern fashion, using material from various 'wisdom traditions'. It has adopted elements of Christianity from African American music culture, but because of their transmission through secular black music culture and gay disco, these elements are alluded to in a transgressional fashion. Also transmitted through African American music traditions are trance practices that have their roots in African possession rituals, with particular similarities to Pygmy and Bushmen traditions. Such trance practices are reinforced by the use of illegal drugs to cybernetically enhance the effects of the trance; they add to the sense of subcultural authority and transgression, with the illegality providing a barrier to re-absorption into the mainstream and the resultant process of disenchantment and deconstruction. The crisis that trance responds to is the crisis of the individualization of society, the homeless self; the trance ritual helps the individual to feel reconnected to or reinserted into a community. Clubbers do not see this activity as religious, which may be because the religion is implicit rather than explicit, with clubs taking the role of what may be described as a secondary institution. However, EDMC functions much like a religion, providing a site of escape and transcendence, a sacred space separate from everyday existence and a key focus of community and identity.

References

Ashworth, Jacinta & Farthing, Ian, *Churchgoing in the UK*, www.tearfund.org [access date 30 October 2007].

Bailey, Edward, *The Secular Faith Controversy: Religion in Three Dimensions* (London: Continuum, 2001).

Bailey, Edward, 'The Notion of Implicit Religion: What It Means, and Does Not Mean', in Edward Bailey (ed.), *The Secular Quest for Meaning in Life: Denton Papers in Implicit Religion* (Lampeter: Edwin Mellen, 2002): 1–15.

Bauman, Zygmunt, *Postmodern Ethics* (Oxford: Wiley-Blackwell, 1993).

Beadle, Jeremy J., *Will Pop Eat Itself? Pop Music in the Soundbite Era* (London: Faber and Faber, 1993).

Bey, Hakim, *T.A.Z.: The Temporary Autonomous Zone, Ontological Anarchy, Poetic Terrorism* (Brooklyn: Autonomedia, 1985).

Boom Festival, *Boom Festival 2006 Website*, www.boomfestival.org/afterboom06/index.html [access date 10 July 2007].

Chernoff, John Miller, *African Rhythm and African Sensibility: Aesthetics and Social Action in African Musical Idioms* (Chicago: University of Chicago Press, 1979).

Deehan, Anne & Saville, Esther, *Calculating the Risk: Recreational Drug Use Among Clubbers in the South East of England*, Home Office Online Report, 43/03 (London: Home Office, 2003).

Demerath III, N.J., 'The Sacred as Surrogate: Notes on Implicit A-Religion', in Edward Bailey (ed.), *The Secular Quest for Meaning in Life: Denton Papers in Implicit Religion* (Lampeter: Edwin Mellen, 2002): 35–55.

Ehrenreich, Barbara, *Dancing in the Streets: A History of Collective Joy* (New York: Metropolitan Books, 2006).

Freeman, Walter J., 'A Neurobiological Role of Music in Social Bonding', in Nils L. Wallin, Bjorn Merker & Steven Brown (eds), *The Origins of Music* (Cambridge MA: MIT Press, 2000): 411–24.

Gablik, Suzi, *The Reenchantment of Art* (London: Thames and Hudson, 1992).

Frith, Simon, *Performing Rites: On the Value of Popular Music* (Oxford: Oxford University Press, 1996).

Gauthier, François, 'Rapturous Ruptures: The "Instituant" Religious Experience of Rave', in Graham St John (ed.), *Rave Culture and Religion* (London: Routledge, 2004): 65–84.

Gauthier, François, 'Orpheus and the Underground: Raves and Implicit Religion – From Interpretation to Critique', *Implicit Religion*, 8/3 (2005): 217–66.

Hebdige, Dick, *Subculture: The Meaning of Style* (London: Routledge, 1979).

Heelas, Paul & Woodhead, Linda, 'Homeless Minds Today?', in Linda Woodhead, Paul Heelas & David Martin (eds), *Peter Berger and the Study of Religion* (London: Routledge, 2001): 43–72.

Lawrence, David H., *Apocalypse and the Writings on Revelation* (Cambridge: Cambridge University Press, 2002).

Lynch, Gordon, *After Religion: 'Generation X' and the Search for Meaning* (London: Darton, Longman and Todd, 2002).

Lynch, Gordon, *Understanding Theology and Popular Culture* (Oxford: Blackwell, 2005).

Lynch, Gordon & Badger, Emily, 'The Mainstream Post Rave Scene as a Secondary Institution: A British Perspective', *Culture and Religion*, 7/1 (2006): 27–40.

Malbon, Ben, *Clubbing: Dancing, Ecstasy and Vitality* (London: Routledge, 1998).

Nettl, Bruno, 'An Ethnomusicologist Contemplates Musical Universals', in Nils L. Wallin, Bjorn Merker & Steven Brown (eds), *The Origins of Music* (Cambridge, 2000): 463–71.

Nicholas, Sian, Kershaw, Chris & Walker, Alison A. (eds), *Crime in England and Wales 2006/2007*, www.homeoffice.gov.uk/rds/crimeew0607.html [access date 26 October 2007].

Obsession, *Obsession Website*, www.obsession.org.uk/history/freedom.htm [access date 9 August 2007].

Olaveson, Tim, '"Connectedness" and the Rave Experience: Rave as New Religious Movement', in Graham St John (ed.), *Rave Culture and Religion* (London: Routledge, 2004): 85–106.

Reynolds, Simon, *Energy Flash: A Journey through Rave Music and Dance Culture* (London: Pan Macmillan, 1998).

Rietveld, Hillegonda, *This is Our House: House Music, Cultural Spaces and Technologies* (London: Ashgate, 1998).

Rietveld, Hillegonda, 'Sacrificial Cyborg and Communal Soul', in Graham St John (ed.), *Rave Culture and Religion* (London: Routledge, 2004): 46–62.

St John, Graham, *Rave Culture and Religion* (London: Routledge, 2004).

Saunders, Nicholas, Saunders, Anja & Pauli, Michelle, *In Search of the Ultimate High: Spiritual Experiences Through Psychoactives* (London: Rider, 2000).

Shapiro, Harry, *Waiting for the Man: The Story of Drugs and Popular Music* (London: William Morrow, 1999).

Small, Christopher, *Music of the Common Tongue: Survival and Celebration in African American Music* (Hanover, NH: Wesleyan University Press, 1987).

Sylvan, Robin, *Trance Formation: The Spiritual and Religious Dimensions of Global Rave Culture* (London: Routledge, 2005).

Rouget, Gilbert, *Music and Trance: A Theory of the Relations between Music and Possession* (Chicago: University of Chicago Press: 1985).

Till, Rupert, 'The Blues Blueprint: The Blues in the Music of the Beatles, the Rolling Stones, and Led Zeppelin', in Neil Wynn (ed.), *Cross The Water Blues* (Mississippi: University of Mississippi Press, 2007): 183–201.

Thornton, Sarah, *Club Cultures: Music Meaning and Subcultural Capital* (Cambridge: Polity Press, 1995).

Weber, Max, *The Protestant Ethic and the Spirit of Capitalism* (New York: Routledge, 1985 [1904]).

Williams, Steve, *dircon*, www.users.dircon.co.uk/~matrix/que/que_club.html/ [access date 9 August 2007].

Chapter 11

Representation of Religion in
Pretty Village, Pretty Flame

Milja Radovic

Introduction

This chapter represents part of my doctoral research on Serbian cinematography in the 1990s. My dissertation is investigating the question whether Serbian films of this period had the potential to criticize the socio-political regime of Slobodan Milosevic. I am examining films which dealt with the break-up of Yugoslavia, together with films which portrayed the consequences of the Milosevic regime for Serbian society—the consequences reaching into areas such as an increase of corruption, instability, violence, crime and disintegration of Serbian society in general.

As my study is interdisciplinary in nature, although I position myself in the field of religion and film, my main focus is the representation of nationalism and its connection with institutional religion, which is the Serbian Orthodox Church. I have chosen the film *Pretty Village, Pretty Flame* (*Lepa sela, lepo gore*, Srdjan Dragojevic, 1995) for this chapter because of its many religious aspects. The central question I wish to address here is: how are religion and religious issues represented in this film? What is their function in this context and what purpose do they serve? Reading Dragojevic's film, I found elements that were not presented in other films at that time and I therefore believe it worthy of attention. These elements are embodied in the film's sub-text, which is a cinematic portrayal of religiousness and the use of religious symbolism. In the existing discussions of this film to date, no film scholar or critic paid attention to this religious 'sub-text' and its place in the overall message portrayed. My focus is on both textual and contextual analysis. I was curious to see whether the text contains subversive messages and whether it informs the viewer about the crucial cultural context of the time. There is, I believe, a general lack of analysis of religious symbols in the studies of Balkan cinematography. It is my contention that this approach will provide greater insight into the culture, its stereotypes and ideological frame and it will help contextualize Balkan films. I will proceed by pointing out places of interest for this subject in the film and their relevance to the issue. Accordingly, I hope to offer new perspectives in reading Serbian films which were produced in the 1990s. This chapter should be of interest to both film scholars concerned with Balkan cinema and those interested in the field of film and religion more generally.

The Socio-Political Background: Religion and Nationalism

Many studies were written about the break-up of Yugoslavia providing analysis of the socio-political climate in Serbia at the time of Milosevic's rise. The significance of what I call 'rediscovered' Orthodoxy in the creation of a nationalistic discourse is the phenomenon that many scholars noted. Understanding some aspects of religious ideology is important in order to see the meaning of religious symbolism in the film. Historically, the Serbian Orthodox Church was closely connected with the state, which had an impact not only on the perception of Christianity, but also on theological thought in Serbia. In that sense, nationhood was often connected with the religious, Orthodox identity and the Serbian Church embraced the role of 'keeper' of Serbian national identity.

In the late 1980s, the Serbian Church returned into the public sphere and regained its social voice. The Church leaders received significant attention in the media and in the public space. The Milosevic regime abandoned the principles of the previous multi-ethnic Yugoslavia under Tito, promoted nationalism as a new political programme and turned to Orthodoxy as a useful source for the creation of new ideology. Leaders of the Serbian Orthodox Church were discussing the 'Serbian national question' in a way which was similar to the way the media, academics and politicians were doing.[1] The Church itself contributed to the formation of religious ideology by equating its ecclesiastical mission with political activities (see also Radic 1996: 268). For example, the civil war was frequently justified as the war which defended Serbian identity, nation, culture and land.[2] In the process of the homogenization of Serbs, one of the main sources was religious myths and ideologies. Similar to the *Memorandum* of the Serbian Academy of Sciences and Arts, Church leaders frequently referred to Yugoslavia as a 'cemetery of Serbs', thereby recognizing Serbs as a nation of martyrs whose cultural identity was the most suppressed.[3] The revival of the 'Kosovo myth'[4] affirmed a

---

[1]   The term 'Serbian national question' refers mainly to the solution of the question of Serbian territories, but also refers to religious and national identity and culture.

[2]   The Church leaders frequently promoted this attitude. One of the books published in the 1990s with the blessing of the Metropolitan of the Serbian Orthodox Church in Montenegro Amfilohije represents an attempt to provide a theological justification of the civil war in Bosnia. The book has an apocalyptic title: *The Lamb of God and the Beast from the Abyss* (see Culibrk & Mladenovic 1996).

[3]   One of the statements to that effect is 'The cultural and spiritual integrity of no other Yugoslav nation is so roughly challenged as that of the Serbian nation …'. The complete text is available at www.haverford.edu/relg/sells/reports/memorandumSANU.htm [access date 17 December 2007].

[4]   The myth is based on the epic reinterpretation of the historical event that occurred on 28 June 1389 on the Kosovo field. The Serbian army was headed by Lazar Hrebeljanovic and the Ottoman army by Sultan Murad, who both died in the battle. The Serbian army lost the battle and consequently lost its independence. The battle remained one of the most famous battles preserved in Serbian epics. The tragedy on Kosovo and a legend of Duke

pseudo-history and a local mythology and represents a politicization of religion. The contemporary use of the Kosovo myth is a blend of national and religious ideology, which combines mythological language and promotes stereotypes, such as the Serbs being a 'heavenly nation', a populist term used at the end of the 1980s and in the 1990s.[5]

Religion became part of everyday life and played an important role in the re-creation of a Serbian national identity. Orthodox symbols and images, such as crosses and icons were widely used, from 'turbo-folk' singers to paramilitary formations.[6] Orthodoxy became inseparable from the idea of a nation and 'being a real Serb' was measured by the extent of one's public portrayal of devotion to the

---

Lazar described, for example, in the epic song *The Fall of the Serbian Empire*, became the basis for the Kosovo myth. Lazar is described as a Christ-like figure, who received a message from God, who confronted him with two possible choices, of the 'kingdom of earth' and the 'kingdom of heaven'. If he chooses the first one, he will win and if he chooses the second one, he will die along with his whole army but will gain Christ's kingdom. As described in the epic poetry, before the battle Lazar had his last supper, where the tragedy to come is revealed by the betrayal of one of his knights, Vuk Brankovic. Vuk Brankovic's character represents Judas. Lazar chooses the 'kingdom of heaven', which represents his acceptance of martyrdom for Christ. This acceptance is the central moral message that an unknown storyteller emphasizes throughout the song. It suggests Christ-likeness as an ideal, and many theologians have referred to Lazar's decision not as an individual act, but, rather, as an act that embodies the orientation of the Serbian nation towards Christ. The story depicts a strictly ethical, moral concept of the battle rather than dealing with concrete historical facts. Its central motif is the idea of Christian suffering and martyrdom for Christ. Before the battle, Lazar calls all Serbs to come to Kosovo, and those who do not come will be cursed by the 'Duke's swear' ('Knezeva kletva'). The words that Lazar supposedly said on this occasion are engraved in the monument of *Gazimestan* where the battle took place. The words of 'Knezeva kletva' were used in the 1980s as a form of political message which was a call to the new national 'battle' for Kosovo through which Serbs would regain their 'lost' national integrity.

[5]   Bishop Jovan used this term in his speech when he welcomed the relics of St Lazarus of Kosovo in 1989 (see Radic 1996: 278).

[6]   Nowadays, many organizations in Serbia, which have clear pro-nationalistic and even pro-fascistic programmes, embrace Orthodox symbolism on their websites. Their programmes are often represented as a fight for the 'moral resurrection' of the Serbs. The notorious brigade Jedinica za Specijalne Operacije (Special Operations Unit), also known as Crvene Beretke (Red Berets), whose leader was convicted for the assassination of the Serbian Prime Minister Dr Zoran Djindjic in 2003, includes on its website links to the Serbian Orthodox Patriarchate and to other web pages of the Serbian Orthodox Church. Its hymn includes verses which evoke the glorious past of the Serbian mediaeval dynasties. One of the songs posted on the same site, called 'Christ Oh God', represents the song of the soldier(s) who is (are) leaving for the battle of Kosovo. The same song is used in the film of Zdravko Sotra, *The Kosovo Battle* (1989) (see www.crveneberetke.com, for other organizations see www.svetijustin.cjb.net/, www.nomokanon.org.yu, http://stari.dverisrpske.com/, www.obraz.org.yu/, www.vidovdan.org/).

nation. Since the late 1980s, public discourse has presented religion and the nation as one, which confronted the Church with the problem of ethnofiletism.[7] The role of Orthodoxy in giving the regime national and political legitimacy resulted in the promotion of nationalism and the justification of the civil war. We will see below how the 'populist version' of Orthodoxy in the 1990s was depicted in the film, *Pretty Village, Pretty Frame.*

The Content of *Pretty Village, Pretty Flame*

The film *Pretty Village, Pretty Flame* (*Lepa sela, lepo gore*, Srdjan Dragojevic, 1995) was made during the time of the Milosevic regime and the civil war, as an independent production of artists who 'tried to resist the destruction and meaninglessness around them' in this way (DVD *Pretty Village, Pretty Flame*, Beograd: Cobra Film, 2001). The film is set in Bosnia and it describes the tragic events in a tunnel where a group of Serbian soldiers are trapped and surrounded by Muslim forces. The tunnel is the site where the two main characters used to play as children; they believed then that 'an ogre' lived there, which 'would set the village on fire', if he awoke. The film focuses on the friendship between a Serbian boy and a Muslim boy, Milan and Halil. Through their personal relationship the director tells the story of civil war. The title *Lepa sela, lepo gore* originally means 'pretty villages burn nicely'; it comes from the comment of one of the characters, a Serbian soldier, after he and others have set a Muslim village on fire. The plot is based around seven characters, Serbian soldiers who are accompanied by a female American journalist. The film exposes an assortment of characters ranging from an ex-communist turned nationalist, an ex-criminal, a professor who stands for the only 'intellectual' among them, to a drug addict who accidentally ended up in the military. Their relationships develop in the tunnel where they are faced with danger, but where they are also confronted with the differences among them. Verbal conflicts reveal their attitudes and personal stories, sometimes in the form of confessions, as recorded by the camera of the American journalist. Each of the main characters is represented in a bold way. Their, to some extent, stereotypical portrayal informs us about the particular mindset of Serbian people during Milosevic's time. It shows the viewer how the regime's ideology affected people from different milieus and backgrounds.

Through the conflicts between some of the characters, the viewer learns not just about ideological differences, but also about different perceptions of recent Yugoslav history. It is interesting that in spite of these differences all the characters are 'unified in a sense of national belonging' (Filip David, '*Pretty Village, Pretty*

---

[7] Ethnofiletism was condemned by the Great Council in Constantinople in 1872. It represents deviation from Orthodox faith because it puts the national ideology above the ecclesiastic dimension of the Church and its basic principle of unity of all in Christ regardless of ethnicity, gender or class. See Radmila Radic: ibid., p. 269.

Flame Questionnaire', personal e-mail 27 November 2007).[8] Nationality seems to be the only element they have in common and only that matters during their time together.

The author uses flashback interruptions to give the viewer a more comprehensive insight into the characters and their backgrounds and to increase the emotional pressure while the plot develops. As the story unfolds, the viewer witnesses the complexity of the ideology which is supported by 'myth-mania' and its connection to the civil war. Two ideologies are addressed in the film: the ideology of 'fraternity and unity' and the ideology of nationalism.

The events shift from one time period to another: from the 1970s to the 1990s. The friendship between Milan and Halil depends on external circumstances or is at least influenced by them. In Tito's Yugoslavia they felt that there were almost no differences between each other. In the film, there is a strong sense of regret about the destroyed friendship; it is not clear who is to blame for the tragedy that took place—the 'ogre' in the tunnel, communists, nationalists? It seems that to a certain extent the story proposes that everyone is to blame for the war and that both sides equally abandoned the ideals of Tito's Yugoslavia.[9] This possible view created a great deal of controversy around the film. My intention is to look into those elements of the film which led critics see it as another Serbian film which states that 'no one is to blame' and those elements which pointed to the film as presenting an ideology that demystified the idea that the war was a 'just war' to defend Serbian 'sacred' lands. The second consideration is unmasked by the subversive portrayal of soldiers as war profiteers and very often as 'predators for fun'.

A Pro-War or an Anti-War Film?

Debates about this film, both in the former Yugoslavia and abroad, were rather controversial. There was a great deal of diversity in the opinions and analysis of the film's meaning. The diversity existed not only among film critics, but also in the perceptions of the audiences. A central question for all viewers was whether this film was created with the intention of being placed in the category of 'pro-war' or 'anti-war' films. The film received positive critical reviews, having been shown at several film festivals, and it was nominated for an Oscar.[10]

Controversy about the film opened a debate as to whether a film coming from Milosevic's Serbia could offer an objective perspective of the conflict. In

---

[8]   My research methodology includes interviews with film directors and critics, which were done mostly through e-mail communication.

[9]   Among many indications for this view, the significant scene is the conversation between two former Yugoslav army colonels, one a Muslim, the other a Serb.

[10]   *Variety* recognized the film as 'one of the biggest anti-war statements ever committed to the big screen' (Credits, Critiques, DVD *Pretty Village Pretty Flame*, Beograd: Cobra Film, 2001).

my opinion the answer is both 'yes' and 'no'. Yes, because bearing in mind the circumstances under which films were produced during the 1990s, one needs to recognize that many films did offer a form of critique by focusing on the impact that the change of political discourse had on Serbian society. Goran Paskaljevic's *Keg of Gunpowder* (*Bure Baruta*) (1998), for example, criticizes the increase of violence by offering a dark picture of 1990s Serbia, although it never directly names those who caused the destruction of society. *Pretty Village, Pretty Flame* deals with the war in Bosnia, offering the Serbian perspective, although this does not necessarily mean that it is taking the Serbian side. My reading is more about observing films in the way they documented the situation as it was. By this I mean 'documenting' the way of thinking in Serbia, the perception of the war, the 'conflict' between village and city as, respectively, retrograde and pro-liberal sites, stereotypes about other nations, the division of the citizens into 'domestic traitors' and patriots and so on. The negative view—the reason why film may be denied objectivity—is embodied in the question whether the film can really operate outside the ideological discourse in which it was made. The film challenges the viewer to think about this problem and to consider to what extent it is possible to operate with stereotypes and ideologies of the local culture and to remain subversive.

This ambiguity of the film is in my opinion what created so many diverse readings, ranging from the very positive to the very negative.[11] What was criticized the most about the film was the lack of a direct message against Milosevic. According to some critics, this resulted in the film being read as one which proposed the idea that it was nobody's fault, similar to Kusturica's *Underground* (see Iordanova 2001: 111–55). There are several indications in the film which critics and film scholars recognized as pointing to a 'pro-Serbian, pro-Milosevic' attitude. Generally, the metaphors, the stereotypical representations of the characters and the character of the American journalist were taken to support such a view. The use of metaphors, such as the 'ogre' in the tunnel, supported the reading that the war was represented through a mythical concept.[12] In other words, according to some views, the 'real' conflict is moved into the mythical sphere representing the war as the 'destiny' of the Balkans.[13] A stereotypical portrayal of the Serbs, but also of Muslims, whose atrocities we also see in the film, can introduce the perspective of the 'wild Balkan man' that Frederick Jameson discussed (see Jameson 2004: 233–4). The American journalist represents, in some opinions,

---

[11]   The director of Viennale, the Austrian film event, refused to screen it, claiming the film was 'Serb fascist propaganda' (Iordanova 2001: 146).

[12]   According to Duijzings (2000: 177), the civil war was presented in Serbian public discourse as 'the mythical conflict between good and evil, an extra-temporal conflict that stands outside the sphere of politics, economics and history'.

[13]   According to Filip David, Serbian screenwriter and professor of dramaturgy, the metaphor of the ogre in the tunnel supports the representation of the war as 'the given state caused by some forces, which are in [the] domain of [the] mythical' (Filip David, '*Pretty Village, Pretty Flame* Questionnaire', personal e-mail 27 November 2007).

the 'Westerner' who gets involved without a real understanding of the locals and their motives for conflict.[14] This film can then also provide a different understanding of the conflict by giving information about the internal perspective, the impact of local mythologies, ideologies and stereotypes, which influenced the escalation of the conflict. I would like to mention, however, that Dragojevic does give certain pointers in the film about the Serbian involvement in the war and the exodus of the Muslim population in the Bosnian areas which had a Serbian majority. The first is embodied in the character of the military doctor and the second is one of the two Muslims we see in the film, Nazim.[15]

Understanding that the film operates with diverse symbolisms and lacks a direct approach of explicitly making the regime responsible for the war, I argue that there is a very strong indirect message which opposes the regime. The film explores the impact of the nationalistic ideology, but above all the mindset of the people. When I say 'the mindset of the people', I do not mean to over-generalize or create a stereotype of the situation in Serbia, but to highlight the impact that the populist propaganda had among the population, at least in the early 1990s.[16]

The weakness of the film in my opinion is not the lack of a direct message against Milosevic, but its stereotypical representation of recent Yugoslav history. The director seems to adopt the common view of the 1990s which saw Yugoslavia as a 'false' country based on false ideals. The viewer sees this in the opening sequence of the inauguration of the tunnel which is symbolically named 'brotherhood and unity tunnel'. The communist commissioner cuts his finger—a symbol of the bloodshed to come. The image of the 'ogre' who 'sleeps' in the 'brotherhood and unity tunnel' gives an indication that Yugoslavia was just a 'break' in the bloodshed which is 'typical' for its people. This is one of the strongest negative stereotypes which the director paints of the Balkan conflict. Conversations between some characters in the tunnel again reveal the idea that ideals on which Yugoslavia was based were false or at least corrupted. The negative review on the recent Yugoslav history is

---

[14]   'This is clearly a comment to the international community's support for Serbia's enemies by using the sub tone of Serbia's self reflection of the border post of Christianity' (Bernd Buder, '*Pretty Village, Pretty Flame* Questionnaire', personal e-mail 19 November 2007).

[15]   At the very beginning of the film, Nazim, a postman, leaves his village with his family. We see his 'fica' car packed with house appliances. Tito's picture is tied to the side of the car. Both the car and the picture of the Marshall represent symbols of a Yugoslavia that no longer exists. Nazim is leaving, which suggests the tragedy which is to come.

[16]   It is important to remember that the media propaganda which promoted a new ideological discourse was very successful in the late 1980s. The nationalistic ideology represented a verbal introduction to the war, a 'call to arms'. At the celebration of the 600 years since the Battle of Kosovo in 1989, Milosevic gathered around two million Serbs who carried Orthodox icons together with Milosevic's pictures. *Politika* recognized this as 'renewed harmony which brings back dignity to Serbia' (*Obnovljena sloga vraca dostojanstvo Srbiji, Politika*, 29 June 1989).

shared by other Serbian directors. It reflects the time in which the films were made, a time of divorce from Yugoslav ideals and the turn towards nationalism.

Religious Identity and Nationalism in the Film

Orthodox Christianity is not specifically analysed in the film nor can one say that Dragojevic's intention was to deal with religious issues *per se*. The film does, however, inform the viewer about institutional religion, Serbian Orthodoxy, its 'populist' version and its impact. Religious elements are to be found in the subtext of the film and are inseparable from the representation of nationalism. Religious intolerance is made visible as an integral part of the conflict. We shall look here at some of the main characters who make their Orthodox identity evident or introduce awareness of the religious diversity between Serbs and Muslims.

One such character in the film is the owner of a roadhouse ironically called Sloga ('Harmony'). His name Sloba, a nickname for Slobodan, can be construed as a reference to Slobodan Milosevic. Sloba is the one who survives the war and profits from it. His roadhouse is turned into the warehouse during the war and remains undamaged despite all the destruction around it. From the very beginning Sloba constantly challenges the friendship between Milan and Halil. In one of the first scenes of the film, he provokes tension between Milan and Halil, drawing attention to the national and religious diversity among Serbs and Muslims in Bosnia. Sloba's language is the same discourse or 'speech of hate' found in Milosevic's media. Sloba uses the term 'belie', a libellous word for Bosnian Muslims. The term actually evokes the 500 years of slavery under the Ottoman Empire, when many Serbs suffered for their Orthodoxy or were forced to convert to Islam. It was not the film director who made this connection—it existed before within the political regime's communications, which continuously reminded citizens of a history of suffering. Later in the film it is Sloba who informs Milan that his mother was murdered and puts the blame on Halil, his Muslim friend, not losing another chance to emphasize how impossible this friendship is and that it was actually never real. For Sloba, conflict is a chance for profit and he is a true war profiteer.

Sloba's story reveals another aspect of the war that the film depicts. After a doctor in the military hospital in Belgrade reminded Milan that all patients are equal to him, whether Serb or Muslim, and that they are all in a foreign country, we see Sloba visiting the hospital with gifts for the doctor. The doctor's attitude may be associated with the official attitude that Serbia was not involved in the Bosnian war. The scene in which the doctor welcomes Sloba cordially when he gives him a painting of the *Kosovo Maiden* suggests that Serbia was not a 'foreign country', but the 'motherland' of the ideology embodied in the painting.[17]

---

[17]   The Kosovo Maiden is again a part of the aforementioned Kosovo Myth. According to the legend, the Kosovo Maiden was a fiancée of one of the Serbian knights who came to the Kosovo field, after the battle, to find her beloved one. She carried wine and bread for

The film shows how the conflict first began in the media, with language which served as an introduction to the war. Dragojevic 'attacks' the media throughout the film. In the scene in which he introduces the next two characters, Fork and Lazar, the viewer discovers more about the media language. In the news that Lazar is watching, Serbs are victimized, while others are identified as the enemies and predators: Croats are identified with 'Ustashi' from the Second World War and Bosnian Muslims with 'Turks' from the Ottoman Empire—the media propaganda also calls them 'jihad warriors'. Motivated by the media's interpretation of the war, Lazar decides to join the army. He is convinced that he is defending Orthodoxy and Serbdom from an Islamic invasion. Ironically, on his trip to the battlefield, a Muslim gives him a ride. Lazar remains confused with the situation, strongly believing as he does in local political mythologies—to the extent that he does not possess a normal perception of reality.

The viewer learns the most about the impact of a religious-national mythology through another main character, Lazar's brother-in-law, whose nickname is Fork. Both Lazar and Fork are metaphors for the population who are 'hooked' on the regime's ideology. Fork wears chetnik marks and demonstrates throughout the film that he belongs to Orthodox Christianity. In one of the first scenes in which Fork appears, the viewer sees him receiving a UN soldier with the traditional Orthodox Easter greeting. The scene takes place somewhere in Bosnia in a battlefield, in the zone protected by the UN. The absurdity of the situation is accentuated by Fork's vulgarity and the dialogue among war profiteers. Like his friend Lazar, Fork believes in the national-religious myth that Serbs are a chosen nation, an idea established on the abuse of the Kosovo myth.

Fork's religious identity reveals a primitive superstitious religiosity: personal faith is replaced with the empty practice of religious customs and with the repetition of phrases, without any deeper meaning or understanding of them by those who subscribe to this kind of religiosity. Fork lives with the delusion that God protects Serbs, because Serbs are a holy nation, and does not examine this myth. How Fork goes into the battlefield is told in a flashback, which connects to the scene of his death. Fork chose to die, the viewer can assume, when he became aware not just of his hopeless situation, but also of the absurdity of the ideas in which they all became trapped. He falls to the ground in a crucified position. This position might represent Fork as a victim. The director does not just provide a 'simple' identification with an anti-hero, but suggests that, although he is a negative character and a participant in a brutal conflict, he is also a victim of the regime's ideology. It does not mitigate his fault, but opens the question of responsibility with regard to those who 'organized' the war. Fork remains a predator, but he is also a victim. Dragojevic's film witnesses not only that the war was bad or that its participants were brutal murderers, but it also proposes that a great deal of responsibility lies with the war ideologists.

---

wounded soldiers. She has a sacral rather than medical role as she is giving the soldiers the 'last communion' and weeps over them.

A significant part of Dragojevic's film deals with war profiteers. In his later film *The Wounds* (*Rane*) (1998), Dragojevic returns to this issue. War profiteers, as we see later on in *Pretty Village, Pretty Flame*, greet Milan with 'God help you' just before they burn down Halil's house. Such a portrayal of the soldiers and the war sites is a demystification of the ideal which projects 'honourable Serbian fighters as peasant-heroes with brave hearts and with the honour of a maiden'.[18]

The reference to the ideological discourse recurs in the obsessive way in which national history is worked into the film. Again, through Fork the viewer discovers the pseudo-historical ideas which were affirmed in Serbia in the early 1990s. When speaking into the camera, the camera of an American journalist, he proclaims that 'the Serbs are the oldest nation', a nation that used a fork at the time when other nations, such as the English or Germans, were eating with their hands. A soldier in the hospital sings a song about 'who says, who lies that Serbia is small', next to a Christmas tree decorated with the sign of the Orthodox cross—a cross with four 's's'. In the place where volunteer soldiers are recruited, the short conversation between Fork and the street salesman, who sells flags and other nationalistic emblems, portrays how mythology has replaced reality, or at least how this reality is just a continuation of the nation's mythological existence. The scene takes place during the night of mobilization and is followed by the strong rhythm of the trumpets, playing under the black flag on which is written: 'With Faith in God— Freedom or Death'. The 'market of history and Orthodoxy', as it was referred to, was common in Serbia, especially in the early 1990s. The film depicts the increase of 'national songs' popularized in Serbia and their political connotation; their aim was to invoke the memory of a glorious and heroic past before Tito's Yugoslavia was established. An awakened sense of national-religious identity was successful because of the reinterpretation of the history and the use of religious myths. The general aim was to show that the civil war was a 'just conflict'.

The film has many scenes which include religious symbols that refer to Serbian Orthodoxy. Religious images in the film are not intrusive and their function is similar to the music in the film: they inform the viewer about the cultural context and the increased use of historical and Orthodox notions in the public sphere. The sign that repeatedly appears in the film is the cross with the four 's's', which one of the characters, the Professor, wears on his helmet (Figure 11.1).[19]

---

[18] See the discussion of anthropologist Ivan Colovic on Serbian political myths in the section 'Skerlic i srpski politicki mitovi' in his *Politika simbola* (2002: 125–42).

[19] Four 's's' usually refers to the slogan: 'Only unity saves Serbs' (*Samo Sloga Srbina Spasava*). Besides this populist interpretation, the four 's's' placed around four sides of the cross actually go back to the Byzantine empire and the navy flag of the dynasty of Palaeologus—according to the historical sources. Originally they were four copies of the Greek letter 'V', which refers to Jesus Christ (Βασιλευς Βασιλεών Βασιλευοντων Βασιλευουσιο, 'The King of Kings who reigns over the queen of cities—Constantinople', and according to the second version it means, 'O King help the King of the Queen

Figure 11.1   Image from *Pretty Village, Pretty Flame* of the cross with the four s's, which the Professor wears on his helmet. Courtesy Cobra Film, Belgrade.

One of the most provocative images is certainly that of Fork, when he is trapped in the tunnel: he has the Orthodox cross hanging next to his head while he is charging a machine gun, giving a Muslim name to each bullet (Figure 11.2).

Figure 11.2   Image from *Pretty Village, Pretty Flame* of the Orthodox cross hanging next to Fork's head while he is charging a machine gun. Courtesy Cobra Film, Belgrade.

of Cities—Constantinople') (see www.nasasrbija.co.yu/skupstina/t_stolica13-1_3.htm, 1 December 2007).

The fist with three fingers up (Figure 11.3) is a symbolic greeting that demonstrates belonging to the Serbian Orthodox nation.[20] Under the sign of the fist with three fingers lifted up is written the slogan 'Serbia to Tokyo', a populist idiom used by the most militant warlords; it says more, despite conveying an element of humour: the tendency to include all Serbian territories in what is called 'Great Serbia'. The greeting with the fist and three fingers up was widely used in the 1990s and its meaning varied, from being a symbol of resistance against Milosevic during the demonstrations in 1991 to being a nationalistic greeting.

Figure 11.3   Image from *Pretty Village, Pretty Flame* of a symbolic greeting that demonstrates one's belonging to the Serbian Orthodox nation. Courtesy Cobra Film, Belgrade.

Bosnian Muslims do not feature so much in the film, except in the characters of Halil and the postman Nazim. On the other hand, both Halil and Nazim are portrayed in a positive light. Nazim's destiny is not revealed to the viewer; only segments of his past are presented, those connected to the friendship between Milan and Halil. Nazim is portrayed as a naïve, ordinary villager, who probably honestly believed in the Yugoslav idea of 'fraternity'. Neither Halil nor Nazim expresses any sense of belonging to particular religious or national communities. This is clearly demonstrated in Tito's picture, mentioned above, that Nazim is taking along to his refugee life.

Regarding other Bosnian Muslim characters, the viewer 'sees' them through the eyes of the main Serbian characters. The viewer's perception of 'others' in that sense depends on the seven soldiers trapped in the tunnel. For Bosnian Muslims, the most common names used in the film are, as mentioned, '*balije*', also

---

[20]   In the Orthodox Church, believers cross themselves with three fingers and the populist interpretation is that it is a symbol for the Serbs being Orthodox.

'circumcised' and 'Turks'. This shows how, for the Serbs, their former neighbours, the Bosnian Muslims, became 'foreigners' and deadly enemies whom they equated with the Turks from the time of the Ottoman rule.

Conclusion

Pretty Village, Pretty Flame opens the possibility for diverse readings and understandings of the film text, its symbolism and context. Its 'sub-text' offers an insight into the ideology which was of crucial importance in the Serbian politics of the 1990s.

My hypothesis is that Dragojevic's film frames the regime's ideology and the nationalistic discourse represented within it constructs clear references to religion. The film depicts religion, Serbian Orthodoxy, as a religious ideology unified with nationalism, which played an important role for the purposes of the Milosevic's propaganda. *Pretty Village, Pretty Flame* with its 'insider' gaze provides a critical depiction of religious-mythological concepts of nationhood.

The film provides pointers to the way nationalism and religious intolerance were directly connected and, further, the way Milosevic's regime presented, through media propaganda, the conflict as a continuation of the historical battle for Serbdom and therefore Orthodoxy as its integral part. There are several ideological assumptions underlying the conflict in Serbia at the time that the film in my opinion 'unmasks': that Serbs are a 'heavenly people' who suffer because of their righteousness, that God protects Serbs (which means he is always on the Serbian side), that Serbs are a martyr nation whose suffering is caused by a world of conspiracy, that Serbs were fighting a defensive war and that the civil war had a 'sacred' purpose. In this way, the return to Orthodoxy in the 1990s is portrayed as a political trend rather than a return to Christian values. Religion as depicted in the film is not as a source of strength for the characters, but as a source of national identity.

The film shows how Serbia replaced a communist ideology with another ideology—a national-religious one. Regardless of whether the director's intention was to describe exactly how similar the impact was to the ideologies in the Balkans—this is, as already mentioned, visible in his approach to recent Yugoslav history—there is a weakness to this lack of direction. It leaves the field open for the possibility of finding different answers. Dragojevic provides a strong sub-text to the film. The cinematic representation of religion and religious symbols delivers a commonly overlooked message in the film. After this the viewer is left with the question whether such a portrayal of religiousness, which, sometimes witty, has a dose of recognizable black humour and is certainly often ironic, can be in the service of Milosevic's propaganda. In my opinion, the answer is that it cannot be, as it deconstructs some of the fundamental stereotypes and myths upon which Milosevic's populist rhetoric was based. Another point that arises is the absurd twist that the nationalistic ideology was supported by the former communists.

The film does not offer solutions, broader explanations or explicit political judgments, which is probably one of the reasons why it was seen as a film which was in favour of the regime. On the other hand, reading the film's sub-text and understanding it within the specific cultural context in which it was made, one might actually be surprised about the amount of critical elements the film contains.

To conclude, *Pretty Village, Pretty Flame* is an ambiguous film. Only when we look at its sub-text will it inform us about the time when it was made and make us think twice about the ideology promoted in Serbia that underpinned the war. The film's portrayal of religion also raises the question what the role of religion was at that time. The film makes connections between religiosity and the rehabilitation of 'chetniks' and many other 'national symbols'. It shows how religion can, when turned into an ideology, be used—in a dangerous way—for political purposes and indoctrination and to legitimate war. In that sense, although made over a decade ago, this film might still have a relevant message in raising this question: is it possible to reconcile the people of the former Yugoslavia without the need to overcome existing trends of national-religious ideology which, even after the war, remains a potential problem in Serbia and therefore for the whole of the Balkan region?

References

Colovic, I., *Politika simbola* (Beograd: Biblioteka XX vek, 2002).

Culibrk, J. & Mladenovic, R.M. (eds), *Jagnje Bozije i zvijer iz bezdana, filosofija rata* (Cetinje: Svetigora, 1996).

Duijzings, G., *Religion and the Politics of Identity in Kosovo* (London: Hurst, 2000).

Iordanova, D., *Cinema of Flames: Balkan Film, Culture and the Media* (London: British Film Institute, 2001).

Jameson, F., 'Thoughts on Balkan Cinema', in A. Egoyan and I. Balfour (eds), *Subtitles: On the Foreignness of Film* (Cambridge, MA: MIT Press: 2004): 231–7.

Radic, R., 'Crkva i srpsko pitanje', in N. Popov (ed.), *Srpska strana rata* (Beograd: Bigz, 1996): 267–304.

Chapter 12

A Secular Gospel for the Marginal:
Two Films of Stephen Chow as
Hong Kong Cinematic Parables

Yam Chi-Keung

Introduction

In the rapidly developing field of religion/theology and film, East Asian cinema is yet to be included on the agenda, notwithstanding its increasing prominence in academic film study and rising popularity among the general worldwide audience. Concomitantly, many film scholars who carry out research on East Asia often focus on the relatively small sample of works distributed in art house cinemas and film festivals, while showing little serious interest in popular commercial cinema. My study breaks these geo-cultural and academic boundaries by attending to the hugely popular cinema in East Asia from a religious–theological perspective.

As part of a larger project on the theological study of Hong Kong cinema, this chapter focuses on two recent films by the Hong Kong actor–filmmaker Stephen Chow, who is arguably the most popular film comedian in Chinese and East Asian societies since the early 1990s.[1] Being the most commercially successful actor in Hong Kong for more than a decade, he is widely regarded as iconic in local popular culture.[2] His unique *moleitau* (non-sensical) style of comedy created the *moleitau* sub-culture in Hong Kong in the 1990s. Stephen Chow has a sizeable fandom not only in his native city, but also in Taiwan, mainland China, South Korea, Japan and some Southeast Asian countries. A considerable number of

---

[1] Stephen Chow (aka Stephen Chiau in earlier transliterations) began his media career in the early 1980s as a host in a highly popular children's television programme. He subsequently became very popular as he started acting in prime-time television drama serials in the late 1980s, because of his unique non-sensical style of playing with words, which came to be known as *moleitau*. His film acting career also began in the late 1980s and he established himself as one of the most well-received actors in Hong Kong in the early 1990s.

[2] According to veteran Hong Kong film critic Sek Kei (石琪), Stephen Chow's films have made more than one billion Hong Kong Dollars in the local box office since 1990; he also recognizes Chow to be a representative of Hong Kong film culture (see Sek Kei 2005).

young intellectuals in China consider his films, especially those from the 1990s, expressions of postmodernism, although Chow repeatedly stresses that he has no idea what that means. Despite his phenomenal popularity, he has been virtually disregarded by film scholars who study Hong Kong cinema. Many of the major scholarly works on Hong Kong film either only mention him briefly or do not mention him at all.[3]

In this chapter, I examine the two films that Stephen Chow made at the beginning of this century, *Shaolin Soccer* (2001) and *Kung Fu Hustle* (2004); I shall look at their immediate socio-cultural and politico-economic context of production as well as their reception by the primary audience and critics in Hong Kong. This study is therefore a combination of textual and contextual analyses, which is enriched by referring to written comments by local critics and audience members at the time when the films were in cinemas in Hong Kong. *Shaolin Soccer* is the first film in which Chow takes full directorial responsibility;[4] both films topped the box office record of local films in Hong Kong.[5] This feat is even more remarkable when seen against the backdrop of the rapid decline of the city's once vibrant film industry since the late 1990s.[6] Popular beliefs, especially those of distant observers, hold that Chow's films are merely frivolous non-sensical comedies which have no value beyond that of pure entertainment.[7] However, I contend that when understood within their original social, political, economic and cultural contexts, the films are parabolic representations of an important aspect of their society of origin. They manifest in irreverent manners some of the deepest collective concerns of contemporary Hong Kong and proffer a vision of hope.

---

[3]   One of the very few examples is the book chapter by Siu Leung Li (2005), which discusses Chow's films in detail.

[4]   Although Stephen Chow formally made his directorial debut as early as 1994 with *From Beijing with Love*, all his films before 2001 were co-directed. In *Shaolin Soccer*, one of his long-time co-directing partners Li Lik-Chee (李力持) is credited as the Associate Director. There are rumours that the two friends became foes in this project, but this is beside the concern of this essay.

[5]   *Shaolin Soccer* was released in Hong Kong in summer 2001; it stayed on screen for almost three months and made over 60 million Hong Kong Dollars to break the box office record of local films. This record was broken by *Kung Fu Hustle* within its first three weeks on screen, during the Christmas period of 2004–2005. At the time of writing this chapter, the latter is still the record holder.

[6]   In the heyday of its film industry during the 1980s and 1990s, Hong Kong boasted the production of more than 300 film titles annually and was the third largest film production centre in the world after Bollywood and Hollywood. This figure has gradually declined since the end of the twentieth century. In the first few years of this century, the annual productivity has amounted to less than a hundred titles.

[7]   Both films were released in the UK and US and DVDs are widely distributed in Europe. A casual glance at the reviews in the 'Western' media indicates that the critics focus almost solely on the films' comic aspects and action.

Shaolin Soccer as Manifestation of the Collective Anxiety of Marginalization

Despite the films' apparent frivolousness and their mix and match of popular appeals from Chinese martial arts, soccer, Japanese *anime* (animation films of uniquely Japanese style and contents) and *manga* (Japanese comic books), and computer role-playing games (RPG), *Shaolin Soccer* and *Kung Fu Hustle* are in essence stories about marginalized underdogs struggling for survival in a changing world that is hostile to them. *Shaolin Soccer* depicts a group of ex-Shaolin monks who have to leave the temple after the death of their master–teacher and find their livelihoods in the 'normal' world. Lacking any practical skills apart from martial arts and thus unable to make their living, they find themselves struggling at subsistence level in the flourishing city. Eventually they gather to form a football team, apply their magnificent martial arts to the sport and make their way to the national tournament against all odds. Echoing this portrayal of the marginal, *Kung Fu Hustle* depicts a grassroots neighbourhood where the poor take refuge at the city's periphery away from the threat of treacherous gangsters. It is, however, within this seemingly powerless community that hidden heroes emerge to defend the people's lives in the face of fatal threats and re-establish a peaceful order.

Certainly, the story of the underdog is a favourite of Stephen Chow's and it is central to many of his previous works. The characterizations and story lines of the two films in question are far from complex. The final victories of the underdogs have been derided as mere commonplace fantasy in popular culture.[8] I argue, however, that, when viewed against their immediate social context, these apparently ordinary narratives take on extraordinary meaning for the local audience: they can be understood as irreverent parables that express important aspects of the mass psychology of the people of Hong Kong in the years following the city's political reunion with China. Even though the relationship between the films and the social milieu is not at all explicit, a considerable portion of the reviews and audience writings that I have perused suggest such an interpretation.

In the case of *Shaolin Soccer*, the aforementioned writings often correlate the experience of the film characters with the latent anxiety of many people in Hong Kong—the fretfulness of being pushed to the margin and eventually becoming obsolete in the face of a gigantic country and its burgeoning economy. These writings suggest that some of the audience relate their own real life experiences with the circumstances of the major characters in the Shaolin football team, which is a group of 'heroes of the past' who find their spectacular skills obsolete in a modernized city of advanced technology and thriving economy.

As is typical of Stephen Chow's *moleitau* style, the characterizations are comically exaggerated and extreme, without any compromise with subtlety. The

---

[8]   This view is strongly articulated by critic Li Cheuk To in the debate with his peers in the Hong Kong Film Critics Society on whether the Best Film Award should be given to *Shaolin Soccer*. A transcript of the discussion is found in *Hong Kong Film Review 2001* (Ng Kwan Yuk (ed.) 2003).

Shaolin cohorts are depicted as devoid of any skills apart from kung fu, to which they have devoted their entire lives before re-entering the ordinary world. While they all reached the pinnacle in their respective specializations at an earlier point in time, in the story they find themselves in a new milieu where their expertise has become useless. In a world where technology dominates, their superb physical capacities have either become derelict due to the lack of practice, or are only put to use in physical labour as a means of livelihood. Henceforth the common fate they share can only be one of displacement. There is a deep sense of angst of having no place in a world which they do not recognize. Being pushed to the margins of their society, these masters of martial arts even renounce the heritage they embody and denounce their core identity in exchange for material subsistence.

Although far from being a direct reference to the situation of Hong Kong people, it is notable that the characters' anxiety of displacement is claimed and owned by some of the Hong Kong audience who relate their frustrations about their own circumstances to those of the film characters. My review of the comments by critics and audience indicates that at the time when *Shaolin Soccer* was shown in Hong Kong cinemas, many residents in the city were going through a period of distress, as they lost confidence in the prospect of the city and perceived the tremendous economic growth of China as a threat to their survival (see, for example, Bono Lee 2002; Long Tin 2003; Tong Ching Siu 2003). The writings also indicate that many of their fellow citizens are overwhelmed by China's rapidly growing economic power and are worried about being supplanted by the country's mounting human resource. In other words, they find resonances in the Shaolin brothers' anxiety of being driven to the margins by this increasingly prosperous country with which they had recently reunited.

The validity of such views is confirmed by the findings of public opinion polls conducted during the same period. According to regular polls carried out in the city since the mid-1990s, around the time when *Shaolin Soccer* was on screen (summer 2001), the confidence of Hong Kong people towards their home city dropped to the lowest point since the change of sovereignty in July 1997; in contrast, there was increasing optimism toward the prospect of China during the same period.[9]

---

[9]   Polls conducted regularly by the Public Opinion Programme of the University of Hong Kong revealed that except for the first quarter after the handover of sovereignty, during which more than 80 per cent of the population expressed confidence in Hong Kong's future, this figure has been on the decrease ever since. In the first half of 2001, slightly more than half of the sampled population was confident; by August that year, the number of those who showed confidence dropped to 46 per cent—the lowest since the launch of the polls in 1994. Over the same period, approximately 80% of the people were optimistic towards the future of China. For details of the polls, see Public Opinion Programme, University of Hong Kong: http://hkupop.hku.hk [access date 1 December 2007]. For the part on the confidence in Hong Kong's future and the comparison with confidence in China, see especially http://hkupop.hku.hk/english/popexpress/trust/conhkfuture/combine/chart/chart1.gif [access date 1 December 2007].

While the audience has regarded the characterization of *Shaolin Soccer* as an expression of their collective anxiety, the tension that underlies this anxiety has also surfaced in the choice of filming locations. Although the narrative is intentionally devoid of any explicit geographical reference, all the major sequences are filmed in two locales in mainland China. Shanghai and Zhuhai (in southern China near Hong Kong) respectively provide the visual characters of the affluent cosmopolitan and the rapidly urbanizing semi-rural town. By abstracting the geographical reference and blending the visual elements of two places into one, the film constructs a 'condensed version' of contemporary China, which is at the same time affluent, highly urbanized, but also poverty-stricken and semi-rural.[10]

Within this visual context, the film situates a crucial moment in the story on a roof top against the panoramic backdrop of cosmopolitan Shanghai. It is the scene in which the Shaolin brothers join hands to form the soccer team, an action which represents their willingness to reconnect with their own tradition, rekindle their brotherhood and struggle for survival in solidarity against a hostile world. By locating this significant moment within the visual embrace of Shanghai, the film positions this leading Chinese city as an opponent against which the Shaolin cohorts decide to fight.[11] In this manner the film conveys an implicit tension between the protagonists and China as a country of rising economic power. The underlying tension finds resonance among some of the Hong Kong audience, as at that time many of them regarded Shanghai as the number one competitor to their own city, set to replace the advantageous economic position that Hong Kong had boasted for decades.

Kung Fu Hustle as Subversive Narrative that Challenges the Hierarchy of Centre and Margin

While many among the local audience and critics regard *Shaolin Soccer* as a manifestation of the fear of marginalization among Hong Kong people, *Kung Fu Hustle* takes the motif of marginalization one step further. It subverts the conventional notion of centre and margin, both through its narrative and through its casting strategy.

---

[10]   Critic Bono Lee (2002: 141) has rightly observed that the story's locale is a constructed non-existent city; yet he focused solely on the affluent side and neglected the semi-rural small town characteristic of this imagined space, which is in fact the predominant geographical aspect of the film.

[11]   The visual character of Shanghai is so dominant in the film that some viewers have mistaken it as the key filming location of the whole film (e.g. Bono Lee 2002: 141) and even the locale of the story (e.g. Siu Leung Li 2005: 53; Yip Yam Chung 2005). In fact only a few scenes are shot in Shanghai and the story's geographical setting is not mentioned or implied.

The story of *Kung Fu Hustle* is set in a haven for those excluded from society's mainstream; the extreme poverty of these people ironically becomes an advantage that keeps them from falling prey to the underworld gangs. The setting of this marginal community as the centre of action is noteworthy. In this world according to Stephen Chow, the marginal people are not at the margin despite their displacement from mainstream society. Instead, they constitute the main players in the film. They are portrayed as heroes who not only exhibit extraordinary physical strength, but also moral courage: they are ready to stand up not just for themselves, but for the lives of others. At a first glance, these residents are ordinary poor people who try to survive at a basic level of subsistence. As the narrative unfolds, however, the audience is presented with one hitherto unrecognized hero after another who emerge from within this marginal community, with all of them having their extraordinariness hidden behind the façade of ordinariness, and who exhibit their own form of power in the seeming powerlessness.

Layer by layer the unexpected power of the marginal community is unveiled. In the drama, this process starts with the comical scene in which the young barber squarely stands up against attempted blackmailing, and soon develops into the solidarity of the whole community in resistance against death threats from the treacherous gangsters. This eventually leads to the emergence of the three hidden *kung fu* masters who had disguised their identities up to that point and to the landlord couple who come out to defend the three masters when the latter are confronted by strong opponents. Before their skills are revealed, these characters are portrayed as weak and flawed. In particular, the landlord is depicted as licentious and timid, while the landlady is depicted as mean and unmerciful. Yet, when the situation demands it, they all put their own lives at stake to defend the others.[12] By focusing the audience's attention on the hidden heroes, the filmmaker places an otherwise disregarded community at centre-stage and tells the story of people who could easily be ignored and even despised, if only given a superficial glance.

Further, the relocation of the marginal people to the centre is not only achieved within the fictitious narrative, but also through the film's casting, as almost all the main actors are not major figures in the local commercial cinema. They include both non-professional talents and actors from an earlier generation who have not been active in the industry for decades. Despite the fact that they lack glamour and are unfamiliar to the audience, the film places these actors into the spotlight. In other words, *Kung Fu Hustle* is more than a story about the marginal; it is in part a collective effort that includes the excluded in its creation. While the ultimate

---

[12]   This phenomenon should be understood within the tradition of Chinese martial arts (*wuxia*) novels. These stories often describe the heroes as having superb mastery of martial arts, but they choose to hide their true identities for the sake of avoiding conflicts and turmoils of the *jianghu* (literally: rivers and lakes, referring to the 'world' of the *wuxia* fiction) in exchange for quiet lives and possibly also to escape assassination at the hands of former enemies. In *Kung Fu Hustle*, the landlord couple explicitly mention this as their reason for hiding their superb martial arts.

hero is played by Stephen Chow himself, the relatively unknown artists are all cast in significant roles, instead of being sidelined to play cosmetic roles, and they have been received with enthusiasm by the local audience. The filmmaker's endeavour, which is seldom seen in mainstream Hong Kong cinema, is applauded by some among the audience as a courageous venture. For instance, one member of the audience humorously called the cast of actors 'broken inside out' and asked the rhetorical question whether there was any other film director in Hong Kong who 'dares cast such actors that are broken inside out to play the leading roles and release their potentials' (Siu Sai 2005). Likewise, cultural critic Bernadette Tsui also appreciates the director's respectful treatment of his unknown cast and comments that in his eyes 'every minor person is lovely and cannot be despised; regardless of who they are, they all have their own lives' (Tsui 2004).

In essence, the film's gesture to locate the marginal at the centre subverts the conventional relationship between the centre and the margin and redefines what is marginal and excluded. In this sense, *Kung Fu Hustle* confronts the collective fear expressed in *Shaolin Soccer* with a subversive spirit. By placing the marginal at the centre, the film essentially suggests to the audience that it is not necessary to follow the conventional definition of what is marginal; by displaying the hidden power of the excluded, it reminds them that power is not necessarily in the hands of those at the centre. As Bernadette Tsui suggests, in this film Chow has 'redefined what are minor persons and small heroes' (ibid.).

Reconnecting the Audience with the Past

In addition to dealing with the issue of marginalization, which concerns many Hong Kong people, the films' treatment of memory is also significant to the local audience. Although memory is not an overriding theme in *Shaolin Soccer* as much as it is in *Kung Fu Hustle*, it is nonetheless the prime motivating force for the Shaolin brothers to gather again and should therefore be regarded as a decisive factor in the narrative.

In *Shaolin Soccer*, the long dispersed cohorts initially despise the protagonist's idea to form a soccer team. As they suffer from discrimination and exclusion from society and find life difficult even at basic subsistence level, they regard the proposal as an impractical day dream that can offer nothing to change their ill fate. In a subsequent montage sequence the audience sees each of them looking at their group photograph taken in the temple. In the scene which immediately follows, they come together to join hands. This visual sequence suggests that it is their common memory of the past that reconnects them and motivates them to gather again as a cohort.

While local critics and the local audience tended to overlook the importance of memory in *Kung Fu Hustle*,[13] it is an indispensable component of the film,

---

[13] None of the writings by local critics and audience that I have reviewed have discussed the importance of memory in the story.

both in terms of the development of the plot and in terms of its connectedness to the social context. Within the drama, the protagonist's childhood memory is the primary trigger of the whole story and also the prime motivation for his drastic change in the latter part of the story when he turns against the evil gang and the invincible Beast.[14] The childhood memory is symbolically represented in the lollipop which appears in key moments throughout the narrative, from the flashback to antecedents until the final scene. It visually embodies the protagonist's recollections of the virtuous values which he used to hold but eventually put aside because of the traumatic experiences of being cheated and bullied when trying to defend the weak.

Concomitantly, however, past memory also leads to the protagonist's return to virtues. When he once again encounters the girl whom he tried to rescue from bullying many years ago, he is confronted by his own past; this marks the starting point of his subsequent change. The memory, although ambivalent, is filled with heroic intention to defend the weak, aspiration to do justice and the little girl whom he failed to save. The protagonist's reconciliation with his memory leads him to reclaim virtues from the past, which eventually entails the discovery of his hitherto unknown identity as the ultimate hero who is to defeat evil.

Apart from being the crux of the plot, memory also emerges in *Kung Fu Hustle* in the film's connection with the collective memory of many Hong Kong people over the last half a century. One of the most prominent elements that immediately catches the attention of the Hong Kong audience is the main locale of the story, Pig Sty Alley. The name of this place and its many characteristics are a parodic re-imagination of an old Hong Kong district, the Kowloon Walled City. Its original Chinese name, *Zhu Long Cheng Zhai* (豬籠城寨), is a pun on the name of the Walled City, which in Chinese is *Jiu Long Cheng Zhai* (九龍城寨).[15] The essential character of Pig Sty Alley as a residential area also resembles Kowloon Walled City—both are physically deplorable, both are marginal communities, populated with the poor and ignored by society's mainstream. In reality, the Walled City was an anomaly within the city of Hong Kong in the course of most of the twentieth

---

[14]   Without the element of memory in perspective, the change of character has been criticized as sudden and unconvincing. As Stephen Chow admits in an interview, the film is not clear enough in relating the protagonist's psychology around this turning point. In the same interview, he gives an explanation of his directorial intent, stating that it is the protagonist's memory of his childhood ideals that leads to his return to conscience (see Ng Chun Hung 2005).

[15]   It should be noted that the play on words can only be fully appreciated by Cantonese speakers, who constitute the majority of the Hong Kong population; for them, it carries a special meaning that is hardly comprehensible for audiences speaking other languages and from other cultures. In Cantonese the name 'Kowloon' is pronounced in exactly the same way as the term for 'dog cage'; this has always been a joke among local children across the generations. It is therefore obvious for the local audience that Pig Sty Alley is in fact a spoof of 'dog cage alley', the Kowloon Walled City.

century, until it was completely demolished by the government in the early 1990s. Due to historic–political reasons, the area was for decades a haven for refugees, illegal residents and the underworld. While many outsiders would have considered it crowded, disorganized, lawless and fearsome, it was relatively untouched by colonial bureaucracy.[16] In other words, both Pig Sty Alley and Kowloon Walled City are inhabited by hidden heroes who try to live their normal lives at the humblest level of society, and both communities are relatively free from interference from outside powers.

Nonetheless, what Pig Sty Alley alludes to is not only the Walled City, but also the living conditions of many people in Hong Kong in the mid twentieth century. When the city experienced a massive influx of refugees who had fled the communist regime in China (in the late 1940s and the 1950s), it became a sanctuary at the margin of a country in turmoil. The sudden and rapid increase of the refugee population resulted in material scarcity and extremely packed living conditions, with several families sharing a small flat. Since the 1950s, the difficult life of that period has been portrayed in numerous local films;[17] *Kung Fu Hustle* dramatically recaptures these circumstances, including restricted water supply, the unscrupulous landlady and the cohabitation of tenants from different parts of China, speaking different dialects under the same roof. Pig Sty Alley is thus a microcosmic representation of the real life situations of common people in Hong Kong in an earlier period. The film thereby connects many among the local audience to the memory of hardship that is common in the city's recent past.

Celebrated Values and Vision of Hope

As pointed out earlier, *Shaolin Soccer* is an irreverent expression of Hong Kong people's collective anxieties of becoming obsolete and marginalized, and *Kung Fu Hustle* confronts this anxiety with a subversive narrative that challenges the conventional understanding of centre and margin. The films also offer a vision of hope through the core values they celebrate, most notably solidarity among the marginal. Although this vision of hope might look unsophisticated and

---

[16]   Constitutionally, due to a special arrangement between the Chinese (imperial) government and the British, Kowloon Walled City never came under colonial governance when the surrounding area became part of the colony of Hong Kong in 1898. For an overview of the earlier history of the Walled City, see Sinn (1987). For a collection of real life stories inside the Walled City towards the latter part of its history, see Lambot & Gerard (1999). A somewhat indirect account of underworld activities can be found in Pullinger (1993).

[17]   Most notably *The House of 72 Tenants* (dir. Chor Yuen 楚原, 1973), which is a free, but fully localized, adaptation of a popular stage comedy of the same title in Shanghai in the 1940s. The first cinematic adaptation of the stage drama was produced by Zhujiang Film Studio in Guangzhou, China (dir. Wang Weiyi 王唯一, 1963).

commonplace, a number of the audience writings indicate that it does inspire a sense of forward-looking sanguinity in local people. Moreover, to criticize the films' message of hope as simplistic is to overlook its significance for the people in that specific geo-historical context.[18]

The primary values celebrated in *Shaolin Soccer* are the protagonist's persistence and determination as well as the accompanying solidarity of the characters at the grassroots level. This solidarity is symbolically embodied in the recurring visual motif of the 'fire in the heart', which appears several times throughout the narrative in the form of CGI (Computer Generated Images). Whenever the narrative involves the rekindling of personal passion, the imagery of the fire literally intrudes in the natural flow of realistic images, in a style that is reminiscent of Japanese *manga* or Hong Kong action comics.

In each of the three key moments in which the fire motif appears, it serves a specific dramatic function and underpins the passionate determination of the characters involved. First, when the protagonist articulates his passion for Shaolin *kung fu* for the first time and his background turns aflame, the fire motif brings out the story's premise and underlines the character's dramatic motivation. Then in the roadside dancing scene which takes place in front of the small *mantou* shop,[19] the fire motif celebrates—in a non-sensical comic style that is typical of Stephen Chow—the bold expression of personal passion and its contagious nature. Finally, the motif culminates in the most crucial turning point of the film, which depicts a friendly match that turns into violent foul play targeted at the Shaolin team. Here, the motif functions as a manifestation of the Shaolin brothers' revitalization in spirit, both individually and collectively.

The film's celebration of grassroots solidarity is demonstrated in the latter two scenes, not only in the plot and the *mise-èn-scene*, but more significantly in the audio-visual style that betrays an unrefined directness often associated with the unsophisticated aesthetics of the grassroots. The unrefined nature and intentional vulgarity are prevalent throughout the film and are in fact consistent with the rest of Stephen Chow's filmography. As local scholar Esther Cheung (2005: 12) suggests in her comments on Stephen Chow's films in general, in Chow's films the *genre* is the carrier of the grassroots' yearnings.

Similarly, grassroots solidarity is also celebrated in *Kung Fu Hustle* where it is crucial in the narrative. The spirit of camaraderie allows the Pig Sty community to survive and resist the first assault of the gangsters, the three hidden *kung fu* masters to discard their concealed identities in order to defend their neighbours,

---

[18]   As suggested by a review posted by Ho Yuet (皓月) in the Hong Kong Movie Database (HKMDB), the success of *Shaolin Soccer* lies exactly in the simplicity and unity of its message, in particular the emphasis on personal persistence which is especially pertinent to the local audience in the midst of the trying time (see Ho Yuet 2003).

[19]   This scene was not included in the original cinematic release, but was added to an 'extended version' after the film had been in the cinema for several weeks and later appeared in DVDs as an optional scene.

and the landlord couple to stand up and fight on behalf of the three masters despite the previous tension between them. Although the story eventually develops into the heroic account of one man, in which the final resolution (the defeat of the evil character named Beast) hinges on the protagonist's miraculous action, the representation of grassroots solidarity is maintained through the portrayal of the protagonist's socio-economic background. Though he is an outsider to Pig Sty Alley and has even tried to take advantage of them in his desperate days, he is essentially one of them in terms of social class. When he discovers and assumes his true identity, he chooses to side with the marginal community and thereby demonstrates his moral superiority to Beast who is solely concerned with excellence in skills and obsessed with winning the fight.

Therefore, in both *Shaolin Soccer* and *Kung Fu Hustle*, the solidarity of the marginal is celebrated as a key value. This is not only portrayed in the narratives, but also exhibited in the films' aesthetic choice: it betrays a form of rawness that is reminiscent of the common folk and the working class rather than the refined taste of intellectuals or the upper middle class. This core value is presented in both films as an important driving force which can change the desperation of the marginal community. In *Shaolin Soccer*, it is the rekindled bonding among the Shaolin brothers, together with their determination and persistence, which lead to their final victory in the tournament and thereby redeem them from socio-economic hopelessness. In *Kung Fu Hustle*, the camaraderie of the Pig Sty Alley residents enables them to survive the life-threatening assault of the treacherous gang; the ultimate hero who later emerges to defeat the ultimate evil is portrayed as coming from the same background. Thus, in the filmmaker's vision, the impetus to transform the destiny of the marginal community has to come from the very socio-economic and cultural stratum of this community rather than from a superior outside elite who breaks into their world as a saviour.

Reconciliation with the Past and Rejuvenation of Tradition

While the two films represent solidarity of the marginal as the ground of hope, the vision of hope proffered in the films is a rejuvenation of past tradition. This rejuvenation is made possible by integrating new elements with old traditions to bring new life to the latter. This idea is presented in the drama of *Shaolin Soccer* and even put into actual practice through the film's creative strategy in *Kung Fu Hustle*.

In *Shaolin Soccer* the idea of revitalizing tradition is encapsulated in the protagonist's urge to renew the heritage of Shaolin martial arts and is explicitly stated to be his mission when he first enters the narrative. His determination and persistence subsequently lead to the formation of the football team, which in fact embodies a double revitalization: the intangible revival of the Shaolin brothers' spiritual heritage and the tangible improvement of their material life. This realizes the protagonist's personal vision to reinvigorate the Shaolin tradition while simultaneously leading to the transformation of his socio-economic status.

The narrative of a double revitalization, including the tension between its spiritual and material dimensions, is symbolically represented in the motif of the shoes, which recurs throughout the film. The protagonist's embrace of the old tradition is seen in his attachment to his old worn-out shoes, while his aspiration for a better material life surfaces in his longing for a better pair. The tension between these two dimensions becomes palpable when he expresses at one point the idea of discarding the old shoes and putting on new ones. The resolution which the filmmaker puts forth pulls together the old and the new into a synthetic whole rather than playing one against the other. Symbolically, the proposed resolution consists in the old pair of shoes being mended—they are given a new vamp and sole—after which the Shaolin team win the final match.

Kung Fu Hustle puts the proposal of old–new integration into practice as it adopts the revitalization of past tradition as its fundamental creative idea. Within the drama, the narrative unveils as a story of memory. Through his reconciliation with the suppressed memory of an unwanted past the protagonist is liberated from the bondage of avoiding his true sense of mission, with the result that he himself and the whole marginal community are saved from destruction. In this sense, *Kung Fu Hustle* presents a paradoxical vision of hope—hope for the future is dependent on reconnecting with the past.

However, the significance of this vision of hope goes beyond the drama itself. As suggested by a number of noted local critics, including veteran film critic Sek Kei (2004) and cultural commentator Ma Ka Fai (2004), *Kung Fu Hustle* as a film project has essentially put into practice the idea of reconnecting with the past. They concur that the film revitalizes an important aspect in the heritage of Hong Kong cinema, which is often ignored: Cantonese *wuxia* (sword fighting) films of the mid twentieth century. This view is confirmed by Stephen Chow when he acknowledged in an interview that he decided to use elements from old Cantonese *wuxia* films because he believes those to be the much neglected hidden gems in local culture (Ng Chun Hung 2005). An audience member further suggests that the film's extensive reference to that tradition not only represents the return of a *genre* in local popular culture, but is also a reminder of the long forgotten martial arts spirit—the courage to stand up against injustice, to defend the weak and to help one another when in need (Ric 2005). Additionally, Ma Ka Kai observes in *Kung Fu Hustle* a spirit of forgiveness towards the enemy and ultimate non-violence that characterizes old Cantonese martial arts films (Ma Ka Fai 2004). As he points out, the hero's most important final achievement in those films is often not to win the fight by crushing the villain, but the villain's repentance. In *Kung Fu Hustle*, this is replicated in both form and essence in the Beast's final move, when he kneels down and weeps in front of the protagonist, admitting defeat as well as the moral superiority of the latter.

Moreover, from the reception of the film in Hong Kong it is evident that the endeavour which reconnects the local audience with their ignored and almost forgotten tradition has vast contemporary implications for Hong Kong society in the early twenty-first century. Commentator Bernadette Tsui (2004) affirms that the film's revitalization of local heritage contributes more substantially to the local cultural scene than the government's controversial plan to build a new cultural district in West Kowloon. By making this contrast, she connects the film to a hotly debated item on the social agenda of the day. Sociologist Ng Chun Hung even claims that Stephen Chow's attempts in *Kung Fu Hustle* can be an exemplary paradigm for Hong Kong society, as it is in a process of redefining its identity as part of China and the world. In the conclusion to his interview with Stephen Chow, Ng Chun Hung commented that this film is 'rooted in tradition and facing the whole world' and that he considered it a 'relaunch of the cultural enterprise of Hong Kong in the era of globalisation' (Ng Chun Hung 2005).

Similar perspectives are found in the mainline press which make use of the film for didactic purposes. For instance, the editorials of two major local broadsheet papers—the *Hong Kong Economic Times* (2004) and *Mingpao Daily News* (2005)—claimed that the film is a model for Hong Kong to find its way forward in the midst of a generally desperate mood. In particular, the editorial in *Mingpao* discussed the film and Hong Kong within the context of global competition and concluded that the film 'has pointed out in concrete terms and in detail the way forward for Hong Kong to revitalise its competitiveness' (16 January 2005). Although different in emphasis, these editorials regard the vision of hope proffered by the film as viable for Hong Kong society in its search for direction during a time of loss, after a series of social crises subsequent to the change of sovereignty.

Concluding Remarks

This chapter has shown that the two films by Stephen Chow dating from the beginning of the century bear extraordinary meaning for its primary audience, the people in Hong Kong. Notwithstanding the apparent senselessness and frivolousness and even vulgarity of Chow's films and despite his being disregarded in serious film studies over the years, *Shaolin Soccer* and *Kung Fu Hustle* engage in their own ways with some of the fundamental issues that confront people and their society during the time of the film's production and release. In different ways, they address the collective anxiety of marginalization that has been prevalent among the people of Hong Kong during these years. Further, the filmmaker presents to the audience a vision of hope which advocates the reconnection with memories of the past as well as the rediscovery and rejuvenation of an often forgotten local cultural legacy. More significantly, the films have been claimed and owned by many among the local audience and critics as telling their stories, and the mainstream press regards the vision put forward by Chow as of considerable importance. Thus, while being commercial entertainment that aims at appealing to a mass audience, the films discussed here echo with some of the deepest concerns in society at large.

In fact the anxiety of being marginalized and the preoccupation with collective memory manifested in the films essentially point towards a more fundamental issue which is at stake on a deeper level. That issue is the puzzle of unresolved identity, which results from the city's political transition in 1997, when Hong Kong ceased to be a British colony and formally reverted to Chinese sovereignty. As mentioned earlier, the fear of marginalization expressed in the film (with which the Hong Kong audience identifies) is the *angst* of becoming obsolete and worthless in the face of the burgeoning Chinese economy. It is also the anguish of losing local uniqueness after being absorbed by a huge and powerful sovereign state. Similarly, the concern about collective memory and local cultural legacy suggests the restlessness resulting from uncertainties and the urge to hold on to what is considered central to the community. As Irwin-Zarecka observes, collective memory is 'one of the most important symbolic resources' that a society can have and is often imbued with 'quasi-sacred meanings' (1994: 67).

In this sense Stephen Chow's films carry a religious undertone. The vision of hope in the films does not involve explicit reference to the transcendent or the religious in a traditional sense, but preaches a 'secular gospel' devoid of sacred content. Yet at the same time the films address fundamental issues that are held to be 'sacred' by many among the local audience at the time. The paradoxical integration of the secular and the sacred is demonstrated in the final resolution of both films. In *Kung Fu Hustle*, the protagonist is depicted as having a brief encounter with the Buddha before he makes a come-back to defeat the ultimate opponent; this consequently ushers in a new order of a peaceful and happy life for the city. In *Shaolin Soccer*, the efforts and eventual victory of the Shaolin team in the national tournament bring about a double revitalization: the rejuvenation of the spiritual tradition of Shaolin and the brothers' socio-economic transformation.

Thus the films present tangible–material–secular and intangible–spiritual–sacred dimensions as complementary rather than oppositional in the human quest for hope. While the primary concern of Stephen Chow's films is the mundane where people have to struggle for survival, it carries spiritual undertones. As emphasized by C.S. Song in his discussion of hope in the Asian context, 'For hope to be hope, it has to address the present as well as the future, perhaps the present more than the future. For hope to be hope, it has to be "contemporary" as well as "proleptic", perhaps more contemporary than proleptic' (1999: 163). Regarded from this perspective, the vision of hope in Stephen Chow's films does 'address the present' and is 'contemporary', albeit lacking a long-term view of the future or an eschatological dimension of any sense. Even so, it is noteworthy that in these irreverent cinematic parables, the dichotomy between the sacred and the secular hardly exists. Hence, attending seriously to such ambiguous unity between the sacred and the secular could be one of the most important values of extending the study of religion/theology and film into East Asian popular cinema. The worldview portrayed in or underlying these films—often a popular manifestation of classical and contemporary Chinese Confucianism—may serve as a corrective to the dichotomized paradigm prevalent in the discipline in the 'Western' academic world.

References

Cheung, Esther (張美君), 'Falling for Master Sing and the Master of the Fox Cave' (情陷星爺與狐狸洞主), in Chan Yuen-ying (陳婉瑩) (ed.), *I am an Actor: Cultural Interpretation of Stephen Chow* (我是一個演員：周星馳的文化解讀) (Guangzhou, China: Nanfang Daily Press, 2005): 10–14.

Ho Yuet (皓月), 'The Unified Performance of *Shaolin Soccer*' (《少林足球》統一圓滿之表演), *Hong Kong Movie Database*, 13 December 2003, www.hkmdb.com/column/wallace/wallace-0011.b5.shtml [access date 2 November 2005].

Hong Kong Economic Times, 'With *Kung Fu* Style Efforts, Hong Kong Will Not Die (肯下『功夫』, 香港不死)', *Hong Kong Economic Times*, Editorial, 22 December 2004.

Irwin-Zarecka, Iwona, *Frames of Remembrance: The Dynamics of Collective Memory* (New Brunswick and London: Transaction Publishers, 1994).

Lambot, Ian & Gerard, Greg, *City of Darkness: Life in Kowloon Walled City* ([Chiddingfold]: Watermark Publications, 1999).

Lee, Bono (李照興), *Hong Kong Postmodern* (香港後摩登) (Hong Kong: Compass Group, 2002).

Li, Siu Leung, 'The Myth Continues: Cinematic Kung Fu in Modernity', in Meaghan Morris *et. al.* (ed.), *Hong Kong Connections: Transnational Imagination in Action Cinema* (Durham, NC: Duke University Press / Hong Kong: Hong Kong University Press, 2005): 49–61.

Long Tin (朗天), 'Computer Game World that Involves Soccer Strategy between China and Hong Kong' (指涉中港足球攻略的電子遊戲世界), in *Hong Kong Film Review 2001*, ed. Ng Kwan Yuk (吳君玉) (Hong Kong: Hong Kong Film Critics Society, 2003): 12–15.

Ma Ka Fai (馬家輝), 'The Boy Who Believes in Miracles (相信奇蹟的男孩)', *Mingpao Daily News*, 27 December 2004, D7.

Mingpao Daily News, 'Local Kung Fu Transformed and Goes Global (地道功夫變身打入國際)', *Mingpao Daily News*, Editorial, 16 January 2005.

Ng Chun Hung (吳俊雄), 'The Treasure is in the Local, Kung Fu is Well Practiced' (地道當係寶, 功夫練得好), *Sunday Mingpao*, 16 January 2005, D2–3.

Ng Kwan Yuk (吳君玉) (ed.), *Hong Kong Film Review 2001* (Hong Kong: Hong Kong Film Critics Society, 2003).

Pullinger, Jackie, *Crack in the Wall: The Life and Death of Kowloon Walled City* (London: Hodder and Stoughton, 1993).

Ric, '*Kung Fu Hustle* Extends the Lost Spirit of the Martial Arts Masters' (『功夫』延續失落的俠義精神), *HK Edcity*, 1 January 2005, www.hkedcity.net/library/review/view.phtml?file_id=40831 [access date 11 February 2007].

Sek Kei (石琪), '*Kung Fu Hustle* Distinctive in Result' (功夫成績優異), *Mingpao Daily News*, 24 December 2004, C9.

Sek Kei (石琪), 'The *Moleitau* Hero of Stephen Chow' (周星馳的無厘頭英雄), *Mingpao Daily News*, 13 January 2005, C3.

Sinn, Elizabeth, 'Kowloon Walled City: Its Origin and Early History', *Journal of the Hong Kong Branch of the Royal Asiatic Society*, 27 (1987): 30–45.

Siu Sai (小西), 'The Change and Unchange of Stephen Chow' (周星馳的變與不變), *Hong Kong Inmedia*, 11 January 2005, www.inmediahk.net/public/article?item_id=7919&group_id=18 [access date 13 February 2007].

Song, C.S., *The Believing Heart: An Invitation to Story Theology* (Minneapolis: Fortress, 1999).

Tong Ching Siu (湯禎兆), 'An Exemplary Work in Shifting Paradigm' (轉型變陣的示範作), in Ng Kwan Yuk (吳君玉) (ed.), *Hong Kong Film Review 2001* (Hong Kong: Hong Kong Film Critics Society, 2003): 72–6.

Tsui, Bernadette (徐詠璇), 'Is *Kung Fu Hustle* Enjoyable?' (《功夫》好看不?), *Mingpao Daily News*, 20 December 2004, D7.

Yip Yam Chung (葉蔭聰), 'Stephen Chow, Please Don't be the Master of the Generation!' (周星馳，請不要做一代宗師!), *Hong Kong Inmedia*, 11 January 2005, www.inmediahk.net/public/article?item_id=7899&group_id=10 [access date 13 February 2007].

Chapter 13

What is '*on*': An Exploration of Iconographical Representation of Traditional Religious Organizations on the Homepages of their Websites

Sarah Lawther

Introduction

Historically, the cultural change that new communication technology brings has provided an 'immense' challenge to traditional religion (Brasher 2004: 12). It is argued that 'technical innovation has ... had a profound impact upon the ways in which religions represent, safeguard and transmit their teachings' (Beckerlegge 2001a: 3). The Internet is perhaps no different. It offers a new way of communicating that is 'rapid' (Beyer 1994: 1), 'boundaryless' (Keenan 2002: 28) and 'truly multimedial' (Dawson & Cowan 2004: 10). It offers new ways of representing and transmitting information; it can be used as a 'communicative tool and/or as a sociocultural environment' (Karaflogka 2003: 193). The web, one aspect of the Internet and the focus of this study, 'appears to be open to mass producers as well as mass consumers' (Ryder 1998); sites can be created easily and are largely unregulated. These are globally transmitted, a 'one-to-the-World communication' (Miller & Mather 1998: ¶2).

What is interesting here is that *traditional* religion is choosing to have a presence on this new medium that not only allows communication in new ways, but also places traditional religion against a backdrop of a multiplicity of other religions and beliefs. That 'involvement in the online world' will change 'religious traditions and religious organizations' (Brasher 2004: xiv) in the offline world is expected, but *how* they will change is 'as yet largely unknown' (Dawson & Cowan 2004: 1). Perhaps one way of assessing how religious traditions are changing is to assess how they are choosing to present themselves in this new medium. With the abundance of choices, information and images for how to present one's religion, what will traditional religious organizations choose to portray themselves in this small space, the homepage, the initial point of contact?

This chapter describes research that explores the representation of traditional religious organizations on the homepages of their websites, focusing on the images that they use—their iconographical representation. Documenting and charting change in this new, evolving medium needs new methodologies, new ways of analysis and interpretation, a 'fresh methodological approach to religion in cyberspace' (Karaflogka 2003: 193). This research thus acts as a methodological case study for further research in the area of iconographical representation of religion on the web.

Religion on the Internet

The Internet, says Bunt (citing Strate, Jacobson & Gibson), can be used as a 'means … *through* which communication takes place', and as a participative environment 'in which communication occurs' (Bunt 2000: 6). Religions are using the Internet in both these ways. Karaflogka uses the terms 'religion *on* cyberspace' and 'religion *in* cyberspace'[1] (2002: 284) to distinguish between religions' use of the Internet to present information and the use of the Internet to provide a participative experience of religion. The former describes 'information uploaded by any religion, church, individual or organisation' and the latter comprises 'religious, spiritual or metaphysical expression which is created and exists exclusively in cyberspace' (ibid.: 285). These typologies, this 'map', Karaflogka argues, is 'fluid' because of the changing nature of the web (ibid.: 287). Helland makes a similar distinction, using the terms 'religion online' which 'presents information about religion' and 'online religion' which 'provides an interactive religious environment' (Helland 2002: 293), such as rituals, prayer and pilgrimage. These distinctions, note Dawson & Cowan, are 'not absolute. An increasing number of websites fall somewhere between these extremes, offering their visitors some combination of the two' (2004: 7). It is predicted that sites will offer an increasingly participative environment in the competition for 'web travellers' among the many other sites available (Helland 2002: 296); there will be a 'probable shift of religions *on* into religions *in*' (Karaflogka 2002: 287).

There is a proliferation of religious sites on the web: official, unofficial, those that also exist offline and those that exist only online. 'There is scarcely a religious tradition, movement, group or phenomenon', observe Hadden and Cowan, that is 'absent entirely from the Net' (qtd in Dawson & Cowan 2004: 6). There are 'official or unofficial sites for every world religion and every major denomination, sect or movement within those religions' (Baker, cited in Beckerlegge 2001b: 224). There are 'New Cyberreligious Movements' that 'mainly exist and function online' (Karaflogka 2002: 286) as well as religious practices that can only be found on the web, such as cybermarriages and cybermemorials (Karaflogka 2003: 200).

---

[1]   Karaflogka (2003) shortens these to 'religion on' and 'religion in'.

Traditional Religion on the Internet

Traditional religion is using this new medium both as a tool and as an environment. It has a presence alongside a multiplicity of different religions and ways of religious expression. The challenge of pluralization, the 'loss of faith in the face of multiplicity' (Woodhead & Heelas 2000: 308) that has faced traditional religions offline can be seen to be a challenge here, too. The 'obviously constructed and pluralistic character of religious expressions online tends to have a relativizing effect on the truth claims of any one religion or its authorities' (Dawson & Cowan 2004: 3). The exposure via the web to new and different views, and the opportunity for new ways of religious expression, 'has the potential to encourage individual religious and spiritual experimentation' (ibid.: 3) which 'manifests itself in ways beyond the conventional channels' (Karaflogka 2003: 199). This may 'prove challenging for ordered, traditional, regulated, hierarchical forms of religion' (ibid.).

To understand how traditional religion is responding to this challenge, we need to understand what its presence *is* here; to do this necessitates the development of a suitable methodology. While the 'information uploaded by any religion, church, individual or organization' also 'exists and can be reached in the offline world' (Karaflogka 2002: 285), once it is online, the nature of the medium shapes the message (McLuhan *et al.* 1967). A presence on the homepage necessitates choices about what to portray on this small (usually 12 inch screen), highly visual, 'worldwide medium' (Cornick 1995). The representation becomes a 'signature' (Karaflogka 2002: 282), a 'fingerprint: unique in design and content' (Karaflogka 2003: 194), projecting 'how a religion or a religious institution is perceived by its leaders and how they convey this perception' (ibid.). In Karaflogka's words, 'The site reflects the identity and mentality of the religion, and clearly illustrates what the leader/s think the essential message of the page should be' (ibid.).

Images are an important part of the representation of religion on these pages and they are used 'in order to achieve maximum strengthening of their transmitted message' (Karaflogka 2002: 282), to add weight to the message conveyed in the 'signature' (ibid.). By looking at what is *'on'* the official pages, and, in particular, at the images used, we have access to the 'public face of the religious organization or tradition' that has been set up 'for an audience defined as "the world"' (Brasher 2004: xiii). A map of iconographical representation of homepages of traditional religious websites thus offers a window (or literally a screen), in which their presence on this highly visual medium, their 'signature', can be captured.

This study began as an exploration of the iconographical representation of traditional religious websites[2] *and* an exploration of methodologies to achieve this aim. The research was limited to images used on the homepage, as this gave clear boundaries for the methodology (it is sometimes difficult to know where a site

---

[2]   Due to sampling issues, this was later narrowed to individual places of worship in the UK.

begins and ends) and captured the essence of the 'signature' as the first, initial point of contact. The websites used were those that appeared to be by traditional religious organizations, the 'official religious representation' as 'distinct from the popular religious sites that may belong to the same tradition' (Helland 2002: 295) and were those belonging to the typology 'religion *on*' as defined by Karaflogka (2002) and Helland's (2002) 'religion online'.

Methodology

Mapping Image Use

Content analysis was used to map the manifest content of images used on homepages. The research drew on methodology used by Lutz & Collins who used a content analysis of images in *National Geographic* to explore 'the making and consuming of images in the non-Western world' (Lutz & Collins, 1993: xii). In her critique of their research, Rose argued that their categories are ambiguous, since 'there is a potential overlap' (2001: 62) which may lead to different interpretations by different researchers. She recommends that the creation and coding of categories should be transparent, 'clearly defined' (ibid.) and documented in detail. To ensure this study is replicable, the initial coding categories were tested and refined in a pilot study of two sites per religion, which was carried out in September 2003. This method does not claim to measure how the images were chosen, the 'site of ... production' (Rose 2001: 67); the images may, for example, have been chosen by a designer paid for by the religious organizations, with little input from the religious organizations themselves. Neither can this method measure how the images are seen—in Rose's words, the 'site of ... audiencing' (ibid.).

The traditional religions studied were Buddhism, Christianity, Hinduism, Islam and Judaism.[3] Operational rules were devised to define categories and a research diary was kept in order to be explicit and reflexive about the reading of images. The categories were not 'exhaustive' (Rose 2001: 60): both in the pilot study and in the main study were images that could not be coded by using existing categories; these were also documented. Methodological issues that arose were also recorded as part of the research process, illustrating how quickly religions are changing their presence on the web and reinforcing the need to document their presence as it evolves. In the main study, for example, there were homepages that had images which changed on the screen (without input from the user) like a slide show. It was decided that all images should be coded as individual images (rather than just the first images on the screen), as the representation included all these

---

[3] On reflection, the sample would have better reflected the traditional religions in the UK, if it had included Sikhism; according to the national census of April 2001, the six largest religious groups in the UK are (in order of size): Christianity, Islam, Hinduism, Sikhism, Judaism and Buddhism (National Statistics 2005).

images. The main study was carried out in June 2004, with 40 sites explored in all (eight for each religion).

Content Analysis Categories

Five types of images emerged from the researcher's initial search of homepages. The researcher noted down all types of images found on all appropriate sites accessed through inputting the names of the five religions into Google during a three-hour period. These were then grouped into categories for further testing in a pilot study. These categories were: 'sacred text', 'traditional religious figure', 'traditional religious symbol', 'localism' and 'commercial information'. The 'sacred text' category included any religious text (such as a quote from the Qu'ran). Each occurrence of 'sacred text' was coded as one image. The 'traditional religious figure' category included images such as Buddha, Balaji and Ganesh. The 'traditional religious symbol' category included, for example, a crucifix, a five-pointed star, a crescent moon. The 'localism' category included images of the local area, local religious figures such as a vicar, the local community, local building or the surrounding area. The 'commercial information' category included images that either illustrated *or* linked to items or services which can be paid for (for example courses or books) or images (such as credit cards) that linked to sites where an online donation could be made.

Pilot Study

In the pilot study, it was observed that the most common image in the 'localism' category was that of a local religious figure, a contemporary religious figure, such as the local priest. It was thought that this was a category that needed further exploration. Brasher argues that, because the web is a place where religions are using the same media (the web) as entertainment, the barriers between celebrity worship and religious worship have been eroded (2004: 137). Could this be what is happening here, that traditional religion is reacting to the changes in communication technology by choosing to portray 'contemporary religious figures' (as opposed to 'traditional religious figures') by giving them local celebrity status? A new coding category, 'contemporary religious figure', was created. The 'localism' category was renamed 'community',[4] which seemed to be a more appropriate name.

There were 10 images (from a total of 46 images) that did not fit into the categories described above. These images were primarily connected with the management of moving around the site, such as a door to go to another site, a link to an Internet host or flags to link to members of other sites in different countries. There was also a calendar and images of awards which sites had received. It was

---

[4]   Any images that were coded as 'contemporary religious figure' were not coded again as 'community'.

felt that the content analysis categories had captured the main types of religious representation present on these sites and that no further categories were needed.

The content analysis categories for the main study were therefore: 'sacred text', 'traditional religious figure', 'traditional religious symbol', 'contemporary religious figure', 'community' and 'commercial information'. While not wholly satisfactory (being rough and reductionist), these categories can begin to provide a picture of what is '*on*', what images are being used in the representation of the religious 'self' of organizations on the homepages used in this study.

Ethics

Although the images on websites are accessible to all, this may not have been the intention of the author(s); they may only be there for a select audience (such as the congregation of a particular religious organization) and they are almost certainly not intended for social scientific analysis. As a researcher, it is important to be self-regulatory and responsible in research (Mann & Stewart 2000: 39) and not take advantage of this 'vulnerability' (Spender 1995: 257). Sites were initially checked for any indication that the site was not to be copied. When this was the case, another site was sought for sampling. When there was no such indication, an e-mail message was sent to site owners stating the aim and purpose of the research and asking for consent to analyse images. Only one site refused permission and this site was not included in the research. Given the nature of the web which makes sites globally available to view and copy, it was assumed in the cases where there was no reply that it was acceptable to copy and analyse the homepage.

Sampling

Websites were found using the meta-search engine www.metacrawler.com. A methodological issue faced in this study was the problem of devising a systematic (Miller 1995) and repeatable method to avoid the danger of being merely an 'electronic tourist' (Fitzpatrick 1999: 102). The aim was to create a sample frame of possible sites from the first 20 hits and then randomly sample from this list. This was a method used by Hine (2000) who explored how to 'develop a methodology for investigating the Internet' (Hine 2000: 2) using Louise Woodward sites (the British nanny who was charged with the murder of a boy who was in her care).

The search engine entries were '+church +UK', '+synagogue +UK', '+mosque +UK', '+Hindu temple +UK' and '+Buddhist temple +UK'. The focus on *individual places of traditional worship* was intended to eliminate inappropriate sites (such as educational or anti-religious sites) that had been found in the pilot study when the name of each religion had been entered (such as 'Buddhism' or Judaism'). The new focus on individual places of UK worship yielded many appropriate sites for Christianity and Judaism, but not eight sites (even going beyond the first 20 hits) for Islam, Buddhism and Hinduism, which was the minimum number of sites needed for the larger study. This may be because there are fewer of these sites: an illustration of the different beliefs on authority and dissemination of knowledge within each religion (Beckerlegge 2001a: 4). This may be due to methodology: that there are many of these sites on the web, but they were not found by using this (English) entry into the search engine. In the case of Islam, Buddhism and Hinduism, directories[5] were used to produce a list of as many appropriate sites as possible. Recommendations of sites that were sometimes given in replies from e-mail requests for permission were also used.

Changing Sites

There were two kinds of Christian sites that posed a problem in the main research that had not occurred in the pilot study. The majority of the first 20 hits recorded for Christian sites consisted of these 'problem' sites. These were typically sites for the headquarters of a Christian organization and came in two categories. The first, such as the 'Official Website of the Methodist Church of Great Britain' (www.methodist.org.uk) contained links to individual sites of worship within that organization from the main site; these were individual in design and thus did not follow a standard format. Such sites were subsumed under the term 'individual umbrella' sites. The second category also consisted of official sites that contained information about individual sites, but this was *within* the main framework of the official homepage, such as the Jesus Army site (www.jesus.org.uk). These sites were subsumed under the term 'inclusive umbrella' sites.

Both categories of sites were not apparent in the pilot study and thus required a methodological decision whether to include them, as their inclusion or exclusion would affected the research focus. The 'umbrella' sites could not be discarded altogether, as they *are* windows for the way the religious organization wants to be seen—one representation, one homepage, for all the smaller places of worship. To include these sites as a sampled site would have meant that like would not be compared with like: some sites would be by the headquarters of an organization ('umbrella' sites), while some sites would be sites of individual places of traditional worship. There were no 'umbrella' sites in the sample for the other religions, which would have allowed for a change in the focus of the study to 'umbrella' sites only.

It was decided to randomly sample one local, subsidiary site from each 'umbrella' site. This would include these sites in the sample, but not so much that it would change the focus to the larger, more organized sites and the focus would remain within the aim of looking at individual places of worship. The sample size was also increased to the first 100 hits, as it was noticed that 'umbrella' sites typically appeared high up in the list of hits. It was hoped that the increase in

---

[5]   A directory is a site that contains lists of links to other sites that have been monitored by an editor, usually on the same subject or area.

sample size would be more likely to include sites which were not 'umbrella' sites. The sample was thus biased and became purposive sampling.

Why do the Sites Appear to be Changing in this Way?

The expertise involved in the creation of such 'umbrella' sites suggests the use of a technical designer or a company, which indicated investment of time and money. This suggests that these religious organizations believe their 'signature' or web presence to be both worthy of investment and an area over which they want to have control.

Helland notes that 'often the nonofficial religious sites appeared on the WWW before the official church representation' (2002: 298). Will there be a decline in these 'nonofficial religious sites' as the 'official church' takes control of religious representation on the homepage? Are some sites in the category 'religion *in*' under increasing control, too? Or is there a difference between the control of information in the categories 'religion *on*' and 'religion *in*'? Are other traditional religious sites likely to follow the same pattern?

Karaflogka suggests that, because the web is 'organized horizontally rather than vertically, there is no central authority' (2002: 285), non-hierarchical religions will fare better. She cites Zaleski who predicts that 'in the long run the Internet will favour those religions and spiritual teachings that tend toward anarchy and that lack a complex hierarchy' (ibid.). Baudrillard's view of the nature of the information age may give insight into the reasons why there seems to be a dichotomy on the web with increasingly uniform 'religion *on*' sites with decreasing individual control *and* the increase of anarchical, 'religion *in*' sites, as noted by Karaflogka. Baudrillard argues that in this information age we are being sold the idea that we must have information for information's sake, that communication becomes about 'the promotion of communication itself as event and as message' (Baudrillard 2003a: 32). The content becomes lost as the medium 'swallows' the message (ibid.: 33). Globalization is 'levelling out every difference' (ibid.: 26), resulting in 'banality' (Baudrillard 2003b: 174) on the one hand and an underground rebellion against this banality on the other hand (Baudrillard 2003a: 26). Are we seeing this here on the web, the 'screen of globality' (ibid.: 34): increasingly uniform sites alongside the rise of the more anarchical New Cyberreligious Movements as noted by Karaflogka (2002: 285)?

It may be that this methodology has highlighted sites that are being 'controlled' and that this is not a general trend. Sites that appear higher in the results list of search engines may be ones that have had more investment and money from higher echelons of the organization and are therefore more likely to be 'controlled'. Some religious organizations, says Helland, are using 'pay for placement' advertising where sites pay 'a significant amount of capital to appear as the "sponsored link" for any searches done for religious material on many search engines' (Helland 2002: 300). The sampling method of this study may have resulted in a concentration of these sites. However, the reason could also be related to the nature of the web, that it may be cheaper and easier to design sites in this way. Any interpretation of results thus needs to bear in mind the influence of the medium itself. The types of questions which this study has raised will only be answered when seen over a period of time, which emphasizes the need to chart the progression of *both* 'religion *on*' and 'religion *in*'.

Results and Analysis

Overall Image Use

There was a high frequency of image use on the homepages used in this study: the total number of images used by the 40 websites was 195.[6] All sites examined in this study had at least one image on their homepage. Christian sites used almost double the amount of images (68) compared to the other religions; all of these used roughly the same amount of images (29–36). The high number of images on Christian sites may not be indicative of an overall pattern, as two of the Christian sites had the most images used in the study (16 and 18, respectively).

Changing Sites

The content of websites was regularly updated and changed. Many sites (and their image use) changed over the course of the research and sometimes the site host changed. Could this continuous updating be an indication of the commercialization of religion? It has been argued that pluralism leads to the 'growth in religion as a free market' (Woodhead & Heelas 2000: 478): religion becomes a product which has to be marketed in order to survive (ibid.: 462). This research alone cannot determine whether sites are viewed as a commodity, as part of a 'pick n mix' approach to religion (Heelas 1996: 7), as this study did not measure how websites are perceived. Or is this updating an indication of regeneration, religion evolving, rather than a marketing activity? Could it be an indication of revitalization (Beyer 1994: 4)? Are the traditional religious organizations alive to change, to new possibilities? If this is the case, this small study cannot determine *how* religions are evolving.

Patterns of Image Use

The results point to a difference in the frequency of types of images used on homepages. Images in the category of 'traditional religious symbol' appeared on homepages most often (48). There were 22 'sacred text' images and 13 images in the 'traditional religious figure' category. Is this an indication of traditional religion reasserting its 'particularisms' (Beyer 1994: 4), in its choice of images?

---

[6] Twenty three of these images were not in the coding categories used in this study.

Online, religion has no 'secondary functions' (politics or education, for example); has more attention been given here to its 'primary function'—has it become 'liberated' (Aldridge 2000: 92)?

Community

There were 34 images in the 'community' category, which perhaps suggests that, for many, religion is about community. Dawson cites Durkheim's definition of religion as 'a unified system of beliefs and practices relative to sacred things ... which unite into one single moral community ... all those who adhere to them' (2004: 75). Although for many people these days, being part of a group 'is more symbolic and subjective than real', 'the notion of religion and community go hand-in-hand' (ibid.). It is not suggested that the presence of these images indicates that there *is* a religious community within these sites or that users are experiencing 'community' when visiting the sites: the presence of 'community' rather than 'mere social interaction' is difficult to define and measure (ibid.: 77). It does illustrate, however, that traditional religions are choosing representations of 'community' instead of, or as well as, other types of image. Why is this the case?

According to Partridge, Campbell's research in 2003 of an online Christian community 'indicates that the primary motivation for Christians who join online communities is *not* information, but rather *relationships*' (2005: 146). Could it be that these sites are reflecting and responding to a need for a religious community by choosing to present 'community' images on their homepages?

It may be that these images of 'community' reflect the nature of the web, that this new technology enables us to go back to 'behaviour patterns that were natural to us' (Adams 1999: 12, citing Risto Linturi): those of living in a small interconnected community, rather than any religious interpretation. Could it be due to the methodology in this study, the choice of sites of individual places of traditional worship? These sites were using images of the building, the local area, but other sites had none of these types of image on their homepage. Was it simply that 'community' images are easier, cheaper to use? They have no copyright and can be uploaded easily from a digital camera. Observations since this study was completed have shown that there has been an increase in the use of 'community' images on the homepages; this would be worthy of further exploration.

'Traditional Religious Figure' vs 'Contemporary Religious Figure'

The same number of images were coded in the categories of 'traditional religious figure' and 'contemporary religious figure' (13). It is a complex process to unpick these results because of the different beliefs about the representation of the divine, but two themes emerged that are worth mentioning.

The Christian sites had no images in the category of 'traditional religious figure' and four images in the category of 'contemporary religious figure'. It is too much of a leap to suggest that this indicates 'celebrity worship' (Brasher 2004:

137), that church and community members are given local celebrity status, but further research on a larger scale could explore whether favouring a more local, personal figure over a traditional one is becoming a trend.

The Hindu sites had ten images in the category 'traditional religious figure' and only one in the category 'contemporary religious figure'. This difference could be because the 'traditional religious figure' images here are being used as *murti*, as sacred images that embody the deity within the image (Beckerlegge, 2001c: 111). Beckerlegge suggests that the Internet 'opens up new opportunities for the creation and use of *murti* and a new, global, interactive electronic medium in which to do this' (ibid.: 109). A further study could look at whether images here are being used as *murti* and, if so, whether the *murti* is being treated here in its 'traditional' sense as the 'embodied deity' (ibid.: 108) or as part of a 'pick n mix' approach to an 'individualistic, informal and privatised religious practice' (ibid.: 89) which may be growing within Hinduism.

Commercial Information

The methodology used for the category of 'commercial information' was slightly different from that used for the other categories: it included images that were representations of items that one could buy or pay for *and* images that linked to a commercial product, service or donation point. Coding was difficult when dealing with such images in any other way, but it has meant that this category was measuring *more than* just representations of commercial information. This must be borne in mind when looking at the results. There were 41 images in the 'commercial information' category, suggesting that religions *are* using the web as a commercial vehicle, as a place to buy and sell goods, but it cannot be assumed that this indicates a reduction to a commercial level of religion, as this study cannot say how images are seen or how they are meant to be seen. It may be that religions that have a website are more commercially developed. Creating a presence on the web involves buying space, which is a commercial act; it follows therefore that religions which are on the web are more likely to be commercially aware and possibly need to have commercial ventures in order to survive.

Screen as 'Signature'

In addition to looking at patterns arising in the types of images used by religious organizations, the analysis also needed to look at *image use as a whole on each homepage* to explore the type of 'signature' being presented. An initial exploration looked at the themes of 'traditional' and 'modern'. The categories 'sacred text', 'traditional religious symbol' and 'traditional religious figure' were combined in an overall category called 'traditional images'. The categories 'contemporary religious figure', 'community' and 'commercial information' were combined in an overall category called 'modern images'. A new coding category was created to explore the idea of a transition phase, the possibility of the co-existence of the 'traditional' and 'modern'; this category was given the heading 'traditional and modern in one image'.

On reflection, naming these themes 'traditional' and 'modern' was too simple, as contemporary religious figures, commercialism and themes of community have always been present in 'traditional' religion. Yet the distinction between 'traditional' and the other types of images found seemed worthy of exploration. The category 'traditional and modern in one image' was difficult to code and there was only one image found: this was an image on a Jewish site that contained a 'contemporary religious figure' and 'sacred text' (see Figure 13.1).

Figure 13.1   Rabbi Romain standing at the Bimah (reading desk) in front of the Ark housing the Torah scrolls. Image courtesy of Rabbi Romain, minister of Maidenhead Synagogue, www.maidenheadsynagogue. org.uk/

A more appropriate conception of themes may be the distinction by Woodhead & Heelas between 'formal', 'hierarchical' and 'impersonal' (2000: 485) religions and religions that are 'more informal', 'less hierarchical', 'more participatory' and 'less tradition determined' (ibid.: 486). Woodhead & Heelas predict that the latter will 'fare well' (ibid.: 493) in modern times:

> Across the whole spectrum of religious types, the religions which seem to be doing well (particularly in modernized western societies) are those which make room for individual participation, self-expression, experience and relationality. By contrast, those which are more traditional, impersonal, hierarchical and

formal, which allow little or no room for participation and choice, and which encourage rejection of this life in favour of the next, are either detraditionalizing fast or losing numbers. (ibid.: 485)

This study cannot measure the nature of the religious organizations presented. It does not, for example, suggest that the relational, the personal, is absent on sites which carry more 'formal' images. It does not measure or assume that formal religions 'allow little or no room for participation and choice, and ... encourage rejection of this life in favour of the next' (ibid.). It does not assume that those with less 'formal' images are offering a participative experience or those that are more 'formal' in presentation are more 'formal' in experience, nor does it predict the success (or failure) of the religious organizations. It does, however, provide a useful starting point from which to explore themes arising in the 'signature' of homepages.

These themes were explored in the way that they are set up for viewing—as a 'signature', the screen as image. The categories 'sacred text', 'traditional religious figure' and 'traditional religious symbol' were combined and coded as 'formal'. The categories 'community', 'contemporary religious figure' and 'commercial information' were combined and coded as 'other'. The analysis examined whether sites were using only formal images, only 'other' images or a combination of 'formal' *and* 'other' images on their homepages.

There were 14 homepages that contained purely 'formal' images. Each religion had at least two sites that were in this category. Is the 'signature' (Karaflogka 2002: 282), the 'public face' (Brasher 2004: xiii), one that reasserts particularisms, fundamental beliefs? Does this suggest 'retraditionalization' or 'tradition maintenance' (Woodhead & Heelas 2000: 347)?

Eight homepages contained only 'other' images. Each religion had at least one site in this category. Is this an indication that these sites are appealing to a one-to-one or more personal experience rather than a traditional or remote experience of religion, appealing to 'a turn away from "life-as"' (Heelas & Woodhead 2005: 3) towards 'the unique subjective lives of the "centred"' (ibid.: 5)? 'Institutions that cater for the unique subjective-lives of the "centred", argue Heelas & Woodhead, 'are on the increase, whilst those that continue to operate in life-as mode find themselves out of step with the times' (ibid.). Are religious organizations that are using this new medium more likely to be those that are more 'modern', more 'in with the times'?

Seventeen sites contained both 'formal' and 'other' images together on the same homepage.[7] Each religion had at least two sites in this category. This suggests a more complex presentation than the suggested dichotomy of 'formal' or 'other'; rather, there is a co-existence of types of images in the 'public face' (Brasher 2004: xiii), the 'signature' (Karaflogka 2002: 282), presented by traditional religious sites.

---

[7]   There was one homepage that contained one image with 'traditional' and 'modern' elements within the same image, as discussed earlier.

On reflection, the inclusion of 'commercial information' in types of 'other' images was problematic, as it did not allow for an exploration of the use of more 'relational' images ('contemporary religious figure' and 'community') with more 'formal' images. A separation of these themes in such an analysis is recommended if a larger scale study is carried out.

Conclusion

This research has provided a mapping of the iconography of 'religion *on*' for a small number of sites at a fixed period of time. It has indicated patterns of image use on homepages: of individual images and the screen as image, the 'signature', both within and between religions which are worthy of further exploration. The content analysis categories that emerged offer a starting point for research on a larger scale that explores these differences on 'religion *on*' sites, 'religion *in*' sites and the 'spectrum' in between (Young 2004: 94).

To answer how 'involvement in the online world' is changing 'religious traditions and religious organizations' (Brasher 2004: xiv), we need now to look at how what has been found here, what is '*on*', is having an affect offline: both for individuals and religious communities. Are online images of traditional religious figures, for example, being used as sacred images, to provide an offline religious experience? Are online images acting in the same way as online information about offline activity, in that they are emphasizing 'the connection the online world maintains with offline religious institutions and communities' (Young 2004: 103)? Can we go further and say that these online images, as Bedell suggests, lead to 'action' offline? (Bedell is here cited by Young 2004: 103). Are, for example, the online images that illustrate a participative experience of religion offline, of 'community', building and sustaining religious communities offline?

This research has, through the process of interpretation of the results, illustrated how interlinked the nature of the web is with what is '*on*': the message cannot easily be separated from the medium. As the medium changes, how will religion on the web fare? As it becomes easier and cheaper for web sites to be centrally designed and controlled (as we have seen here of Christian sites), will there be increased participation by religious organizations in the design and content of information on these sites? Will these sites become more uniform in design and content: perhaps more formal, less local? Perhaps. A bigger change on the Internet horizon may counteract this. It is argued that the Internet is currently not worldwide but Western in that it 'only works for those communities whose native language is Latin-based' (Fattal cited by McCarthy 2006: 1), because the current domain name system 'only works with Western languages' (ibid.: 7). China and Israel, for example, have their own internal system of domains (in Chinese and Hebrew respectively) but these are not fully accessible worldwide (ibid.: 11). As domain names become 'truly multilingual' (Fattal 2008: 1) that is, in any language, not just Latin-based, then individuals will be able to access the Internet in their own native language: it will become a worldwide (as opposed to a Western)[8] community. My prediction is that as a counterbalance to this, we will see more local, relational, community images on websites of individual places of religious worship,[9] but that these will not wholly replace the more 'formal' images seen here, but will be alongside 'formal' images, offering the 'signature of co-existence' that has been seen on sites in this study. Whether this will be the case, and if it is, what affect this will have on offline communities remains to be seen.

Most of all, this research has raised many more questions than it has answered, illustrating how much work there is to be done here, and serves as a methodological case study from which to document the changing iconography of traditional religious websites in this emerging and exciting area of the study of religion.

References

Adams, Douglas, *How to Stop Worrying and Learn to Love the Internet* (1999), www.douglasadams.com/dna/19990901-00-a.html [access date 23 August 2005].

Aldridge, Alan, *Religion in the Contemporary World: A Sociological Introduction* (Cambridge: Polity Press, 2000).

Baudrillard, Jean, 'The Global and the Universal', in Victoria Grace, Heather Worth & Laurence Simmons (eds), *Baudrillard West of the Dateline* (Palmerston North: Dunmore Press, 2003a): 23–36.

Baudrillard, Jean, 'The Violence of the Image and the Violence done to the Image', in Victoria Grace, Heather Worth & Laurence Simmons (eds), *Baudrillard West of the Dateline* (Palmerston North: Dunmore Press, 2003b): 171–81.

Beckerlegge, Gwilym, 'Introduction', in Gwilym Beckerlegge (ed.), *From Sacred Text to Internet* (Aldershot: Ashgate, 2001a): 1–7.

Beckerlegge, Gwilym, 'Computer–mediated Religion: Religion on the Internet at the Turn of the Twenty-First Century', in Gwilym Beckerlegge (ed.), *From Sacred Text to Internet* (Aldershot: Ashgate, 2001b): 219–66.

Beckerlegge, Gwilym, 'Hindu Sacred Images for the Mass Market', in Gwilym Beckerlegge (ed.), *From Sacred Text to Internet* (Aldershot: Ashgate, 2001c): 57–116.

Beyer, Peter, *Religion and Globalization* (London: Sage, 1994).

Brasher, Brenda, *Give Me that Online Religion* (London: Rutgers University Press, 2004).

---

[8] Baudrillard (2003a: 35) talked of this shift from the Western, arguing that the 'Western vantage point ... is no more a vantage point'.

[9] In the same way as Woodhead & Heelas argue that 'social dislocation ... leads to a counterbalancing desire for strong and supportive community' (Woodhead & Heelas 2000: 495).

Bunt, Gary, *Virtually Islamic: Computer-mediated Communication and Cyber Islamic Environments* (Cardiff: University of Wales Press, 2000).

Cornick, Delroy L., 'Cyberspace: Its Impact On The Conventional Way of Doing and Thinking About Research' (Baltimore, Maryland: 1995), paper presented at the Sixth Annual Conference of the Urban Business Association, www.csaf. org/cyber.htm [access date 27 May 2001].

Dawson, Lorne L., 'Religion and the Quest for Virtual Community', in Lorne L. Dawson & Douglas E. Cowan (eds), *Religion Online: Finding Faith on the Internet* (London: Routledge, 2004): 75–89.

Dawson, Lorne L. & Cowan, Douglas E., 'Introduction', in Lorne L. Dawson & Douglas E. Cowan (eds), *Religion Online: Finding Faith on the Internet* (London: Routledge, 2004): 1–16.

Fattal, Khaled, 'Multilingual Internet Names Consortium', 2008, www.minc.org/ Default.aspx?&lang=en [access date 12 January 2008].

Fitzpatrick, Tony, 'Social Policy for Cyborgs', *Body and Society*, 5/1 (1999): 93–116.

Heelas, Paul, 'Introduction: Detraditionalization and its Rivals', in Paul Heelas, Scott Lash & Paul Morris (eds), *Detraditionalization: Critical Reflections on Authority and Identity* (Oxford: Blackwell, 1996): 1–20.

Heelas, Paul & Woodhead, Linda, with Seel, Benjamin, Szerszynski, Bronislaw & Tusting, Karin, *The Spiritual Revolution: Why Religion is Giving Way to Spirituality* (Oxford: Blackwell, 2005).

Helland, Christopher, 'Surfing for Salvation', *Religion*, 32 (2002): 293–302.

Hine, Christine, *Virtual Ethnography* (London: Sage, 2000).

Karaflogka, Anastasia, 'Religious Discourse and Cyberspace', *Religion*, 32 (2002): 279–91.

Karaflogka, Anastasia, 'Religion on – Religion in Cyberspace', in Grace Davie, Paul Heelas & Linda Woodhead (eds), *Predicting Religion: Christian, Secular and Alternative Futures* (Aldershot: Ashgate, 2003): 191–202.

Keenan, William, 'Rediscovering the Theological in Sociology: Foundation and Possibilities', *Body and Society*, 5/1 (2002): 19–42.

Lutz, Catherine & Collins, Jane, *Reading National Geographic* (London: University of Chicago Press, 1993).

Mann, Chris & Stewart, Fiona, *Internet Communication and Qualitative Research: A Handbook for Researching Online* (London: Sage, 2000).

McCarthy, Kieren, 'Divided by a common language', *The Guardian*, Thursday July 27 2006, www.guardian.co.uk/technology/2006/jul/27/ guardianweeklytechnologysection5 [access date 12 January 2008].

McLuhan, Marshall & Fiore, Quentin, with Agel, Jerome, *The Medium is the Massage: An Inventory of Effects* (Harmondsworth: Penguin, 1967).

Miller, Hugh, 'The Presentation of Self in Electronic Life: Goffman on the Internet' (Nottingham: The Nottingham Trent University, 1995), www.ntu.ac.uk/soc/ psych/miller/goffman.htm [access date 27 July 2001].

Miller, Hugh & Mather, Russell, 'The Presentation of Self in WWW Home Pages' (Iriss 98: Conference papers), www.intute.ac.uk/socialsciences/archive/iriss/papers/paper21.htm [access date 14 October 2007].

National Statistics, *Religious Populations* (2005), www.statistics.gov.uk/cci/nugget.asp?id=954 [access date 25 May 2005].

Partridge, Christopher, *The Re-Enchantment of the West: Alternative Spiritualities, Sacralization, Popular Culture, and Occulture*, vol. 2 (London: T&T Clark International, 2005).

Rose, Gillian, *Visual Methodologies* (London: Sage, 2001).

Ryder, Martin, 'The World Wide Web and the Dialectics of Consciousness', paper presented to the Fourth Congress of the International Society for Cultural Research and Activity Theory, Aarhus, Denmark, 7–11 June 1998, http://carbon.cudenver.edu/~mryder/iscrat_98.html [access date 3 June 2006].

Spender, Dale, *Nattering on the Net: Women, Power and Cyberspace* (Melbourne: Spinifex, 1995).

Woodhead, Linda & Heelas, Paul (eds), *Religion in Modern Times: An Interpretive Anthology* (Oxford: Blackwell, 2000).

Young, Glenn, 'Reading and Praying Online: The Continuity of Religion Online and Online Religion in Internet Christianity', in Lorne L. Dawson & Douglas E. Cowan (eds), *Religion Online: Finding Faith on the Internet* (London: Routledge, 2004).

Chapter 14

Researching Theo(b)logy: Emerging Christian Communities and the Internet

Katharine Sarah Moody

Introduction

A man talks of pulling threads:

> … unravelling and ravelling, I was both. They mean the same thing. I started
> to see that unravelling didn't need the negative appendage, the *un-* prefix. As if
> unravelling were to be avoided, to be considered the ruin of my belief, as if this
> dissection indicated the death of my faith … My faith didn't unravel, it ravelled
> … I learned to revel in ravelling … Tearing apart what I love is evidence that I
> love it. (Caswell 2007)

He speaks as part of a 'theodrama' performed by Ikon, an 'iconic, apocalyptic, heretical, emerging, and failing' 'transformance art' collective from Belfast, Northern Ireland (wiki.ikon.org.uk, access date 21 February 2008). Those gathered take part in this '(un)ravelling' through a laptop and an interactive software programme. Under the title 'Ikon Creed Editor 2007', the Apostles' Creed is projected on to a screen to our left, along with this invitation: 'The creed is a statement of belief. This is an opportunity to engage with the creed. Feel free to interact with the text below by editing and changing it.' Throughout Ikon's performance, people use the laptop to edit what appears in the window.[1]

In this gathering, Ikon uses a technology which is facilitating the online activities of a growing number of communities who also articulate their religious identity in the language of emergence and in particular through the markers 'emergent' or 'emerging church'. While such communities remain resistant to definition,

---

[1] This performance, entitled 'The God Delusion', was staged at the Greenbelt Arts Festival, Cheltenham, UK, on 26 August 2007. At the end of the event, the Edited Creed was posted on Ikon's website, wiki.ikon.org.uk/wiki/index.php/The_Edited_Creed [access date 21 February 2008].

the Internet is a space where self-identity is being worked out.[2] This chapter examines the role of two Internet-based technologies for their emergence and development—blogging and open source software. I suggest that an exploration of emerging Christian communities is incomplete without an investigation into their manifestation in cyberspace. I clarify the nature of the two technologies under consideration and argue for their relevance for what I shall call 'theo(b)logy' and 'open source Christianity'.

This chapter is also an exploration of the methodological possibilities in the intersecting spaces between religion and Internet media. I present the difficulties of locating blogs and measuring their validity and influence and suggest a participatory research methodology for the blogosphere. I close with practical and ethical reflections on a blog which I created in the hope of encouraging interaction between research participants.

Researching Emerging Christian Communities

In active conversation with emerging cultures, emerging Christian communities are critical of Christianity's capitulations to modernism and explore Christian identity, theology and community in shifting paradigms. The use of technology in these endeavours mirrors the theologies and sociologies of these communities.[3] There is what one prolific 'emerging church' blogger calls a 'cross-over of values—new media values and new church values' (Tallskinnykiwi, 22 January 2004).

A review of the theoretical and empirical research conducted with emerging Christian communities reveals a form of reductionism which stems from research methodologies that do not provide data from a cross-section of emerging Christian community members. These approaches, both supportive and critical, produce unrealistic pictures of emerging Christian communities: they neglect the possible disparity between the way in which individual authors and leaders articulate their identities in books (Carson 2005; Smith 2005), interviews (Gibbs & Bolger 2006) and public mission/values/descriptive statements (Flores 2005) and the way in which these communities express themselves in more informal and everyday

---

[2]   With regard to terminology, I use the phrase 'emerging Christian communities' to reflect some of the unease with the institutional connotations of 'church', a clear emphasis on community and relationality and an understanding of Christian identity as something which one is continually becoming or emerging 'into' rather than ever fully being, having or inhabiting. The phrase 'emerging *Christian* communities' remains inappropriate for some participants, however, considering their resistance to labelling themselves with a Christian religious identity. Where I refer to the terminology used by others, I use single quotation marks, for example, 'emerging church'.

[3]   On the technological transformation of the Church, see La Grou & Hjalmarson (2007).

situations, in the ordinary life of the community. Further, these approaches largely ignore the online aspects of emerging Christian communities.[4]

A more careful research design can attempt to be inclusive in its approach to data collection, gathering information from as many levels of resource as possible, in order to facilitate the inclusion of seldom heard voices from emerging Christian communities. This multi-methodology needs to incorporate Internet-based research for two interlinked reasons. Firstly, these communities tend to be technologically proficient and comfortable with a variety of media in their communal and individual lives. They are very quick to apply and/or adapt new technologies, articulating them within a discourse which constructs these technologies as apposite for religion and spirituality (Campbell 2005). Secondly, the Internet is vital for the emergence and development of emerging Christian communities. Those who acknowledge the connection between such communities and the direct and dynamic interactions facilitated by the advent of the Internet are right to speculate that 'without ready access to this form of instant communication, the emerging church may not exist at all' (Drane 2006: 9). The Internet is, as Paul Teusner has observed, 'the only medium in which "emerging church" [should be] understood as a movement beyond local faith communities' (Teusner 2006: 4–5). The Church must emerge from its context and be incarnate in this locality, but the Internet provides a global space for encouragement, experiment, inspiration and challenge between and beyond these geographically dispersed communities. Through it, the communities can become 'glocal'.

A chosen research methodology must always be apt for the research question(s) and the research subject(s) rather than primarily benefiting the researcher. The efficacy of Internet methodologies lies, therefore, with their relevance for a particular study rather than with their cost efficiency or novelty.[5] A consideration of emerging Christian communities' use of the Internet and their manifestation within this kind of media is therefore central to an understanding of these communities. Their use of blogging and open source software is instrumental for their construction of what I shall call 'theo(b)logy' and 'open source Christianity'. These activities (which occur both on- and offline) will not be fully understood without first being placed in their technological context.

---

[4]   Two researchers who focus specifically on 'emerging church' blogs are Bryan Murley and Paul Teusner. Murley investigates the extent to which Technorati.com's top 50 ranking 'emerging church' blogs function as an interpretive community for the global 'emerging church' and Teusner explores bloggers' offline impact on 'emerging church' identity in Australia. See further emergingchurch.bryanmurley.com [access date 21 February 2008] and teusner.org [access date 21 February 2008].

[5]   Many proponents of Internet methodologies focus solely on the time and cost benefits, while the detractors focus on the lack of representativeness in sampling and thus the lack of general applicability to the population at large. Increasingly, however, researchers are questioning the previously presumed lack of diversity among Internet users (Hewson *et al.* 2003: 30–6).

Blogging and Theo(b)logy

Blogs are diary-like interactive websites containing regularly updated entries or 'posts', with the most recent posts displayed at the top of the page and previous entries below, in reverse chronological order. Blogs can be personal and/or more purposive, with authors ('bloggers') blogging about their lives, uploading photographs, video and sound files from daily or special events, or about specialized topics of interest. Blogs are published on the Internet for anyone with web access to read and interact with; such interaction most often comes in the form of commenting. Below the blog post, which is contained in the main body of the page, is space for comments from readers of the blog. Comments can be viewed by all visitors to the site, which fosters dialogue not only between reader and blogger, but also amongst readers themselves. Hyperlinks are used by both bloggers and those who comment to move the cognitive and affective conversations in new discursive and virtual directions, creating a web of texts between different locations in cyberspace or what I have called elsewhere a 'text between texts' (Moody 2008).

Blogs allow individuals to store, organize, process and distribute information, but the mechanisms for interaction encourage new patterns of thinking and new ideas to emerge communally, beyond any meanings and experiences intended by the originating blogger. These features make active collaboration in knowledge building and identity formation possible. The processes and products of discussion become interdisciplinary, as individuals come together from a wide range of educations and experiences, both expert and amateur. Blogs are understood as tools for the distribution of ideas, which are then extended and reformed in dialogue (or dia(b)logue)[6] with others, to produce richer understandings and to construct notions of identity, theology and society *in community*.

In their study of the construction of religious identities on the Internet, Mia Lövheim and Alf Linderman (2005) emphasize the importance of a single definition of the situation in which interaction takes place, while also recognizing that the nature of computer-mediated communication means that these interactions are 'more vulnerable to the impact of individual users who through their participation may uphold, transform, or challenge the essential common setting' (ibid.: 126). The nature of emerging Christian communities is still being debated, both on- and offline, so that no single definition of the community, of the 'essential common setting', has yet been reached. This observation is the basis on which Teusner argues that 'the "emerging church" blogosphere has great authority in constructing the identity of the "emerging church" in the world offline' (Teusner 2006: 5). This identity includes theological, missiological, ecclesiological, philosophical, sociological, economical, ecological and political questions which have yet to be

---

[6] Emerging Christian communities follow postmodern philosophers in their fondness for word play, a tradition which I also continue with my use of the neologism 'theo(b)logy'.

exhausted through interactions in the blogosphere. Using Radical Orthodoxy's post-secular understanding of theology, but alluding to the medium in which they are produced, I refer to all these varied blog theorizings as 'theo(b)logy'.[7]

Radical Orthodoxy recognizes that even supposedly secular realms hide fundamental commitments to certain beliefs, ways of thinking and practices. In short, they are 'theologies or anti-theologies in disguise' (Milbank 2006: 3). A call to recognize this post-secular nature of the contemporary (Western) world re-admits Christianity into the public realm as one theology among many. For Christians, their theorizings should be *Christianly* theological or, as James K.A. Smith prefers, 'confessional' (Smith 2004: 173)—grounded in the Christian narrative of creation, fall, redemption and consummation in order to out-narrate the other narratives available.

'Emerging church' bloggers reflect Christianly upon a host of contemporary phenomena. Their blog postings are tagged and categorized into a wide range of subjects, including: technologically supported human creations (such as blogs, music, film, art, Godcasts, vjing[8]); other cultural artefacts (football, beer, TV, fashion, food); social networks (family, friends, work, Ireland, Manchester, Greenbelt); political issues (the environment, justice, Middle East, democracy, economics, gender equality, poverty); more narrowly defined theological and ecclesiological concerns (mission, monasticism, labyrinth, Kingdom of God, truth, Bible, liturgy, youth ministry); and fluid markers of religious identity (emerging church, alternative worship, emergent). Theology, conventionally understood as the systematic study of Christian revelation found in the Bible, the Church and history, is exploded into Radical Orthodoxy's post-secular theology: a theology which reflects *Christianly* on all the realms of creation previously denied it by the myth of secularism. This theology finds a concrete example in the theo(b)logy of emerging Christian communities.

Open Source Software and Open Source Christianity

Collective construction can also be seen in the use made of other Internet technologies, particularly websites using an innovation in information technology design. Open source software follows a mode of production and development that allows open access to the product's source materials—in the case of software, to the source code. Source code is made publicly available for modification and redistribution, so that progress is made by any number of people working on a problem in community (for example, MediaWiki). This approach evolved

---

[7] This neologism is also used by Tony Jones, the US national coordinator of the 'emerging church' organization 'Emergent', as the title of his (old) blog, www.theoblogy. blogspot.com [access date 21 February 2008].

[8] A 'Godcast' is the neologism given to podcasts which take religion as their subject matter, and vjing, video jockeying, is a term modified from the practice of DJ-ing.

in contrast to closed access software, where problems are dealt with by a select number of individuals who have exclusive access to the source code (for example, Microsoft). The latter mode of functioning translates into a hierarchical structure of power, with a few at the top of the pyramid possessing the most knowledge and holding the most power. By publishing source code alongside its software products, the former approach attempts to give as many people as possible access to the knowledge, and therefore the power, to change and improve software, encouraging constructive collaboration in software creation (Raymond 1997).

A well-known product of the open source software MediaWiki is the interactive online encyclopaedia Wikipedia (en.wikipedia.org). Users can update entries, thereby sharing their knowledge on a range of encyclopaedic subjects and producing definitions and explanations in community with other users.[9] This open source software is used by a number of emerging Christian communities and the network of websites which support their online activities. For example, Ikon uses the Wiki model for its community website, where visitors are invited to edit the pages using the tools provided on the site to alter page content, layout and skin and upload resources (wiki.ikon.org.uk). The principle behind open source software was also used in the (un)ravelling event described above, where the page containing the Creed could be edited by those gathered in an act of 'tearing apart what I love'. The website Open Source Theology (www.opensourcetheology.net) is an online community of users who are engaged in the reconstruction of theology following an open source methodology. The site acts as a forum for the theological discussions of emerging Christians, among others, as they question, reinterpret and modify the source code of the Christian religion. Users can start and contribute to threads on a variety of theological topics, including hermeneutics, eschatology and ethics.[10]

In practice, the potential openness is restricted to those with the relevant expertise of software programming, although its use on the Internet is generally accompanied by instructions for new users. When open sourcing is extended beyond software into a model for political, social and religious community, however, such particular expertise is not a prerequisite. Writing in favour of a participatory 'network democracy' on the open source model, Douglas Rushkoff recognizes the precondition that 'participants in an open source collaboration must

---

[9]   The openness (or, rather, the neutrality) of Wikipedia has come into question, with some users feeling that there is a secular liberal bias to the site, which results in their additions being deleted by other users. Conservapedia (www.conservapedia.com) has been set up by conservative Christian users as an alternative.

[10]   The founder of this website, Andrew Perriman, published a collection of essays in 2007 which featured as threads on the site. However, as the publication contains only these originating threads, without the collaborative conversations which followed their posting, it serves to undermine the project in its translation into print media. Published blogs (sometimes known as 'plogs') often also fall into this trap by publishing posts without the comments. Penner & Barnes (2007) are more successful, including alongside the reproduced post several different conceptual threads created in the accompanying comments.

be educated in the field they are developing' (2003: 57). While it might not require acquaintance with software programming, what is required to construct open source religions is an education in that religion which then enables questioning, reinterpretation and modification of the religion's 'source code'.

Among emerging Christian communities, socialization in the Christian community is often emphasized above doctrinal confirmation. Authors, leaders and bloggers frequently refer to a reversal of the 'believing > behaving > belonging' understanding of community involvement, so that socialization (belonging) is the form of education which enables the open sourcing of Christianity (behaving > believing). Without wishing to draw false boundaries around what elements can be considered as this religion's source code, these communities draw upon the history of Christianity for inspiration and guidance. That socialization is the ground for knowledge and experience (rather than academic or pastoral training) once again explodes the conventional understanding of theology as a bounded discipline reserved for 'the experts'.

While theo(b)logy and open source Christianity represent the coming together of individuals from a range of expertise and life experiences to construct Christianly theological theories in dialogue with each other, it is both on- and offline where emerging Christian communities are (un)ravelling. As Heidi Campbell has noted, the ways online communities describe themselves are providing models for how these communities wish to be structured offline (2003: 223) and these communities place a high emphasis on new software models that stress the importance of networking, full participation and evolution through community. The 'new media values' associated with blogging and open source software reflect the 'new church values' of inclusive theo(b)logy, participatory open source Christianity and egalitarian social structuring of emerging Christian communities.

Researching Theo(b)logy

Studying the online activities of emerging Christian communities is problematic when difficulties are encountered by those undertaking fieldwork in the blogosphere. 'Emerging church' blogs must be successfully identified, their validity assessed and their influence considered. However, blogging and open source software also exhibit the 'new research values' that have developed within the social sciences, largely due to the work of feminist researchers. Conducting research in the blogosphere therefore also presents opportunities for participatory research; opportunities which may facilitate an open sourcing of the research process itself.

The methods used to locate blogs have an impact upon the extent to which they are relevant for the research project. For example, using a blog aggregator such as Technorati (www.technorati.com), it is possible to search for blogs that contain the phrase 'emerging church' in their self-identity or in posts and tags in the blog. The criteria which Technorati uses in its searches are, however, self-awarded and unregulated, so that any blog which uses the search term will be ranked, regardless of the relevance of the blog for the research project. Further, blogs have to 'opt-in' to a Technorati search by registering free and compiling a list of relevant search entries with which they wish to be associated. The particular features of Technorati can thereby limit the research process. A more serendipitous method should consequently also be employed, involving random non-linear Internet journeys in the blogosphere to uncover widely linked blogs that do not turn up in more systematic searches.

It cannot be assumed that ranked blogs will be considered valid sites by the research subjects. The validity of a blog as an 'emerging church' blog must be measured by careful analysis of its content. Many returned blogs within a Technorati 'emerging church' search can be described as 'anti-emerging church' blogs, such as Pyromaniacs (teampyro.blogspot.com/). Secondly, searches rank sites which, while related to the 'emerging church', have a wider readership and are not specifically 'emerging church' blogs. Dave Walker's CartoonBlog is one such blog (www.cartoonchurch.com/blog).

It is also important to consider a blog's validity in representing (certainly not all, but at least some of) the research subjects. While a multi-methodological approach will in many ways serve to confirm or modify the conclusions that can be drawn from a study of blogs, the format of blogs themselves also provides methods by which the online community can scrutinize the views contained within. Collating all the posts on a particular subject allows for fact checking and analyses of argument and commenting enables these interactions to constitute, as Mark Brady believes, 'a peer-review system' (2005: 10). Readers can comment on content, argument, language, style, mistakes and omissions.

Tallskinnykiwi's 'The Girls Post' is an example of the ways in which blogs encourage online emerging Christian communities to validate or overturn their content.[11] In his 'definitive history' of the exchanges, Tallskinnykiwi addresses blog dynamics (Tallskinnykiwi, 24 February 2004). In particular, he mentions the problems that ensue if bloggers like himself do not properly hyperlink the conversation, as many readers came to the discussion halfway through, without being properly directed to the context of the original post. The episode indicates one way in which blogging provides methods which allow these communities to either corroborate or correct the kinds of statements and sentiments published online by individual members.

A related issue in researching blogs is the levels of influence which particular blogs have on other bloggers and, as part of a multi-methodology approach, the influence they have on research participants at later or concurrent stages of data

---

[11]   Tallskinnykiwi made a remark that juxtaposed men with girls, instead of women, appearing to belittle the status of women. While he maintains that these were posts about age discrimination (pointing out that God's mission favours teenage girls rather than women and mentioning Mary and Esther as biblical examples), responses from readers began as friendly warnings, but soon changed to disappointment and outrage.

collection. Given the stress which emerging Christian communities place on the Internet and the extent to which this is the only context in which these communities can be said to form a 'movement', of an albeit heterogeneous nature, there is a high possibility that theorizings from online emerging Christian communities will be read, assessed and assimilated by offline communities (or rather by online individuals, who then influence their local communities when offline).

The facilities inherent in blogging can aid the researcher in determining blog influence. Hyperlinks within the text of Blog B to the specific permanent URL of a post of Blog A reveals that Blog A has been read and that Blogger B has engaged with it, thus suggesting that Blogger A has been influential in some way. These are the measures by which aggregators such as Technorati rank blogs according to influence, or in their language, 'authority' (Sifry 2006). While this feature is useful for social network analysts, who can determine both authorities (blogs with a high number of links to them) and hubs (blogs with a high number of links to other blogs), and can be used to establish which blogs are influential on a macro-level—as in Teusner's and Murley's research into the influence of national (Australian) and global 'emerging church' blogs—such rankings are less useful for determining the influence of blogs on a micro-level.

The current multi-method project does not wish to construct an entity that can be identified as 'the UK emerging church'. Therefore, an investigation into the most influential blogs among these communities, as measured by blog ranking systems, is not pertinent here. Instead, an exploration of influential blogs is significant on an individual participant basis. While a 'power law distribution' model can be shown to exist among 'emerging church' blogs (Moody 2008),[12] whereby the cumulative linking preferences of previous users make it highly likely that blog readers reinforce the reading and linking choices made by others before them (Shirky 2003), participants may also be influenced by other low-ranked blogs, because they are important within the context of their local emerging Christian community or because of many other possible reasons beyond their Technorati rankings. Questions regarding interactions in the blogosphere can be figured into other stages of data collection to allow exploration of individual participants' networks of online influence.

A Participatory Research Methodology for the Blogosphere

Despite the difficulties and ambiguities to be negotiated, the blogosphere presents researchers with an opportunity for increasing the levels of participation open to

---

[12]   A power law distribution curve can be roughly described thus: whatever is being ranked (here, inbound links from other blogs), the value for the Nth position will be $1/N$, so that the value for the second ranked item will be $1/2$ the value of the first ranked item; the value for the tenth ranked item will be $1/10$ the value of the first ranked item; the value for the one hundredth ranked item will be $1/100$ of the first ranked item; and so on.

those involved in the research, an increase that might be otherwise constrained by more conventional research methods. While the interactivity of the blogosphere complicates certain aspects of Internet research, it can be harnessed in the project's favour. A methodology for this kind of research should make the most of these aspects of the Internet rather than shy away from them because of the possibility for complicating the relationship between researcher and research subject(s). The Internet constitutes an appropriate medium in which to provide a space for continued dialogue with participants and gives researchers the opportunity to conduct research publicly. This can produce what Liz Stanley refers to as 'accountable knowledge': the participant will have 'access to details of the contextually-located reasoning processes which give rise to "the findings", the outcomes' (cited in Cotterill & Letherby 1993: 68). I suggest that a participatory research methodology for the blogosphere should include the creation of a project-specific blog for interactions between researcher and research subjects (as well as many others).

A blog allows participants to gather in a clearly designated (though not delineated) space and discuss the research project and their experiences of being involved.[13] However, it also allows participants to 'outgrow' the specific role of participation with which they entered the relationship with the researcher and other participants. Thus discussion topics that spring from the research questions will be given a place to develop, whereas in interview situations the researcher may be unable to allow such flexibility. Subsequently, this can aid individuals in their own personal theorizings by engaging with other voices, produce a resource for future research both for participants and other readers of the blog and ultimately result in a conversation which would be a collective, accessible and on-going alternative to my single-authored, time-constrained, academic and library-destined PhD thesis. Just as I have had the privilege of listening to others' voices and the freedom to construct an argument based on their insights, a gathering of participants enables others to engage in the same activities.

Another benefit is that data pertaining to the research questions are not understood to be the property of the researcher. While returned questionnaires and/or interview transcripts might be considered the researcher's property, by providing public space for participants to interact with the research questions, the researcher shows that they are not attempting to hoard the intellectual property of participants for their own gain. Further, as the blog will last beyond the submission date of the research, the relationship between participants and researcher also outlasts its initial configuration. Researchers do not abandon the relationship, once

---

[13]   While my use of other blogs as data is based upon the conviction that these texts are in the public domain, in the event that I wish to quote comments posted on my own blog, I intend to ask permission of individual commenters as far as possible; also, a comments policy (akin to an informed consent form) appears in the pop-up comments window. Commenters are free to disclose their identities or remain anonymous and, although I have yet to reflect on interview data in the blog, I will do so without disclosing identifiable characteristics.

it has produced a written piece of research, as there has been an investment in a blog and the relationships it generates, which will exist beyond submission or publication.

Research in the blogosphere is complex, but blogging and open source software can be used to increase the involvement of research subjects so that the research process becomes open sourced and participatory. The advantages of a project-specific blog appear to be clear for an Internet methodology which desires to be participatory.[14]

Concluding Thoughts: Reflections on Open Source Research

In April 2007, I launched a research blog entitled Open Source Research (opensourceresearch.blogspot.com), intended to increase the levels of participation open to research participants and to communicate my 'reasoning processes' as I conducted the research and constructed a thesis. I reflect here on some practical and ethical issues which were not anticipated before the implementation of this participatory methodology for the blogosphere.

At the outset of the project I was concerned that I would be unable to adequately monitor whether participants blogged about their experiences of participating or to accurately judge whether others might read these blogs before participating themselves.[15] I hoped more easily to keep track of the conversations about my research by providing participants with a space in which to conduct conversations. However, in blogging about their experiences of taking part, participants either e-mailed me to let me know that they had just posted some reflections or hyperlinked to my blog, in which case I was made aware of their contributions (through my blog host, Blogger.com) without their appearance in the designated space for comments. While not acting in precisely the way I had imagined, the blog (and an online presence in general) is enabling me to keep abreast of the various conversations about my research taking place in the blogosphere.

---

[14]   Both Bryan Murley and Paul Teusner have project-specific blogs. After his original blog (emergingchurch.bryanmurley.com/ [access date 21 February 2008]) crashed in 2006, Murley has not posted frequently about his research at his main site (bryanmurley. wordpress.com/ [access date 21 February 2008]). While Teusner seems to have intended his blog as a convenient platform for the feedback of information and work in progress (in line with his interests in new media, see www.collegemediainnovation.org/blog/ [access date 21 February 2008]), he increasingly regards it (teusner.org/ [access date 21 February 2008]) as a place 'where not only I, but my research subjects, engage in the study of emerging church bloggers' (Tuesner 2007: 6).

[15]   I was even uncertain of the extent to which these were valid concerns, as no participant in any research project is ever divorced from their surroundings which are influential in any number of potential ways; there is often an impact on research, which is beyond the researcher's ability to identify or measure.

Blogging demands frequent postings and has thus been a useful (although at times distracting and time-consuming) writing exercise. I have blogged about conferences I have attended, papers I have given and chapters I have written. I have also reflected upon events hosted by emerging Christian communities in relation to my research questions. Interactions facilitated by the blog have included comments by participants, 'anonymous' commenters, other 'emerging church' researchers, 'emerging church' sceptics, researchers in related fields and authors whose work I have reviewed. While I informed participants of the existence of my blog, these other commenters found Open Source Research through other means. The blog has also facilitated e-mail conversations with some of these individuals.

However, these interactions are more infrequent than anticipated. From the *ability* of participants to access my blog, it does not necessarily follow that participants *will* access it nor that they will read it and comment on it. Similarly, the relative youth of my blog and the scarcity of links to it mean that it does not rank high in systems such as Technorati, which might be used by non-participants to locate my blog. I can e-mail participants each time I post a new entry, but, in order to gain awareness among general Internet users, other possible methods raise ethical considerations.

What is needed to increase ranking and therefore visibility is to receive more links from other blogs. This is achieved through frequent posting and through interesting, novel, humorous or pertinent blog content. As I write and engage with others in the blogosphere, linking to other sites in the process, these linked-to individuals and communities are made aware of my presence; however, the linking patterns only go one way. As I begin to reflect on my data and blog about preliminary themes, I can hope that the relevance of my research for emerging Christian communities will begin to raise interest and start to generate more links to my blog, but three months after launching the blog I was faced with an opportunity for generating *reciprocal* links, the kinds of links which enable a blog to gain readership and therefore a higher rank and even further increased readership.

A fellow postgraduate researcher tagged me and, as with e-mails of this kind, I was required to pass it on.[16] I was asked to link to the blogger who tagged me and then tag eight others by linking to them in a post. I was tempted; by tagging eight influential 'emerging church' bloggers, who would then link to me in return, I could increase the visibility of my blog among the very communities I was exploring. However, this raised ethical concerns. Through this 'game', bloggers who were ranked highly, but did not respond to my call for participants could be pressured into acknowledging my project, when they had chosen not to before. This form of 'link slutting'—linking to highly ranked blogs in the hope of receiving a link in return—concerned me. While Jill Walker identifies this practice as a logical 'consensual exchange of favours' (2002: 79), being a 'link whore' is not viewed

---

[16]   Unlike the tagging involved in the classification of blog posts and other data to enable keyword-based information retrieval systems, this form of tagging modifies the child's game 'tag' into a game of being linked to by and linking to other participants.

positively among bloggers who adhere to often strict 'netiquette'.[17] I therefore decided not to take part and instead blogged about the ethical decision which motivated me to 'break the chain'.

Creating a research blog does not automatically produce the desired interaction with and between participants. It requires the dedication of regular posting and a commitment to spending time reading and engaging with other bloggers. Just as the time and cost benefits of Internet methodologies can mask the new practical, theoretical and ethical concerns and opportunities, hyperbole about the interactivity of the blogosphere can mask the varied activities in which bloggers engage in order to generate and then cultivate that interactivity. In order to do this myself, I am participating in the 'emerging church' blogosphere beyond my own blog, (un)ravelling on both personal and professional levels, and taking part in their/our theo(b)logical endeavour to explore open source Christianity.

References

Brady, Mark, 'Blogging: Personal Participation in Public Knowledge Building on the Web' (Colchester: University of Essex, 2005), www.essex.ac.uk/chimera/content/pubs/wps/CWP-2005-02-Blogging-in-the-Knowledge-Society-MB.pdf [access date 21 February 2008].

Campbell, Heidi, *Exploring Religious Community Online: We Are One In The Network* (New York: Peter Lang, 2003).

Campbell, Heidi, 'Spiritualising the Internet: Uncovering Discourses and Narratives of Religious Internet Usage', *Online – Heidelberg Journal of Religions on the Internet*, 1/1 (2005), http://archiv.ub.uni-heidelberg.de/volltextserver/volltexte/2005/5824/pdf/Campbell4a.pdf [access date 21 February 2008].

Carson, D.A., *Becoming Conversant with the Emerging Church: Understanding a Movement and Its Implications* (Grand Rapids: Zondervan, 2005).

Caswell, Stephen, '(Un)ravelling' (2007), http://wiki.ikon.org.uk/wiki/index.php/%28Un%29ravelling [access date 21 February 2008].

Cotterill, Pamela & Letherby, Gayle, 'Weaving Stories: Personal Auto/biographies in Feminist Research', *Sociology*, 27/1 (1993): 67–79.

Drane, John, 'Editorial: The Emerging Church', *International Journal for the Study of the Christian Church*, 6/1 (2006): 3–11.

Flores, Aaron O., 'An Exploration of the Emerging Church in the United States: The Missiological Intent and Potential Implications for the Future', Unpublished Masters Dissertation (Vanguard University, Costa Mesa, California, 2005), www.thevoiz.com/media/aoflores_ecstudy0605.pdf [access date 21 February 2008].

---

[17] While the Internet Engineering Task Force produced an Internet memo on netiquette in 1995 (tools.ietf.org/html/rfc1855), in practice the conventions which the concept contains vary among online communities.

Gibbs, Eddie & Bolger, Ryan K., *Emerging Churches: Creating Christian Community in Postmodern Cultures* (London: SPCK, 2006).

Hewson, Claire, Yule, Peter, Laurent, Dianna & Vogel, Carl, *Internet Research Methods: A Practical Guide for the Social and Behavioural Sciences* (London: Sage Publications, 2003).

La Grou, John & Hjalmarson, Len (eds), *Voices of the Virtual World: Participative Technology and the Ecclesial Revolution* (Wikiklesia Press, 2007).

Lövheim, Mia & Linderman, Alf G., 'Constructing Religious Identity on the Internet', in Højsgaard, Morten T. & Warburg, Margit (eds), *Religion and Cyberspace* (London: Routledge, 2005): 121–37.

Milbank, John, *Theology and Social Theory: Beyond Secular Reason* (Oxford: Blackwell, 2006).

Moody, Katharine Sarah, 'The Desire for Interaction and the Emerging Texts of the Blogosphere', in Sawyer, Deborah F. & Llewellyn, Dawn (eds), *Reading Spiritualities* (Aldershot, Hampshire: Ashgate, 2008): 99–113.

Penner, Myron Bradley & Barnes, Hunter, *A New Kind of Conversation: Blogging Toward a Postmodern Faith* (Colorado Springs: Paternoster, 2007).

Perriman, Andrew, *Otherways: In Search of an Emerging Theology – selected posts from www.opensourcetheology.net 2002 –2007* (Open Source Theology, 2007).

Raymond, Eric, 'The Cathedral and the Bazaar' (1997), www.catb.org/~esr/writings/cathedral-bazaar/cathedral-bazaar/ [access date 21 February 2008].

Rushkoff, Douglas, *Open Source Democracy: How Online Communication is Changing Offline Politics* (Demos, 2003).

Shirky, Clay, 'Power Laws, Weblogs, and Inequality' (2003), www.shirky.com/writings/powerlaw_weblog.html [access date 21 February 2008].

Sifry, Dave, 'State of the Blogosphere, October, 2006' (2006), www.sifry.com/alerts/archives/000443.html [access date 21 February 2008].

Smith, James K.A., *Introducing Radical Orthodoxy: Mapping a Post-secular Theology* (Grand Rapids: Baker Academic, 2004).

Smith, R. Scott, *Truth and the New Kind of Christian: The Emerging Effects of Postmodernism in the Church* (Wheaton, IL: Crossway, 2005).

Tallskinnykiwi, 'Blogging and Emerging Church', 22 January 2004, tallskinnykiwi.typepad.com/tallskinnykiwi/2004/01/blogging_and_em.html [access date 21 February 2008].

Tallskinnykiwi, 'The Girls Post: A Definitive History', 24 February 2004, tallskinnykiwi.typepad.com/tallskinnykiwi/2004/02/the_whole_story.html [access date 21 February 2008].

Teusner, Paul, 'Identity Construction in the "Emerging Church" blogosphere: Building a Theoretical Framework' (2006), paulteusner.org/docs/theory.pdf [access date 21 February 2008].

Teusner, Paul, 'Researching Individual and Communal Identity among Religious Blogs' (2007), paulteusner.org/docs/aoir8paper2.pdf [access date 21 February 2008].

Walker, Jill, 'Links and Power: the Political Economy of Linking on the Web', Proceedings of Hypertext 2002 (Baltimore: ACM Press, 2002), jilltxt.net/txt/ linksandpower.html [access date 21 February 2008].

Index